T'think it's actually still gaanin'.

STRANGE, ISN'T IT?

What's that supposed to mean?

"I WORKED HARD."

—Rikdo Koshi

STORY AND ART BY
RIKDO KOSHI

EXCEL SAGA 02

STORY AND ART BY
RIKDO KOSHI

ENGLISH ADAPTATION BY
DAN KANEMITSU & CARL GUSTAV HORN

TRANSLATION
DAN KANEMITSU

LETTERING & TOUCH-UP BY
CATO

COVER DESIGN
BRUCE LEWIS

GRAPHIC DESIGNER
CAROLINA UGALDE

EDITOR
CARL GUSTAV HORN

MANAGING EDITOR
ANNETTE ROMAN

EDITOR IN CHIEF
WILLIAM FLANAGAN

DIRECTOR OF LICENSING & ACQUISITIONS
RIKA INOUYE

VP OF SALES & MARKETING
LIZA COPPOLA

SR. VP OF EDITORIAL
HYOE NARITA

PUBLISHER
SEIJI HORIBUCHI

Published by VIZ, LLC
P.O. Box 77064
San Francisco, CA 94107

Action Edition
10 9 8 7 6 5 4 3 2 1
First printing, August 2003

www.viz.com

ANIMERICA
ANIME & MANGA MONTHLY

storeviz.com

For advertising rates or media kit, e-mail advertising@viz.com

5.   MISSION 1
DESTINIES AT THE CROSSROADS
29.   MISSION 2
THE OPENING WINDS
59.   MISSION 3
THE RELATIVE SPEED OF FOOLS
91.   MISSION 4
AN EQUATION FOR LIBERATION
113.   MISSION 5
VICTIMS AND PERPETRATORS
143.   MISSION 6
SHIFT IN TACK
149.   MISSION 7
UNHAPPY HAPPINESS
171.   MISSION 8
THE JOYS OF DEFEAT
192.   OUBLIETTE
(EXCEL SAGA BONUS SECTION)

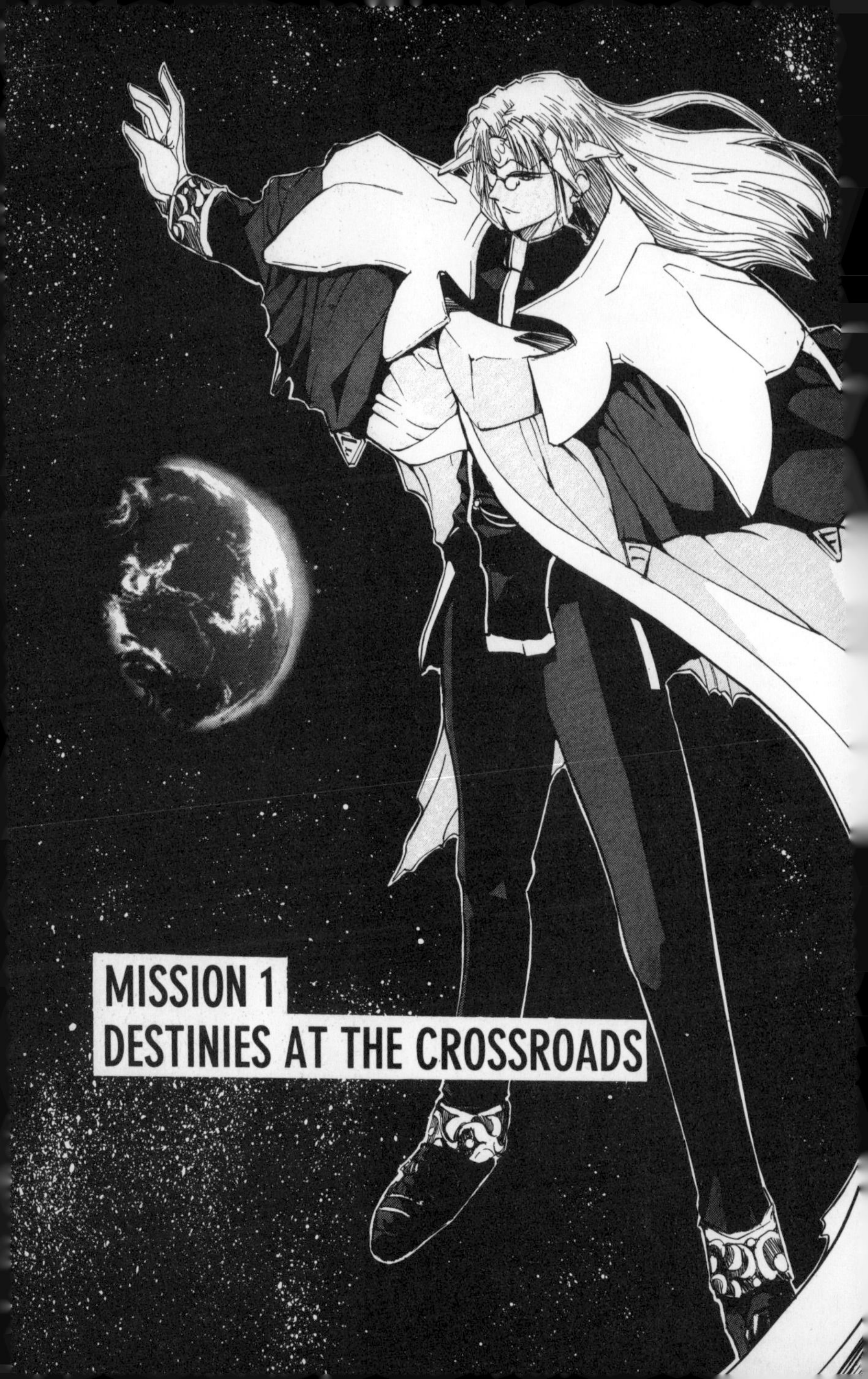
MISSION 1
DESTINIES AT THE CROSSROADS

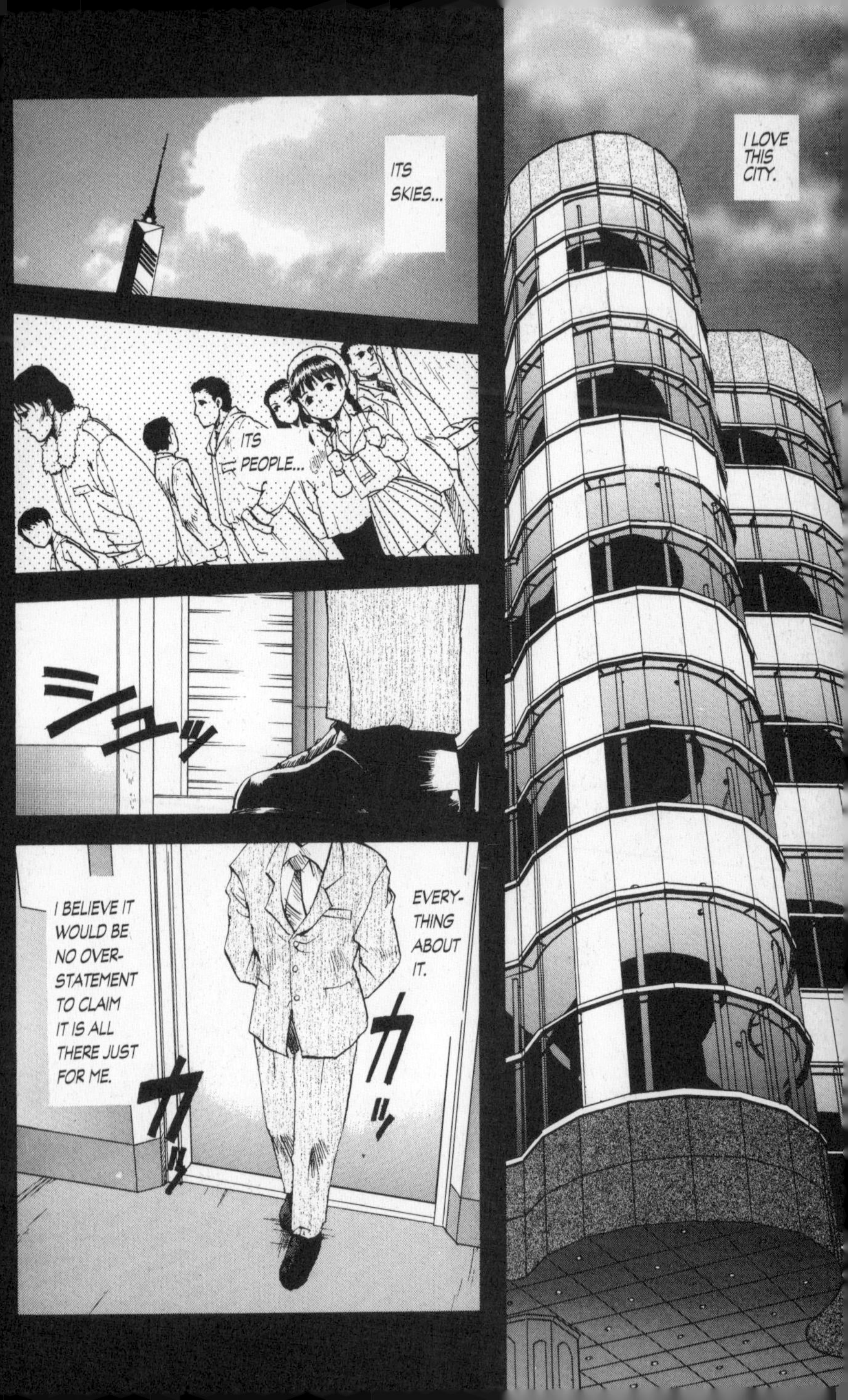
I LOVE THIS CITY.
ITS SKIES...
ITS PEOPLE...
シュッ
EVERYTHING ABOUT IT.
I BELIEVE IT WOULD BE NO OVERSTATEMENT TO CLAIM IT IS ALL THERE JUST FOR ME.
カッ
カッ

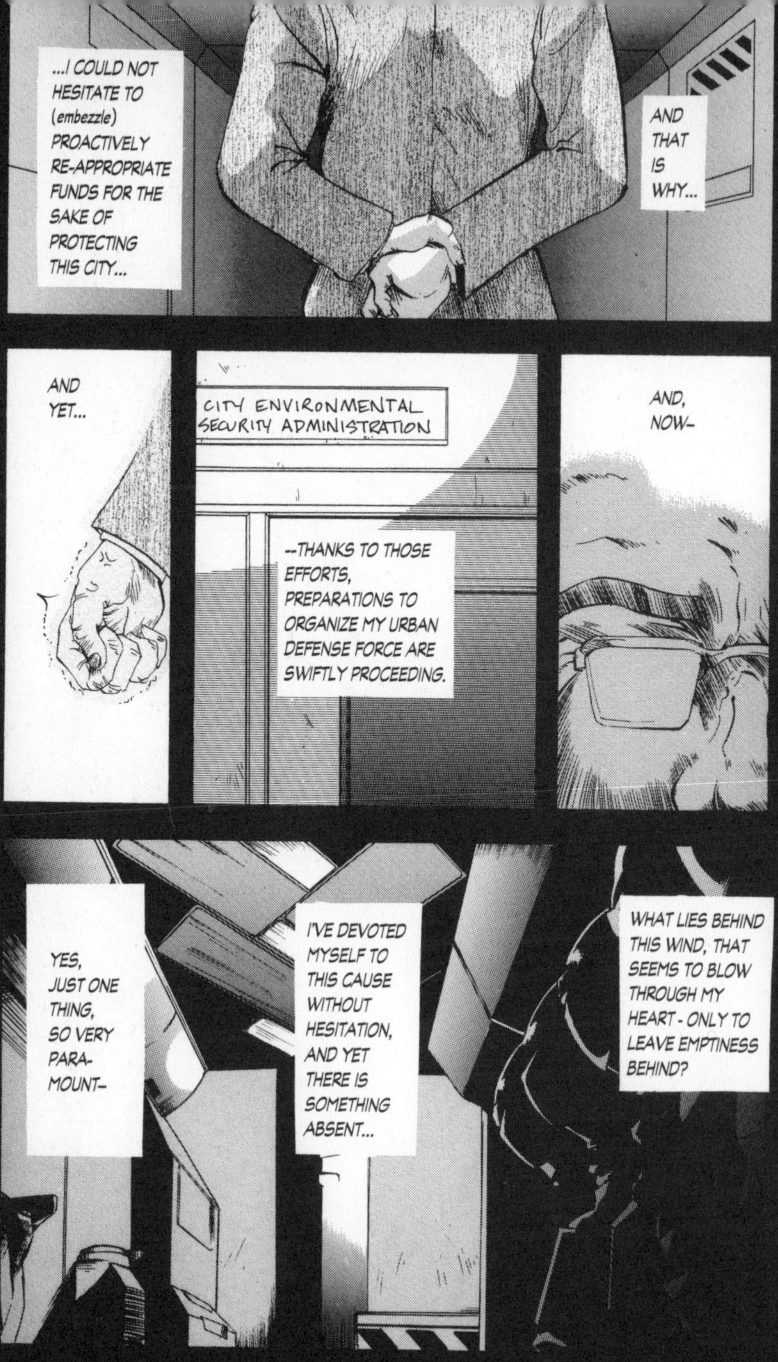
AND THAT IS WHY...
...I COULD NOT HESITATE TO (embezzle) PROACTIVELY RE-APPROPRIATE FUNDS FOR THE SAKE OF PROTECTING THIS CITY...
AND, NOW-
CITY ENVIRONMENTAL SECURITY ADMINISTRATION
--THANKS TO THOSE EFFORTS, PREPARATIONS TO ORGANIZE MY URBAN DEFENSE FORCE ARE SWIFTLY PROCEEDING.
AND YET...
WHAT LIES BEHIND THIS WIND, THAT SEEMS TO BLOW THROUGH MY HEART - ONLY TO LEAVE EMPTINESS BEHIND?
I'VE DEVOTED MYSELF TO THIS CAUSE WITHOUT HESITATION, AND YET THERE IS SOMETHING ABSENT...
YES, JUST ONE THING, SO VERY PARA-MOUNT-

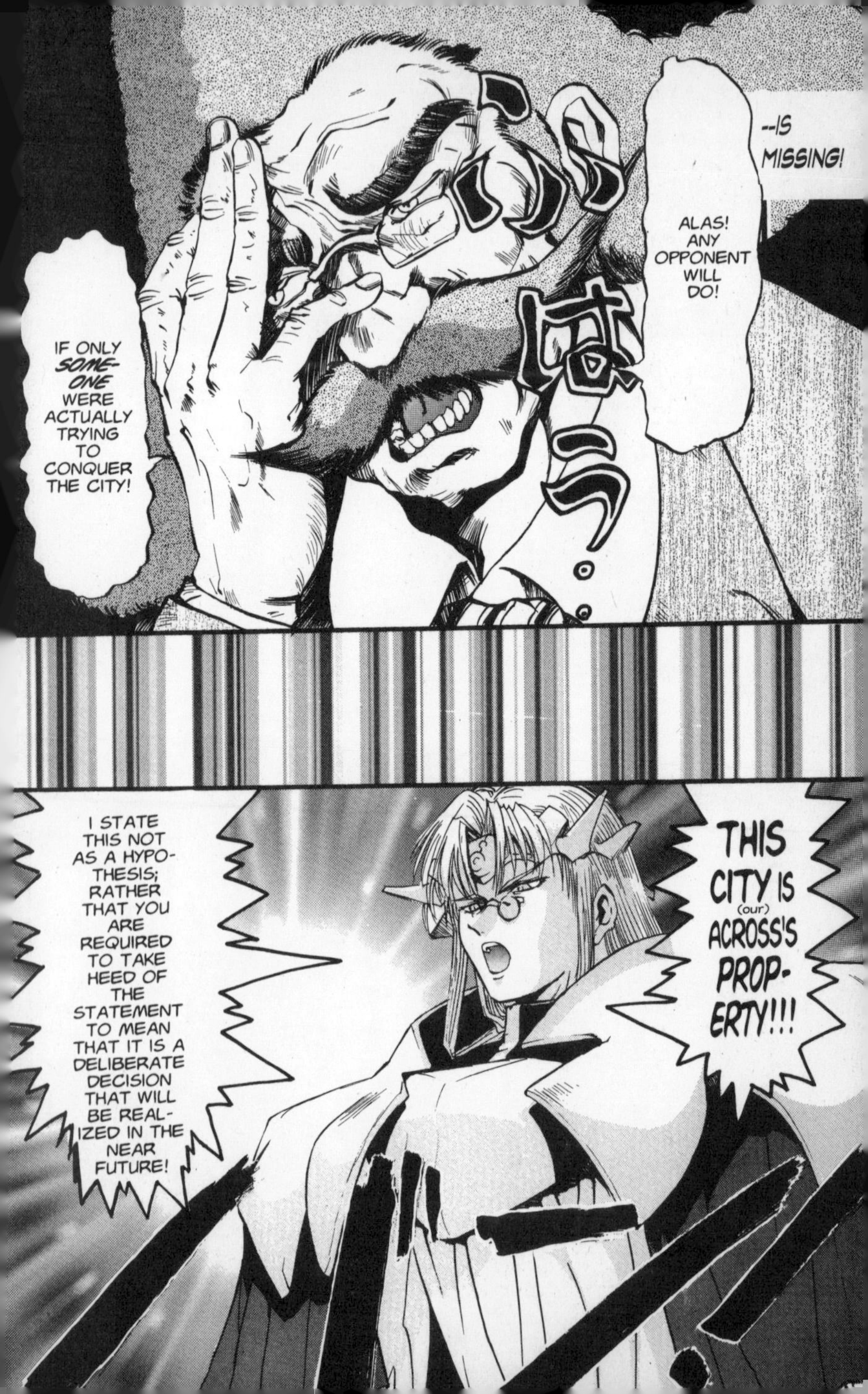
--IS MISSING!
ALAS! ANY OPPONENT WILL DO!
IF ONLY *SOME-ONE* WERE ACTUALLY TRYING TO CONQUER THE CITY!
THIS CITY IS (our) ACROSS'S PROP-ERTY!!!
I STATE THIS NOT AS A HYPO-THESIS; RATHER THAT YOU ARE REQUIRED TO TAKE HEED OF THE STATEMENT TO MEAN THAT IT IS A DELIBERATE DECISION THAT WILL BE REAL-IZED IN THE NEAR FUTURE!

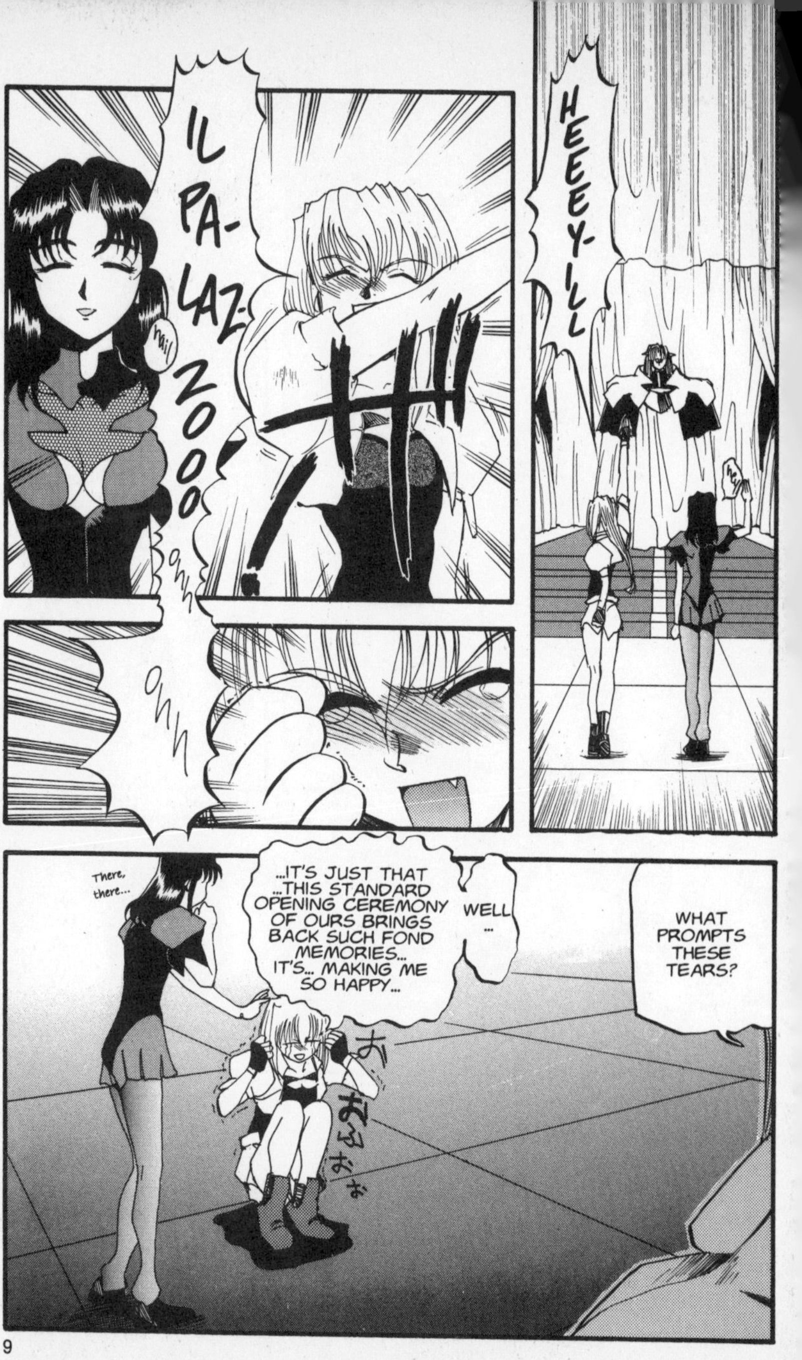
HEEEEY-LLLL
hey
IL PA-LAZ-ZOOOO
hail
ohhh
WHAT PROMPTS THESE TEARS?
WELL...
...IT'S JUST THAT ...THIS STANDARD OPENING CEREMONY OF OURS BRINGS BACK SUCH FOND MEMORIES... IT'S... MAKING ME SO HAPPY...
There, there...
お

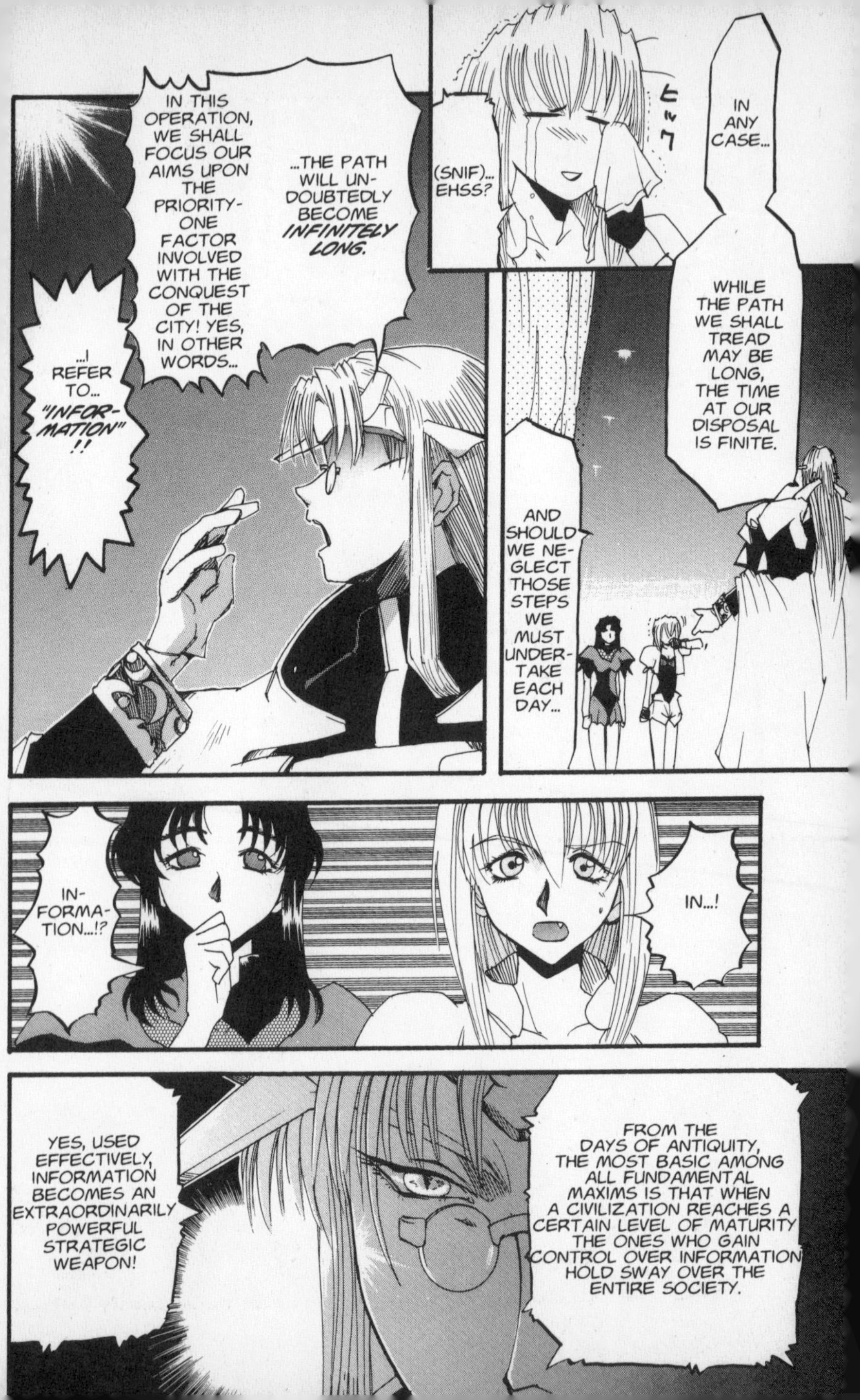
IN ANY CASE...
(SNIF)... EHSS?
ヒック
WHILE THE PATH WE SHALL TREAD MAY BE LONG, THE TIME AT OUR DISPOSAL IS FINITE.
AND SHOULD WE NEGLECT THOSE STEPS WE MUST UNDERTAKE EACH DAY...
...THE PATH WILL UNDOUBTEDLY BECOME *INFINITELY LONG.*
IN THIS OPERATION, WE SHALL FOCUS OUR AIMS UPON THE PRIORITY-ONE FACTOR INVOLVED WITH THE CONQUEST OF THE CITY! YES, IN OTHER WORDS...
...I REFER TO... *"INFORMATION"!!*
IN...!
INFORMATION...!?
FROM THE DAYS OF ANTIQUITY, THE MOST BASIC AMONG ALL FUNDAMENTAL MAXIMS IS THAT WHEN A CIVILIZATION REACHES A CERTAIN LEVEL OF MATURITY THE ONES WHO GAIN CONTROL OVER INFORMATION HOLD SWAY OVER THE ENTIRE SOCIETY.
YES, USED EFFECTIVELY, INFORMATION BECOMES AN EXTRAORDINARILY POWERFUL STRATEGIC WEAPON!

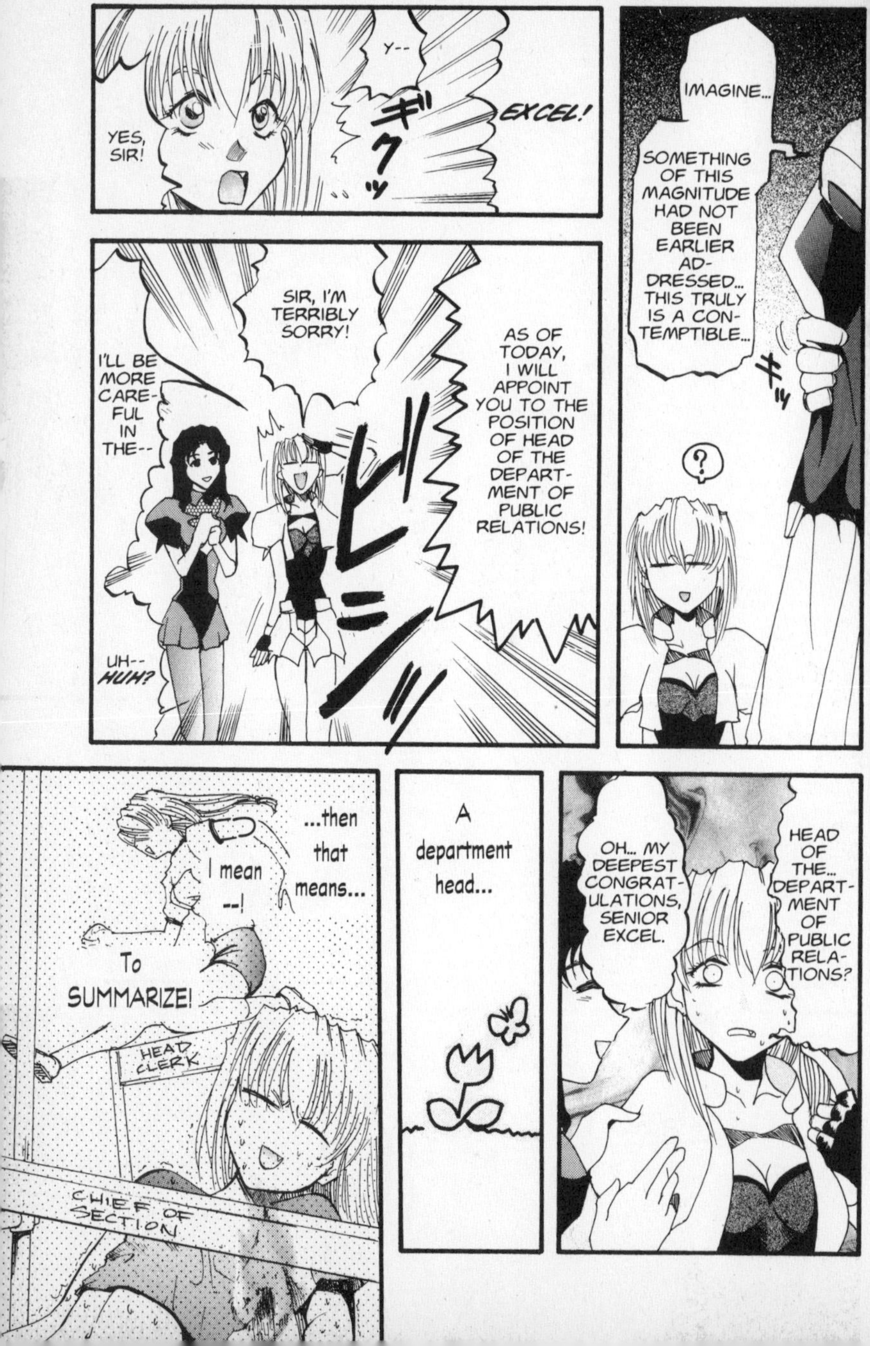
IMAGINE...
SOMETHING OF THIS MAGNITUDE HAD NOT BEEN EARLIER AD-DRESSED... THIS TRULY IS A CON-TEMPTIBLE...
ギッ
?
EXCEL!
Y--
ギクッ
YES, SIR!
AS OF TODAY, I WILL APPOINT YOU TO THE POSITION OF HEAD OF THE DEPART-MENT OF PUBLIC RELATIONS!
SIR, I'M TERRIBLY SORRY!
I'LL BE MORE CARE-FUL IN THE--
UH-- HUH?
HEAD OF THE... DEPART-MENT OF PUBLIC RELA-TIONS?
OH... MY DEEPEST CONGRAT-ULATIONS, SENIOR EXCEL.
A department head...
...then that means...
I mean --!
To SUMMARIZE!
HEAD CLERK
CHIEF OF SECTION

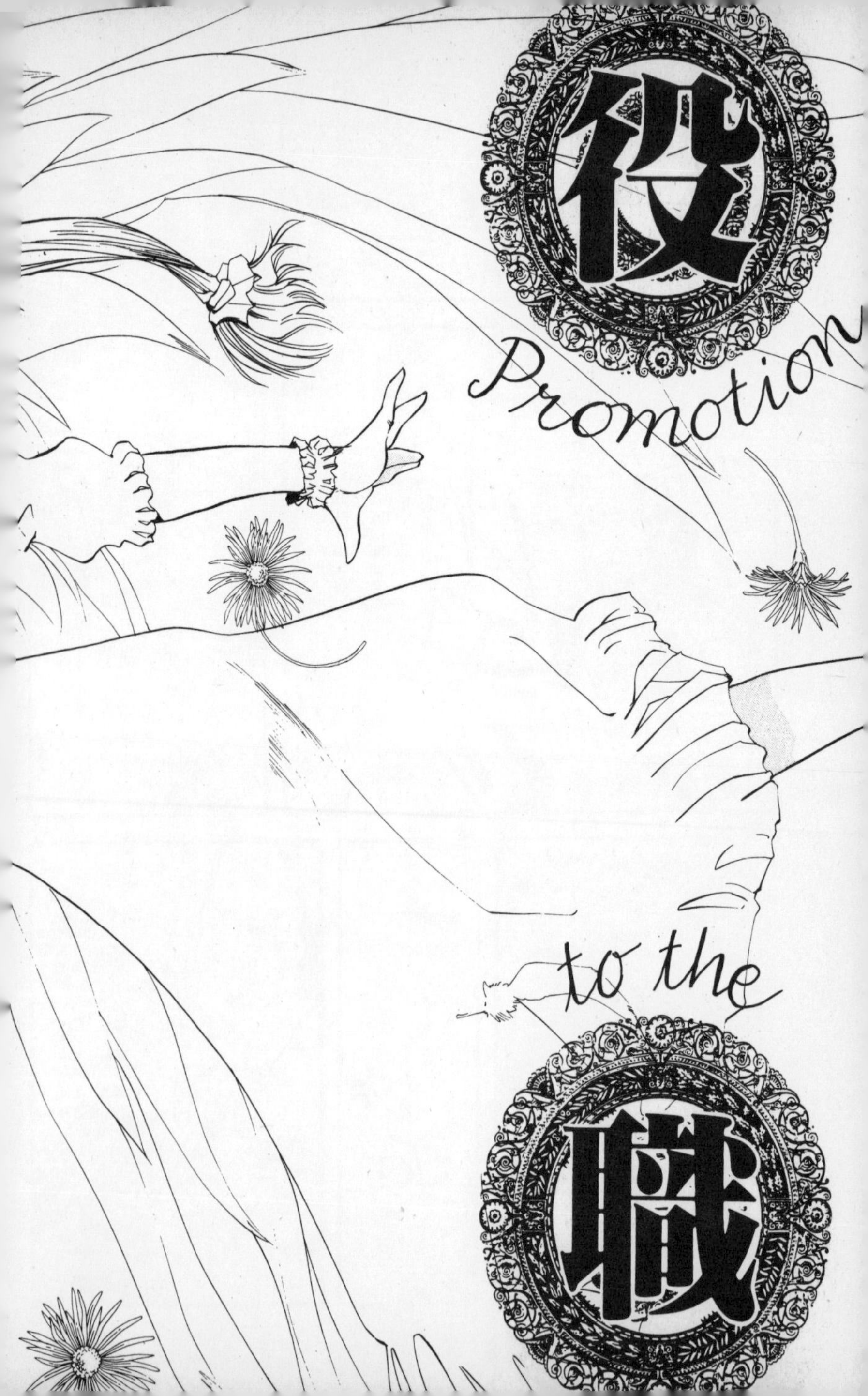

役
Promotion
to the
職

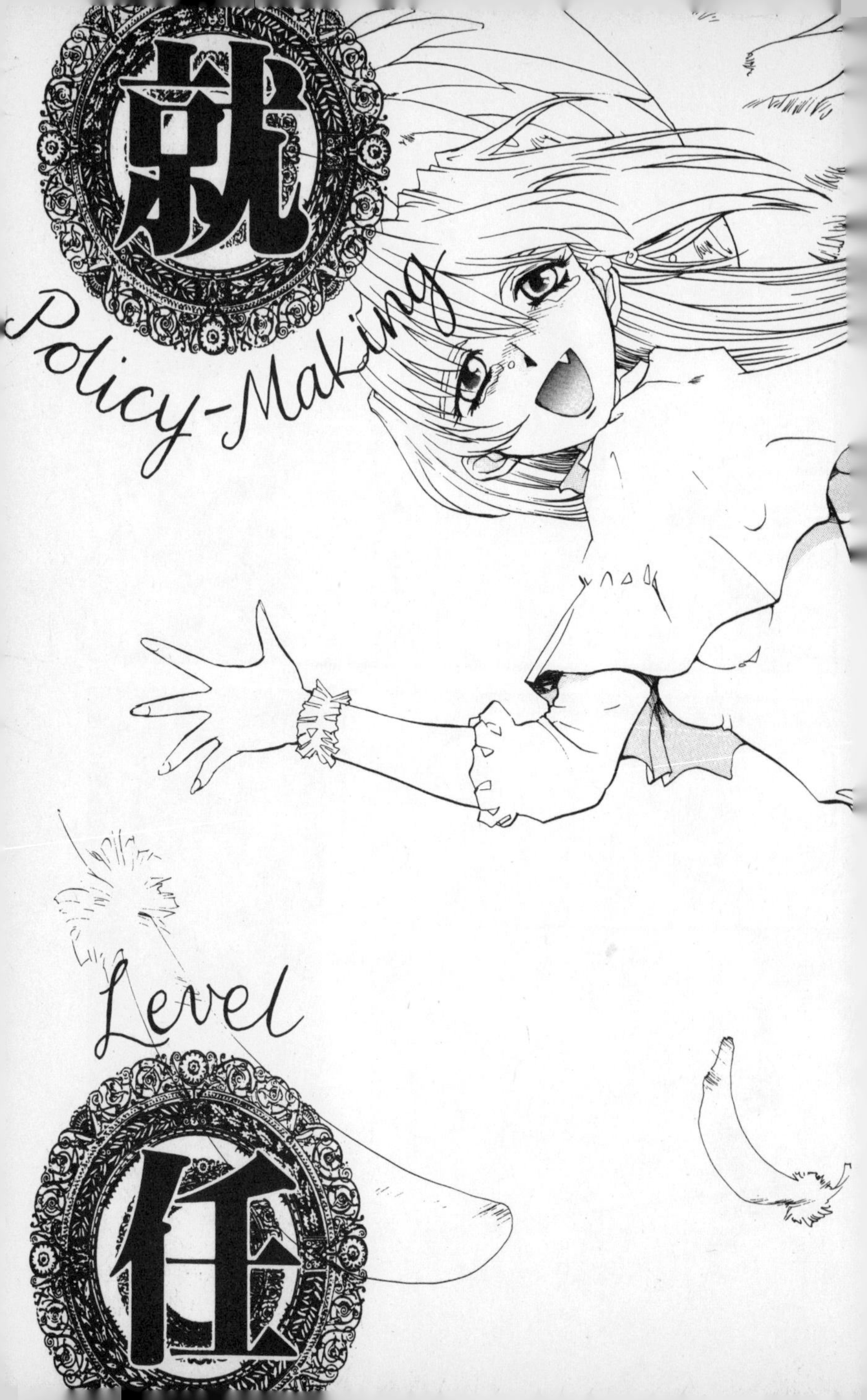
就
Policy-Making
Level
任

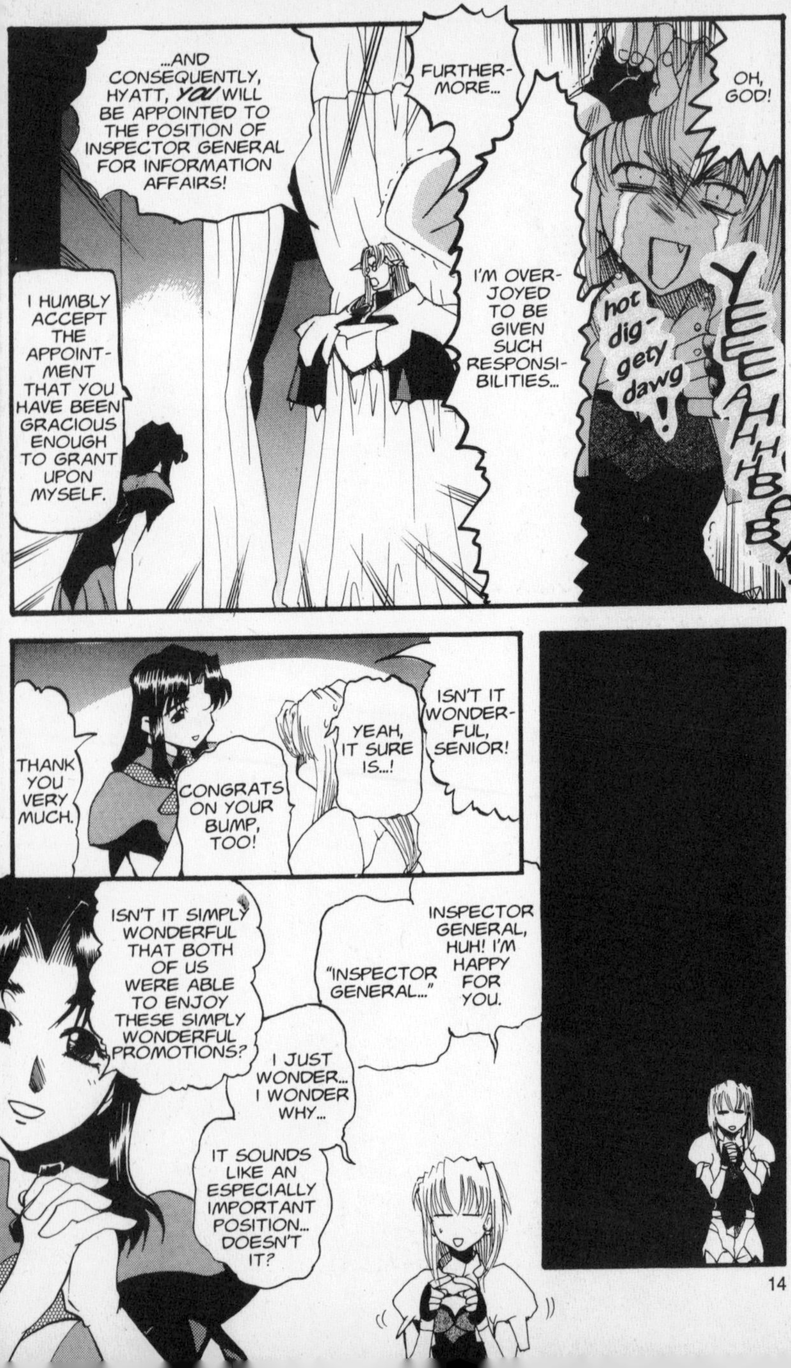
OH, GOD!
YEEEAHHHBeBY!
hot diggety dawg!
FURTHERMORE...
...AND CONSEQUENTLY, HYATT, *YOU* WILL BE APPOINTED TO THE POSITION OF INSPECTOR GENERAL FOR INFORMATION AFFAIRS!
I'M OVERJOYED TO BE GIVEN SUCH RESPONSIBILITIES...
I HUMBLY ACCEPT THE APPOINTMENT THAT YOU HAVE BEEN GRACIOUS ENOUGH TO GRANT UPON MYSELF.
ISN'T IT WONDERFUL, SENIOR!
YEAH, IT SURE IS...!
CONGRATS ON YOUR BUMP, TOO!
THANK YOU VERY MUCH.
INSPECTOR GENERAL, HUH! I'M HAPPY FOR YOU.
"INSPECTOR GENERAL..."
ISN'T IT SIMPLY WONDERFUL THAT BOTH OF US WERE ABLE TO ENJOY THESE SIMPLY WONDERFUL PROMOTIONS?
I JUST WONDER... I WONDER WHY...
IT SOUNDS LIKE AN ESPECIALLY IMPORTANT POSITION... DOESN'T IT?

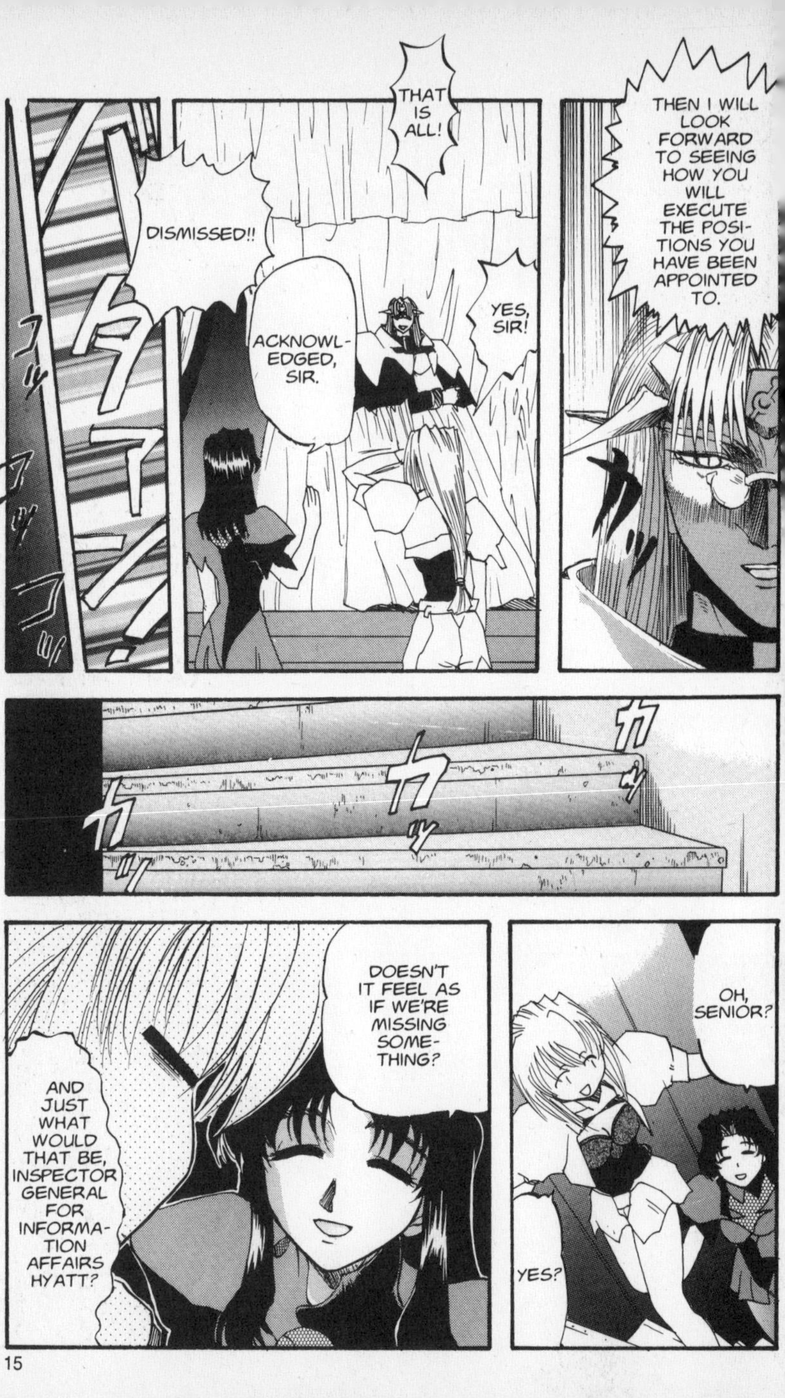
THEN I WILL LOOK FORWARD TO SEEING HOW YOU WILL EXECUTE THE POSITIONS YOU HAVE BEEN APPOINTED TO.
THAT IS ALL!
YES, SIR!
ACKNOWLEDGED, SIR.
DISMISSED!!
OH, SENIOR?
YES?
DOESN'T IT FEEL AS IF WE'RE MISSING SOMETHING?
AND JUST WHAT WOULD THAT BE, INSPECTOR GENERAL FOR INFORMATION AFFAIRS HYATT?

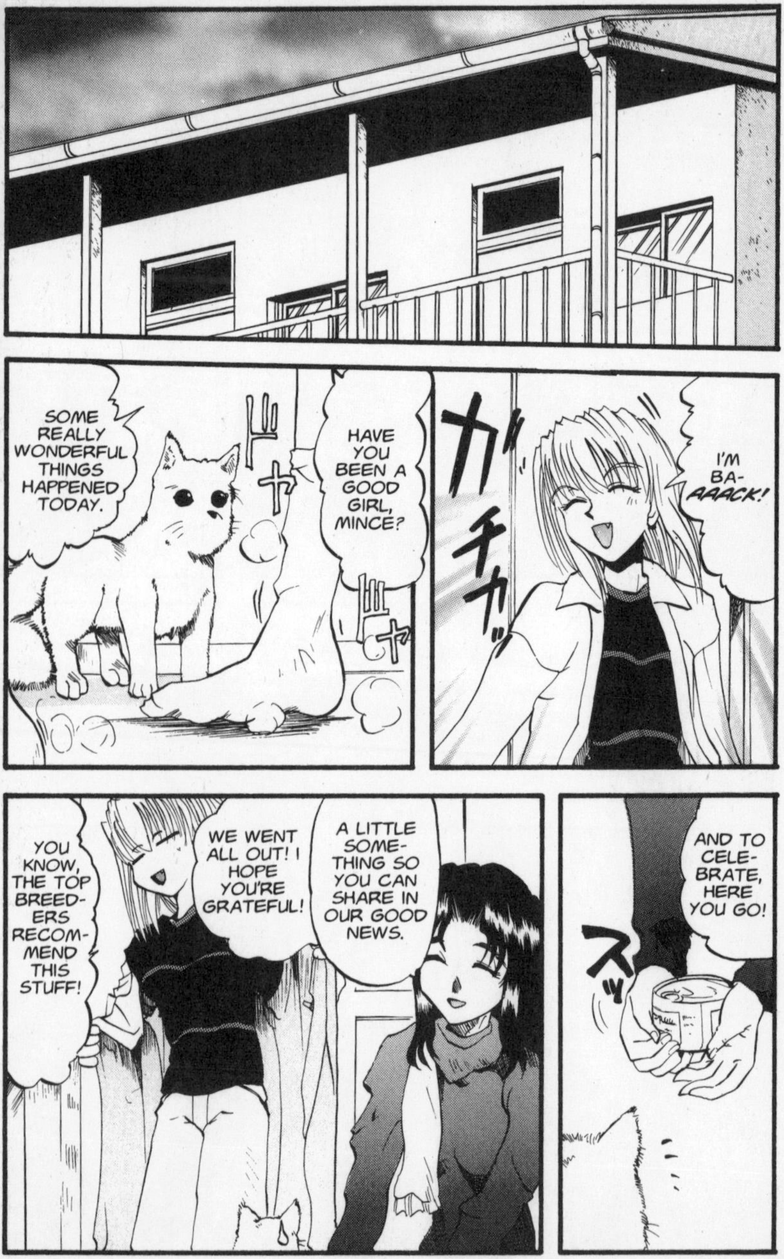
I'M BA-AAACK!
HAVE YOU BEEN A GOOD GIRL, MINCE?
SOME REALLY WONDERFUL THINGS HAPPENED TODAY.
AND TO CELE-BRATE, HERE YOU GO!
スッ
A LITTLE SOME-THING SO YOU CAN SHARE IN OUR GOOD NEWS.
WE WENT ALL OUT! I HOPE YOU'RE GRATEFUL!
YOU KNOW, THE TOP BREEDER-ERS RECOM-MEND THIS STUFF!

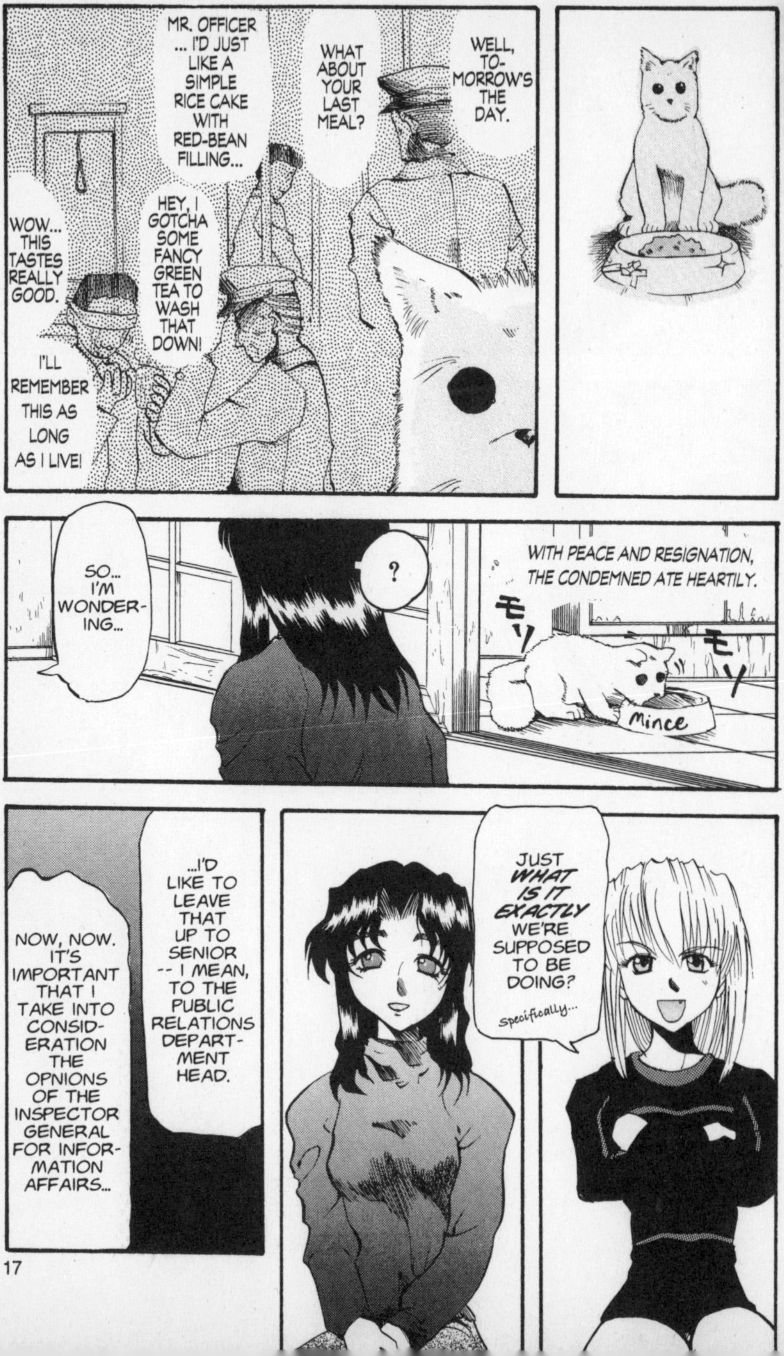
WELL, TOMORROW'S THE DAY.
WHAT ABOUT YOUR LAST MEAL?
MR. OFFICER ... I'D JUST LIKE A SIMPLE RICE CAKE WITH RED-BEAN FILLING...
HEY, I GOTCHA SOME FANCY GREEN TEA TO WASH THAT DOWN!
WOW... THIS TASTES REALLY GOOD.
I'LL REMEMBER THIS AS LONG AS I LIVE!
WITH PEACE AND RESIGNATION, THE CONDEMNED ATE HEARTILY.
モソ
モソ
Mince
?
SO... I'M WONDERING...
JUST ***WHAT IS IT EXACTLY*** WE'RE SUPPOSED TO BE DOING?
Specifically...
...I'D LIKE TO LEAVE THAT UP TO SENIOR -- I MEAN, TO THE PUBLIC RELATIONS DEPARTMENT HEAD.
NOW, NOW. IT'S IMPORTANT THAT I TAKE INTO CONSIDERATION THE OPNIONS OF THE INSPECTOR GENERAL FOR INFORMATION AFFAIRS...

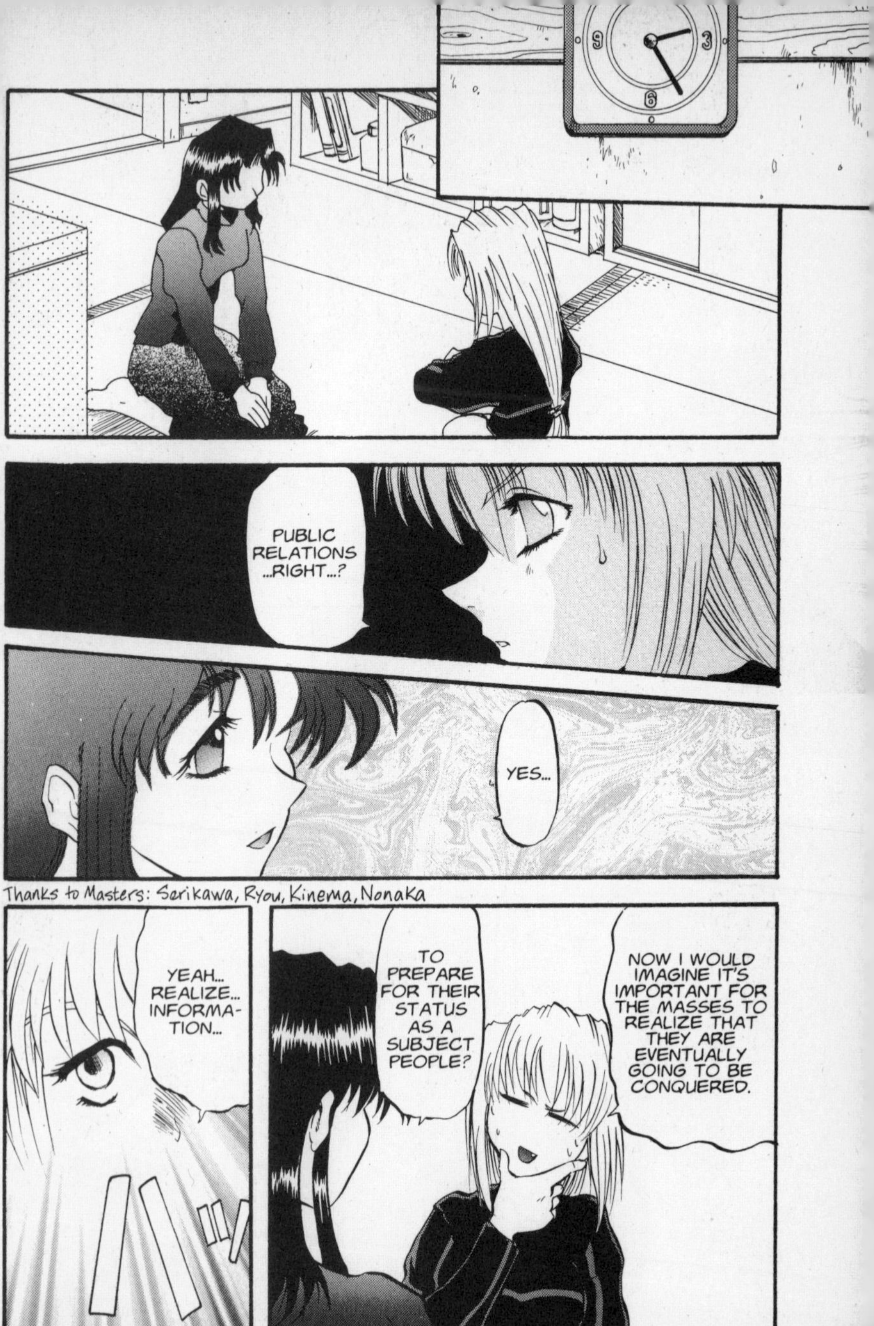
PUBLIC RELATIONS ...RIGHT...?
YES...
Thanks to Masters: Serikawa, Ryou, Kinema, NonaKa
NOW I WOULD IMAGINE IT'S IMPORTANT FOR THE MASSES TO REALIZE THAT THEY ARE EVENTUALLY GOING TO BE CONQUERED.
TO PREPARE FOR THEIR STATUS AS A SUBJECT PEOPLE?
YEAH... REALIZE... INFORMATION...

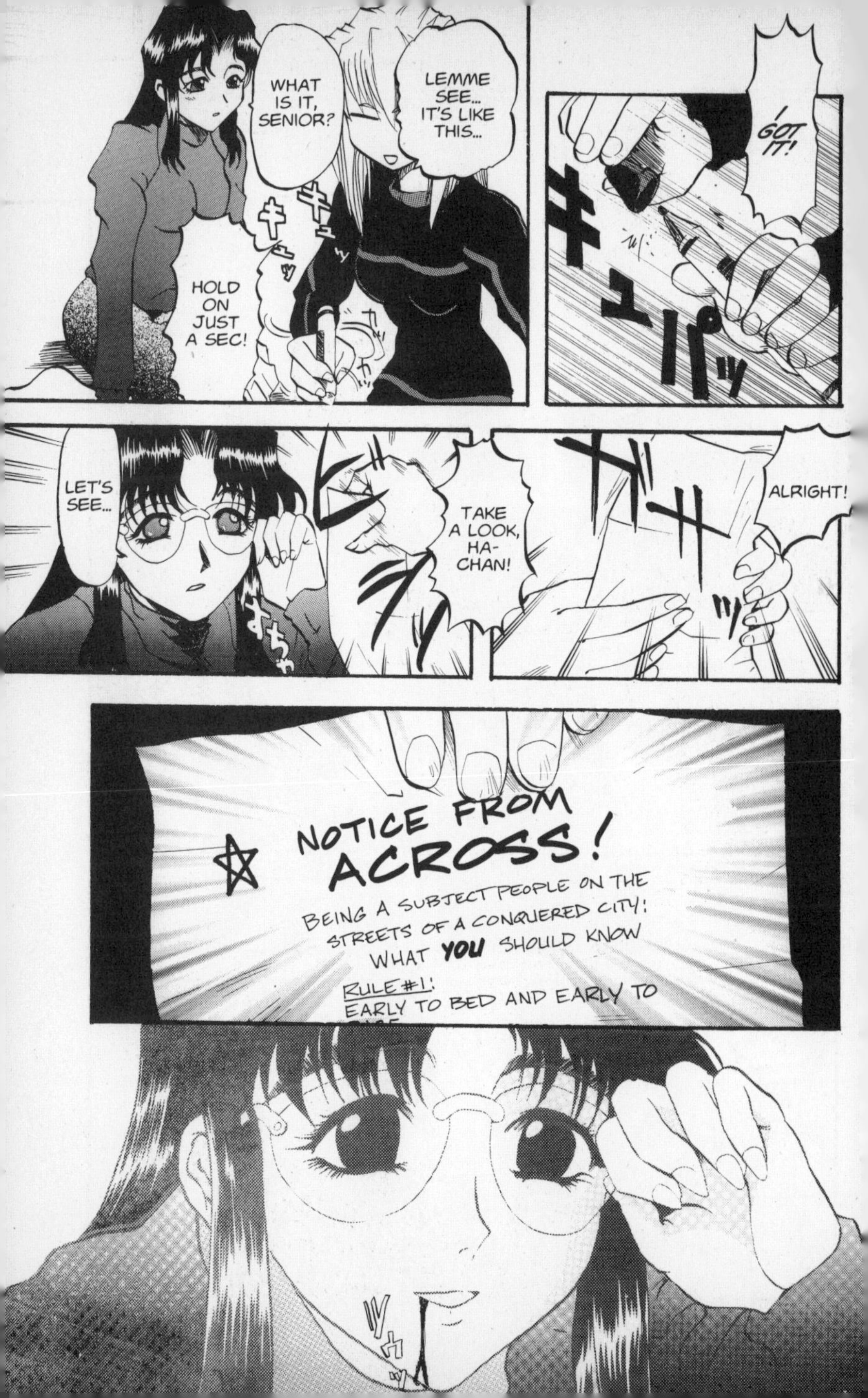
I GOT IT!
LEMME SEE... IT'S LIKE THIS...
WHAT IS IT, SENIOR?
HOLD ON JUST A SEC!
ALRIGHT!
TAKE A LOOK, HA-CHAN!
LET'S SEE...
NOTICE FROM ACROSS!
BEING A SUBJECT PEOPLE ON THE STREETS OF A CONQUERED CITY: WHAT YOU SHOULD KNOW
RULE #1:
EARLY TO BED AND EARLY TO

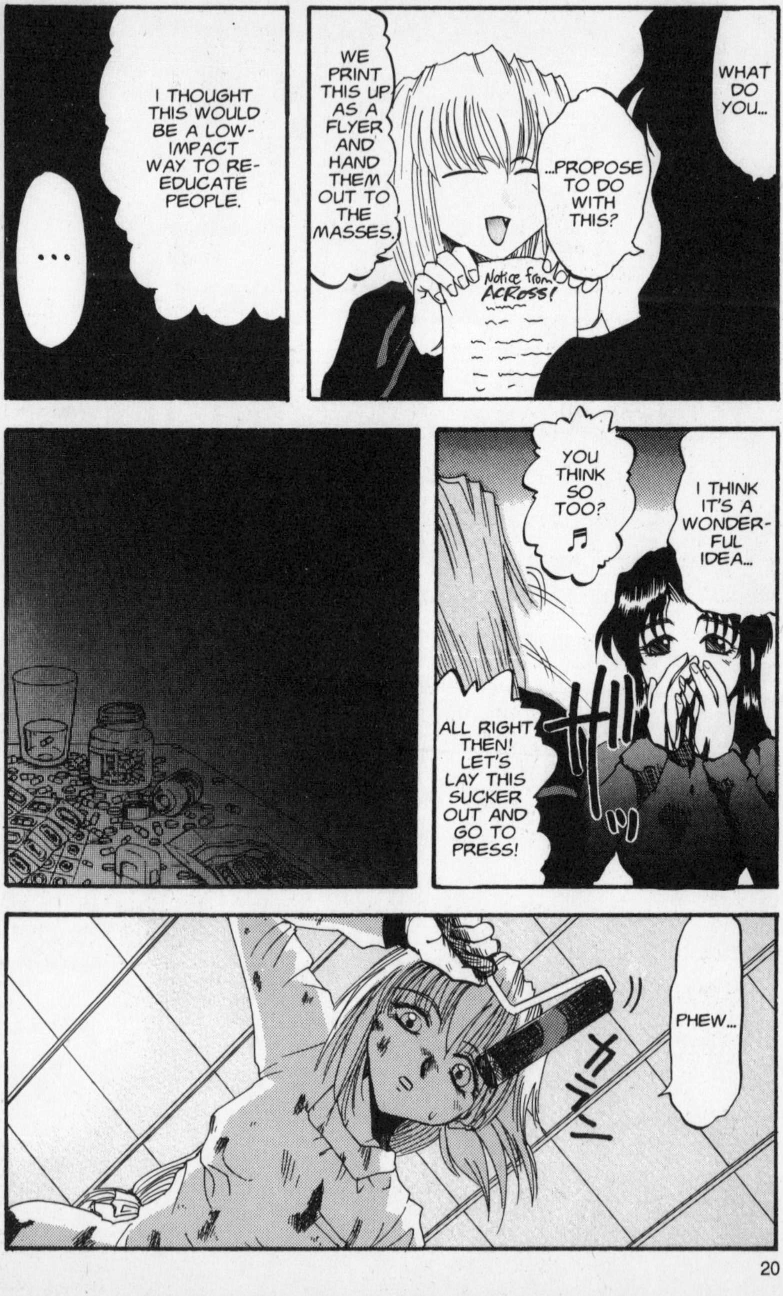
WHAT DO YOU...
...PROPOSE TO DO WITH THIS?
WE PRINT THIS UP AS A FLYER AND HAND THEM OUT TO THE MASSES.
Notice from ACROSS!
I THOUGHT THIS WOULD BE A LOW-IMPACT WAY TO RE-EDUCATE PEOPLE.
...
I THINK IT'S A WONDERFUL IDEA...
YOU THINK SO TOO? ♪
ALL RIGHT THEN! LET'S LAY THIS SUCKER OUT AND GO TO PRESS!
PHEW...

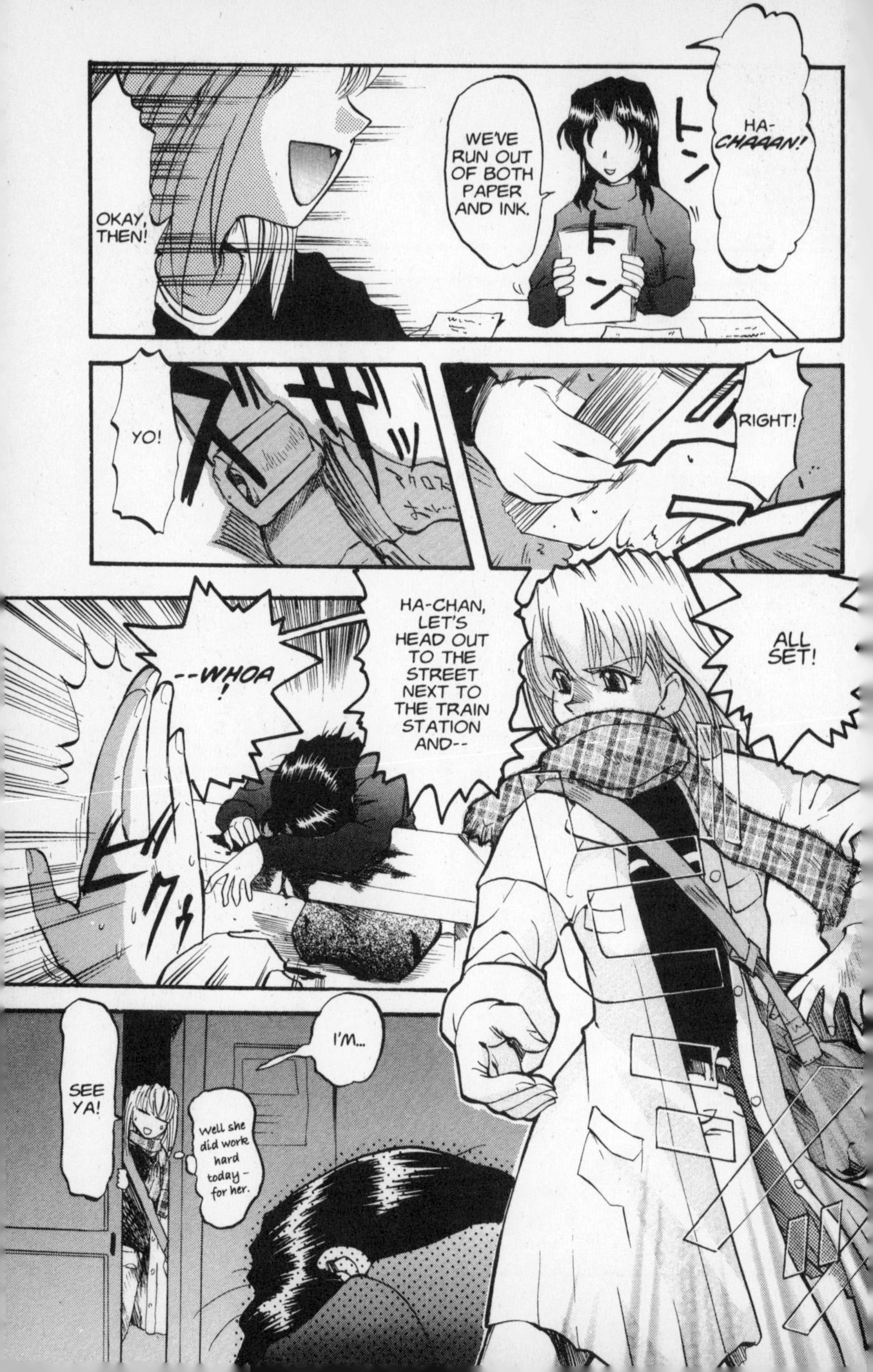
HA-CHAAAN!
WE'VE RUN OUT OF BOTH PAPER AND INK.
OKAY, THEN!
RIGHT!
YO!
ALL SET!
HA-CHAN, LET'S HEAD OUT TO THE STREET NEXT TO THE TRAIN STATION AND--
--WHOA!
I'M...
SEE YA!
Well she did work hard today - for her.

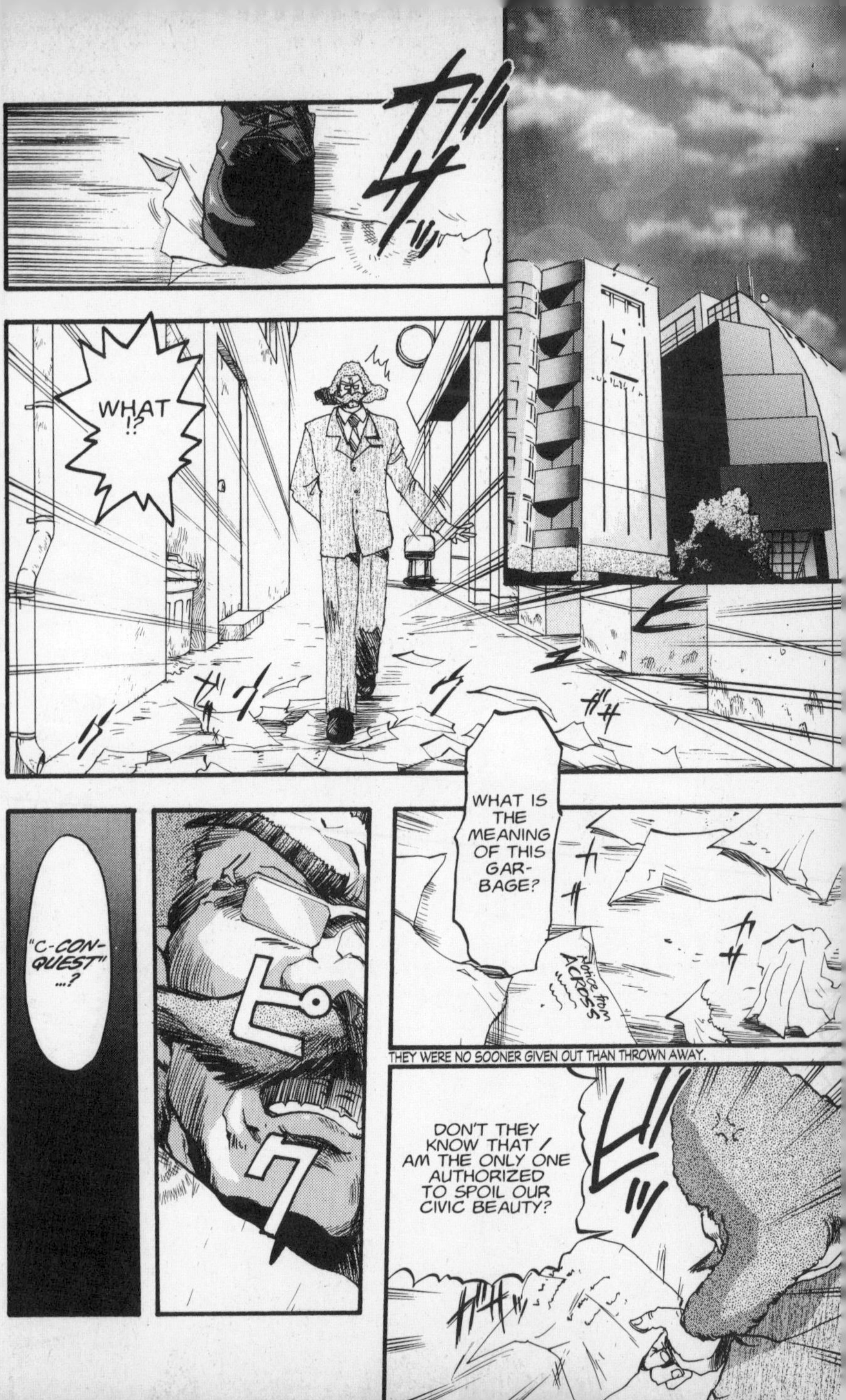
WHAT !?
WHAT IS THE MEANING OF THIS GAR-BAGE?
Notice from ACROSS
THEY WERE NO SOONER GIVEN OUT THAN THROWN AWAY.
DON'T THEY KNOW THAT I AM THE ONLY ONE AUTHORIZED TO SPOIL OUR CIVIC BEAUTY?
"C-CON-QUEST" ...?

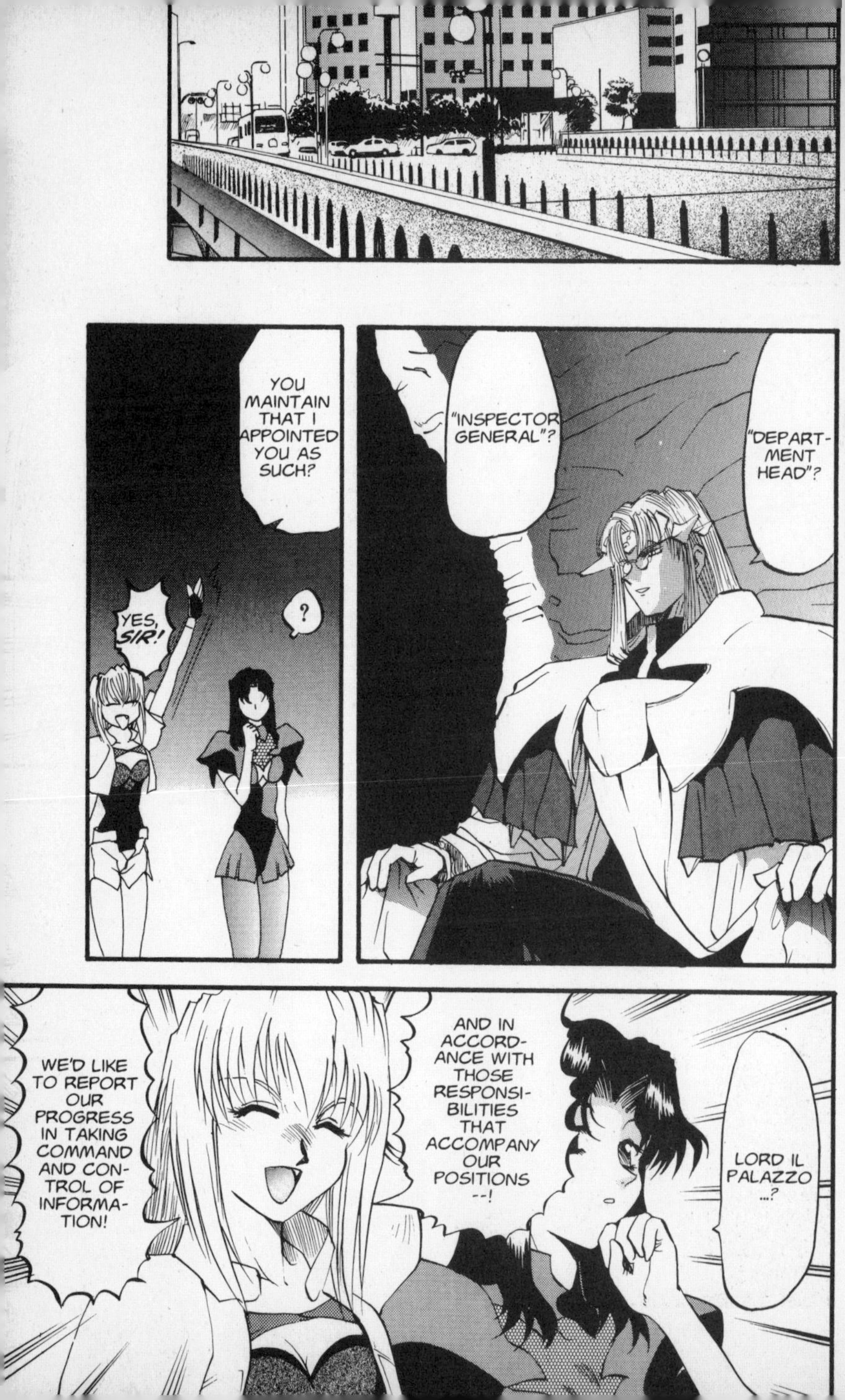
"DEPART-MENT HEAD"?
"INSPECTOR GENERAL"?
YOU MAINTAIN THAT I APPOINTED YOU AS SUCH?
YES, *SIR!*
?
LORD IL PALAZZO ...?
AND IN ACCORD-ANCE WITH THOSE RESPONSI-BILITIES THAT ACCOMPANY OUR POSITIONS --!
WE'D LIKE TO REPORT OUR PROGRESS IN TAKING COMMAND AND CON-TROL OF INFORMA-TION!

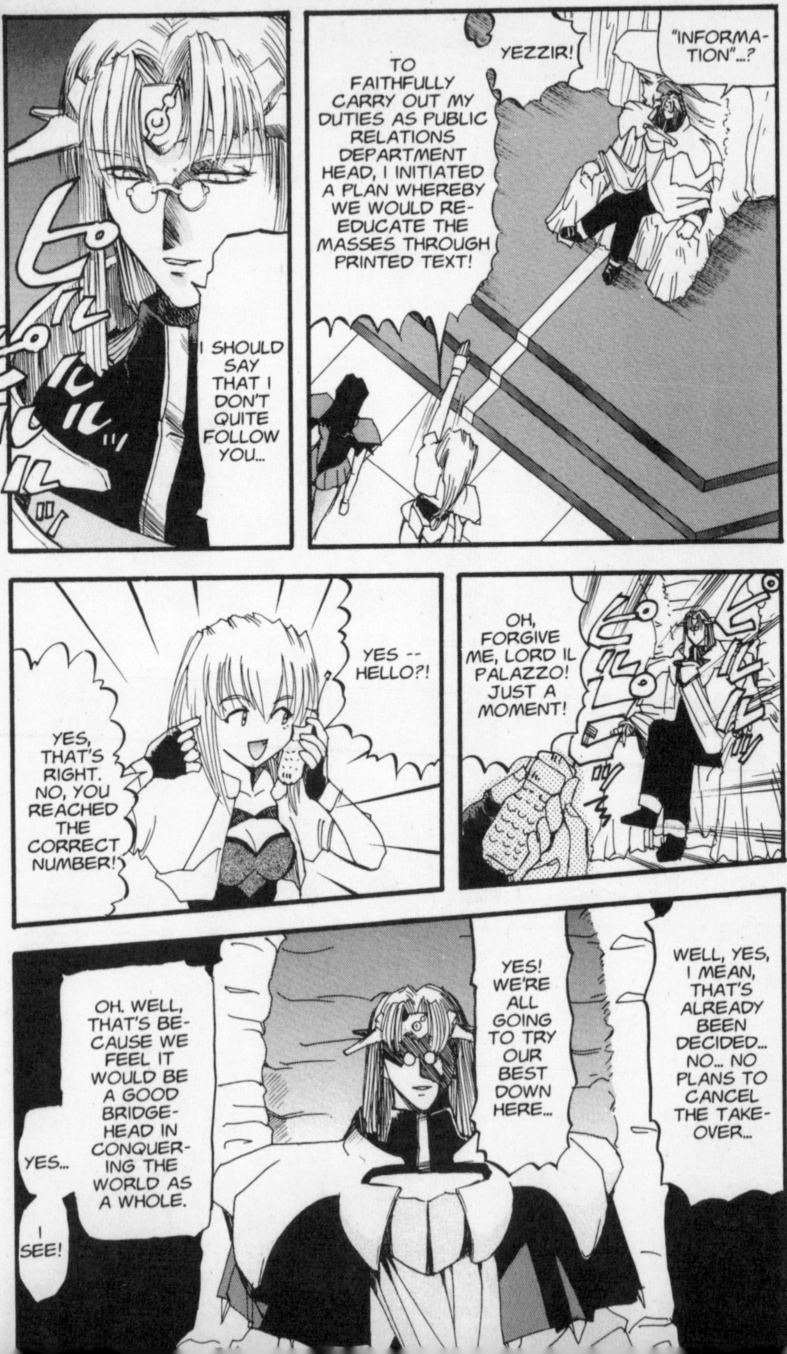
"INFORMATION"...?
YEZZIR!
TO FAITHFULLY CARRY OUT MY DUTIES AS PUBLIC RELATIONS DEPARTMENT HEAD, I INITIATED A PLAN WHEREBY WE WOULD RE-EDUCATE THE MASSES THROUGH PRINTED TEXT!
I SHOULD SAY THAT I DON'T QUITE FOLLOW YOU...
OH, FORGIVE ME, LORD IL PALAZZO! JUST A MOMENT!
YES -- HELLO?!
YES, THAT'S RIGHT. NO, YOU REACHED THE CORRECT NUMBER!
WELL, YES, I MEAN, THAT'S ALREADY BEEN DECIDED... NO... NO PLANS TO CANCEL THE TAKE-OVER...
YES! WE'RE ALL GOING TO TRY OUR BEST DOWN HERE...
OH. WELL, THAT'S BE-CAUSE WE FEEL IT WOULD BE A GOOD BRIDGE-HEAD IN CONQUER-ING THE WORLD AS A WHOLE.
YES...
I SEE!

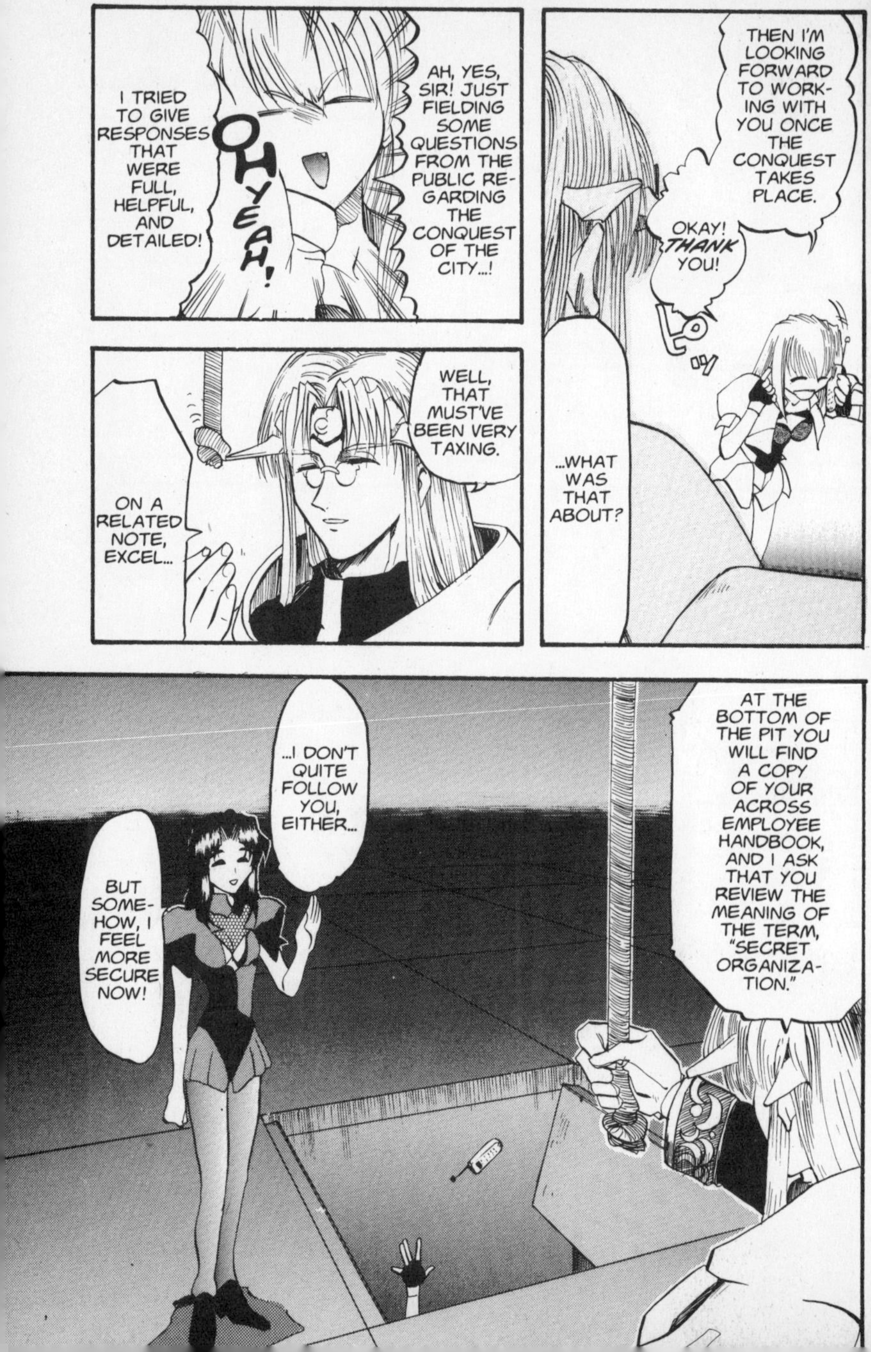
THEN I'M LOOKING FORWARD TO WORKING WITH YOU ONCE THE CONQUEST TAKES PLACE.
OKAY! THANK YOU!
...WHAT WAS THAT ABOUT?
AH, YES, SIR! JUST FIELDING SOME QUESTIONS FROM THE PUBLIC REGARDING THE CONQUEST OF THE CITY...!
OH YEAH!
I TRIED TO GIVE RESPONSES THAT WERE FULL, HELPFUL, AND DETAILED!
WELL, THAT MUST'VE BEEN VERY TAXING.
ON A RELATED NOTE, EXCEL...
AT THE BOTTOM OF THE PIT YOU WILL FIND A COPY OF YOUR ACROSS EMPLOYEE HANDBOOK, AND I ASK THAT YOU REVIEW THE MEANING OF THE TERM, "SECRET ORGANIZATION."
...I DON'T QUITE FOLLOW YOU, EITHER...
BUT SOMEHOW, I FEEL MORE SECURE NOW!

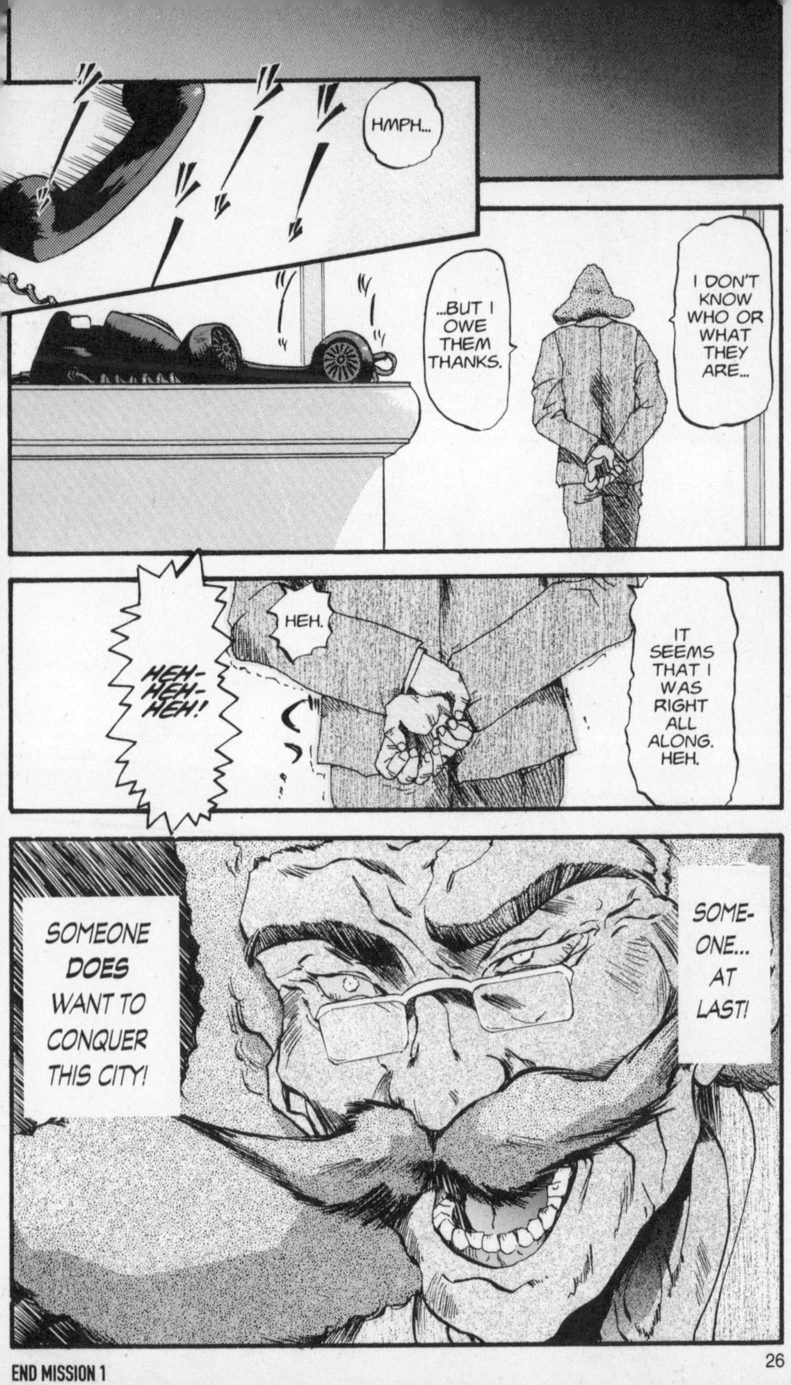
HMPH...
I DON'T KNOW WHO OR WHAT THEY ARE...
...BUT I OWE THEM THANKS.
IT SEEMS THAT I WAS RIGHT ALL ALONG. HEH.
HEH.
HEH-HEH-HEH!
SOME-ONE... AT LAST!
SOMEONE DOES WANT TO CONQUER THIS CITY!

END MISSION 1

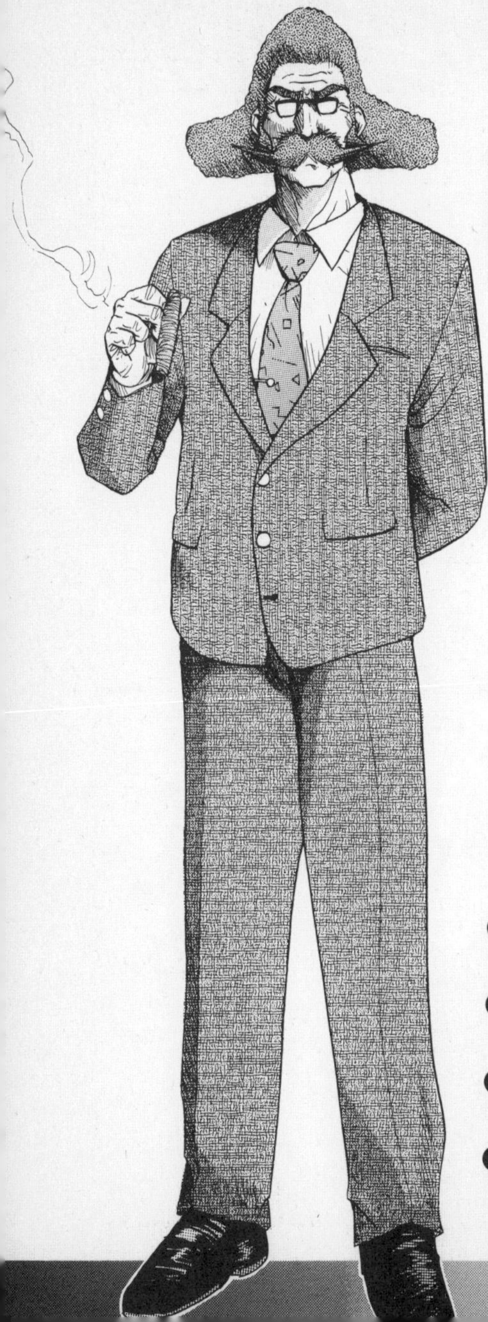

Featured Characters # (Whole Lot) + 1

"Call me *'Doc-tor'* (Emphasize both syllables

DOCTOR KABAP

His most prominent ~~strengths~~ characteristics

- His hairstyle
- ...and his mustache
- While he's a fun person to draw...
- ...doing close-ups of that face doe tend to wear you down.

EXCEL SAGA

PRESCRIPTION MEDICATION
Rx
TO BE INGESTED

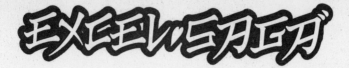

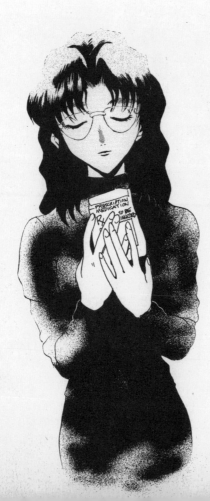

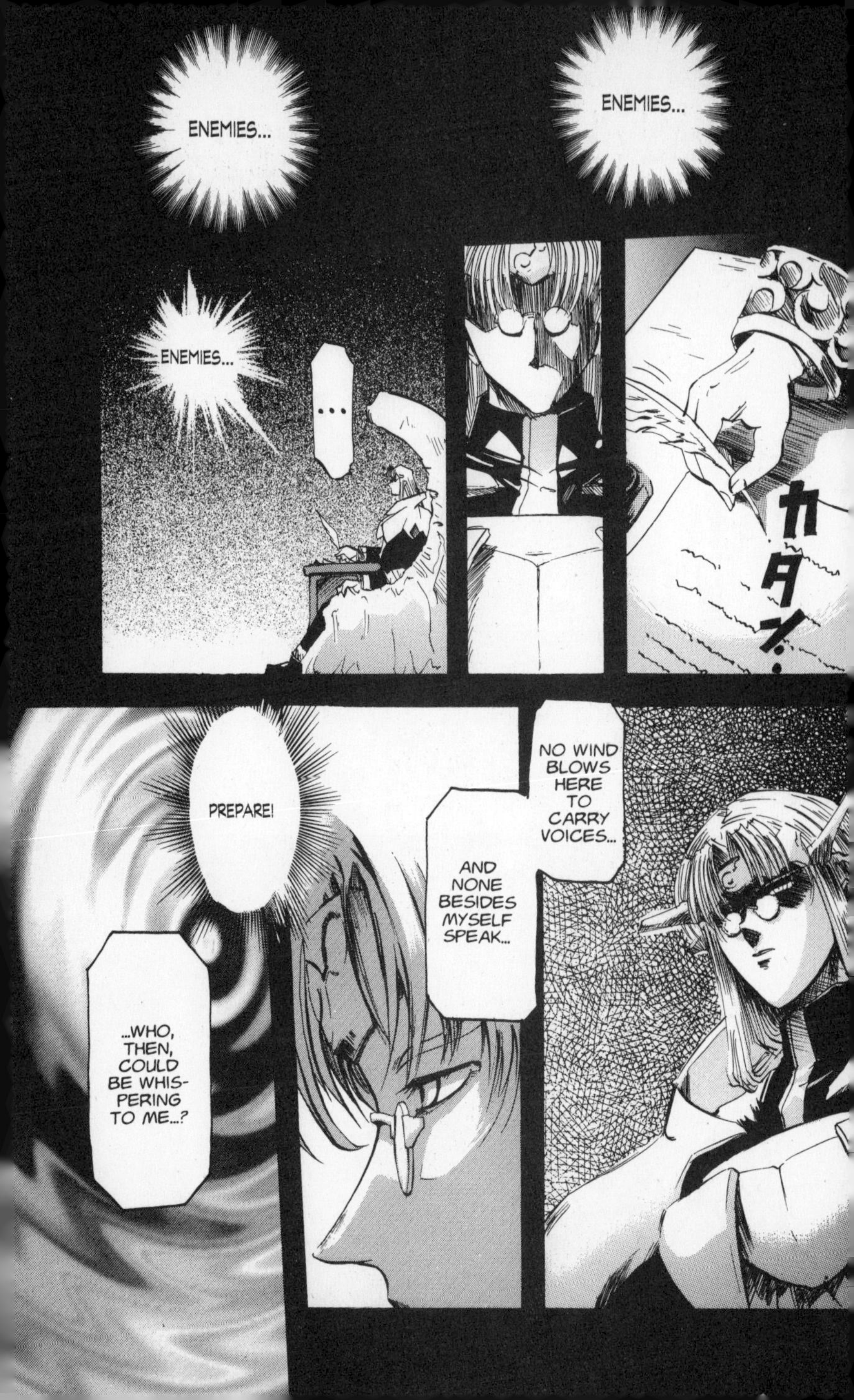
ENEMIES...
ENEMIES...
カタン
ENEMIES...
...
NO WIND BLOWS HERE TO CARRY VOICES...
AND NONE BESIDES MYSELF SPEAK...
PREPARE!
...WHO, THEN, COULD BE WHIS-PERING TO ME...?

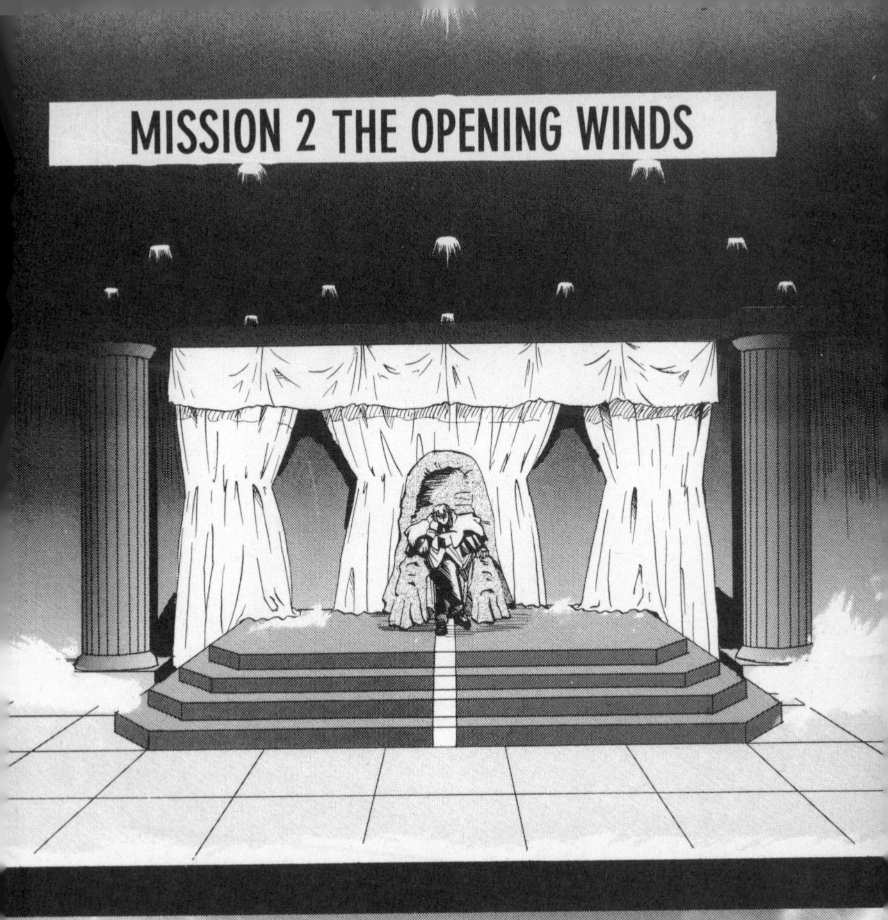
MISSION 2 THE OPENING WINDS

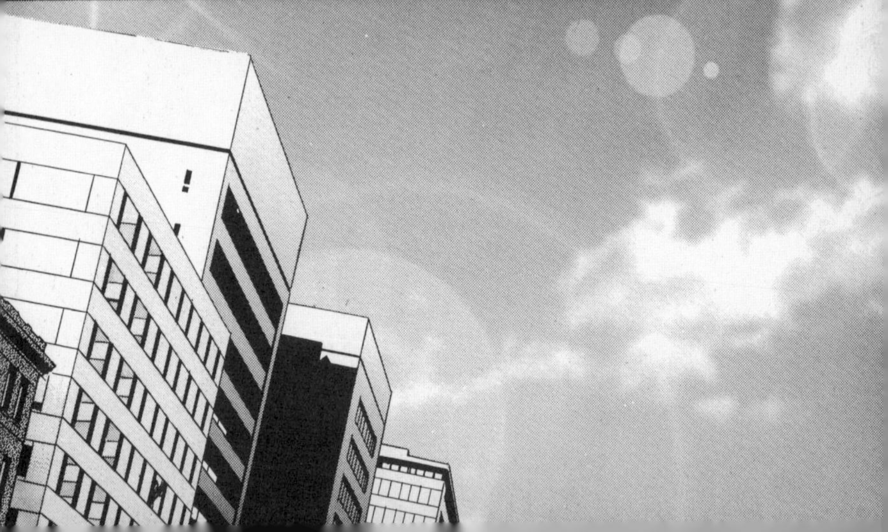

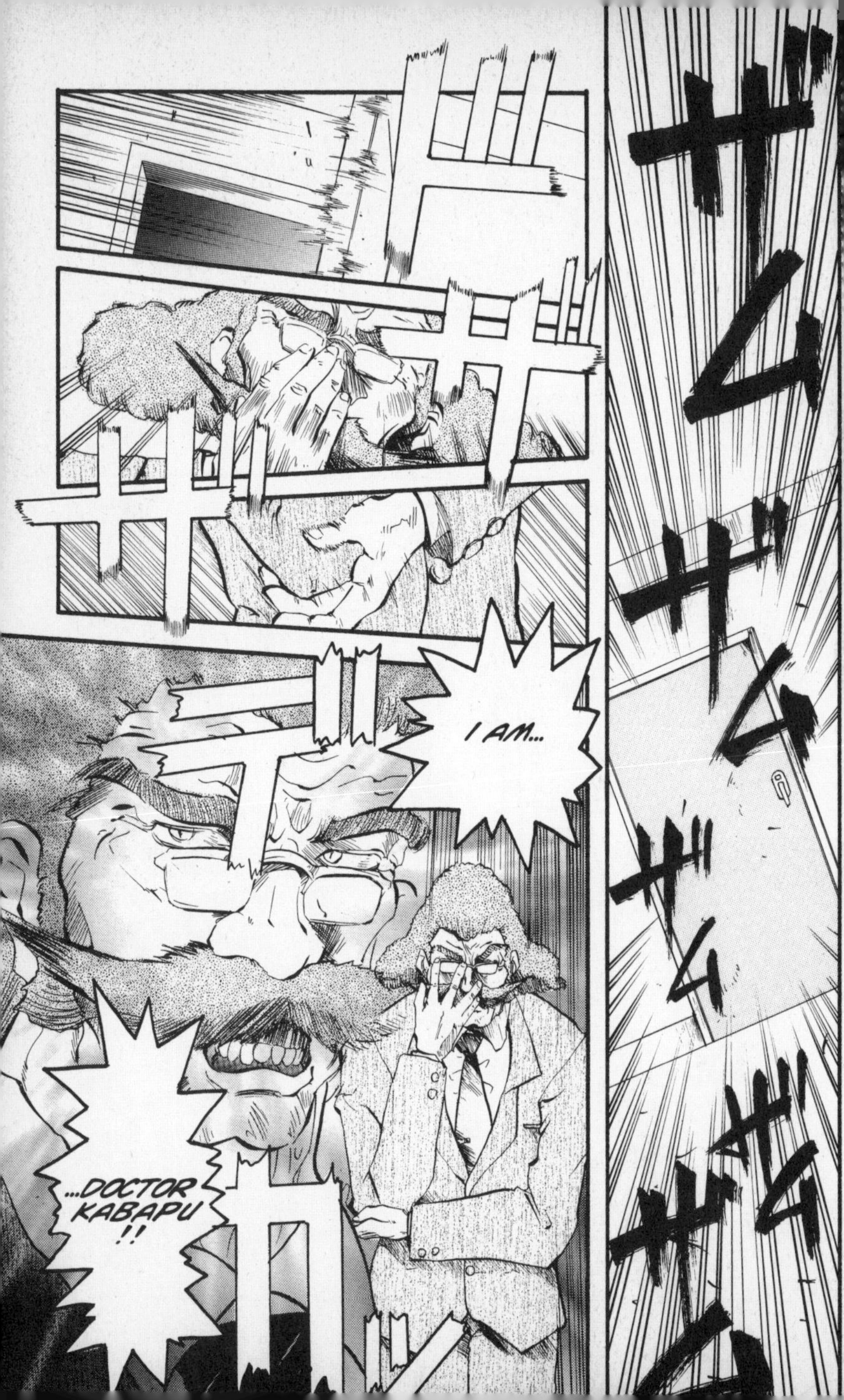
I AM...
...DOCTOR KABAPU !!

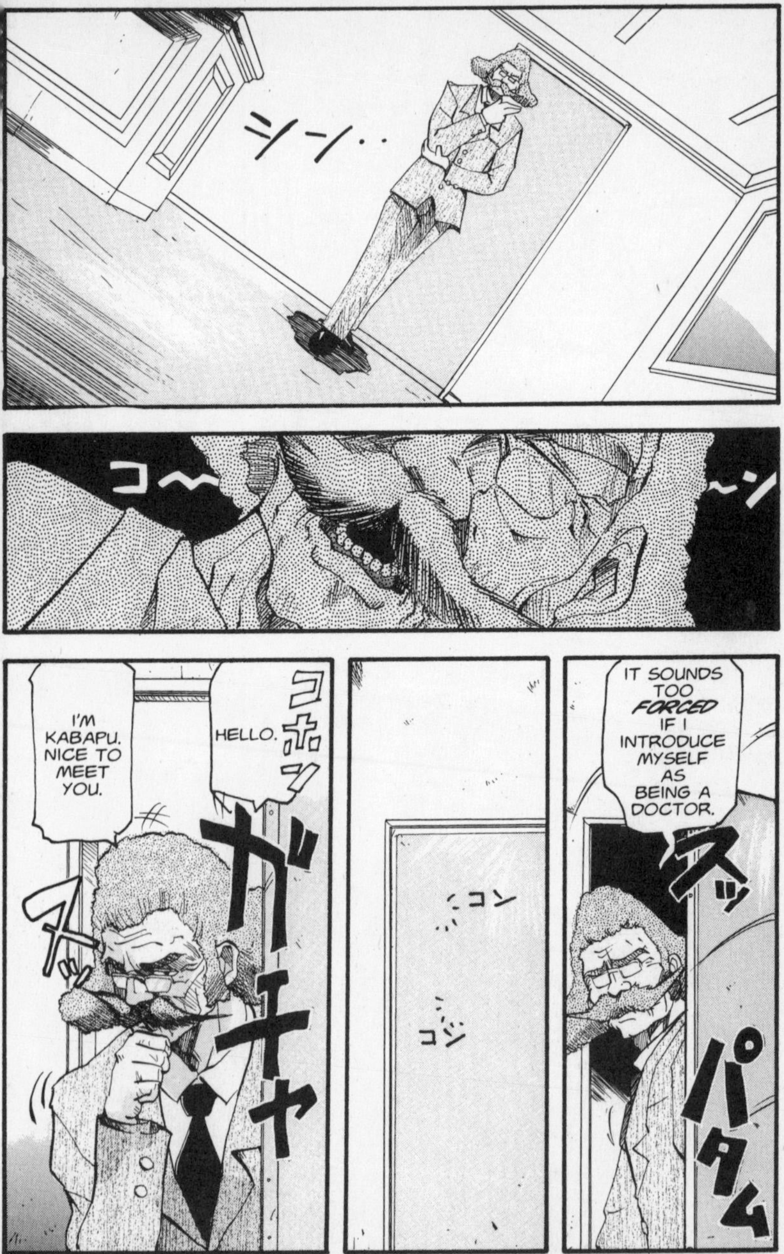
シーン‥
コ～
～ン
IT SOUNDS TOO FORCED IF I INTRODUCE MYSELF AS BEING A DOCTOR.
スッ
パタム
コン
コン
コホン
HELLO.
ガチャ
I'M KABAPU. NICE TO MEET YOU.
スッ

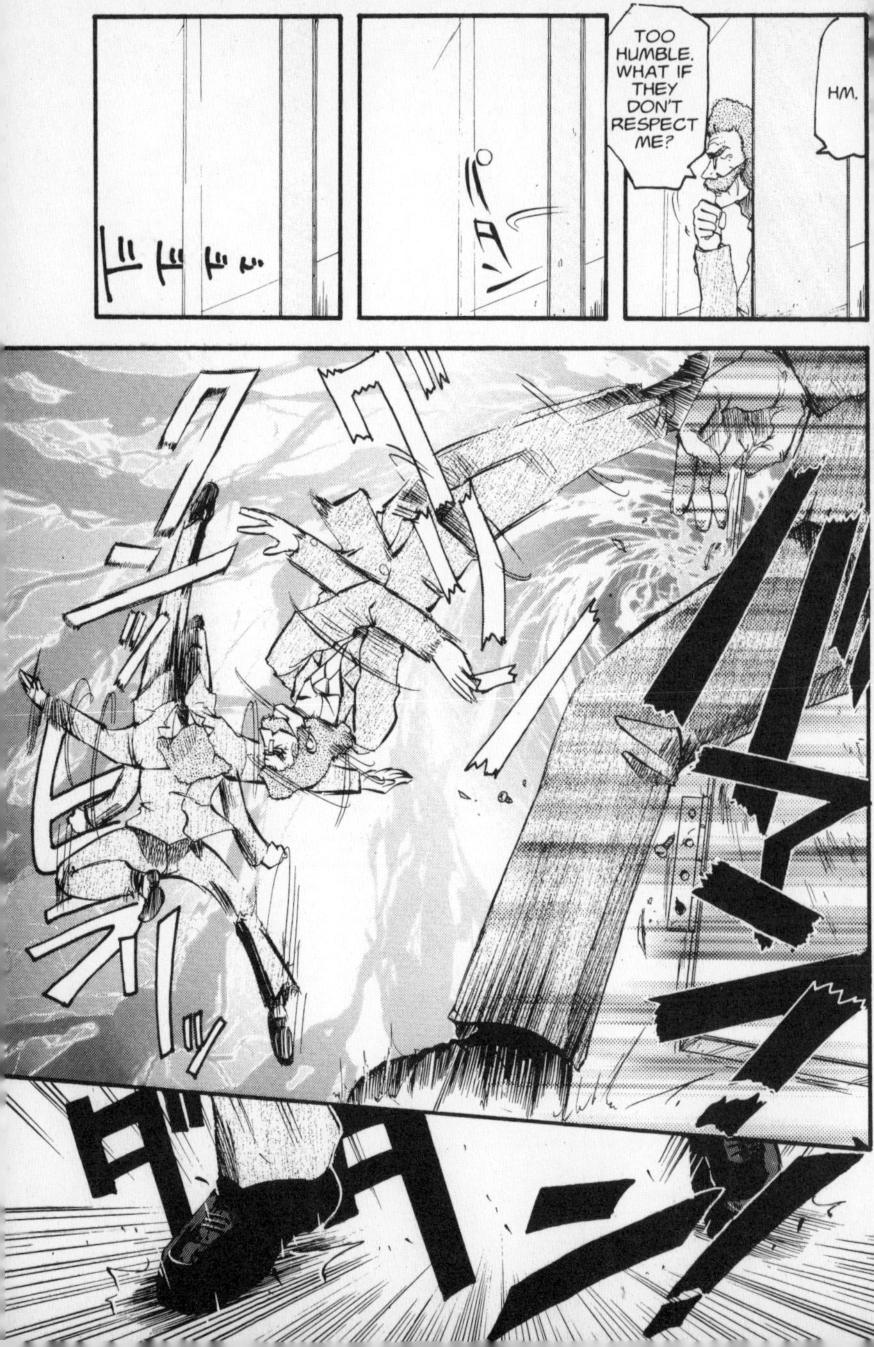
HM.
TOO HUMBLE. WHAT IF THEY DON'T RESPECT ME?

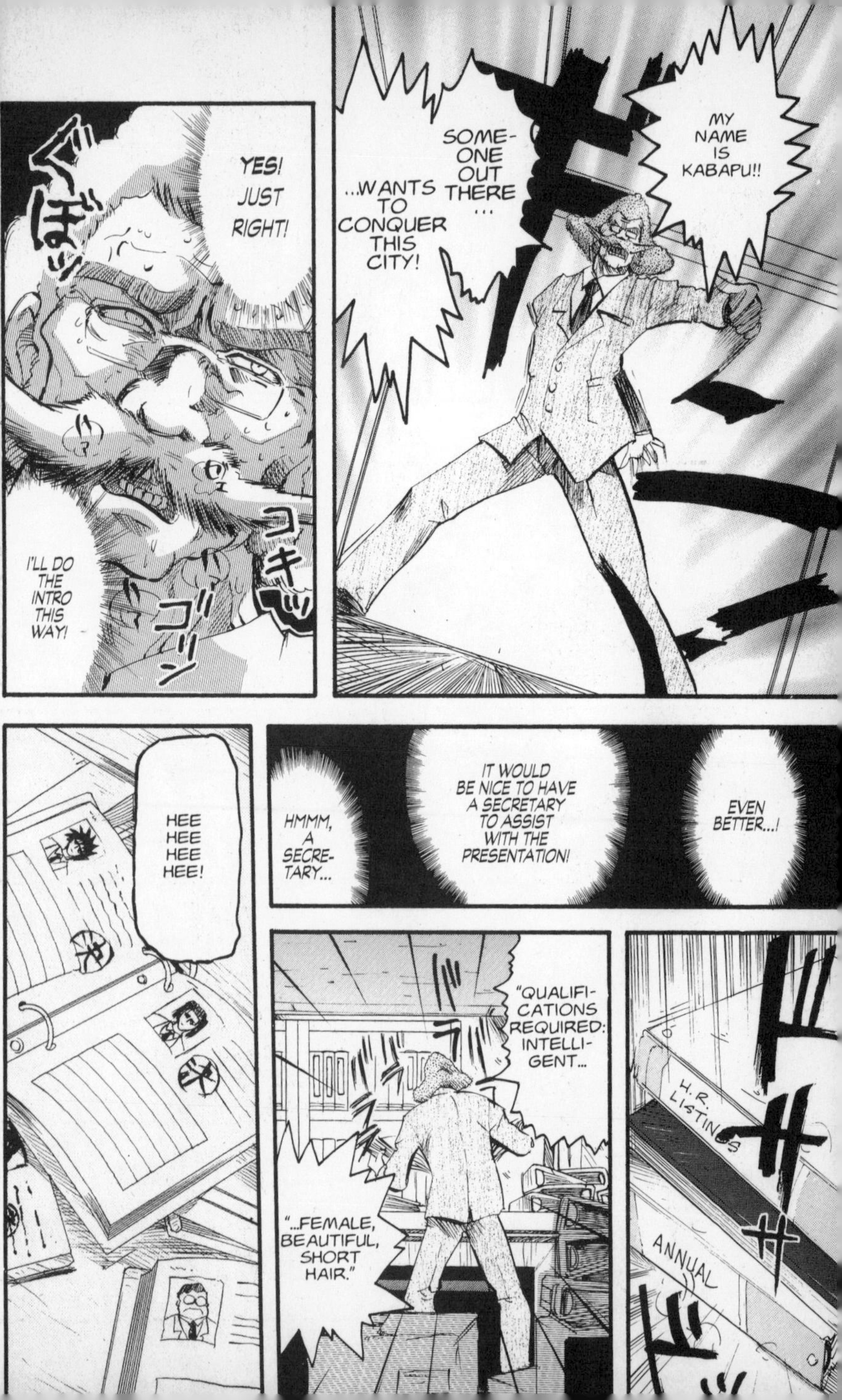
MY NAME IS KABAPU!!
SOME-ONE OUT THERE ...
...WANTS TO CONQUER THIS CITY!
YES! JUST RIGHT!
I'LL DO THE INTRO THIS WAY!
EVEN BETTER...!
IT WOULD BE NICE TO HAVE A SECRETARY TO ASSIST WITH THE PRESENTATION!
HMMM, A SECRE-TARY...
H.R. LISTINGS
ANNUAL
"QUALIFI-CATIONS REQUIRED: INTELLI-GENT...
"...FEMALE, BEAUTIFUL, SHORT HAIR."
HEE HEE HEE HEE!

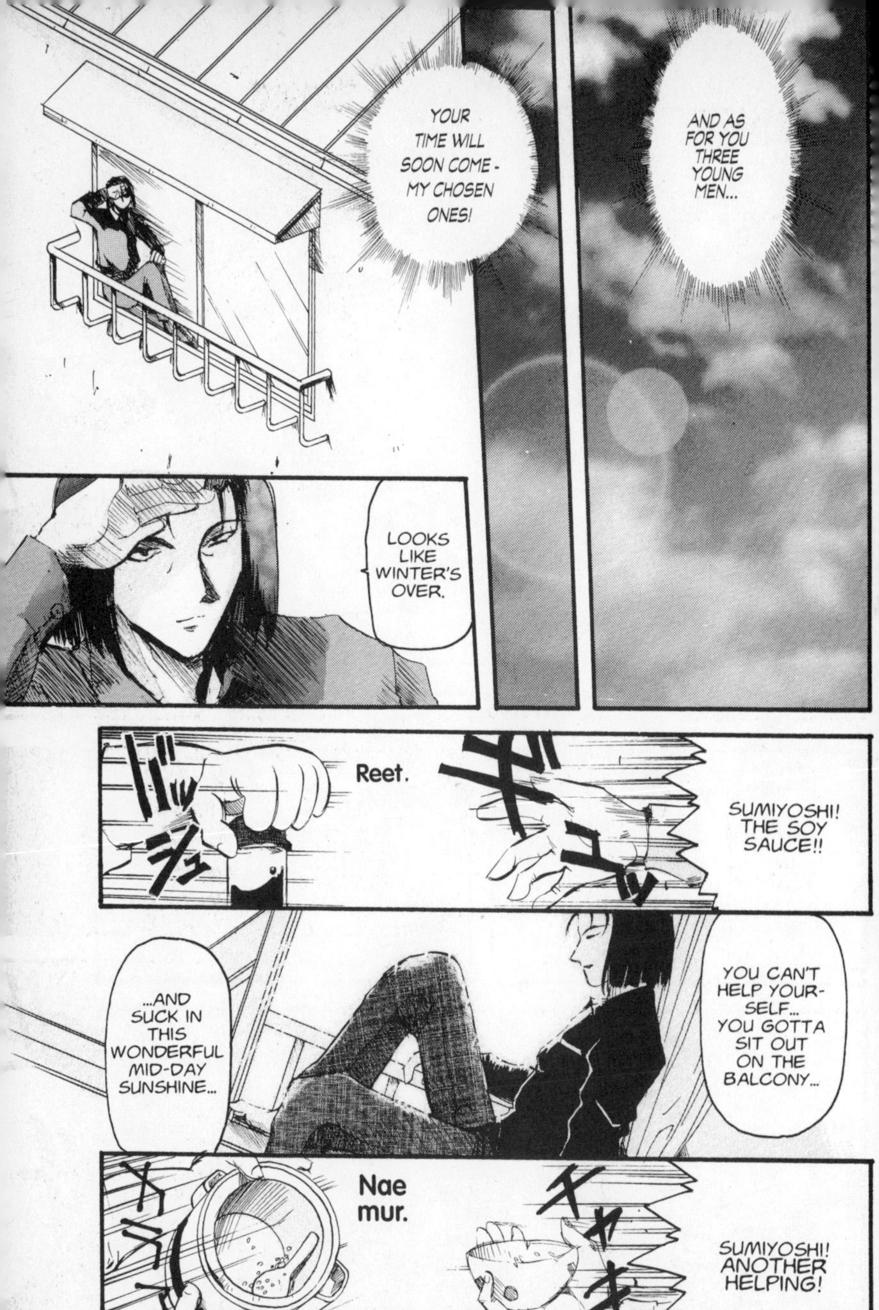
AND AS FOR YOU THREE YOUNG MEN...
YOUR TIME WILL SOON COME - MY CHOSEN ONES!
LOOKS LIKE WINTER'S OVER.
SUMIYOSHI! THE SOY SAUCE!!
Reet.
YOU CAN'T HELP YOUR-SELF... YOU GOTTA SIT OUT ON THE BALCONY...
...AND SUCK IN THIS WONDERFUL MID-DAY SUNSHINE...
SUMIYOSHI! ANOTHER HELPING!
Nae mur.

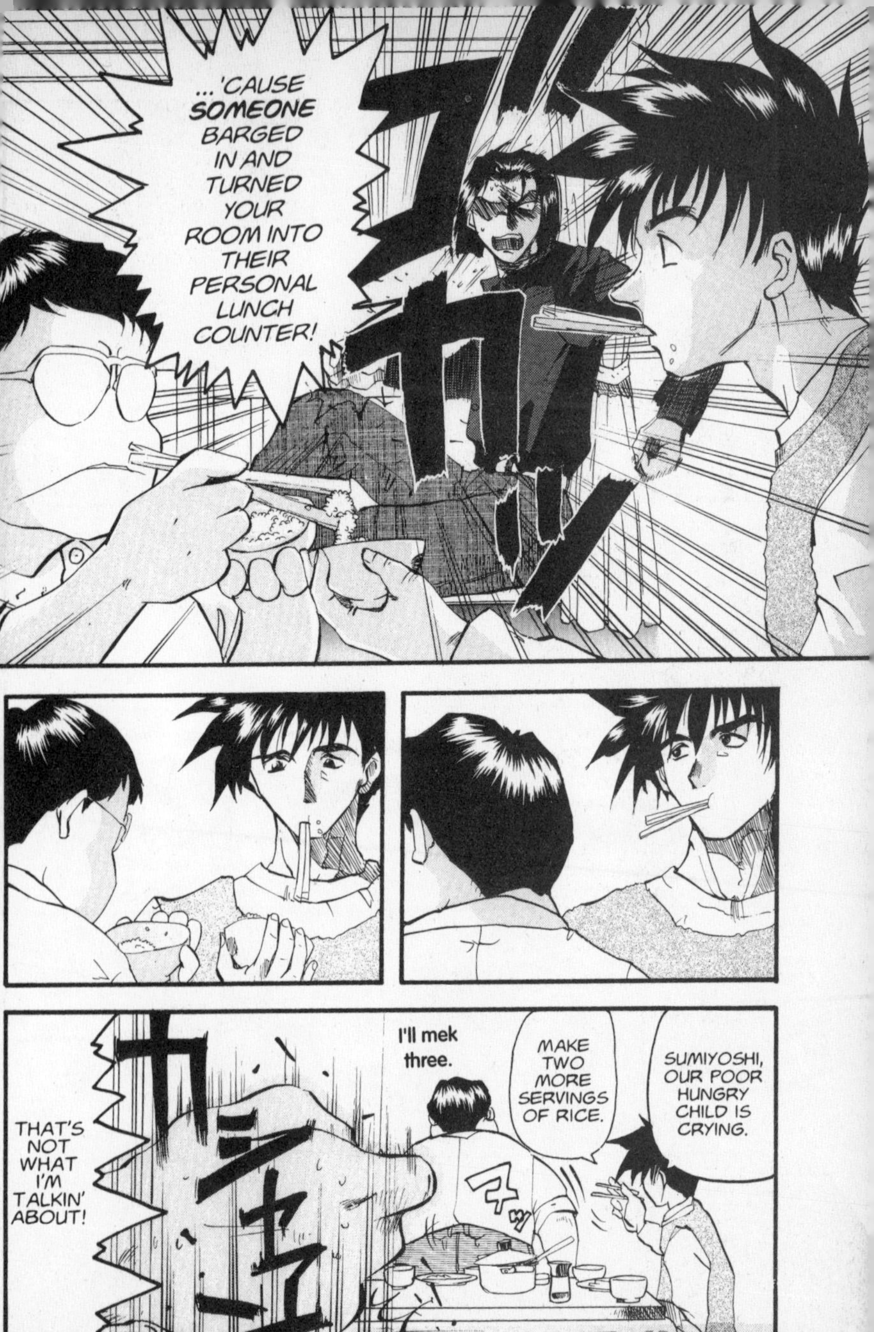
...'CAUSE SOMEONE BARGED IN AND TURNED YOUR ROOM INTO THEIR PERSONAL LUNCH COUNTER!
SUMIYOSHI, OUR POOR HUNGRY CHILD IS CRYING.
MAKE TWO MORE SERVINGS OF RICE.
I'll mek three.
THAT'S NOT WHAT I'M TALKIN' ABOUT!

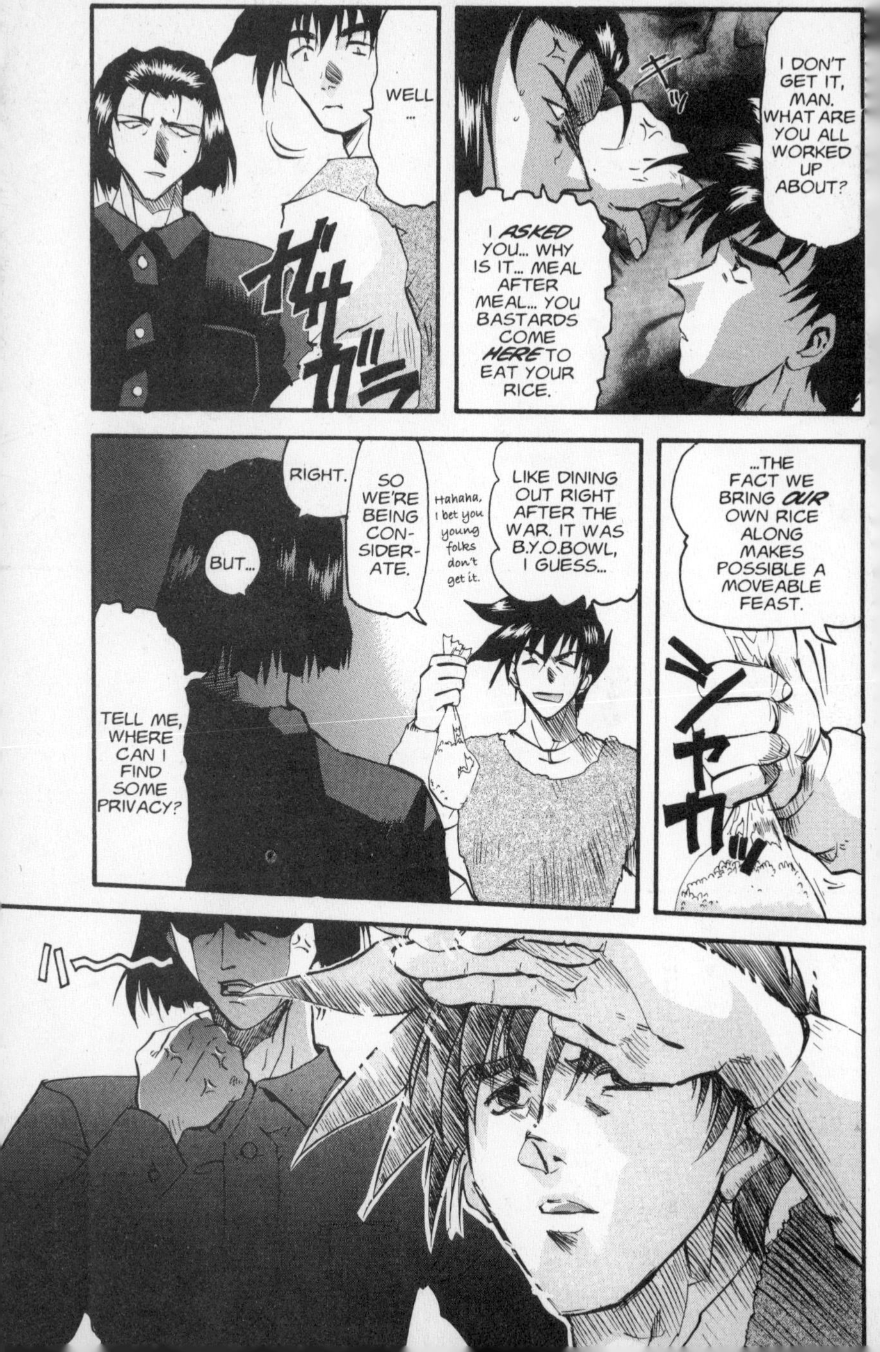
I DON'T GET IT, MAN. WHAT ARE YOU ALL WORKED UP ABOUT?
I *ASKED* YOU... WHY IS IT... MEAL AFTER MEAL... YOU BASTARDS COME *HERE* TO EAT YOUR RICE.
WELL ...
...THE FACT WE BRING *OUR* OWN RICE ALONG MAKES POSSIBLE A MOVEABLE FEAST.
LIKE DINING OUT RIGHT AFTER THE WAR. IT WAS B.Y.O.BOWL, I GUESS...
Hahaha, I bet you young folks don't get it.
SO WE'RE BEING CON-SIDER-ATE.
RIGHT.
BUT...
TELL ME, WHERE CAN I FIND SOME PRIVACY?

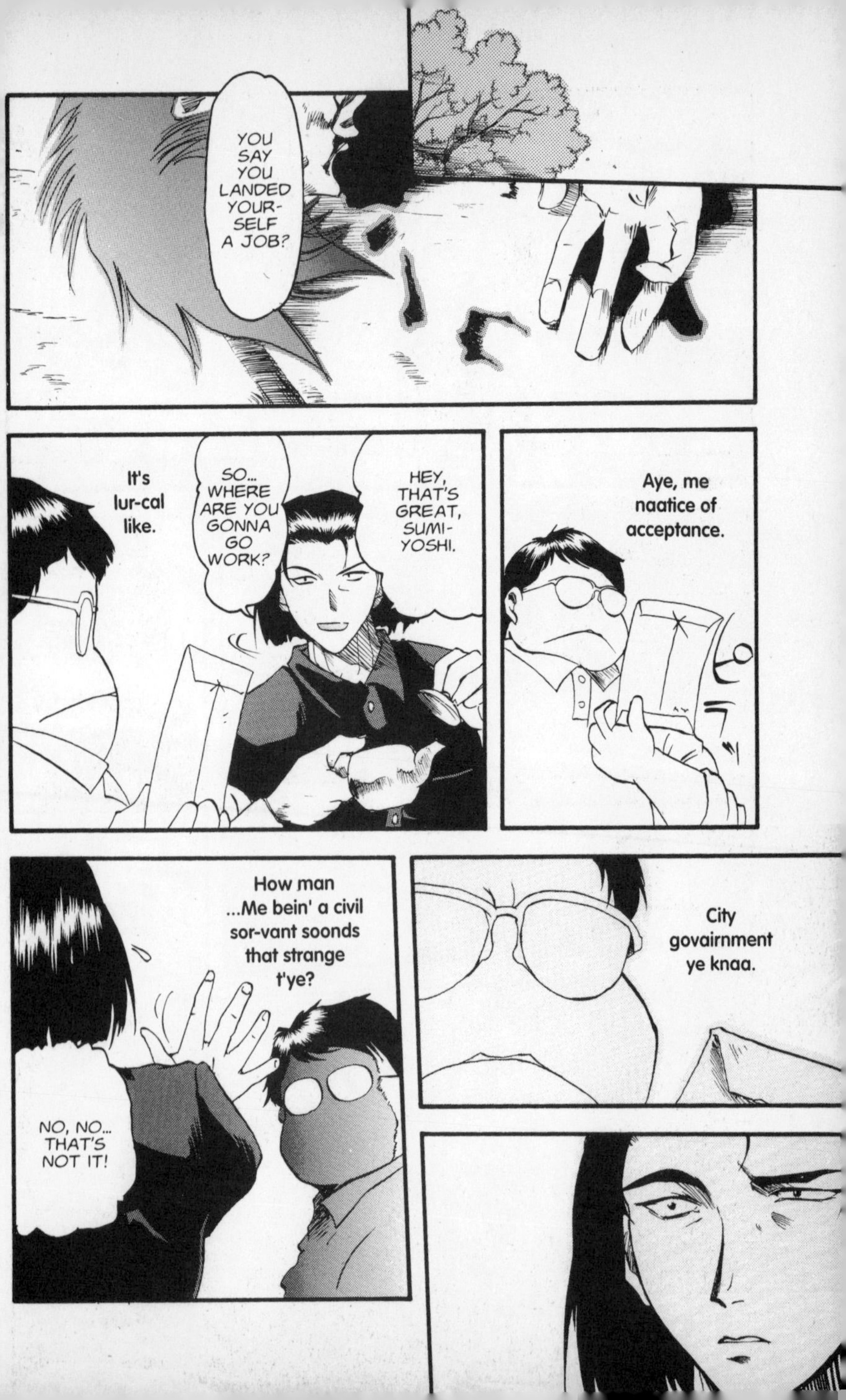
YOU SAY YOU LANDED YOURSELF A JOB?
Aye, me naatice of acceptance.
HEY, THAT'S GREAT, SUMIYOSHI.
SO... WHERE ARE YOU GONNA GO WORK?
It's lur-cal like.
City govairnment ye knaa.
How man ...Me bein' a civil sor-vant soonds that strange t'ye?
NO, NO... THAT'S NOT IT!

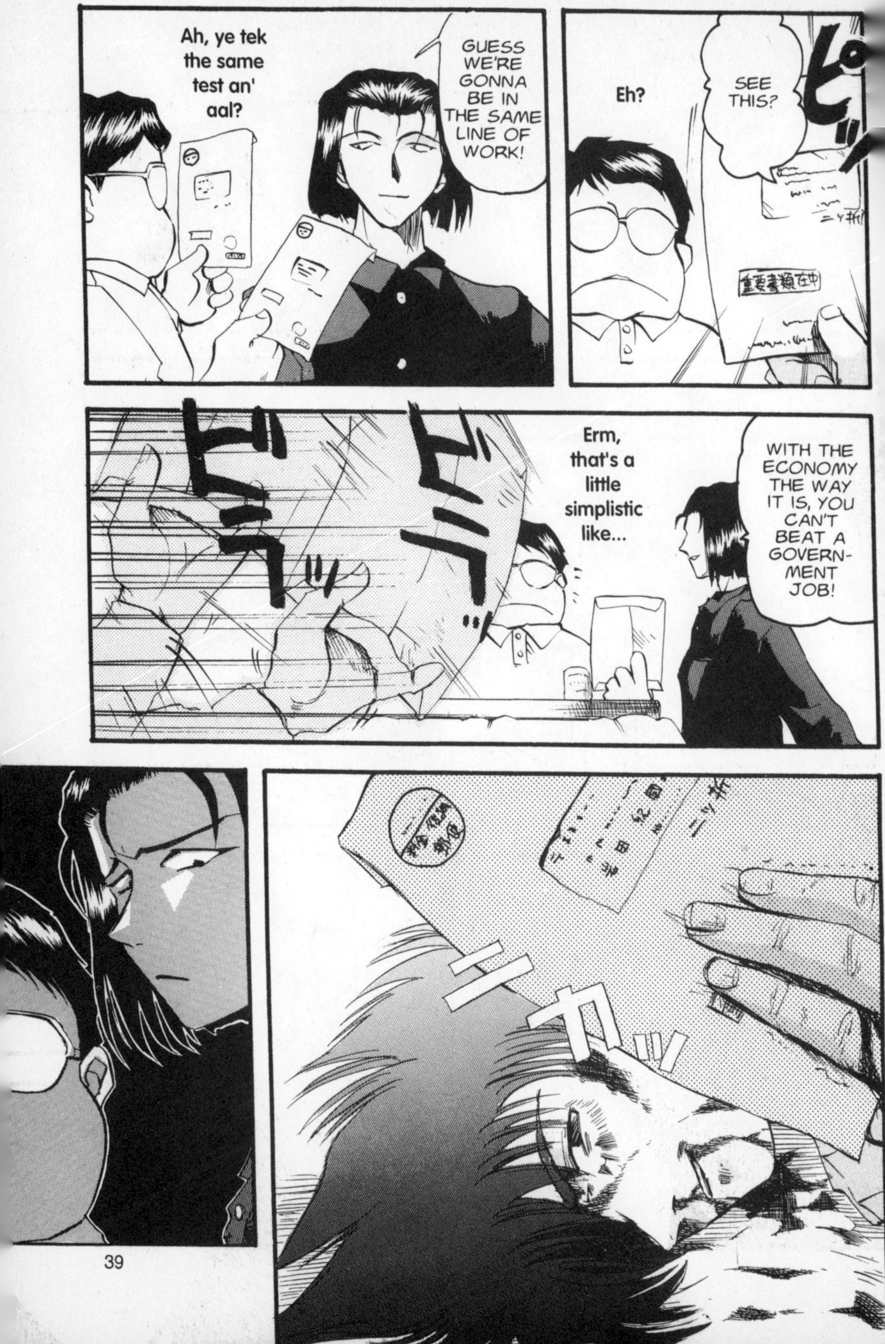
SEE THIS?
Eh?
GUESS WE'RE GONNA BE IN THE SAME LINE OF WORK!
Ah, ye tek the same test an' aal?
WITH THE ECONOMY THE WAY IT IS, YOU CAN'T BEAT A GOVERNMENT JOB!
Erm, that's a little simplistic like...

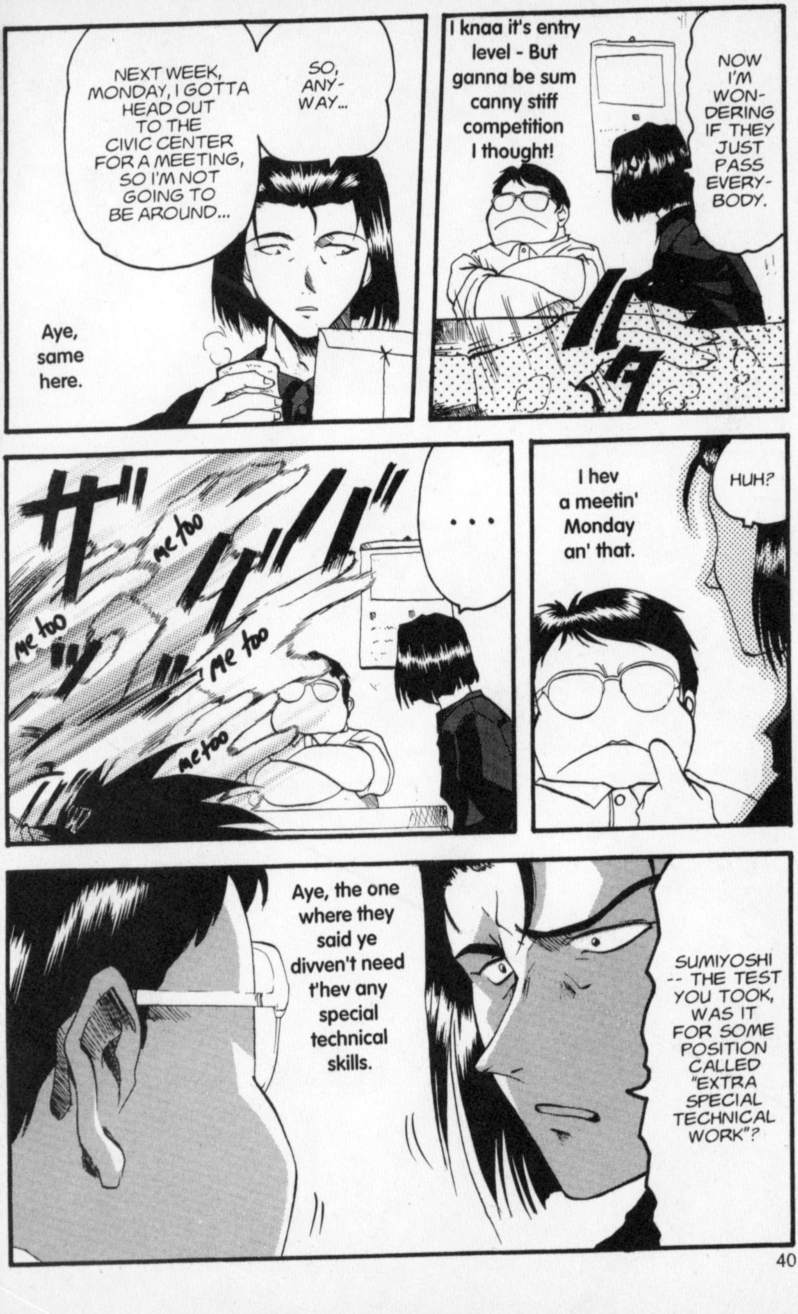
NOW I'M WONDERING IF THEY JUST PASS EVERYBODY.
I knaa it's entry level - But ganna be sum canny stiff competition I thought!
SO, ANYWAY...
NEXT WEEK, MONDAY, I GOTTA HEAD OUT TO THE CIVIC CENTER FOR A MEETING, SO I'M NOT GOING TO BE AROUND...
Aye, same here.
HUH?
I hev a meetin' Monday an' that.
. . .
me too
me too
me too
me too
SUMIYOSHI -- THE TEST YOU TOOK, WAS IT FOR SOME POSITION CALLED "EXTRA SPECIAL TECHNICAL WORK"?
Aye, the one where they said ye divven't need t'hev any special technical skills.

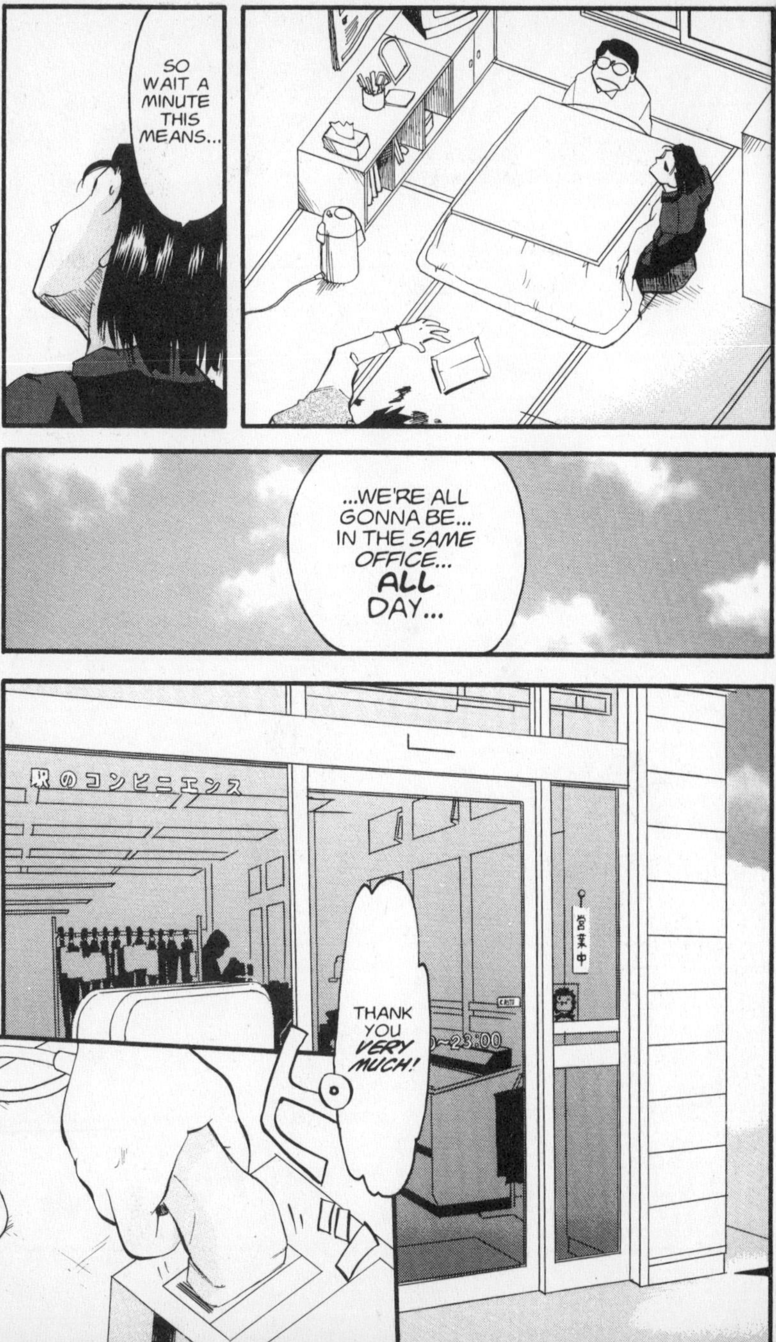
SO WAIT A MINUTE THIS MEANS...
...WE'RE ALL GONNA BE... IN THE SAME OFFICE... ALL DAY...
駅のコンビニエンス
営業中
THANK YOU VERY MUCH!

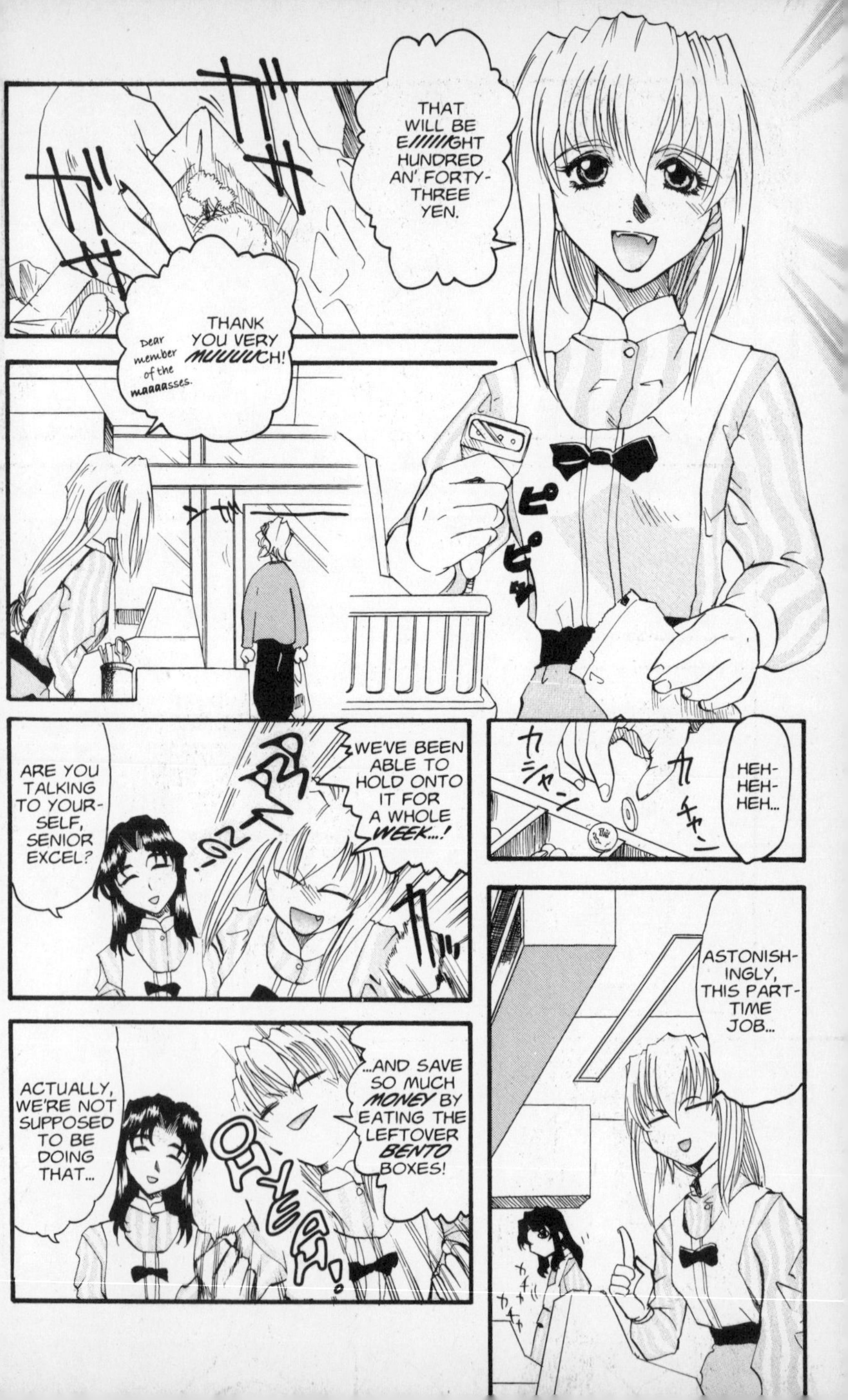
THAT WILL BE E//////GHT HUNDRED AN' FORTY-THREE YEN.
THANK YOU VERY MUUUUCH!
Dear member of the maaaasses.
HEH-HEH-HEH...
ASTONISHINGLY, THIS PART-TIME JOB...
WE'VE BEEN ABLE TO HOLD ONTO IT FOR A WHOLE WEEK...!
ARE YOU TALKING TO YOURSELF, SENIOR EXCEL?
...AND SAVE SO MUCH MONEY BY EATING THE LEFTOVER BENTO BOXES!
OH YEAH!
ACTUALLY, WE'RE NOT SUPPOSED TO BE DOING THAT...

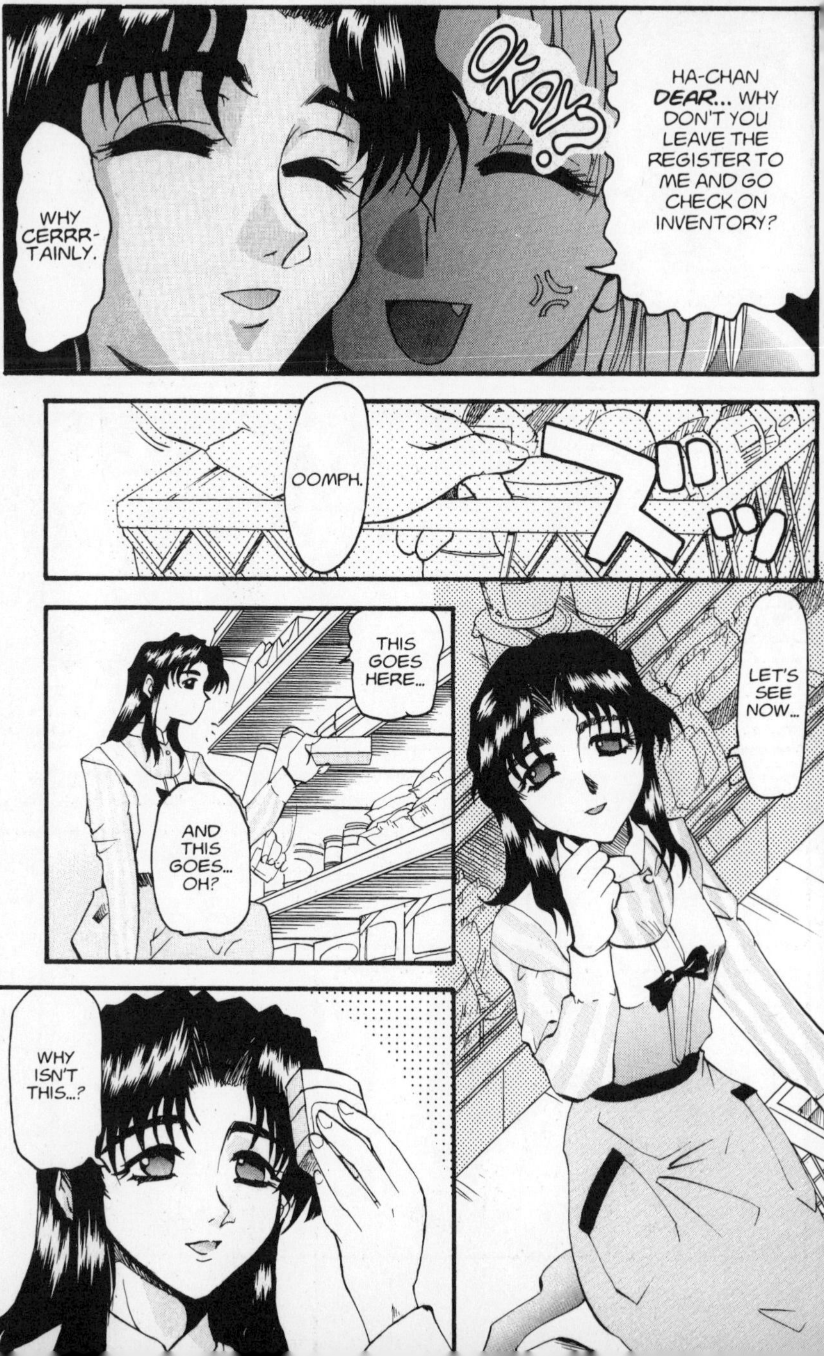
HA-CHAN DEAR... WHY DON'T YOU LEAVE THE REGISTER TO ME AND GO CHECK ON INVENTORY?
OKAY?
WHY CERRR-TAINLY.
OOMPH.
LET'S SEE NOW...
THIS GOES HERE...
AND THIS GOES... OH?
WHY ISN'T THIS...?

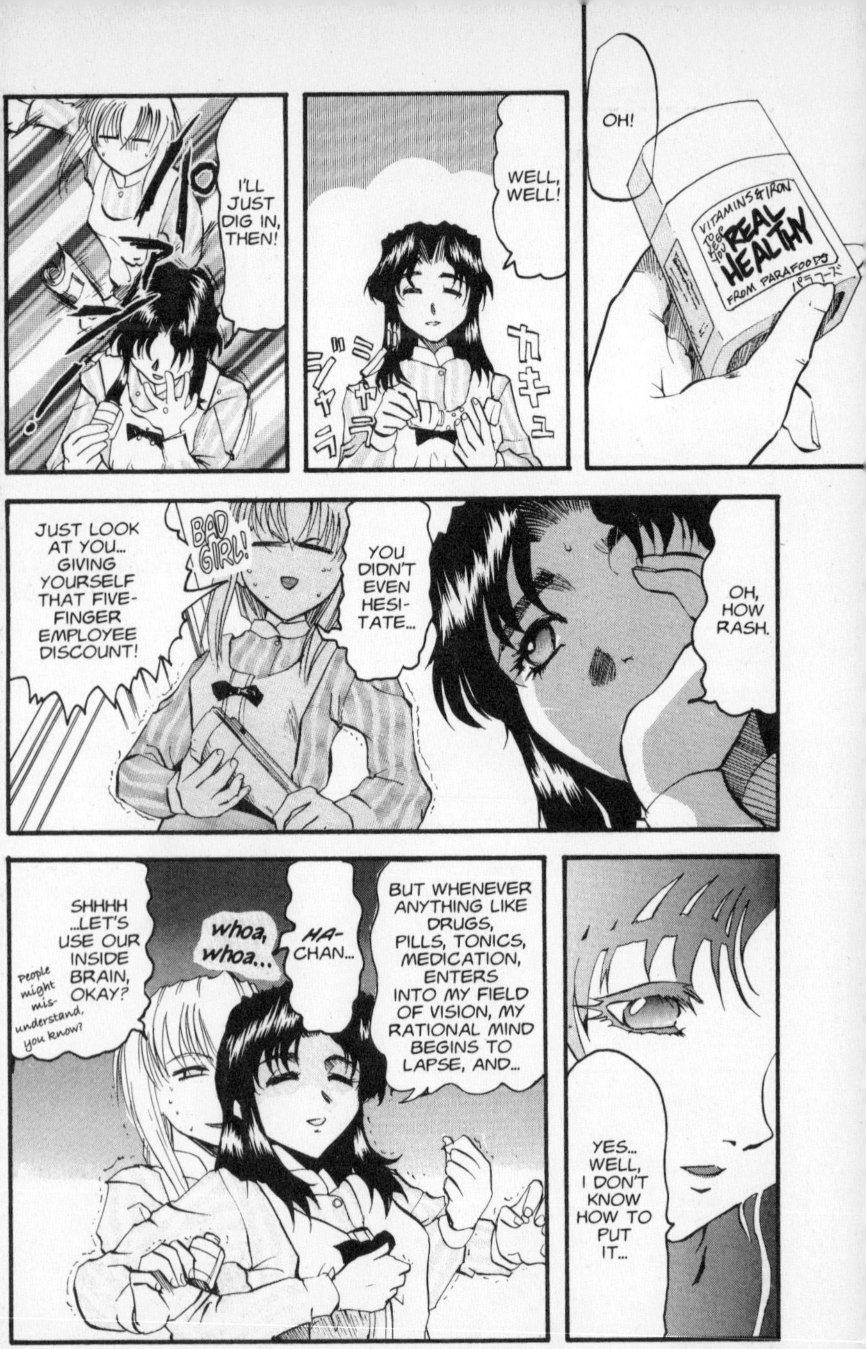
OH!
VITAMINS & IRON
TO KEEP YOU
REAL HEALTHY
FROM PARAFOODS
パラフーズ
WELL, WELL!
カキュ
I'LL JUST DIG IN, THEN!
OH, HOW RASH.
YOU DIDN'T EVEN HESI-TATE...
BAD GIRL!
JUST LOOK AT YOU... GIVING YOURSELF THAT FIVE-FINGER EMPLOYEE DISCOUNT!
YES... WELL, I DON'T KNOW HOW TO PUT IT...
BUT WHENEVER ANYTHING LIKE DRUGS, PILLS, TONICS, MEDICATION, ENTERS INTO MY FIELD OF VISION, MY RATIONAL MIND BEGINS TO LAPSE, AND...
HA-CHAN...
whoa, whoa...
SHHHH ...LET'S USE OUR INSIDE BRAIN, OKAY?
People might mis-understand, you know?

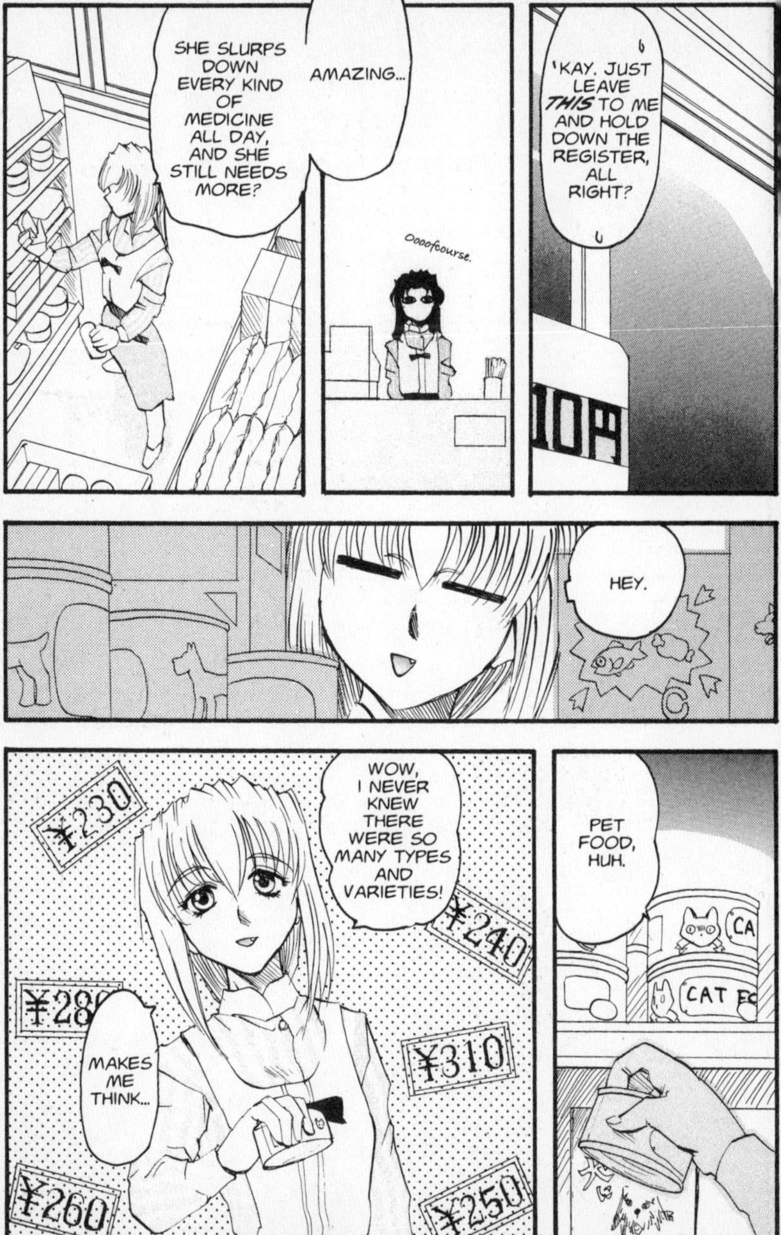
'KAY. JUST LEAVE THIS TO ME AND HOLD DOWN THE REGISTER, ALL RIGHT?
AMAZING...
Oooofcourse.
SHE SLURPS DOWN EVERY KIND OF MEDICINE ALL DAY, AND SHE STILL NEEDS MORE?
HEY.
PET FOOD, HUH.
WOW, I NEVER KNEW THERE WERE SO MANY TYPES AND VARIETIES!
¥230
¥240
¥310
¥250
¥260
MAKES ME THINK...

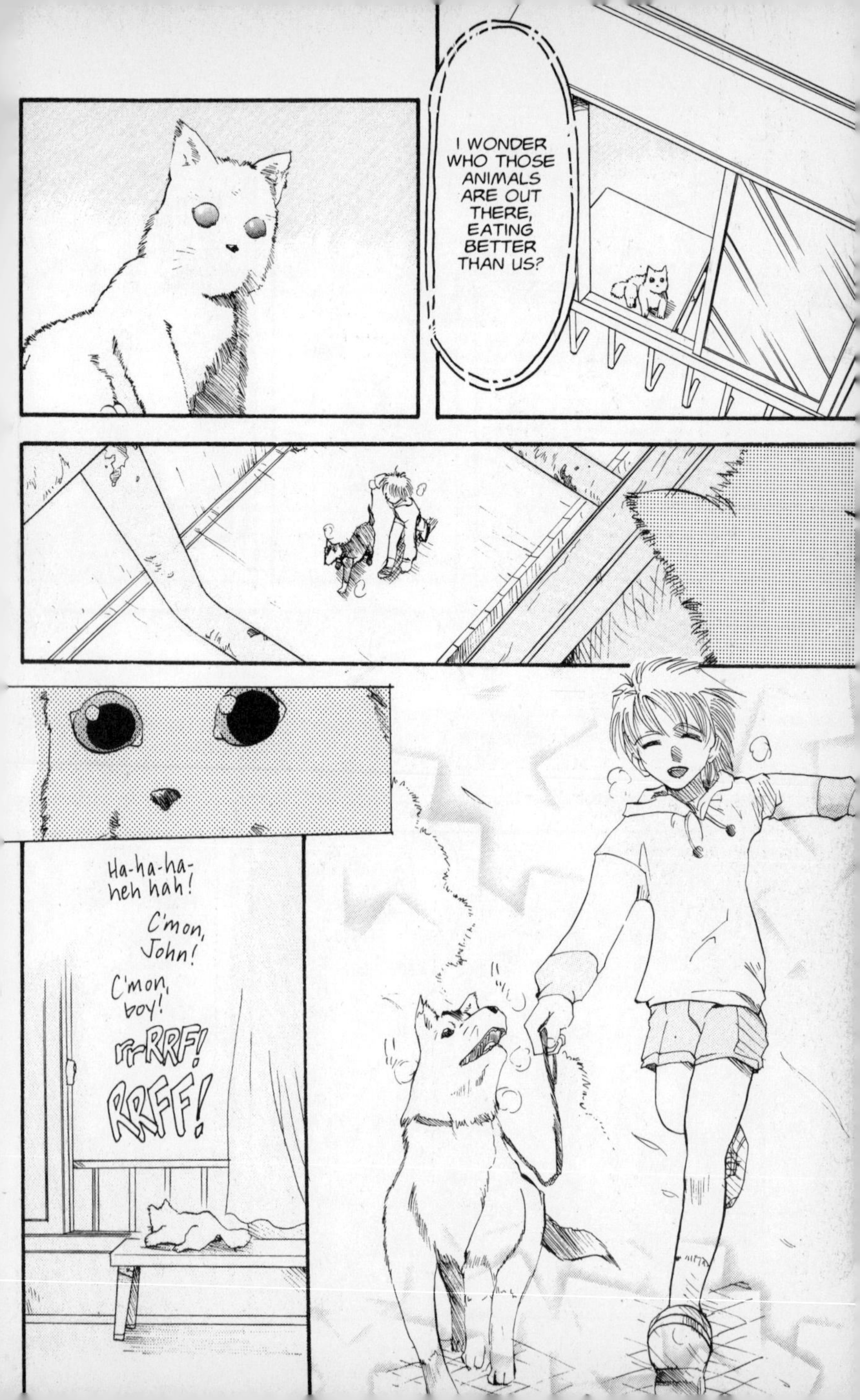
I WONDER WHO THOSE ANIMALS ARE OUT THERE, EATING BETTER THAN US?
Ha-ha-ha-heh hah!
C'mon, John!
C'mon, boy!
rrRRF!
RRFF!

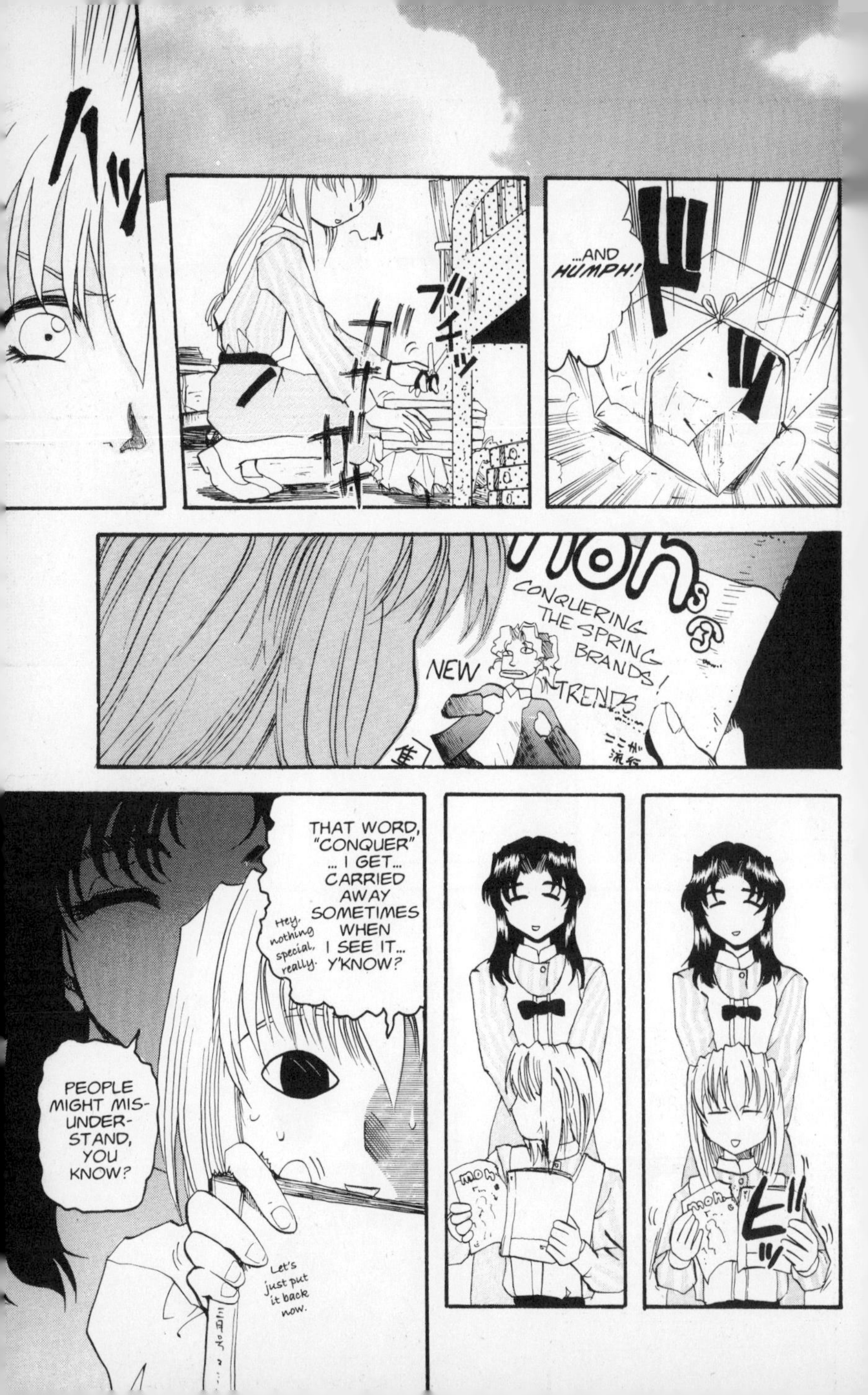
...AND HUMPH!
CONQUERING THE SPRING BRANDS!
NEW TRENDS
THAT WORD, "CONQUER" ... I GET... CARRIED AWAY SOMETIMES WHEN I SEE IT... Y'KNOW?
Hey, nothing special, really.
PEOPLE MIGHT MIS-UNDER-STAND, YOU KNOW?
Let's just put it back now.

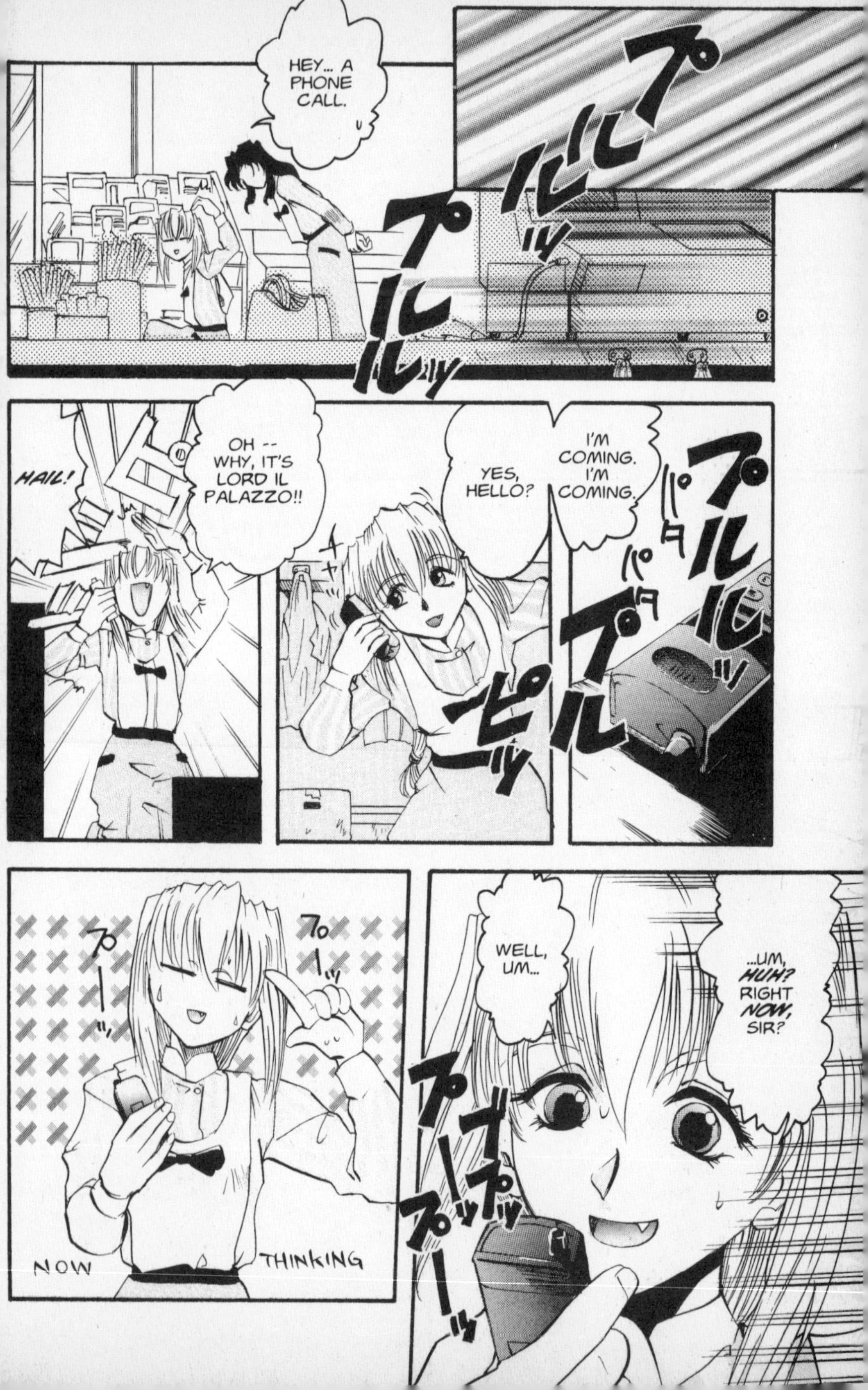
プルルッ
プルルッ
HEY... A PHONE CALL.
プルルッ
パタ パタ
プルル
I'M COMING. I'M COMING.
YES, HELLO?
ピッ
OH -- WHY, IT'S LORD IL PALAZZO!!
HAIL!
WELL, UM...
...UM, *HUH?* RIGHT *NOW,* SIR?
プーッ
プーッ
プーッ
プー
プーッ
NOW THINKING

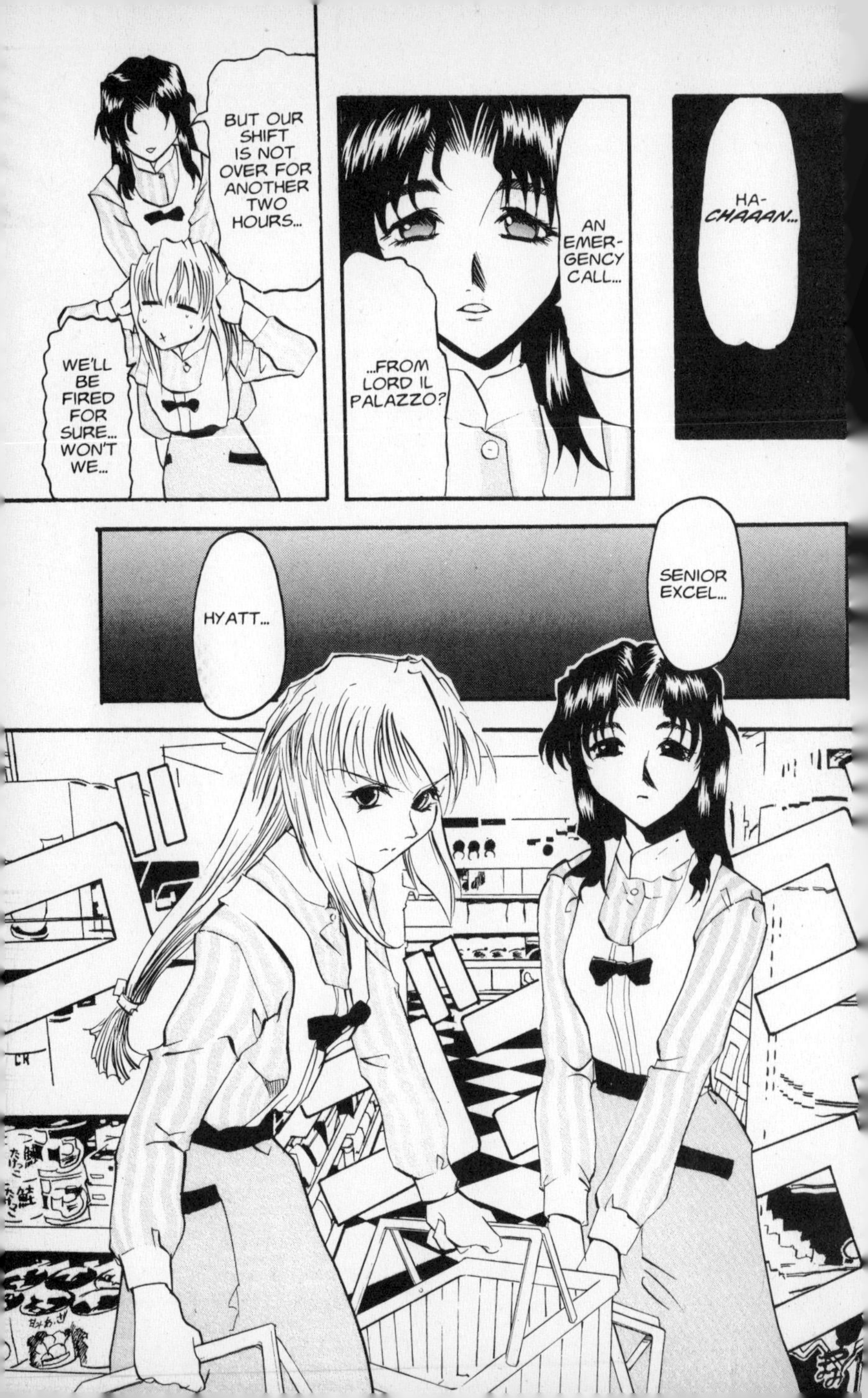
HA-CHAAAN...
AN EMERGENCY CALL...
...FROM LORD IL PALAZZO?
BUT OUR SHIFT IS NOT OVER FOR ANOTHER TWO HOURS...
WE'LL BE FIRED FOR SURE... WON'T WE...
SENIOR EXCEL...
HYATT...

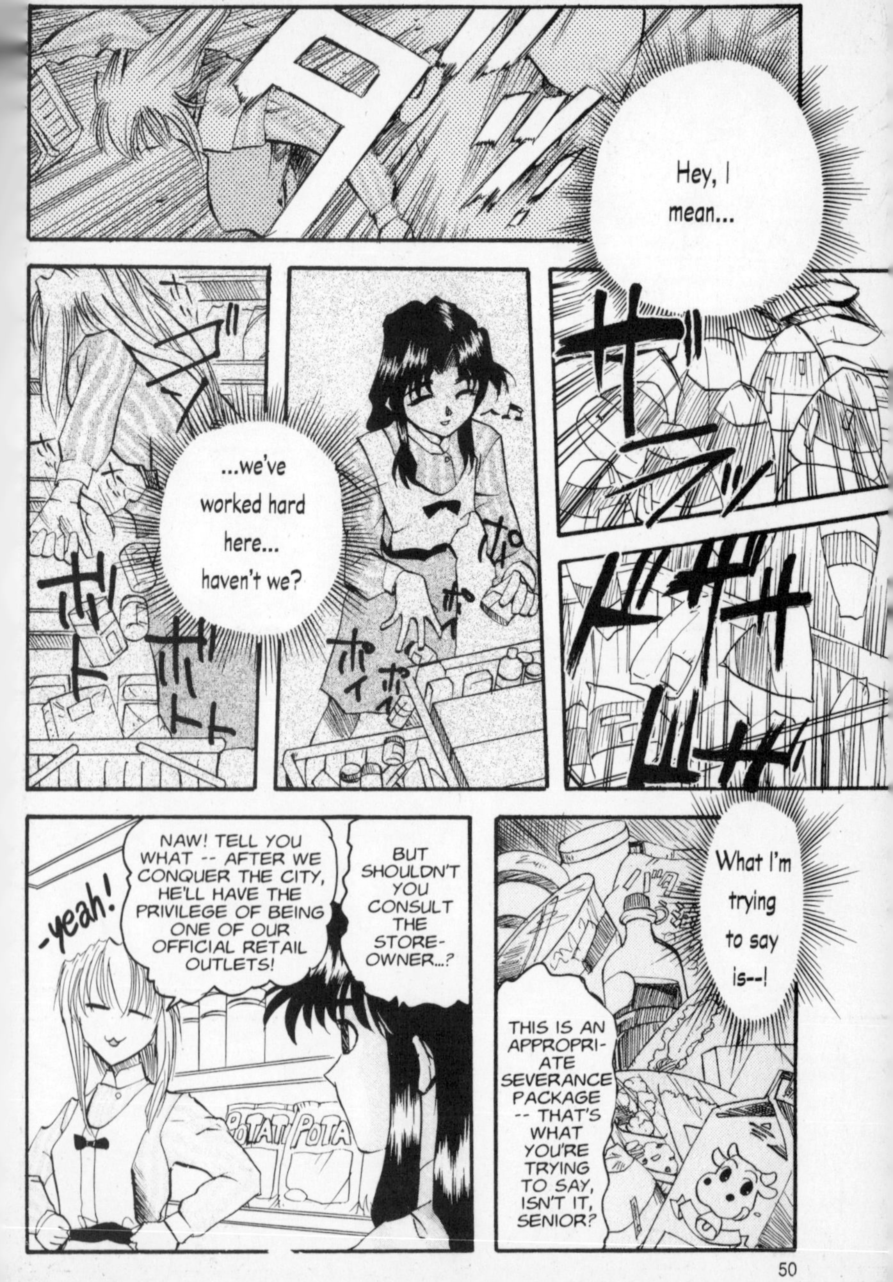
Hey, I mean...
...we've worked hard here... haven't we?
What I'm trying to say is--!
THIS IS AN APPROPRIATE SEVERANCE PACKAGE -- THAT'S WHAT YOU'RE TRYING TO SAY, ISN'T IT, SENIOR?
BUT SHOULDN'T YOU CONSULT THE STORE-OWNER...?
NAW! TELL YOU WHAT -- AFTER WE CONQUER THE CITY, HE'LL HAVE THE PRIVILEGE OF BEING ONE OF OUR OFFICIAL RETAIL OUTLETS!
-yeah!

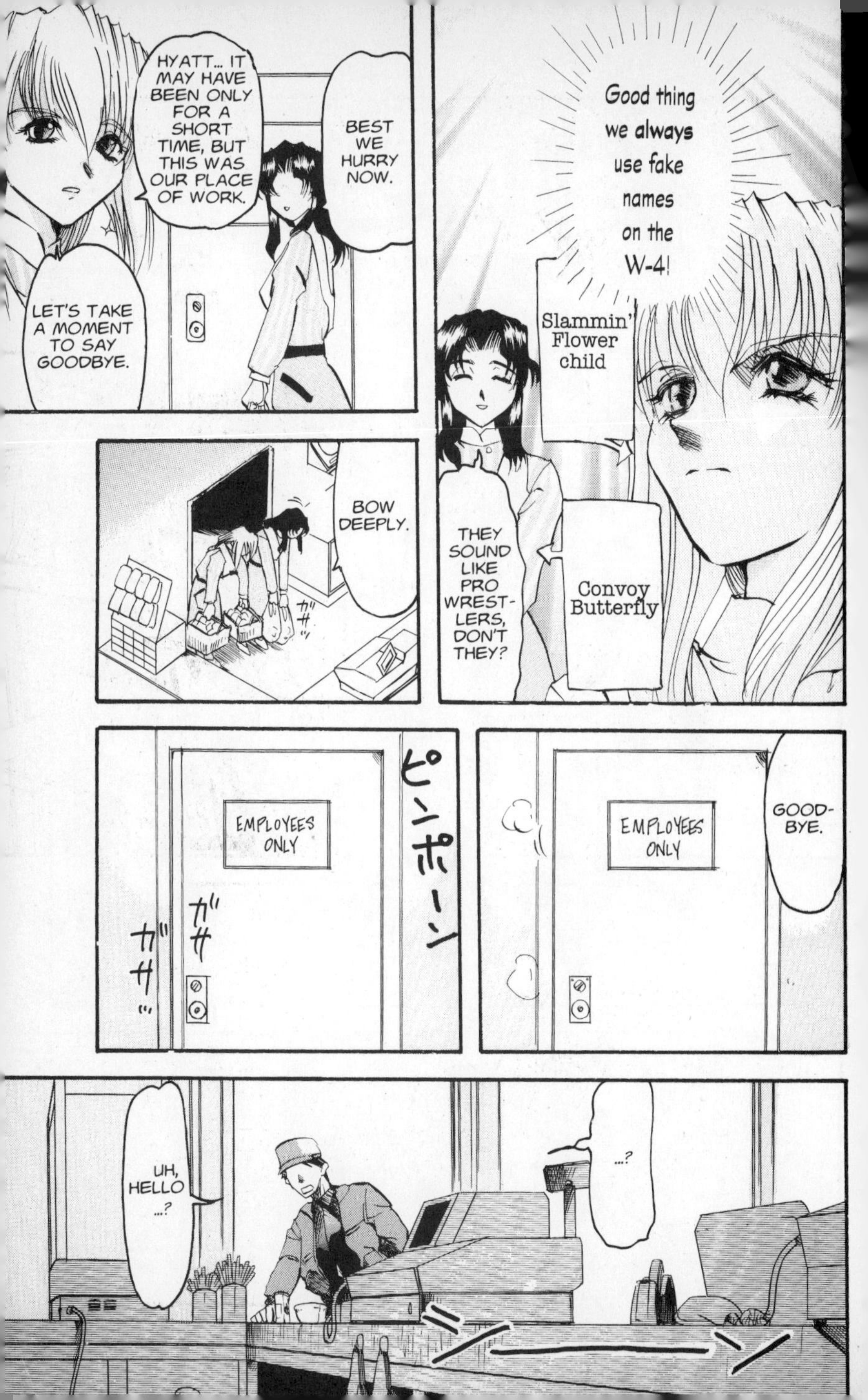
Good thing we always use fake names on the W-4!
Slammin' Flower child
Convoy Butterfly
THEY SOUND LIKE PRO WRESTLERS, DON'T THEY?
BEST WE HURRY NOW.
HYATT... IT MAY HAVE BEEN ONLY FOR A SHORT TIME, BUT THIS WAS OUR PLACE OF WORK.
LET'S TAKE A MOMENT TO SAY GOODBYE.
BOW DEEPLY.
ガサッ
GOOD-BYE.
EMPLOYEES ONLY
ピンポーン
EMPLOYEES ONLY
ガサ
ガサッ
...?
UH, HELLO ...?

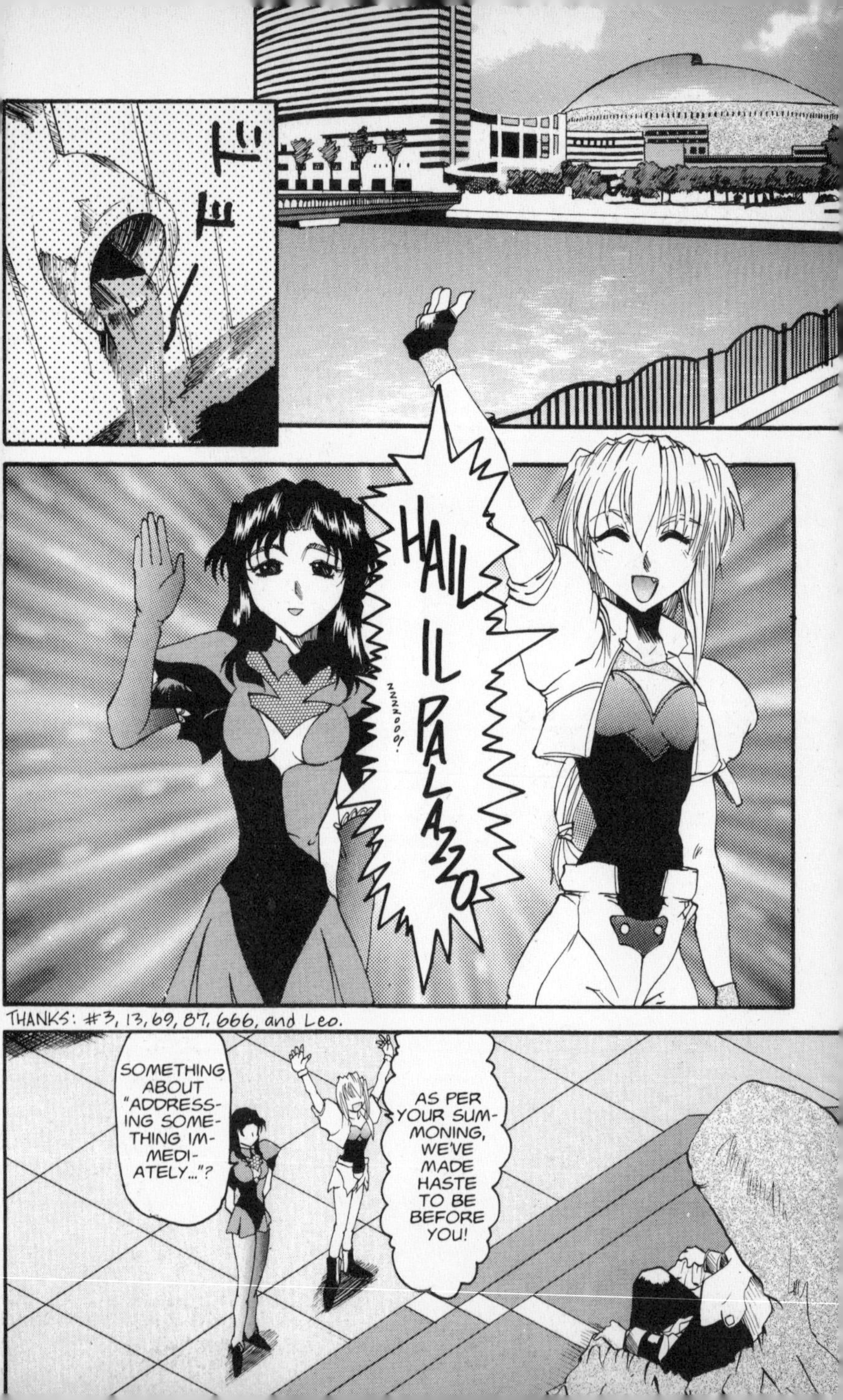

HAIL IL PALAZZO
ZZZZOOO!
THANKS: #3, 13, 69, 87, 666, and Leo.
AS PER YOUR SUMMONING, WE'VE MADE HASTE TO BE BEFORE YOU!
SOMETHING ABOUT "ADDRESSING SOMETHING IMMEDIATELY..."?

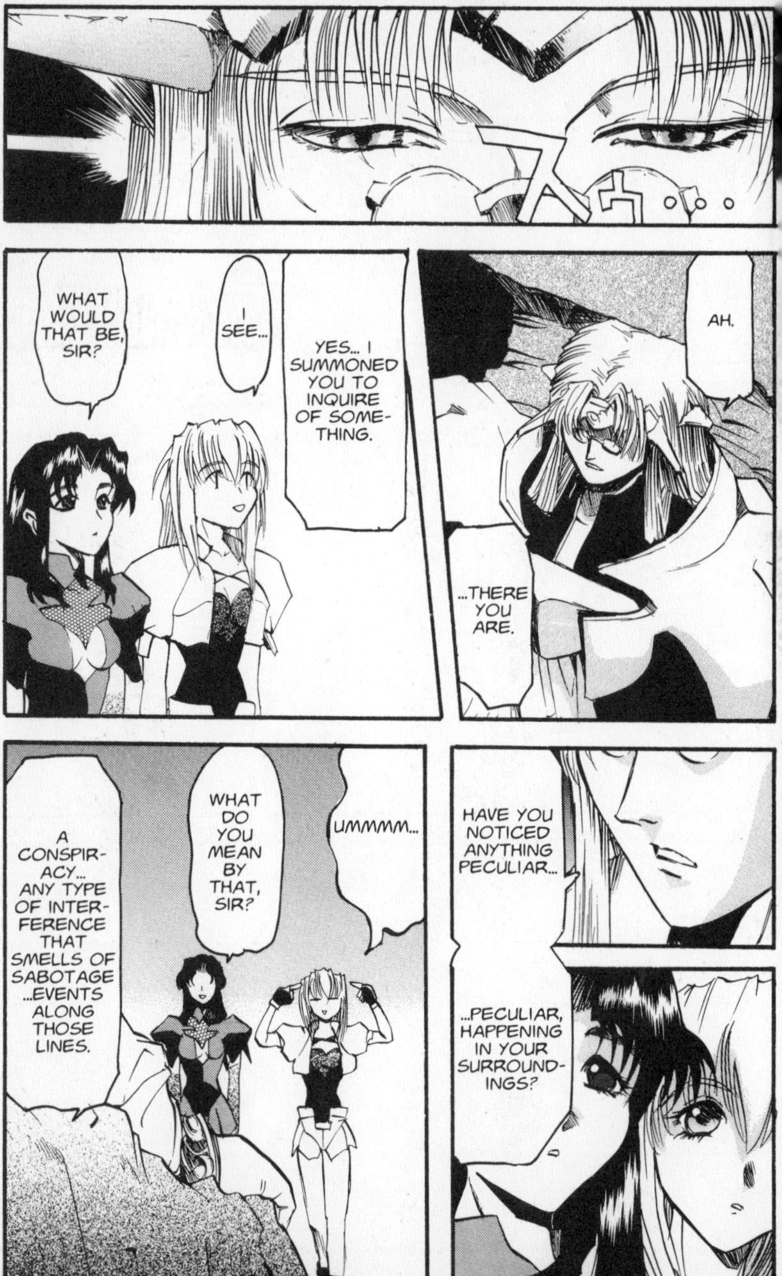
AH.
...THERE YOU ARE.
YES... I SUMMONED YOU TO INQUIRE OF SOME-THING.
I SEE...
WHAT WOULD THAT BE, SIR?
HAVE YOU NOTICED ANYTHING PECULIAR...
...PECULIAR, HAPPENING IN YOUR SURROUND-INGS?
UMMMM...
WHAT DO YOU MEAN BY THAT, SIR?
A CONSPIR-ACY... ANY TYPE OF INTER-FERENCE THAT SMELLS OF SABOTAGE ...EVENTS ALONG THOSE LINES.

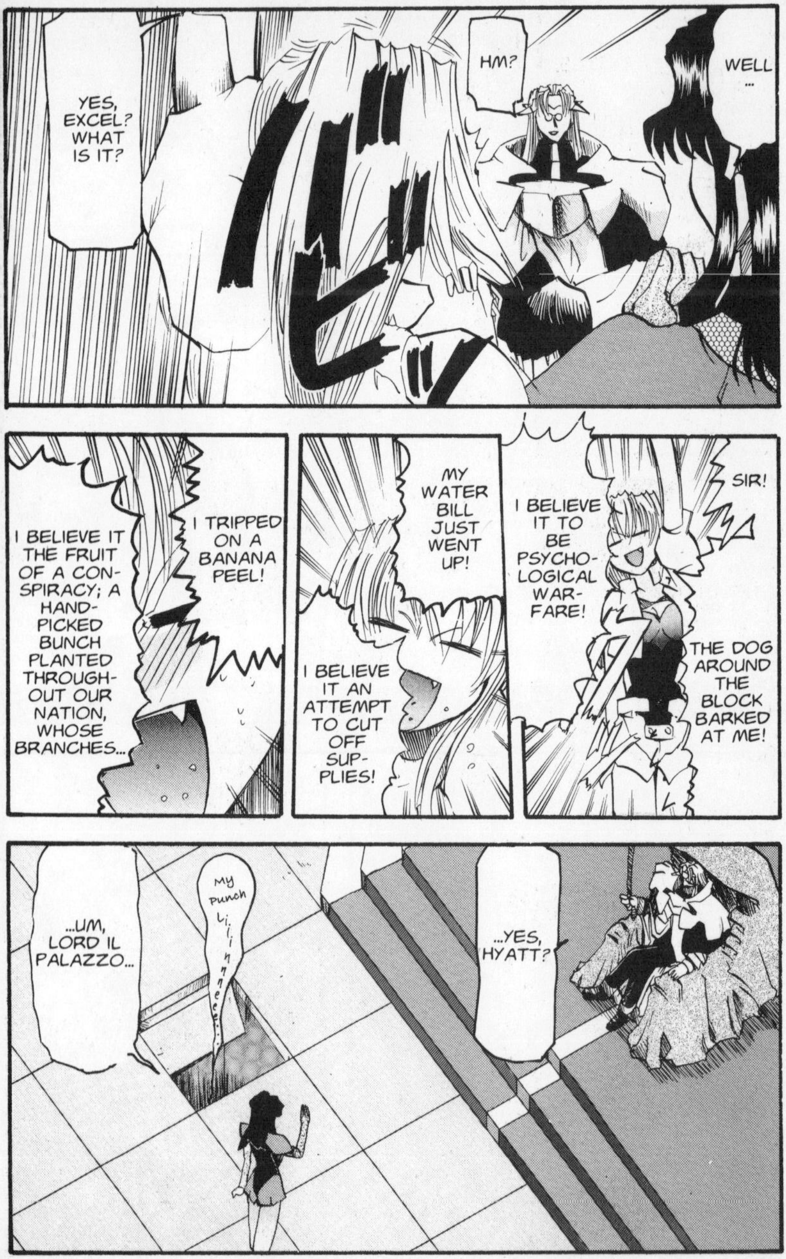
WELL ...
HM?
YES, EXCEL? WHAT IS IT?
SIR!
I BELIEVE IT TO BE PSYCHOLOGICAL WARFARE!
THE DOG AROUND THE BLOCK BARKED AT ME!
MY WATER BILL JUST WENT UP!
I BELIEVE IT AN ATTEMPT TO CUT OFF SUPPLIES!
I TRIPPED ON A BANANA PEEL!
I BELIEVE IT THE FRUIT OF A CONSPIRACY; A HANDPICKED BUNCH PLANTED THROUGHOUT OUR NATION, WHOSE BRANCHES...
...YES, HYATT?
My Punch Liiinneee...
...UM, LORD IL PALAZZO...

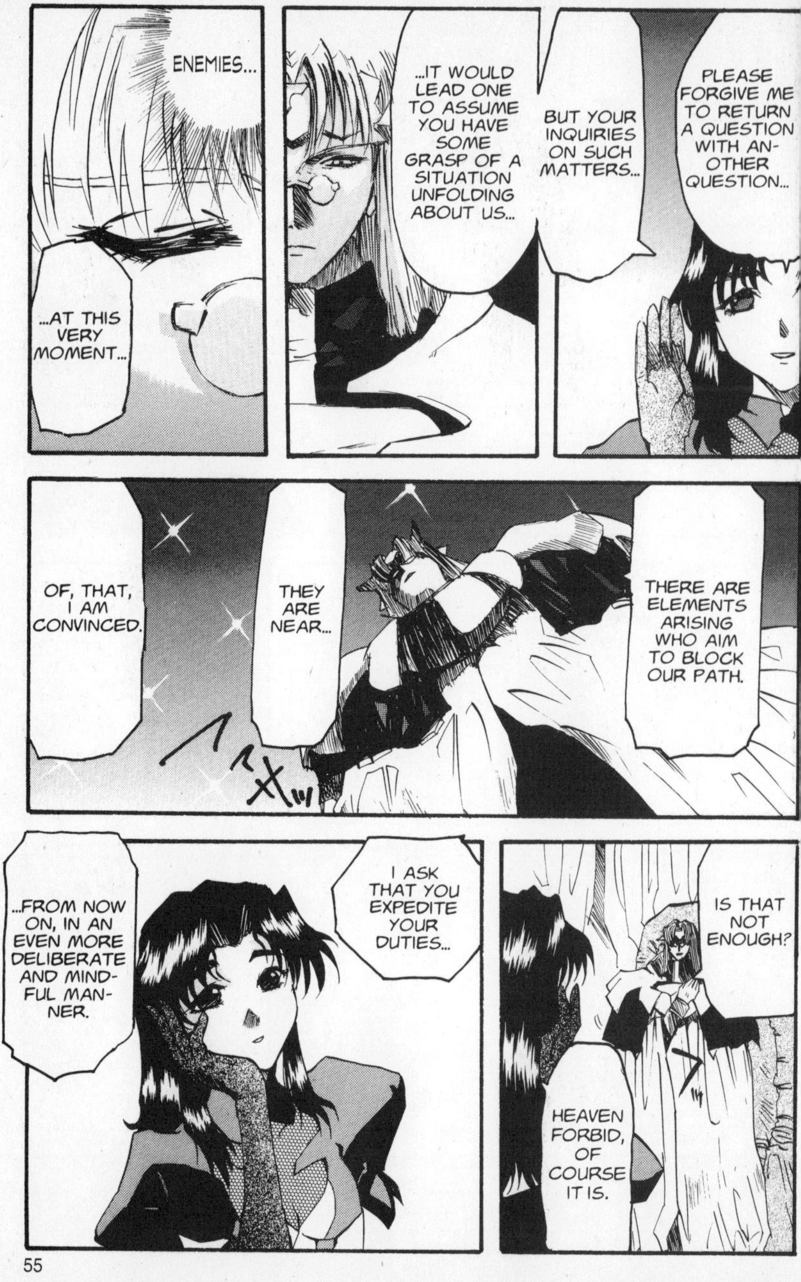
PLEASE FORGIVE ME TO RETURN A QUESTION WITH AN-OTHER QUESTION...
BUT YOUR INQUIRIES ON SUCH MATTERS...
...IT WOULD LEAD ONE TO ASSUME YOU HAVE SOME GRASP OF A SITUATION UNFOLDING ABOUT US...
ENEMIES...
...AT THIS VERY MOMENT...
THERE ARE ELEMENTS ARISING WHO AIM TO BLOCK OUR PATH.
THEY ARE NEAR...
OF, THAT, I AM CONVINCED.
IS THAT NOT ENOUGH?
HEAVEN FORBID, OF COURSE IT IS.
I ASK THAT YOU EXPEDITE YOUR DUTIES...
...FROM NOW ON, IN AN EVEN MORE DELIBERATE AND MINDFUL MANNER.

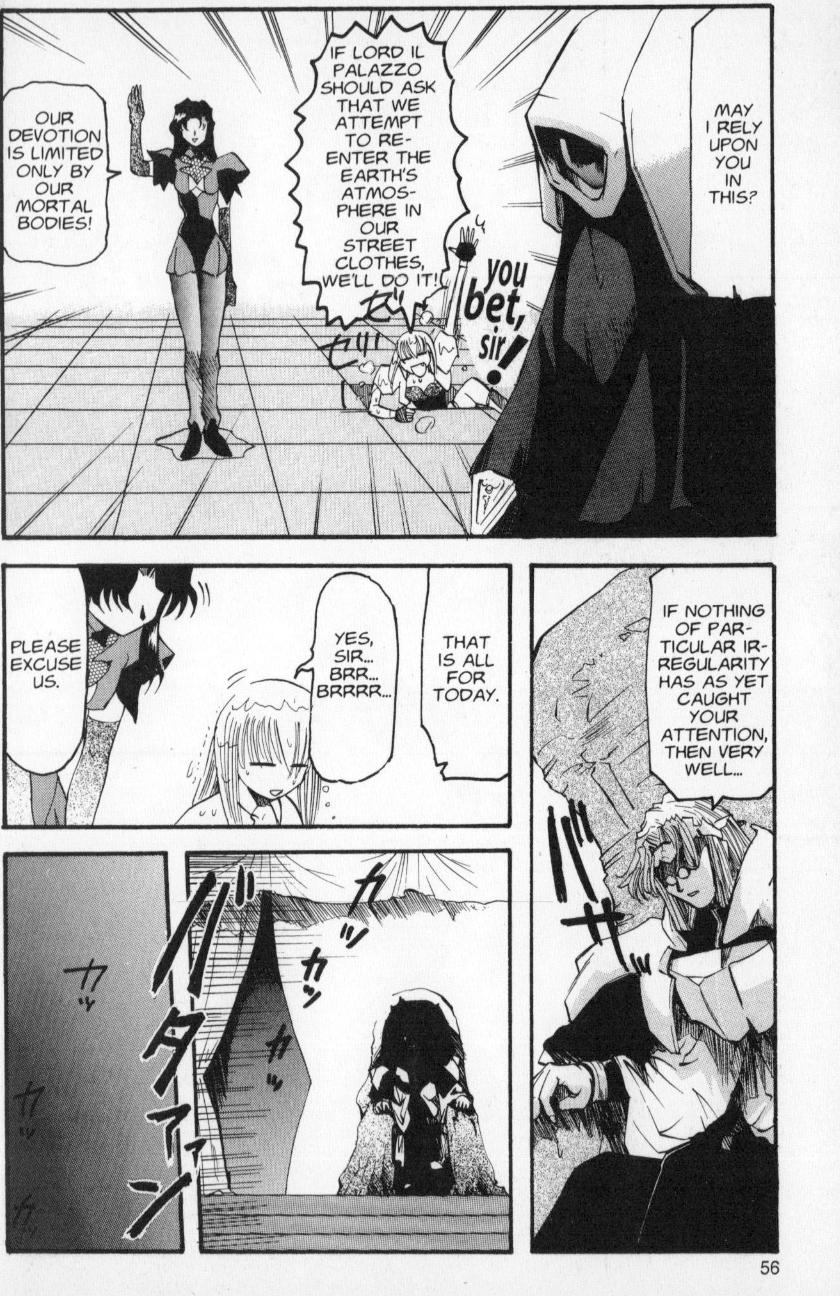
MAY I RELY UPON YOU IN THIS?
IF LORD IL PALAZZO SHOULD ASK THAT WE ATTEMPT TO RE-ENTER THE EARTH'S ATMOSPHERE IN OUR STREET CLOTHES, WE'LL DO IT!
you bet, sir!
OUR DEVOTION IS LIMITED ONLY BY OUR MORTAL BODIES!
IF NOTHING OF PARTICULAR IRREGULARITY HAS AS YET CAUGHT YOUR ATTENTION, THEN VERY WELL...
THAT IS ALL FOR TODAY.
YES, SIR... BRR... BRRRR...
PLEASE EXCUSE US.

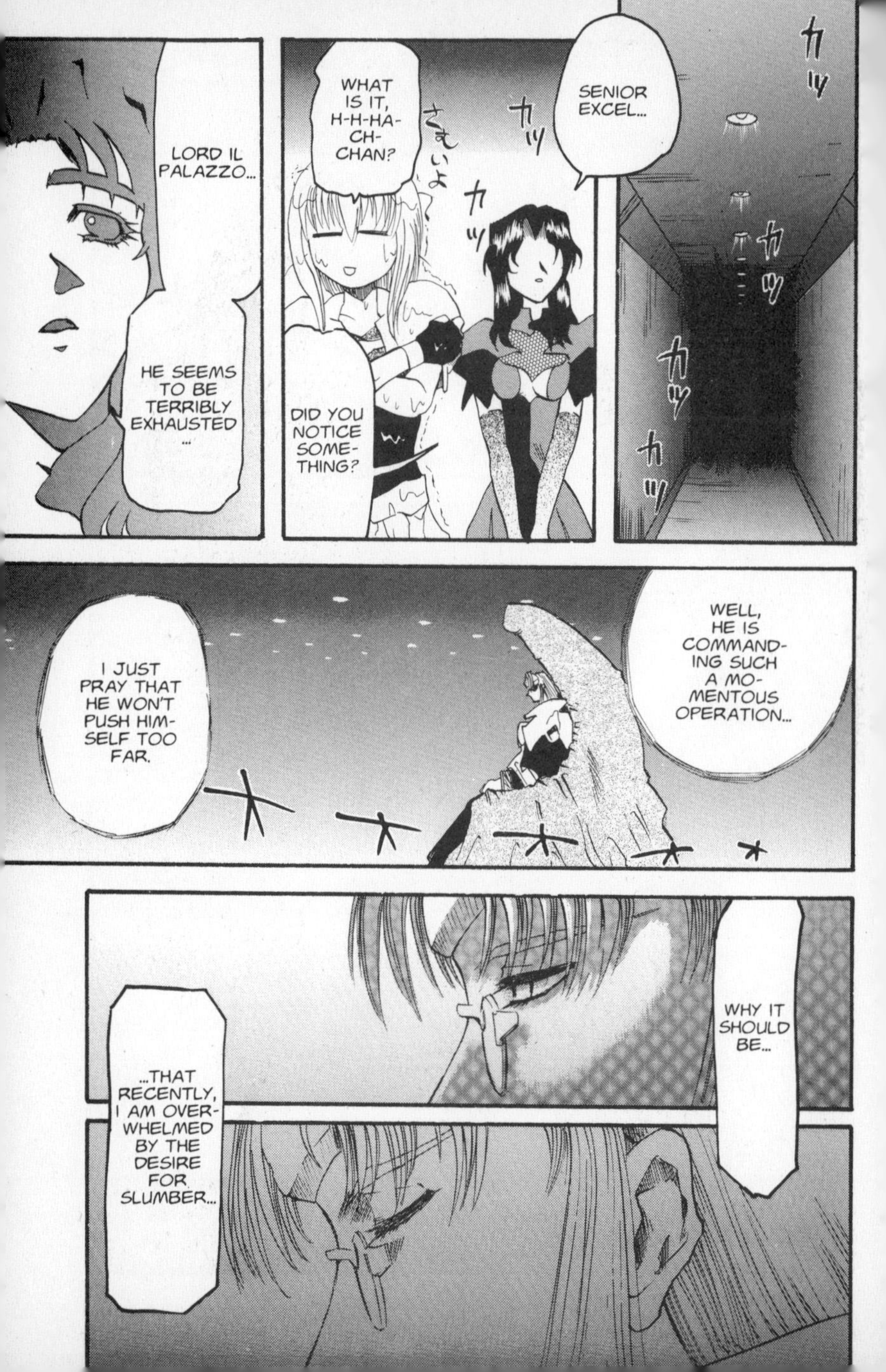

カッ
カッ
カッ
カッ
カッ
カッ
SENIOR EXCEL...
WHAT IS IT, H-H-HA-CH-CHAN?
さむいよ
DID YOU NOTICE SOMETHING?
LORD IL PALAZZO...
HE SEEMS TO BE TERRIBLY EXHAUSTED...
WELL, HE IS COMMANDING SUCH A MOMENTOUS OPERATION...
I JUST PRAY THAT HE WON'T PUSH HIMSELF TOO FAR.
WHY IT SHOULD BE...
...THAT RECENTLY, I AM OVERWHELMED BY THE DESIRE FOR SLUMBER...

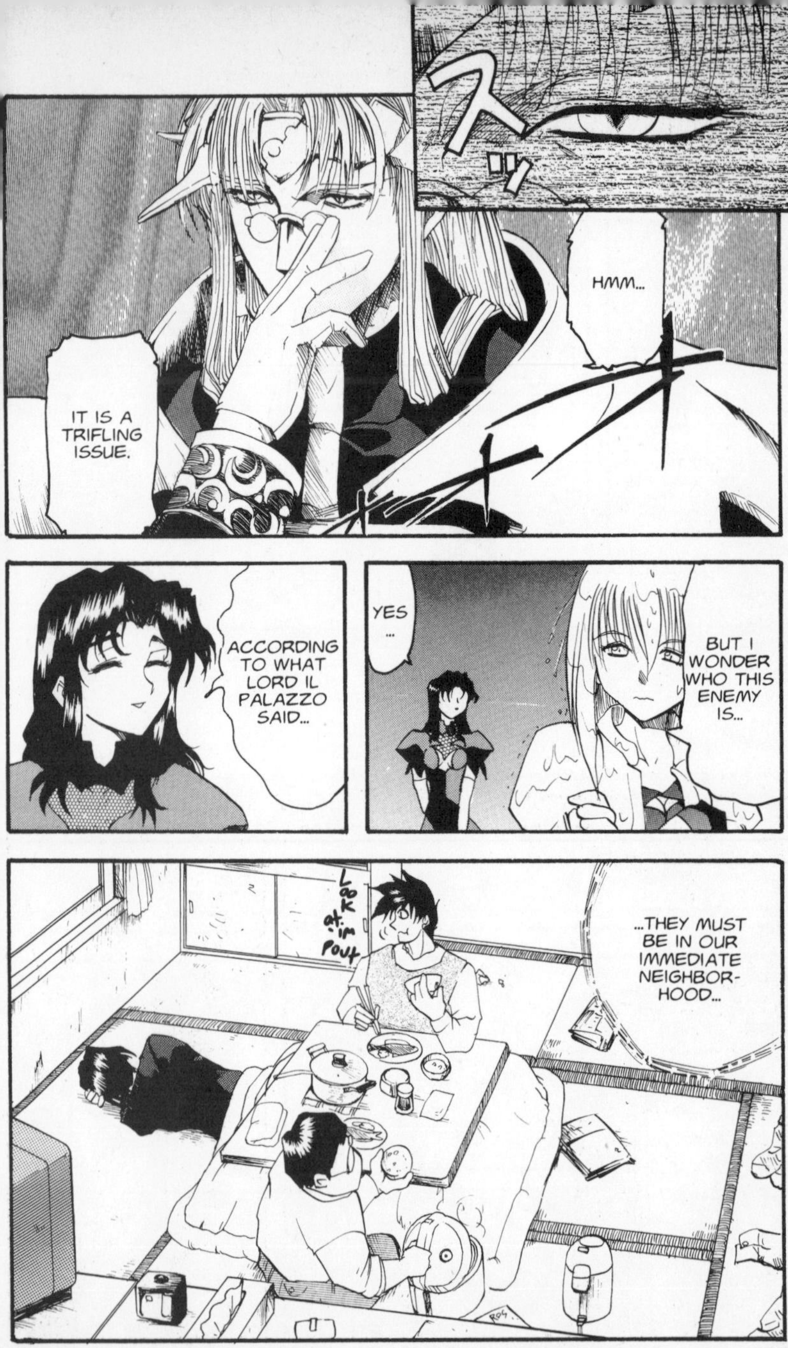

スッ
HMM...
IT IS A TRIFLING ISSUE.
YES ...
BUT I WONDER WHO THIS ENEMY IS...
ACCORDING TO WHAT LORD IL PALAZZO SAID...
LOOK AT 'IM POUT
...THEY MUST BE IN OUR IMMEDIATE NEIGHBOR-HOOD...

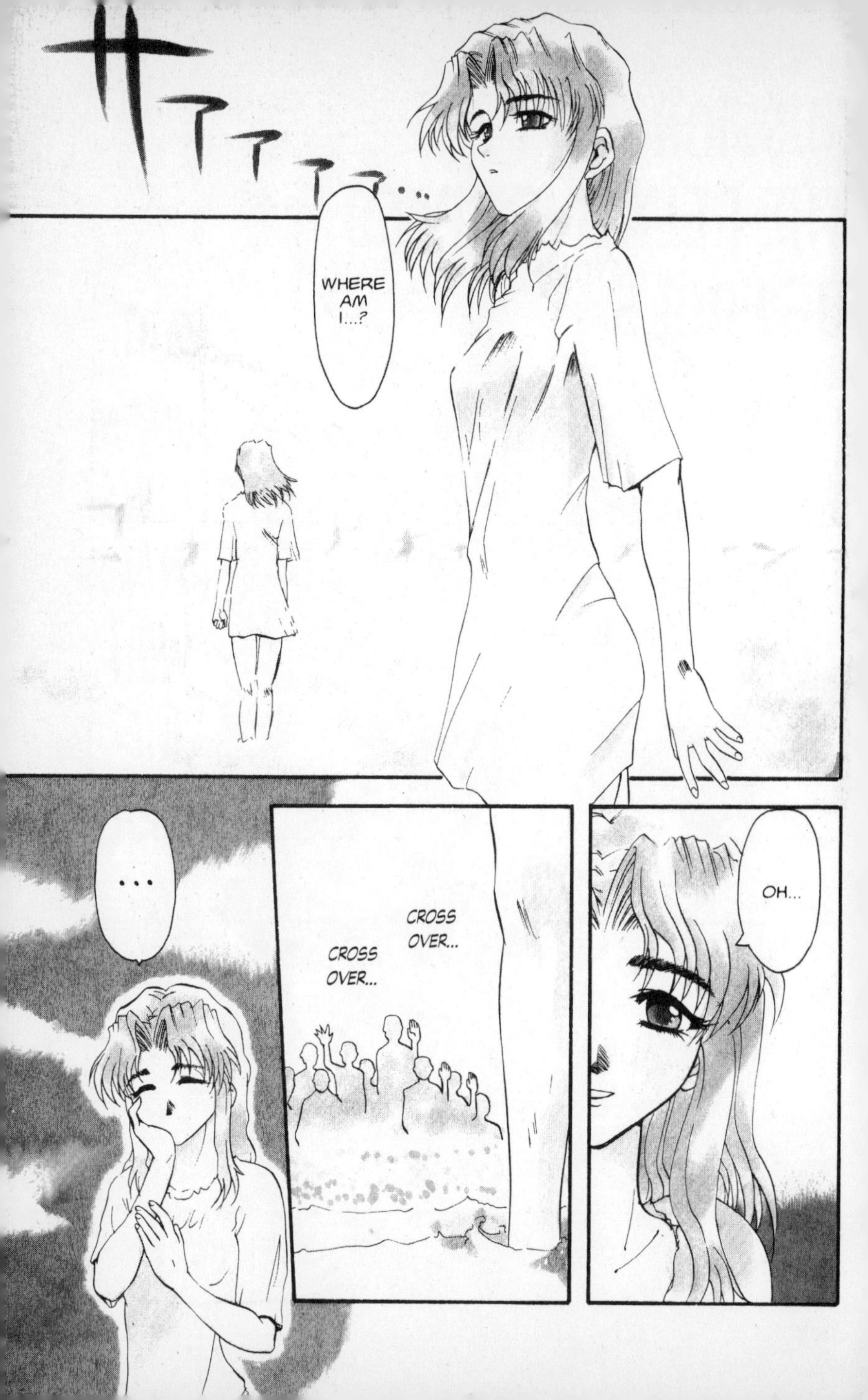
サァァァ…
WHERE AM I...?
OH...
CROSS OVER...
CROSS OVER...
. . .

MISSION 3
THE RELATIVE SPEED OF FOOLS

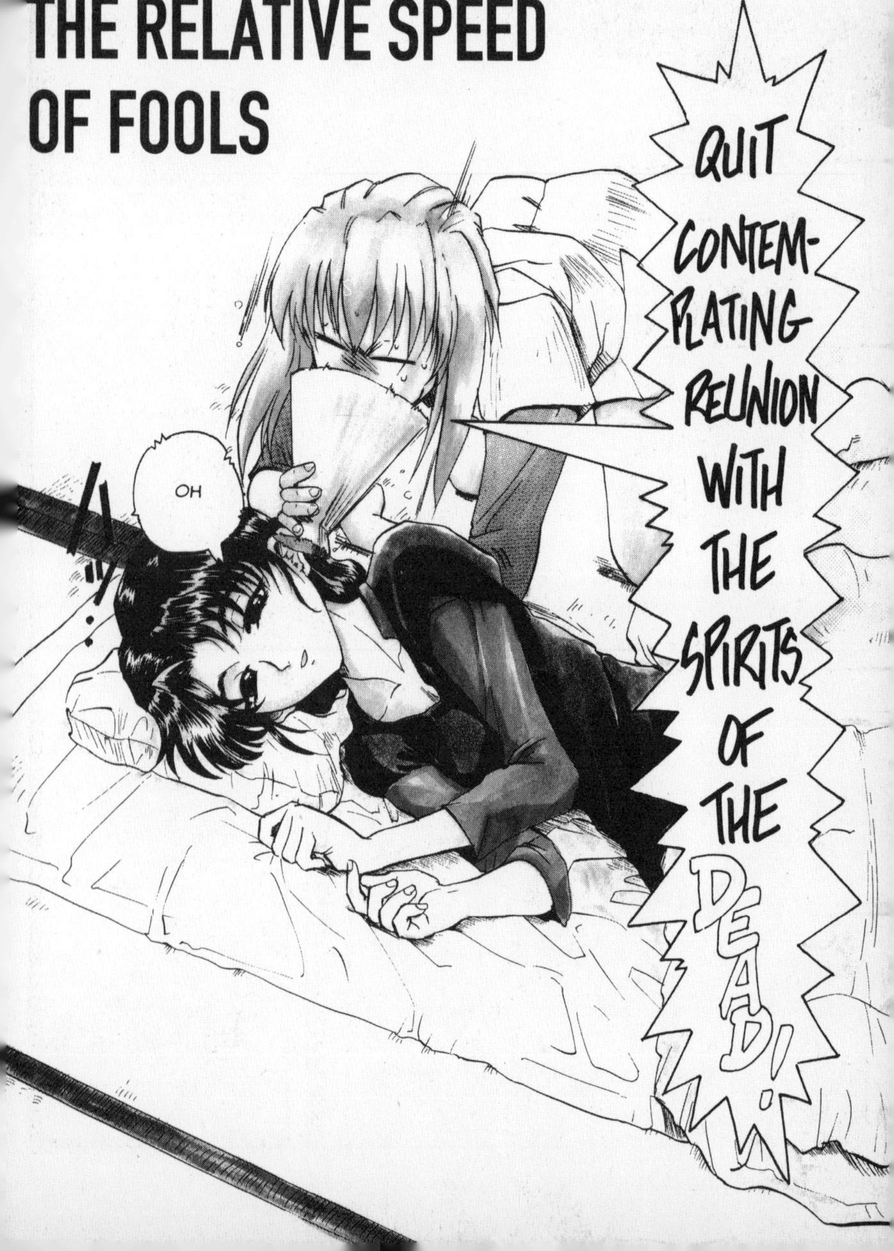
QUIT CONTEM-PLATING REUNION WITH THE SPIRITS OF THE DEAD!
OH

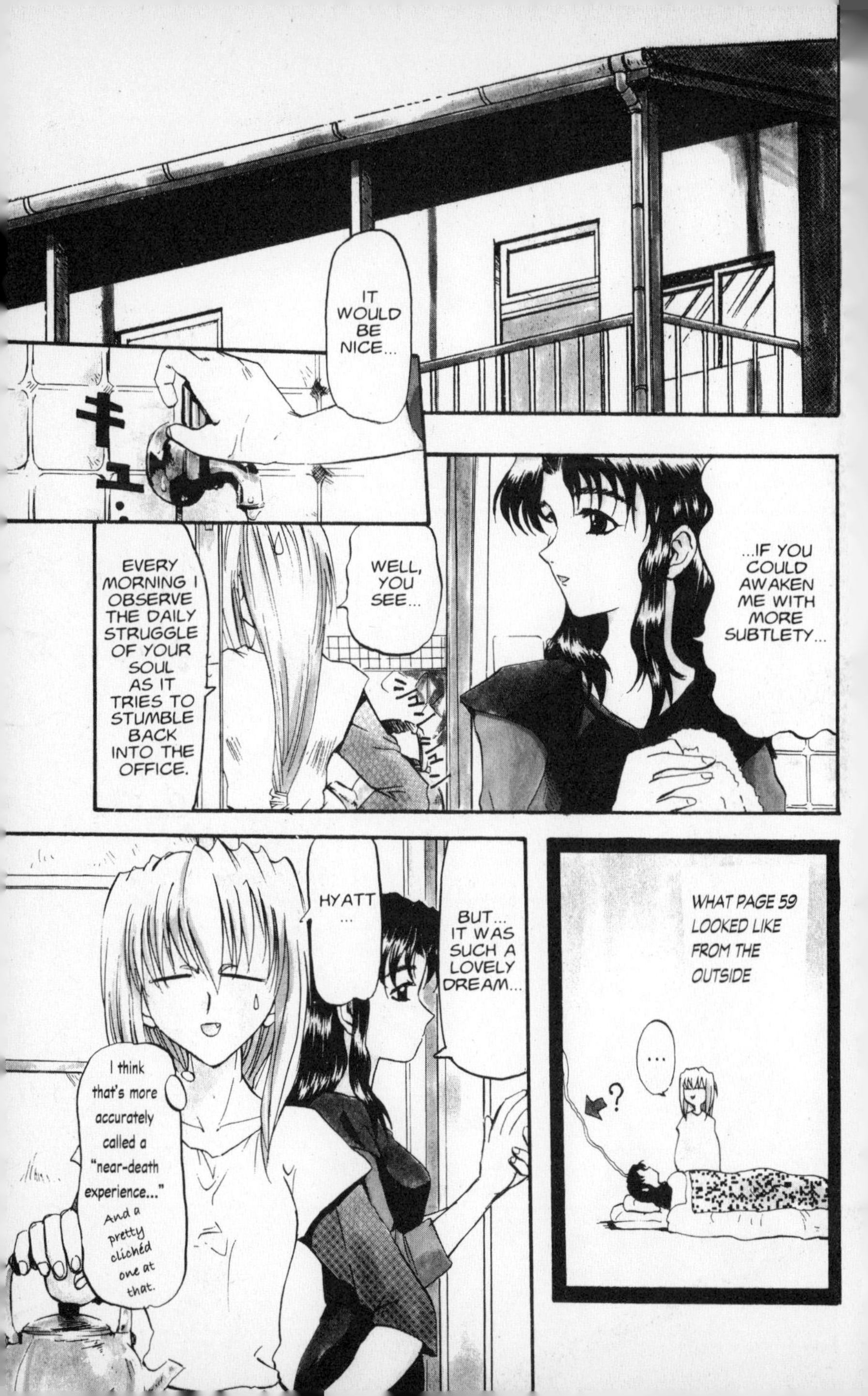

IT WOULD BE NICE...
キュ
...IF YOU COULD AWAKEN ME WITH MORE SUBTLETY...
WELL, YOU SEE...
EVERY MORNING I OBSERVE THE DAILY STRUGGLE OF YOUR SOUL AS IT TRIES TO STUMBLE BACK INTO THE OFFICE.
WHAT PAGE 59 LOOKED LIKE FROM THE OUTSIDE
...
?
BUT... IT WAS SUCH A LOVELY DREAM...
HYATT...
I think that's more accurately called a "near-death experience..." And a pretty clichéd one at that.

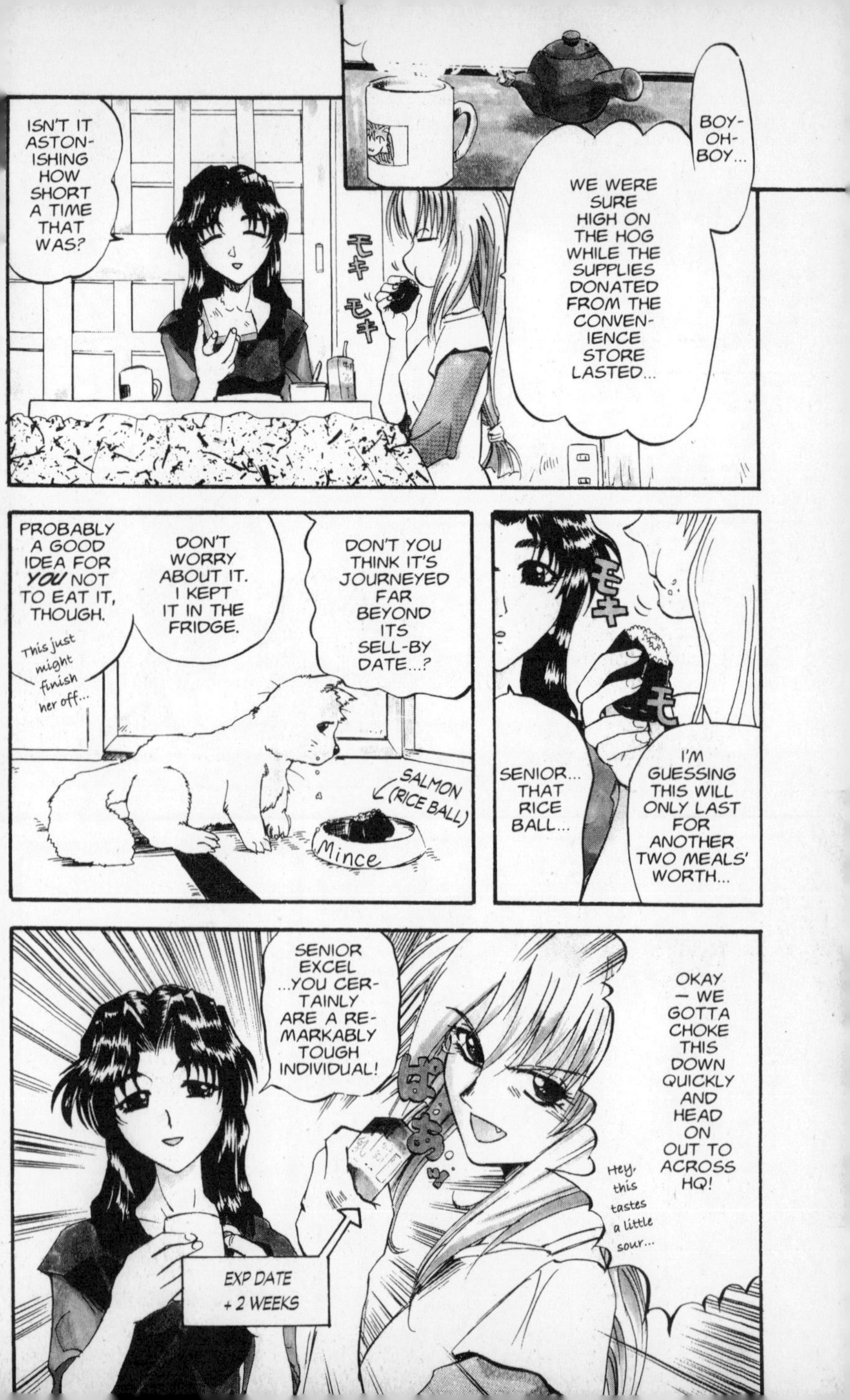
BOY-OH-BOY...
WE WERE SURE HIGH ON THE HOG WHILE THE SUPPLIES DONATED FROM THE CONVENIENCE STORE LASTED...
ISN'T IT ASTONISHING HOW SHORT A TIME THAT WAS?
モキ モキ
モキ
モ
I'M GUESSING THIS WILL ONLY LAST FOR ANOTHER TWO MEALS' WORTH...
SENIOR... THAT RICE BALL...
DON'T YOU THINK IT'S JOURNEYED FAR BEYOND ITS SELL-BY DATE...?
DON'T WORRY ABOUT IT. I KEPT IT IN THE FRIDGE.
PROBABLY A GOOD IDEA FOR ***YOU*** NOT TO EAT IT, THOUGH.
This just might finish her off...
SALMON (RICE BALL)
Mince
OKAY — WE GOTTA CHOKE THIS DOWN QUICKLY AND HEAD ON OUT TO ACROSS HQ!
Hey, this tastes a little sour...
SENIOR EXCEL ...YOU CERTAINLY ARE A REMARKABLY TOUGH INDIVIDUAL!
EXP DATE + 2 WEEKS

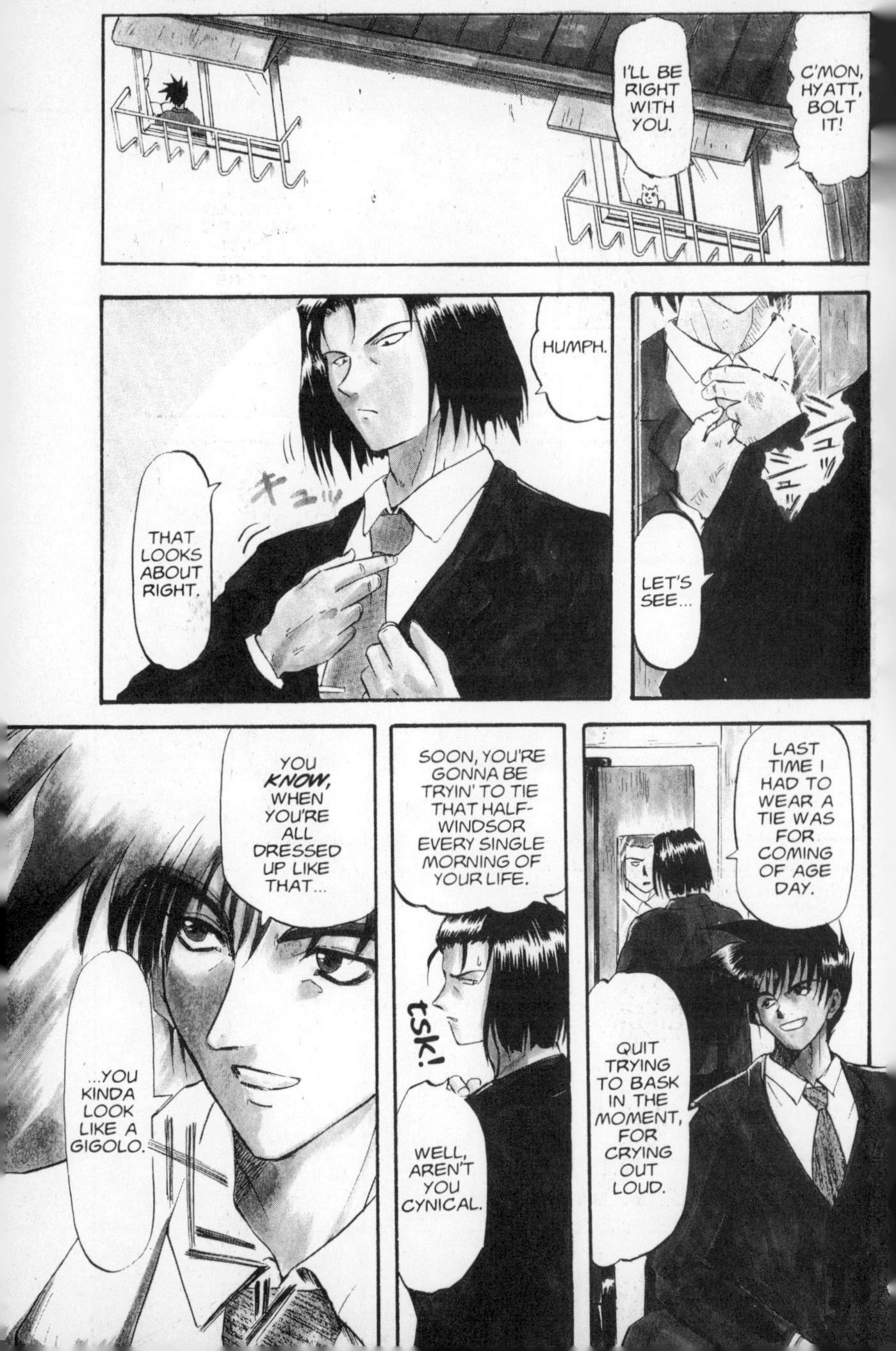
C'MON, HYATT, BOLT IT!
I'LL BE RIGHT WITH YOU.
LET'S SEE...
HUMPH.
キュッ
THAT LOOKS ABOUT RIGHT.
LAST TIME I HAD TO WEAR A TIE WAS FOR COMING OF AGE DAY.
QUIT TRYING TO BASK IN THE MOMENT, FOR CRYING OUT LOUD.
SOON, YOU'RE GONNA BE TRYIN' TO TIE THAT HALF-WINDSOR EVERY SINGLE MORNING OF YOUR LIFE.
TSK!
WELL, AREN'T YOU CYNICAL.
YOU ***KNOW,*** WHEN YOU'RE ALL DRESSED UP LIKE THAT...
...YOU KINDA LOOK LIKE A GIGOLO.

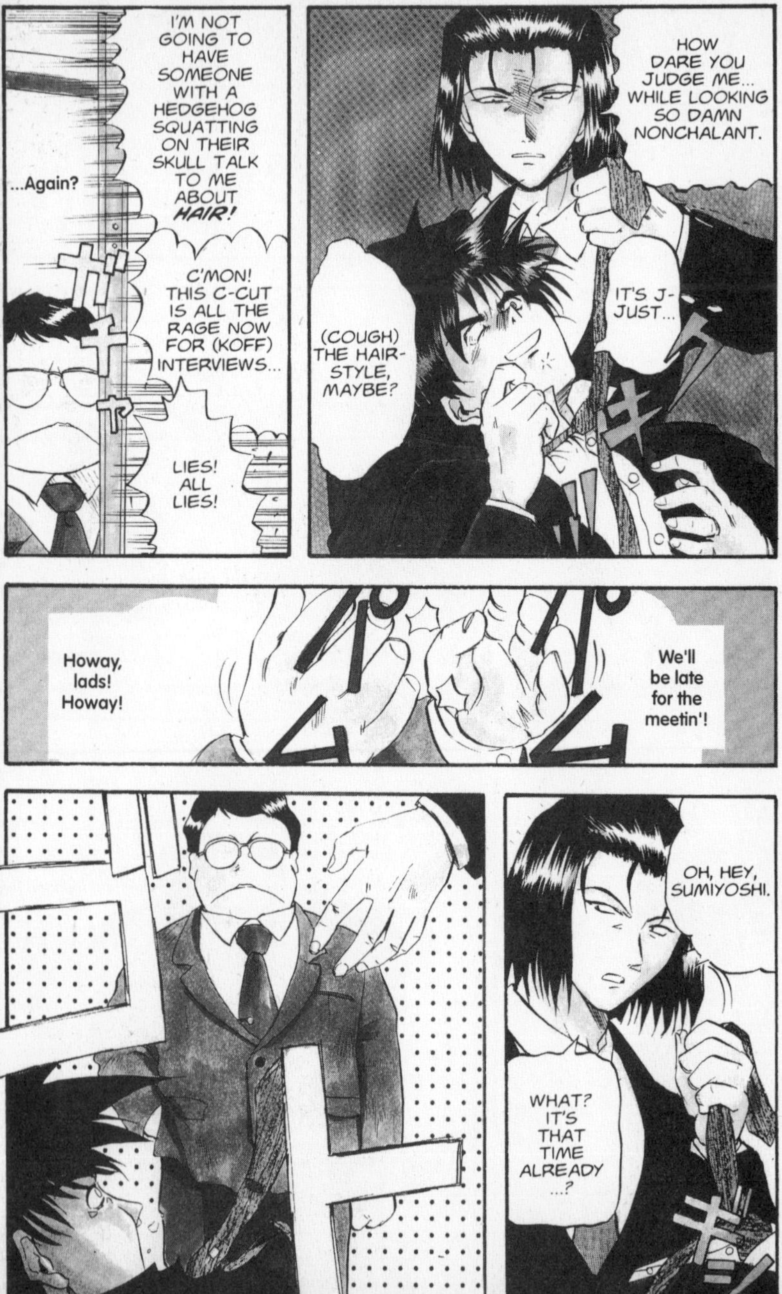
HOW DARE YOU JUDGE ME... WHILE LOOKING SO DAMN NONCHALANT.
IT'S J-JUST...
(COUGH) THE HAIR-STYLE, MAYBE?
I'M NOT GOING TO HAVE SOMEONE WITH A HEDGEHOG SQUATTING ON THEIR SKULL TALK TO ME ABOUT HAIR!
...Again?
ガチャ
C'MON! THIS C-CUT IS ALL THE RAGE NOW FOR (KOFF) INTERVIEWS...
LIES! ALL LIES!
We'll be late for the meetin'!
Howay, lads! Howay!
OH, HEY, SUMIYOSHI.
WHAT? IT'S THAT TIME ALREADY ...?

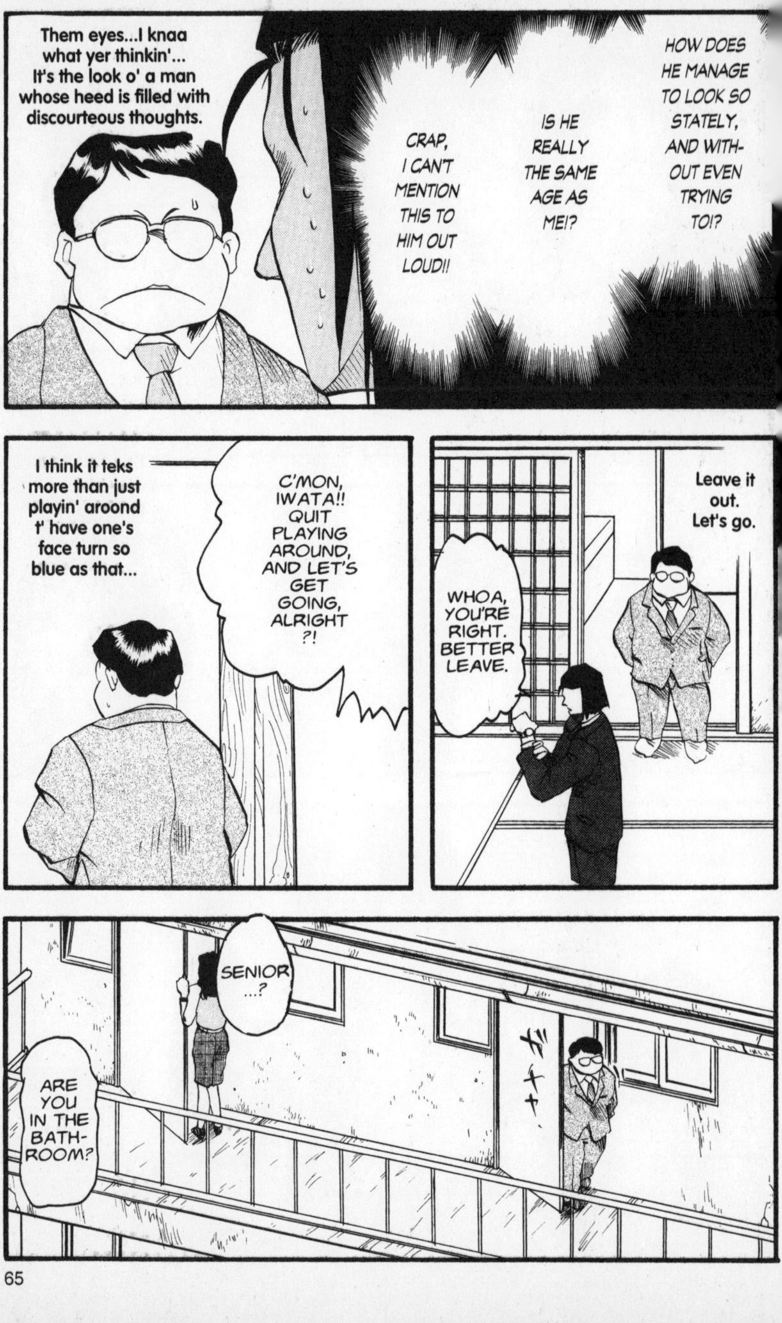
HOW DOES HE MANAGE TO LOOK SO STATELY, AND WITHOUT EVEN TRYING TO!?
IS HE REALLY THE SAME AGE AS ME!?
CRAP, I CAN'T MENTION THIS TO HIM OUT LOUD!!
Them eyes...I knaa what yer thinkin'... It's the look o' a man whose heed is filled with discourteous thoughts.
Leave it out. Let's go.
WHOA, YOU'RE RIGHT. BETTER LEAVE.
C'MON, IWATA!! QUIT PLAYING AROUND, AND LET'S GET GOING, ALRIGHT?!
I think it teks more than just playin' aroond t' have one's face turn so blue as that...
ガチャ
SENIOR...?
ARE YOU IN THE BATHROOM?

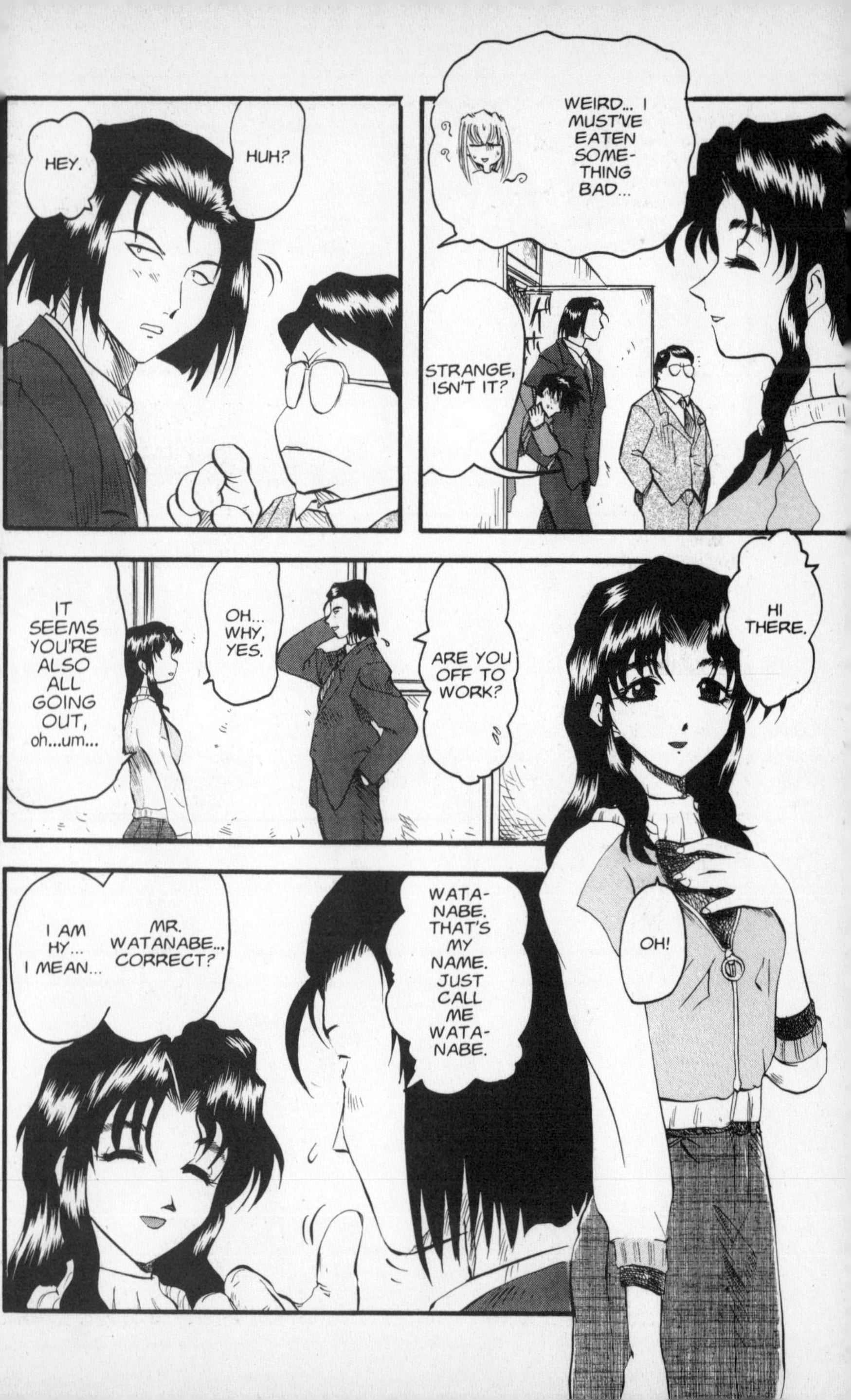
WEIRD... I MUST'VE EATEN SOME-THING BAD...
STRANGE, ISN'T IT?
HUH?
HEY.
HI THERE.
ARE YOU OFF TO WORK?
OH... WHY, YES.
IT SEEMS YOU'RE ALSO ALL GOING OUT, oh...um...
OH!
WATA-NABE. THAT'S MY NAME. JUST CALL ME WATA-NABE.
MR. WATANABE... CORRECT?
I AM HY... I MEAN...

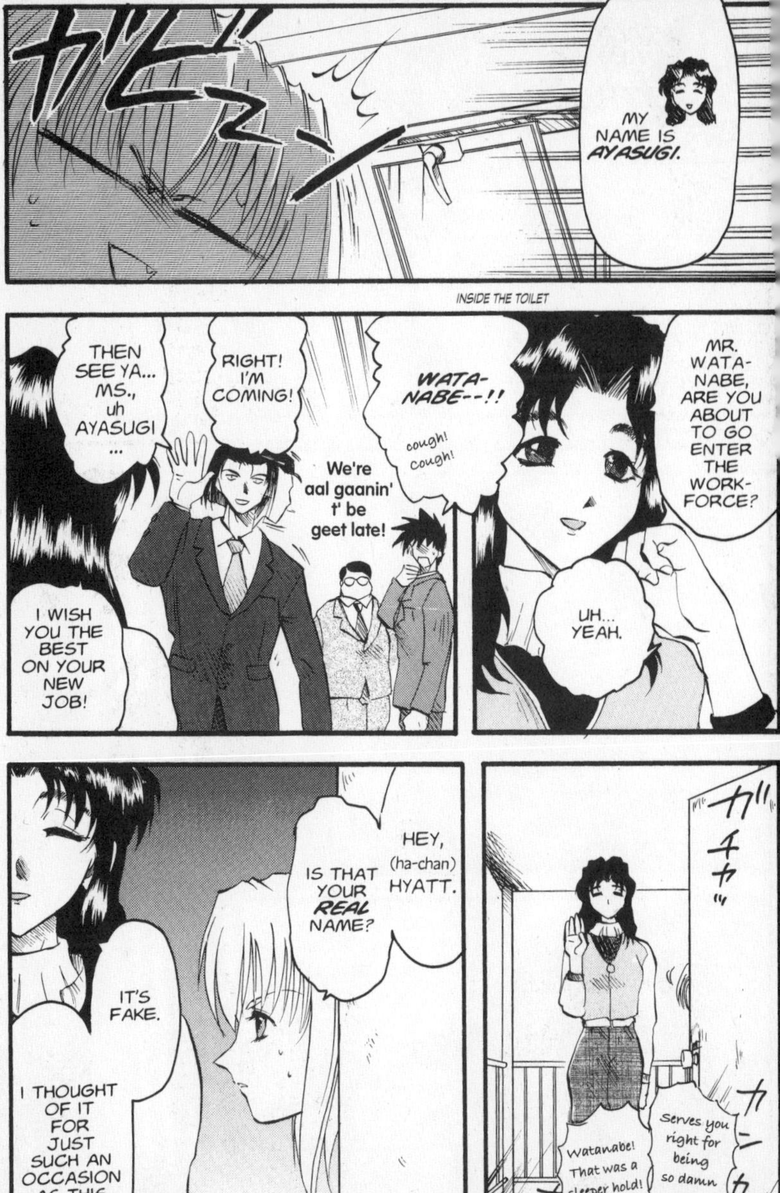
MY NAME IS AYASUGI.
INSIDE THE TOILET
MR. WATA-NABE, ARE YOU ABOUT TO GO ENTER THE WORK-FORCE?
UH... YEAH.
WATA-NABE--!!
cough! cough!
We're aal gaanin' t' be geet late!
RIGHT! I'M COMING!
THEN SEE YA... MS., uh AYASUGI ...
I WISH YOU THE BEST ON YOUR NEW JOB!
Serves you right for being so damn crass!
Watanabe! That was a sleeper hold!
HEY, (ha-chan) HYATT.
IS THAT YOUR REAL NAME?
IT'S FAKE.
I THOUGHT OF IT FOR JUST SUCH AN OCCASION AS THIS.

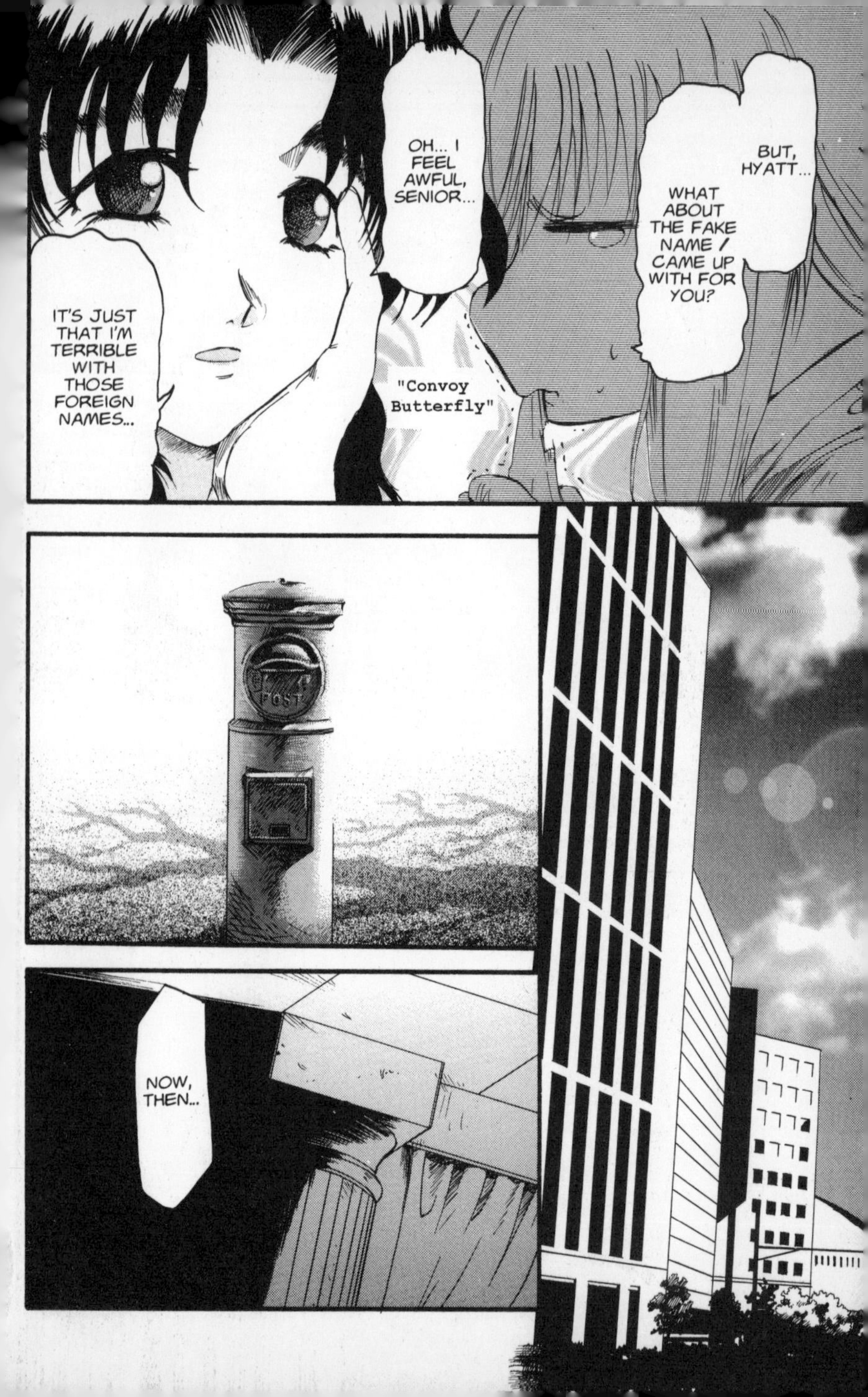
BUT, HYATT...
WHAT ABOUT THE FAKE NAME I CAME UP WITH FOR YOU?
"Convoy Butterfly"
OH... I FEEL AWFUL, SENIOR...
IT'S JUST THAT I'M TERRIBLE WITH THOSE FOREIGN NAMES...
POST
NOW, THEN...

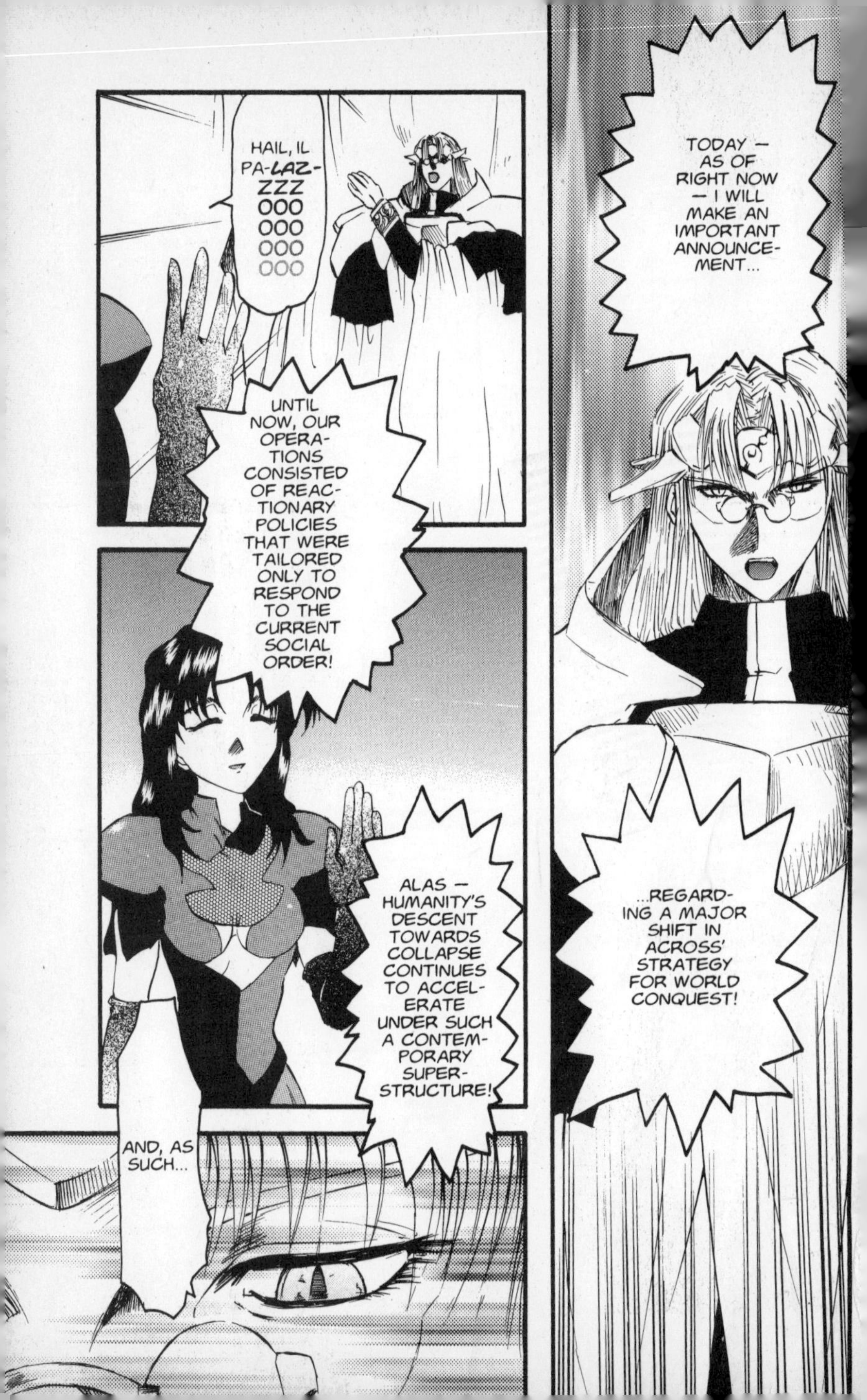
TODAY — AS OF RIGHT NOW — I WILL MAKE AN IMPORTANT ANNOUNCEMENT...
...REGARDING A MAJOR SHIFT IN ACROSS' STRATEGY FOR WORLD CONQUEST!
HAIL, IL PA-LAZ-ZZZ OOO OOO OOO OOO
UNTIL NOW, OUR OPERATIONS CONSISTED OF REACTIONARY POLICIES THAT WERE TAILORED ONLY TO RESPOND TO THE CURRENT SOCIAL ORDER!
ALAS — HUMANITY'S DESCENT TOWARDS COLLAPSE CONTINUES TO ACCELERATE UNDER SUCH A CONTEMPORARY SUPERSTRUCTURE!
AND, AS SUCH...

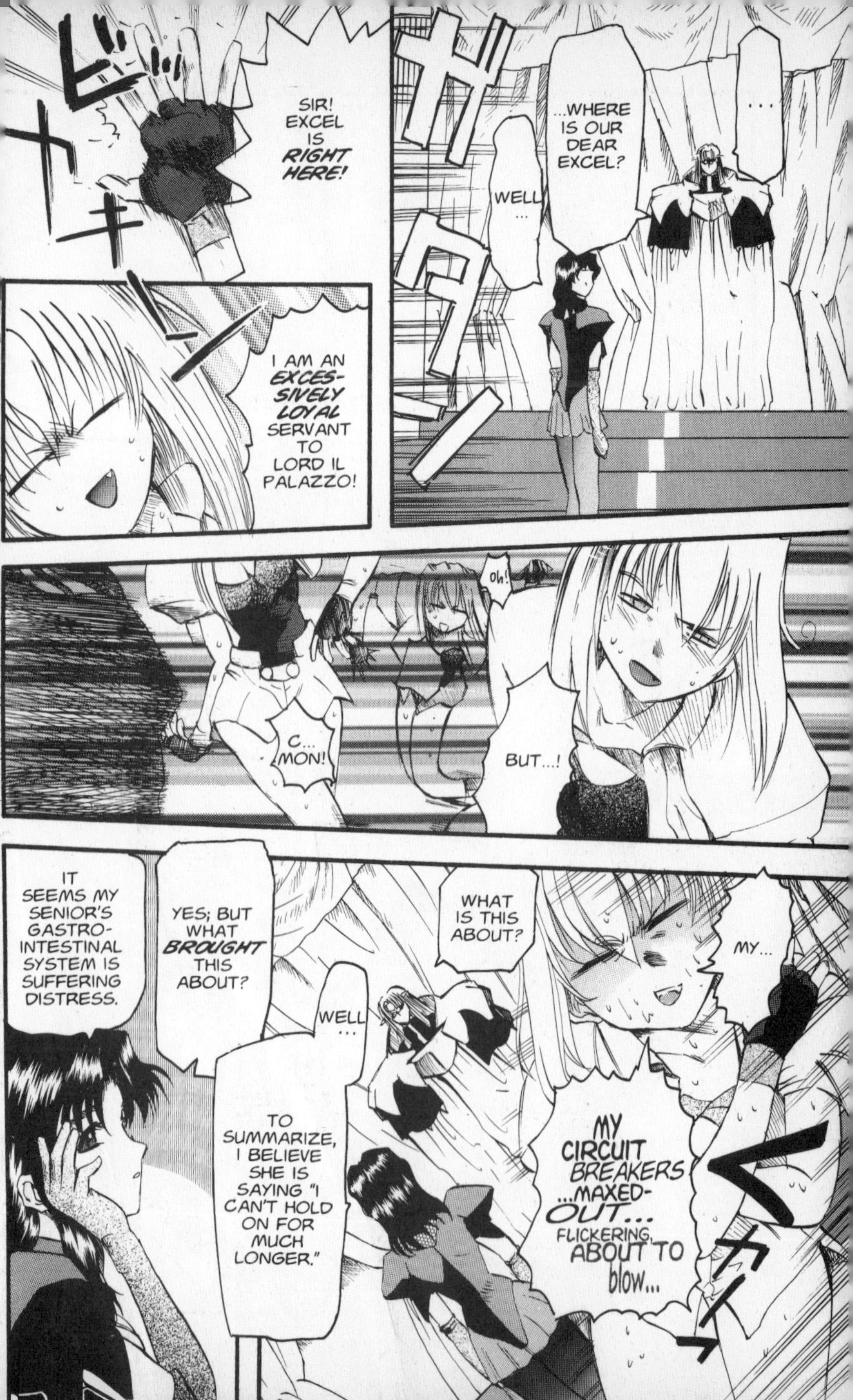
. . .
...WHERE IS OUR DEAR EXCEL?
WELL ...
SIR! EXCEL IS RIGHT HERE!
I AM AN EXCESSIVELY LOYAL SERVANT TO LORD IL PALAZZO!
Oh!
BUT...!
C... MON!
MY...
WHAT IS THIS ABOUT?
MY CIRCUIT BREAKERS ...MAXED-OUT... FLICKERING, ABOUT TO blow...
IT SEEMS MY SENIOR'S GASTRO-INTESTINAL SYSTEM IS SUFFERING DISTRESS.
YES; BUT WHAT BROUGHT THIS ABOUT?
WELL ...
TO SUMMARIZE, I BELIEVE SHE IS SAYING "I CAN'T HOLD ON FOR MUCH LONGER."

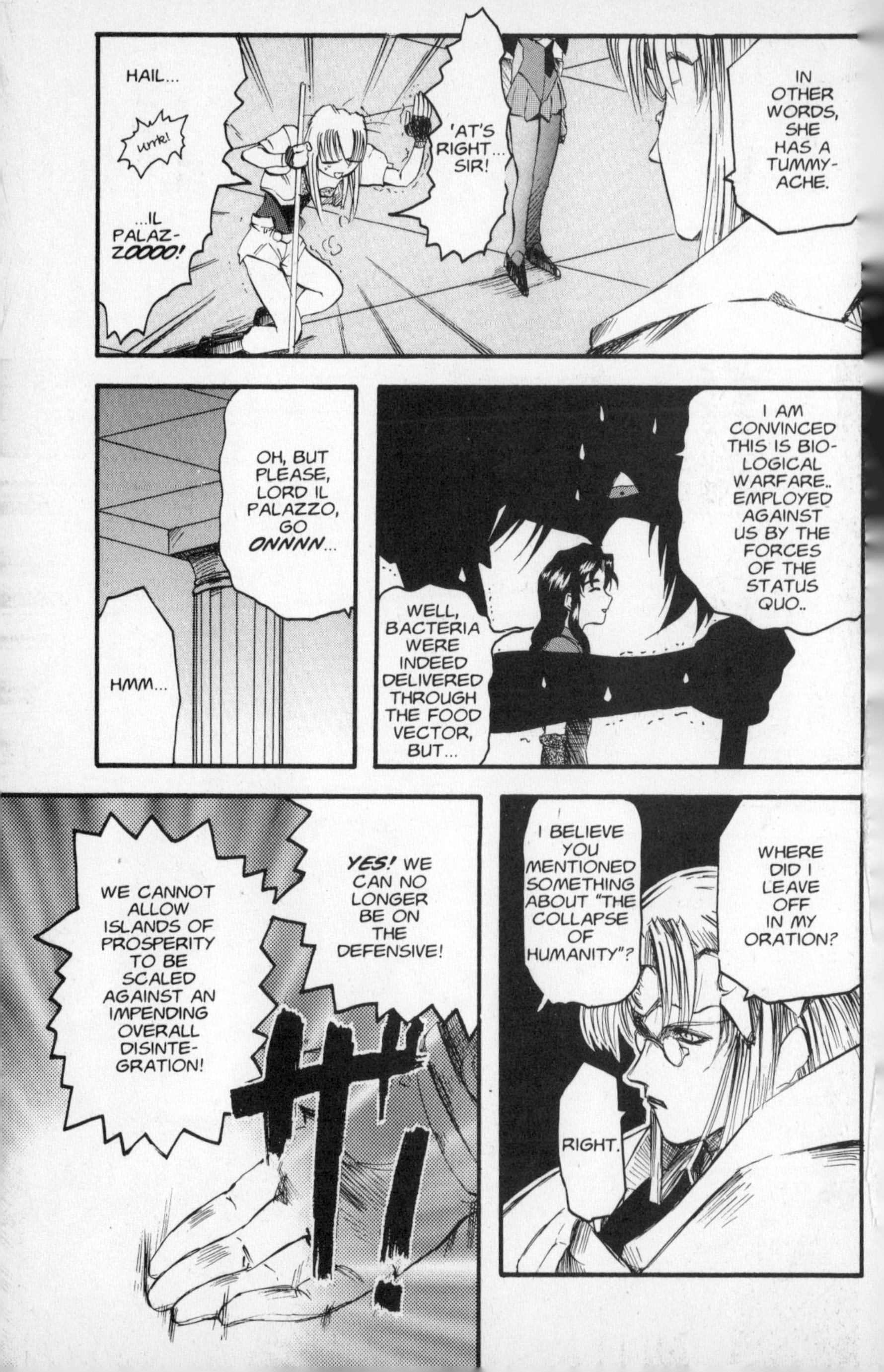
IN OTHER WORDS, SHE HAS A TUMMY-ACHE.
'AT'S RIGHT... SIR!
HAIL...
urrk!
...IL PALAZ-ZOOOO!
I AM CONVINCED THIS IS BIO-LOGICAL WARFARE.. EMPLOYED AGAINST US BY THE FORCES OF THE STATUS QUO..
WELL, BACTERIA WERE INDEED DELIVERED THROUGH THE FOOD VECTOR, BUT...
OH, BUT PLEASE, LORD IL PALAZZO, GO ONNNN...
HMM...
WHERE DID I LEAVE OFF IN MY ORATION?
I BELIEVE YOU MENTIONED SOMETHING ABOUT "THE COLLAPSE OF HUMANITY"?
RIGHT.
YES! WE CAN NO LONGER BE ON THE DEFENSIVE!
WE CANNOT ALLOW ISLANDS OF PROSPERITY TO BE SCALED AGAINST AN IMPENDING OVERALL DISINTE-GRATION!

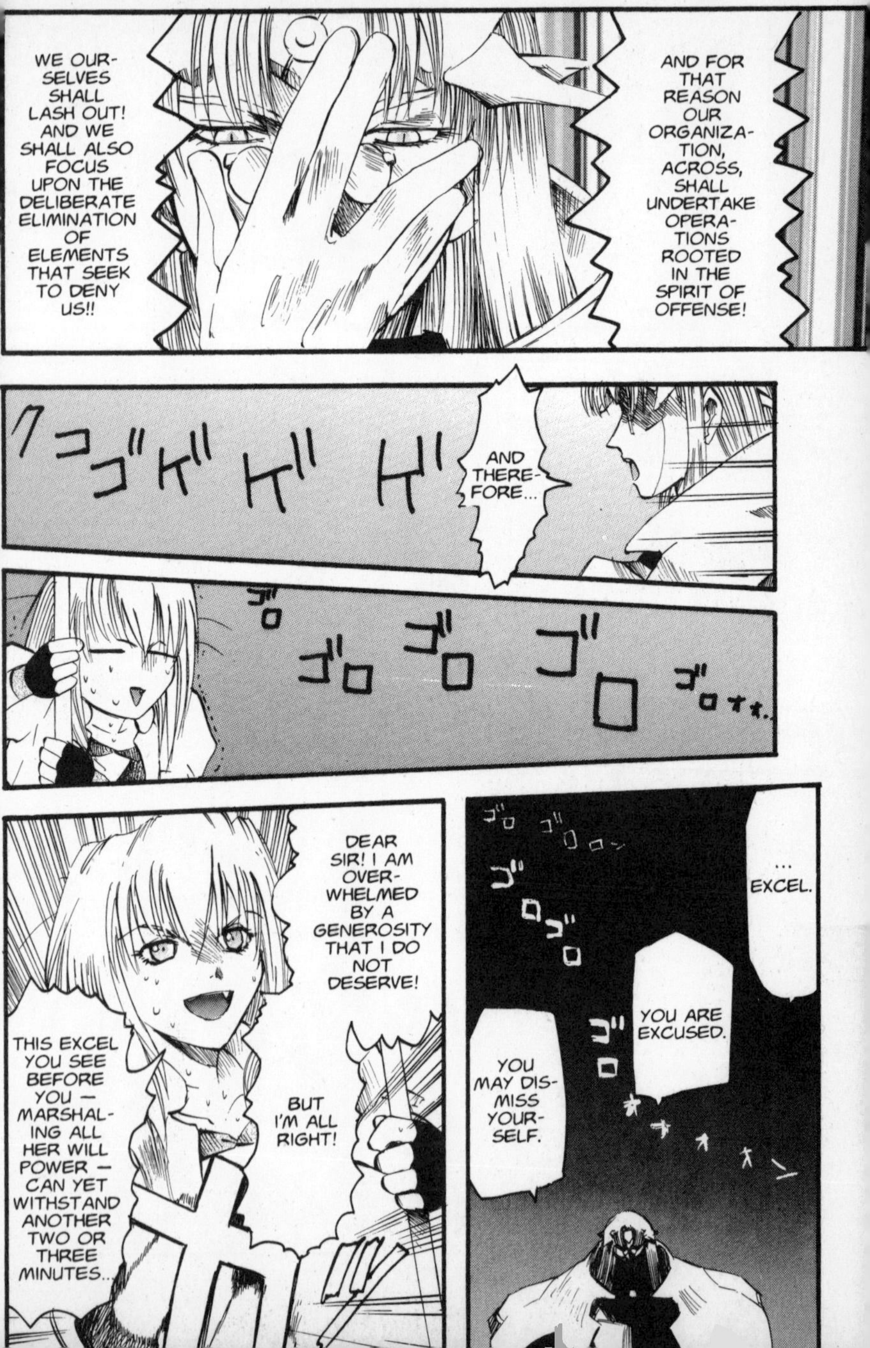
AND FOR THAT REASON OUR ORGANIZATION, ACROSS, SHALL UNDERTAKE OPERATIONS ROOTED IN THE SPIRIT OF OFFENSE!
WE OURSELVES SHALL LASH OUT! AND WE SHALL ALSO FOCUS UPON THE DELIBERATE ELIMINATION OF ELEMENTS THAT SEEK TO DENY US!!
AND THEREFORE...
...EXCEL.
YOU ARE EXCUSED.
YOU MAY DISMISS YOURSELF.
DEAR SIR! I AM OVERWHELMED BY A GENEROSITY THAT I DO NOT DESERVE!
BUT I'M ALL RIGHT!
THIS EXCEL YOU SEE BEFORE YOU — MARSHALING ALL HER WILL POWER — CAN YET WITHSTAND ANOTHER TWO OR THREE MINUTES...

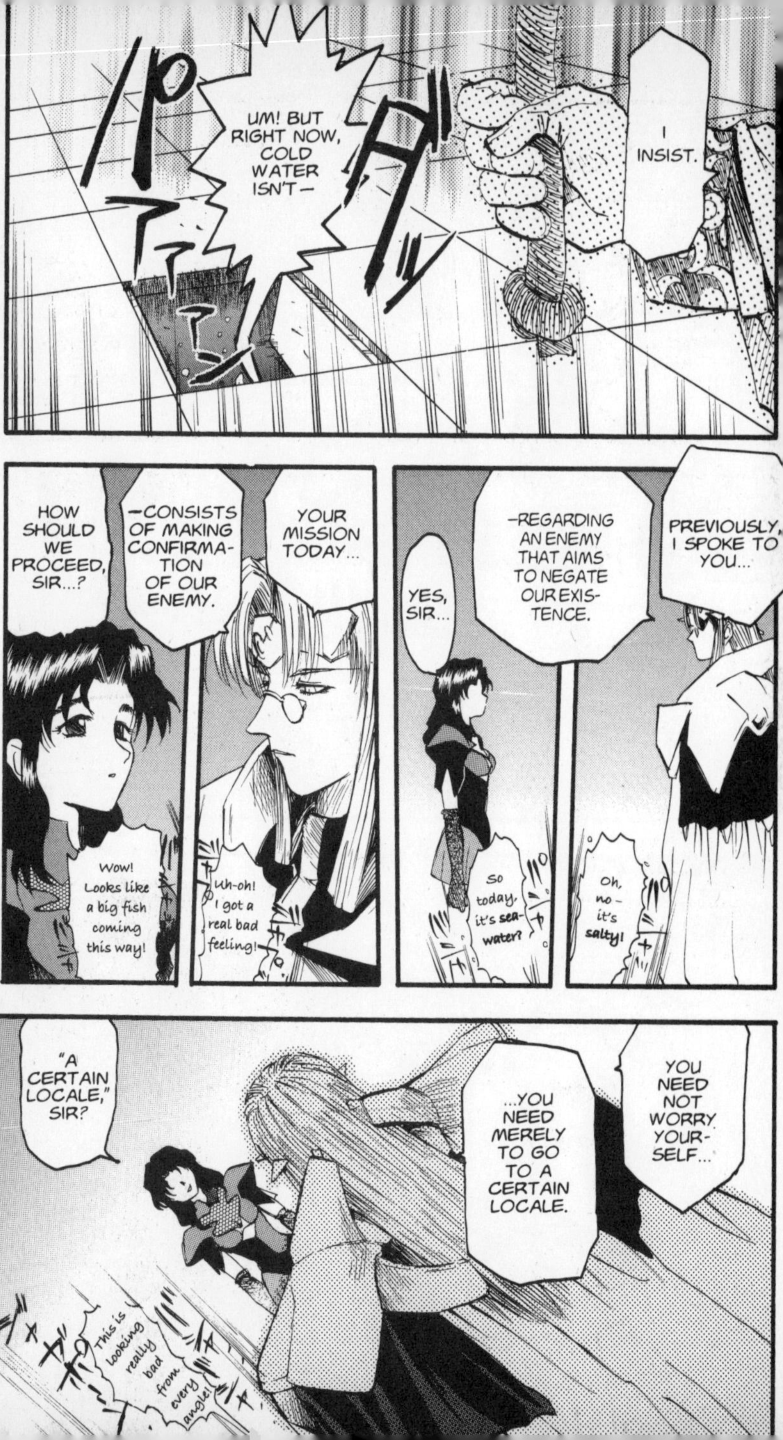
I INSIST.
UM! BUT RIGHT NOW, COLD WATER ISN'T—
PREVIOUSLY, I SPOKE TO YOU...
Oh, no— it's salty!
—REGARDING AN ENEMY THAT AIMS TO NEGATE OUR EXISTENCE.
YES, SIR...
So today, it's sea-water?
YOUR MISSION TODAY...
—CONSISTS OF MAKING CONFIRMATION OF OUR ENEMY.
Uh-oh! I got a real bad feeling!
HOW SHOULD WE PROCEED, SIR...?
Wow! Looks like a big fish coming this way!
YOU NEED NOT WORRY YOURSELF...
...YOU NEED MERELY TO GO TO A CERTAIN LOCALE.
"A CERTAIN LOCALE," SIR?
This is looking really bad from every angle!

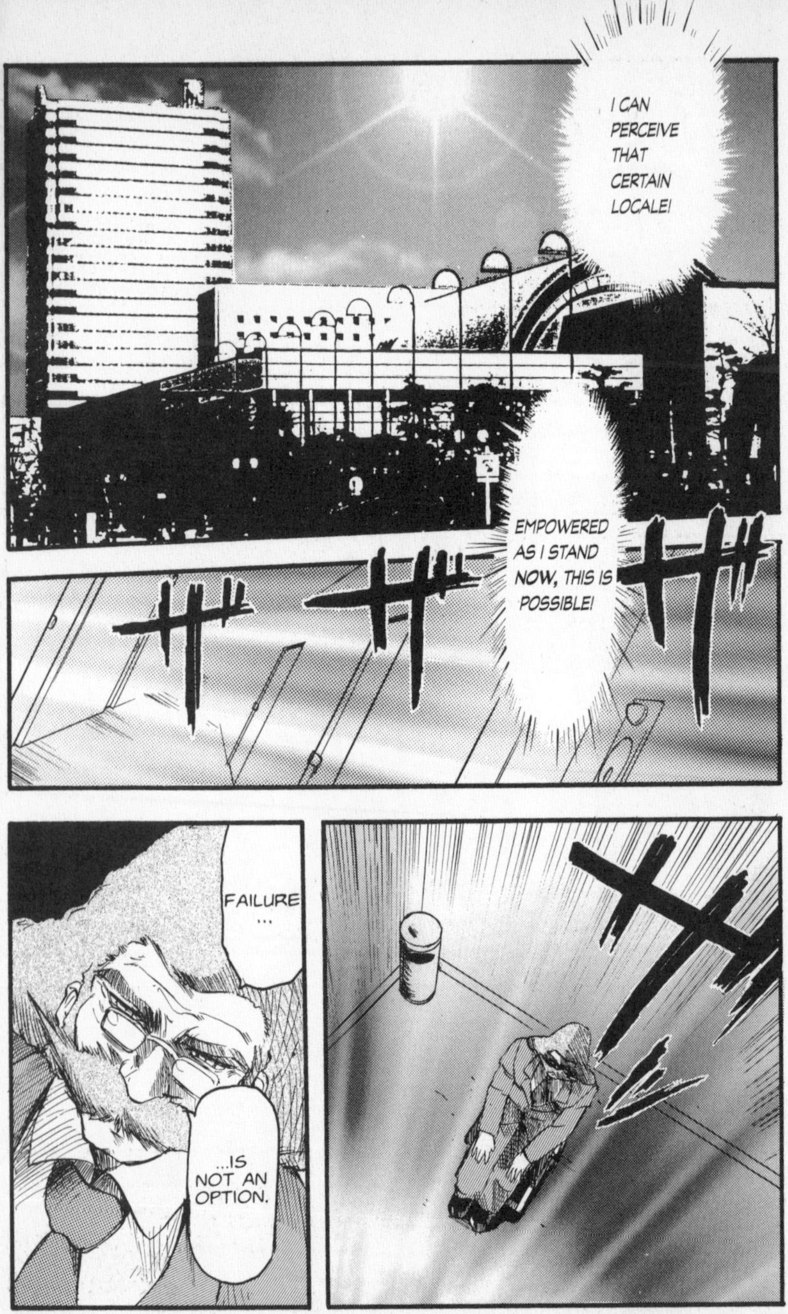
I CAN PERCEIVE THAT CERTAIN LOCALE!
EMPOWERED AS I STAND NOW, THIS IS POSSIBLE!
FAILURE ...
...IS NOT AN OPTION.

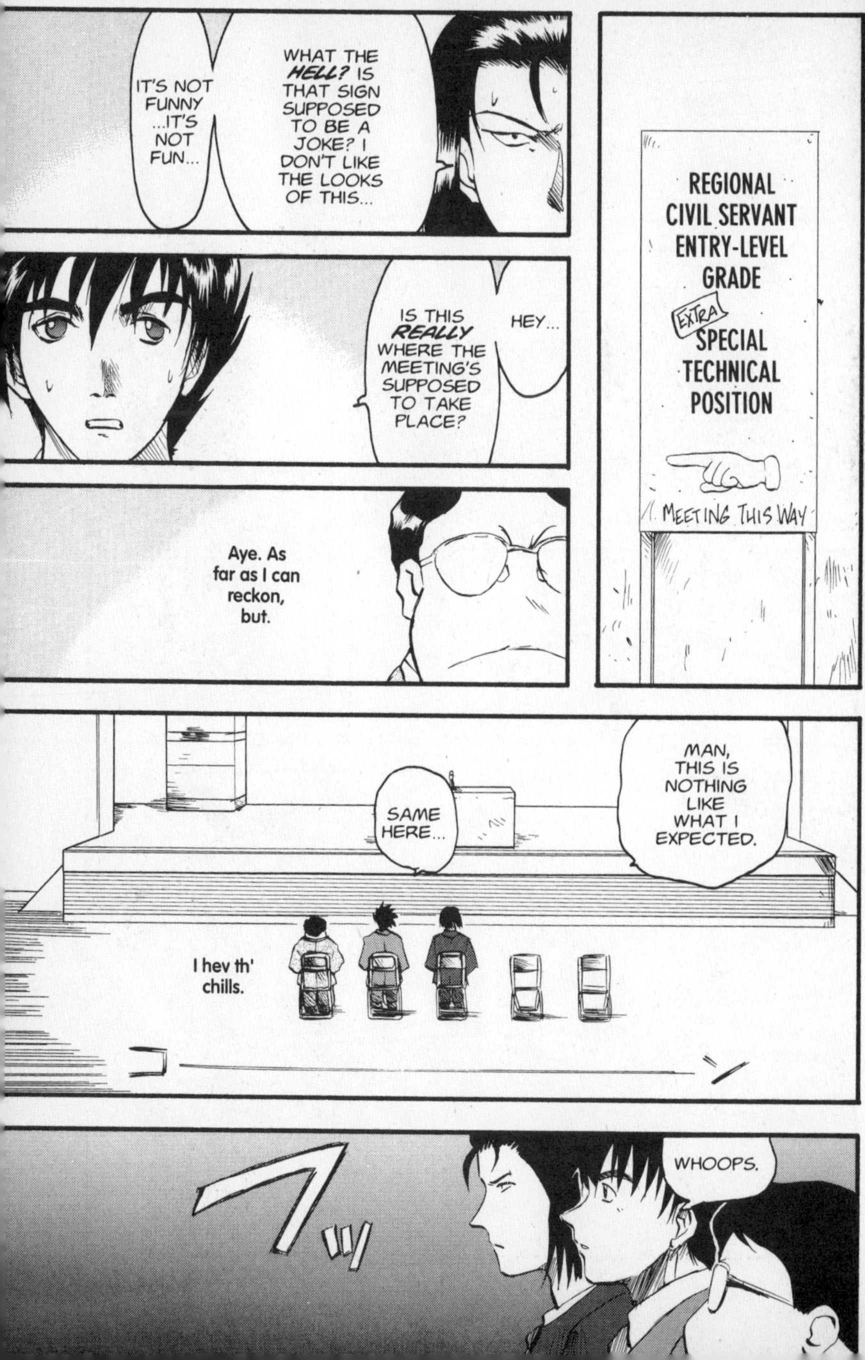
REGIONAL CIVIL SERVANT ENTRY-LEVEL GRADE EXTRA SPECIAL TECHNICAL POSITION
MEETING THIS WAY
WHAT THE HELL? IS THAT SIGN SUPPOSED TO BE A JOKE? I DON'T LIKE THE LOOKS OF THIS...
IT'S NOT FUNNY ...IT'S NOT FUN...
HEY...
IS THIS REALLY WHERE THE MEETING'S SUPPOSED TO TAKE PLACE?
Aye. As far as I can reckon, but.
MAN, THIS IS NOTHING LIKE WHAT I EXPECTED.
SAME HERE...
I hev th' chills.
WHOOPS.

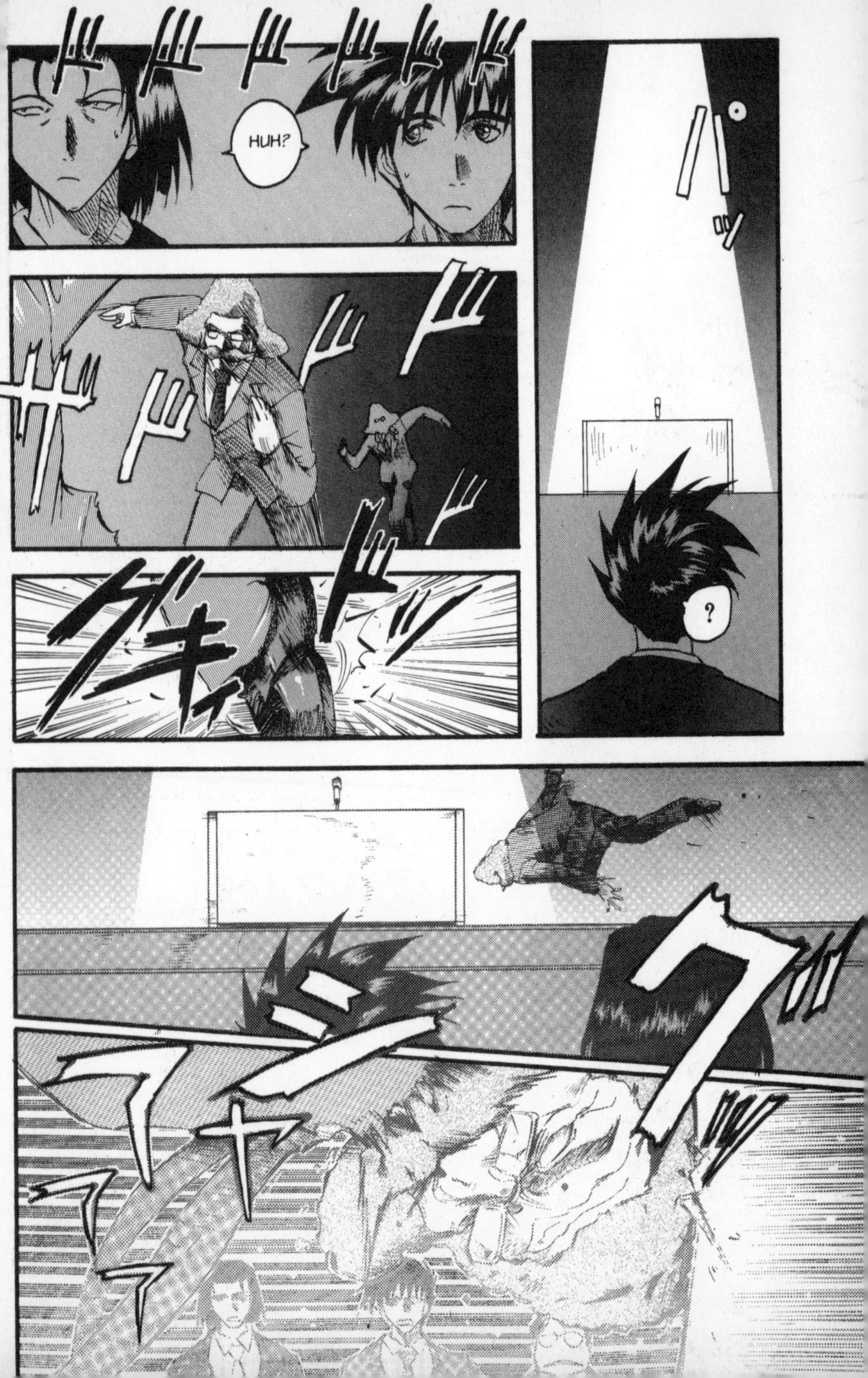
?
HUH?

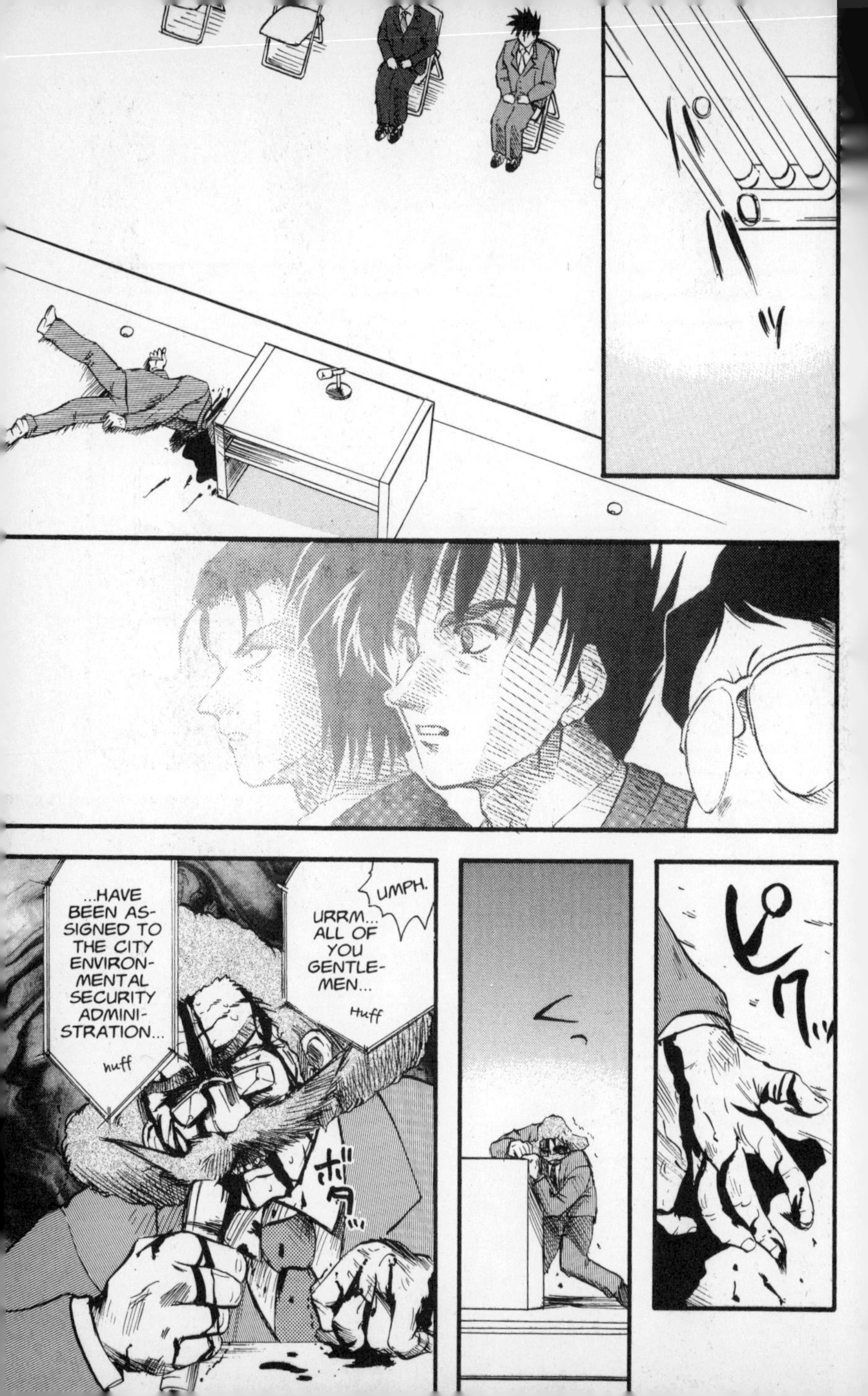
ピクッ
UMPH.
URRM... ALL OF YOU GENTLE-MEN...
Huff
...HAVE BEEN AS-SIGNED TO THE CITY ENVIRON-MENTAL SECURITY ADMINI-STRATION...
huff
ボタ

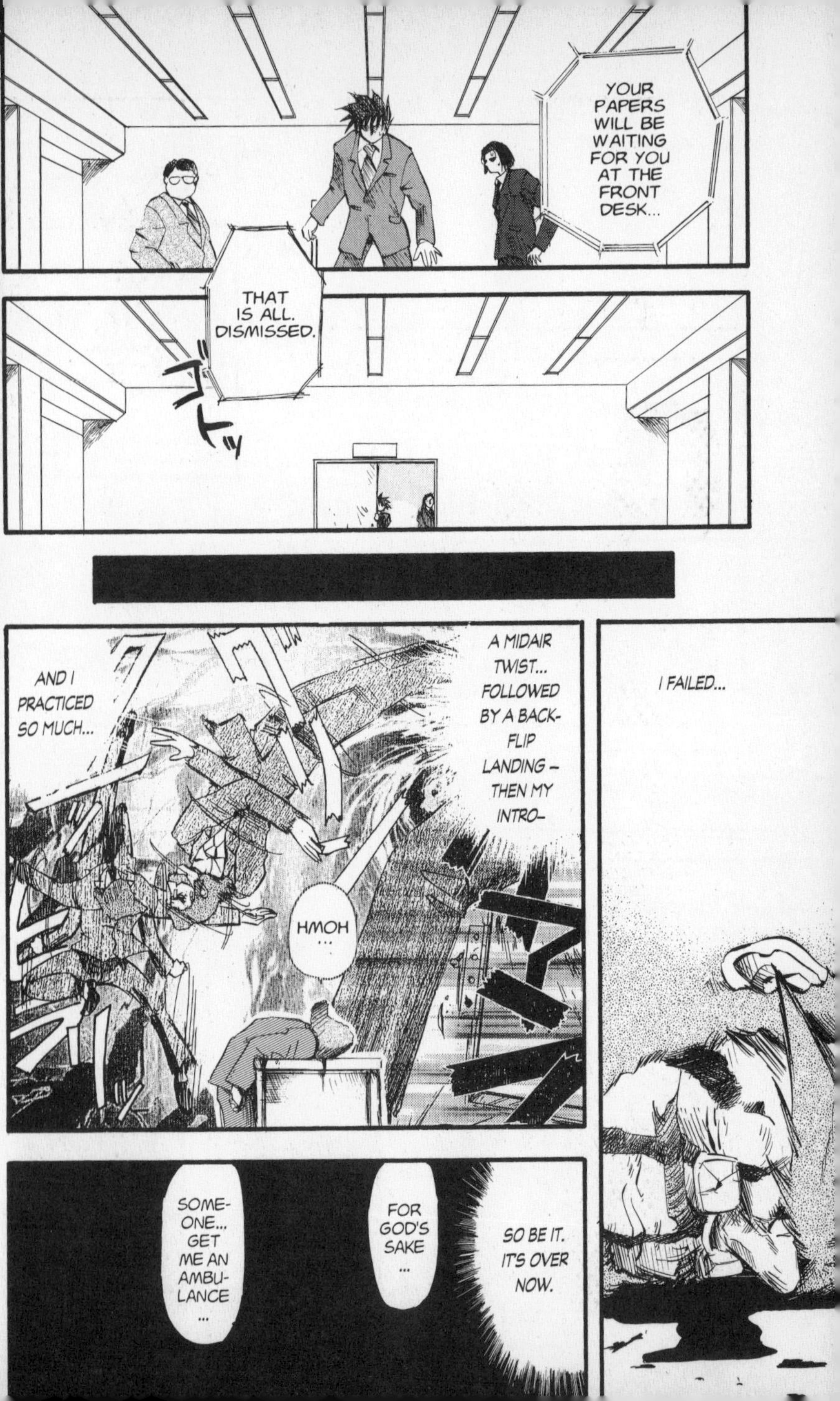
YOUR PAPERS WILL BE WAITING FOR YOU AT THE FRONT DESK...
THAT IS ALL. DISMISSED.
ゴトッ
I FAILED...
A MIDAIR TWIST... FOLLOWED BY A BACK-FLIP LANDING — THEN MY INTRO—
AND I PRACTICED SO MUCH...
HMOH ...
SO BE IT. IT'S OVER NOW.
FOR GOD'S SAKE ...
SOME-ONE... GET ME AN AMBU-LANCE ...

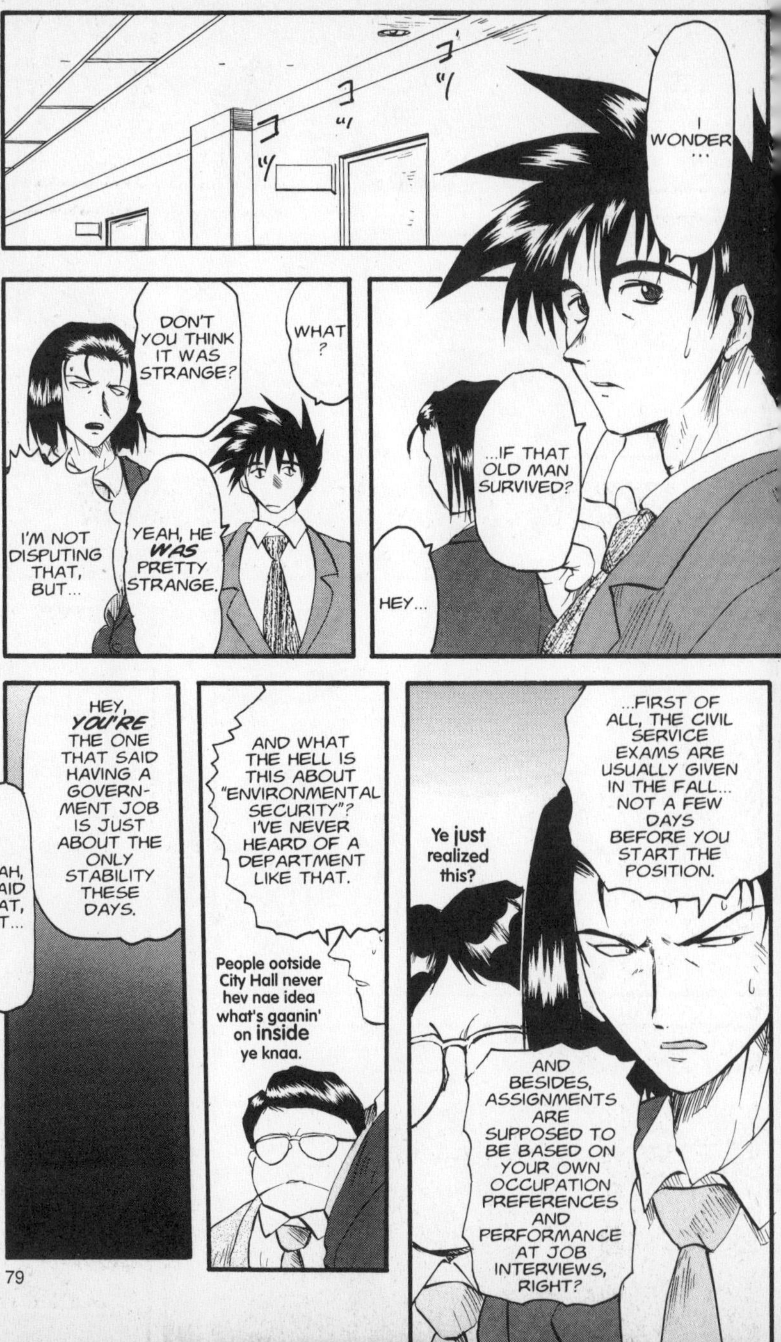

I WONDER...
...IF THAT OLD MAN SURVIVED?
HEY...
WHAT?
DON'T YOU THINK IT WAS STRANGE?
YEAH, HE *WAS* PRETTY STRANGE.
I'M NOT DISPUTING THAT, BUT...
...FIRST OF ALL, THE CIVIL SERVICE EXAMS ARE USUALLY GIVEN IN THE FALL... NOT A FEW DAYS BEFORE YOU START THE POSITION.
Ye just realized this?
AND BESIDES, ASSIGNMENTS ARE SUPPOSED TO BE BASED ON YOUR OWN OCCUPATION PREFERENCES AND PERFORMANCE AT JOB INTERVIEWS, RIGHT?
AND WHAT THE HELL IS THIS ABOUT "ENVIRONMENTAL SECURITY"? I'VE NEVER HEARD OF A DEPARTMENT LIKE THAT.
People ootside City Hall never hev nae idea what's gaanin' on inside ye knaa.
HEY, *YOU'RE* THE ONE THAT SAID HAVING A GOVERNMENT JOB IS JUST ABOUT THE ONLY STABILITY THESE DAYS.
YEAH, I SAID THAT, BUT...

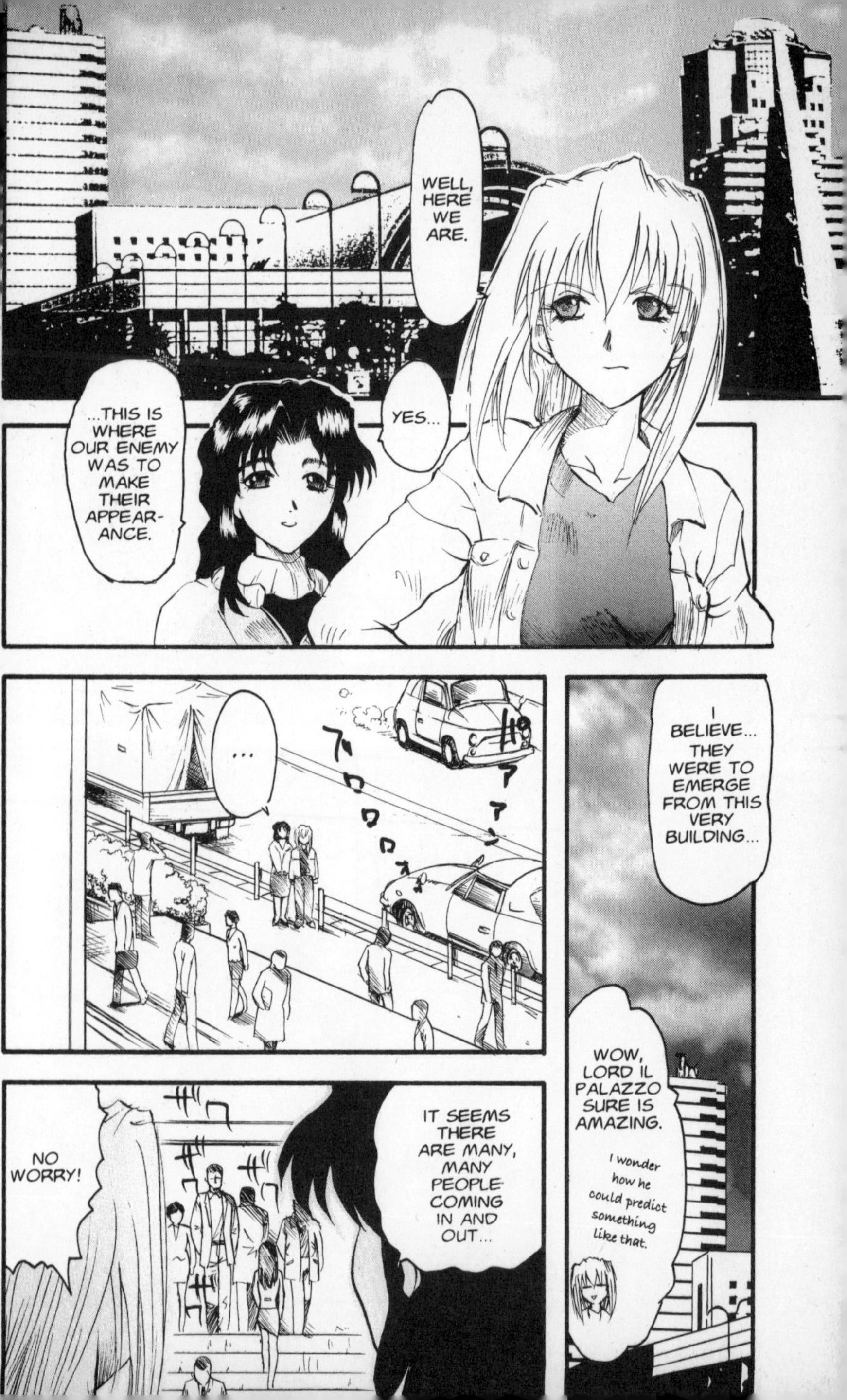
WELL, HERE WE ARE.
YES...
...THIS IS WHERE OUR ENEMY WAS TO MAKE THEIR APPEARANCE.
I BELIEVE... THEY WERE TO EMERGE FROM THIS VERY BUILDING...
WOW, LORD IL PALAZZO SURE IS AMAZING.
I wonder how he could predict something like that.
パアアン
ブロロロオ
...
IT SEEMS THERE ARE MANY, MANY PEOPLE COMING IN AND OUT...
NO WORRY!

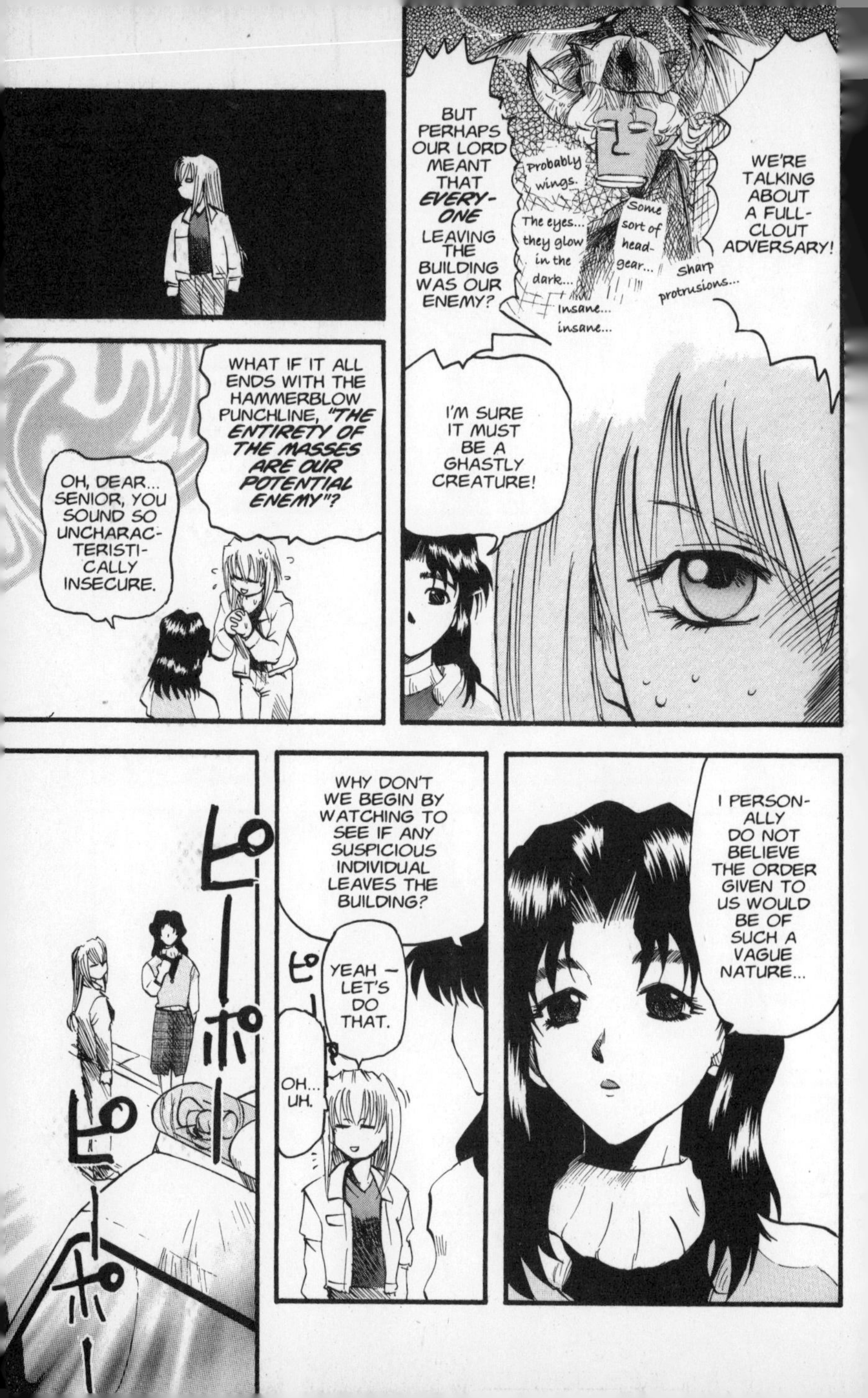
WE'RE TALKING ABOUT A FULL-CLOUT ADVERSARY!
Some sort of head-gear...
Sharp protrusions...
Probably wings.
The eyes... they glow in the dark...
insane... insane...
BUT PERHAPS OUR LORD MEANT THAT ***EVERYONE*** LEAVING THE BUILDING WAS OUR ENEMY?
I'M SURE IT MUST BE A GHASTLY CREATURE!
WHAT IF IT ALL ENDS WITH THE HAMMERBLOW PUNCHLINE, ***"THE ENTIRETY OF THE MASSES ARE OUR POTENTIAL ENEMY"***?
OH, DEAR... SENIOR, YOU SOUND SO UNCHARACTERISTICALLY INSECURE.
I PERSONALLY DO NOT BELIEVE THE ORDER GIVEN TO US WOULD BE OF SUCH A VAGUE NATURE...
WHY DON'T WE BEGIN BY WATCHING TO SEE IF ANY SUSPICIOUS INDIVIDUAL LEAVES THE BUILDING?
YEAH — LET'S DO THAT.
OH... UH.
ピーポー
ピーポー

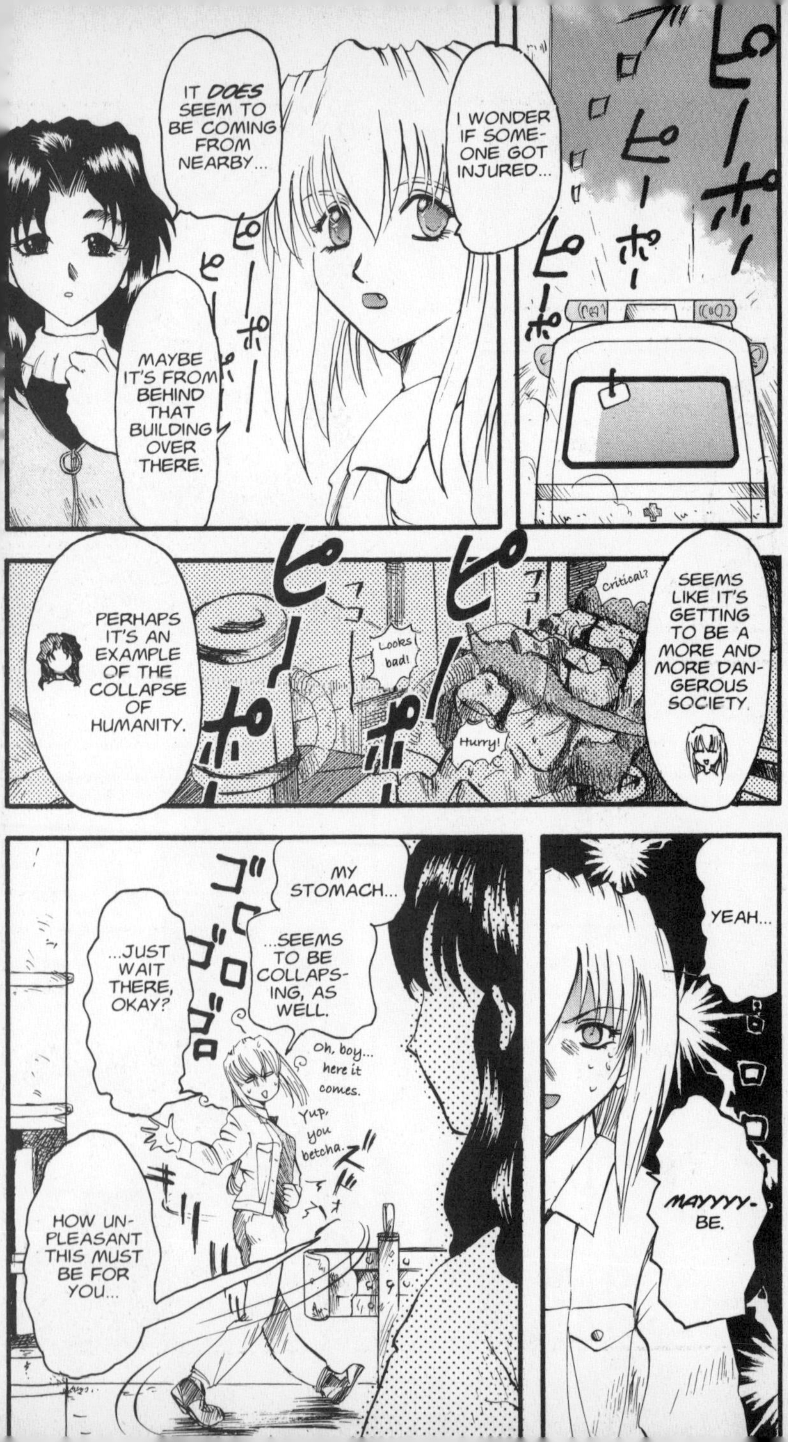
I WONDER IF SOME-ONE GOT INJURED...
IT *DOES* SEEM TO BE COMING FROM NEARBY...
MAYBE IT'S FROM BEHIND THAT BUILDING OVER THERE.
SEEMS LIKE IT'S GETTING TO BE A MORE AND MORE DAN-GEROUS SOCIETY.
Critical?
Looks bad!
Hurry!
PERHAPS IT'S AN EXAMPLE OF THE COLLAPSE OF HUMANITY.
YEAH...
MAYYYY- BE.
MY STOMACH...
...SEEMS TO BE COLLAPS-ING, AS WELL.
...JUST WAIT THERE, OKAY?
Oh, boy... here it comes.
Yup, you betcha.
HOW UN-PLEASANT THIS MUST BE FOR YOU...

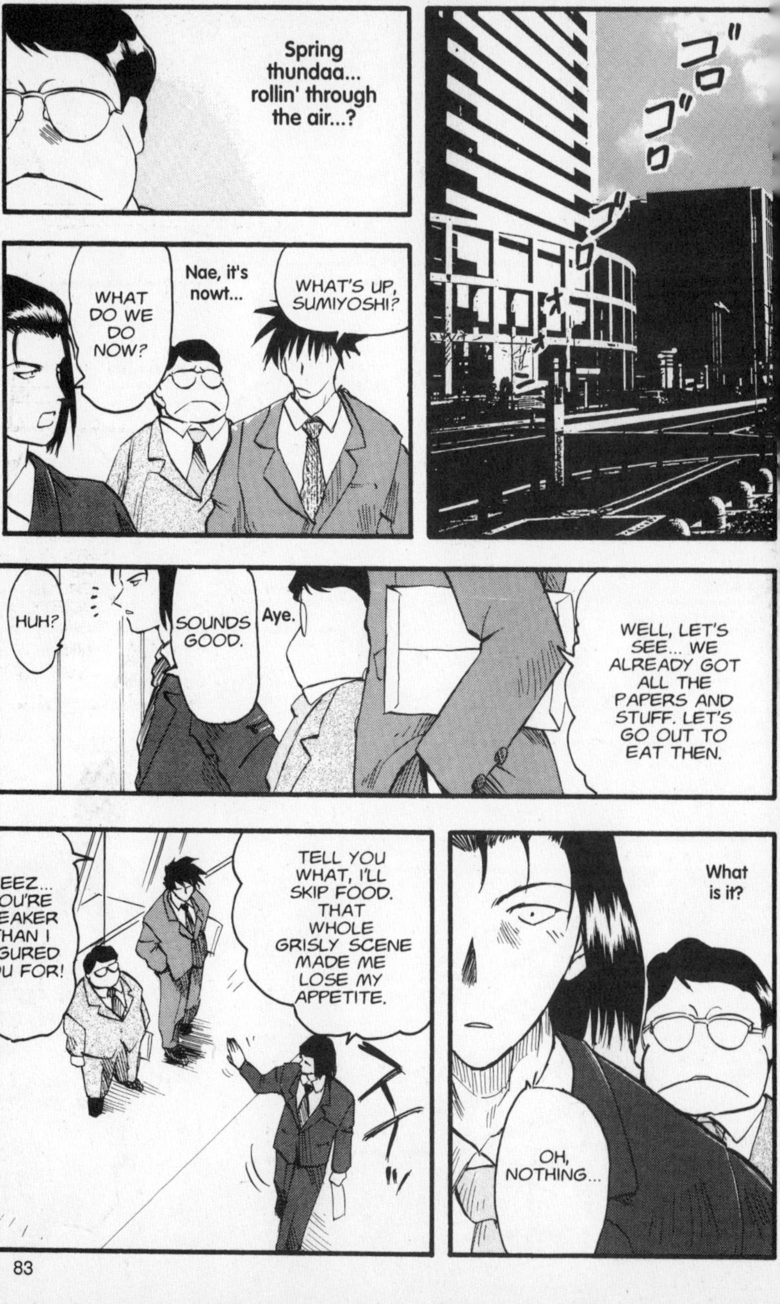
ゴロゴロ
ゴロオオン
Spring thundaa... rollin' through the air...?
WHAT'S UP, SUMIYOSHI?
Nae, it's nowt...
WHAT DO WE DO NOW?
WELL, LET'S SEE... WE ALREADY GOT ALL THE PAPERS AND STUFF. LET'S GO OUT TO EAT THEN.
Aye.
SOUNDS GOOD.
HUH?
What is it?
OH, NOTHING...
TELL YOU WHAT, I'LL SKIP FOOD. THAT WHOLE GRISLY SCENE MADE ME LOSE MY APPETITE.
JEEZ... YOU'RE WEAKER THAN I FIGURED YOU FOR!

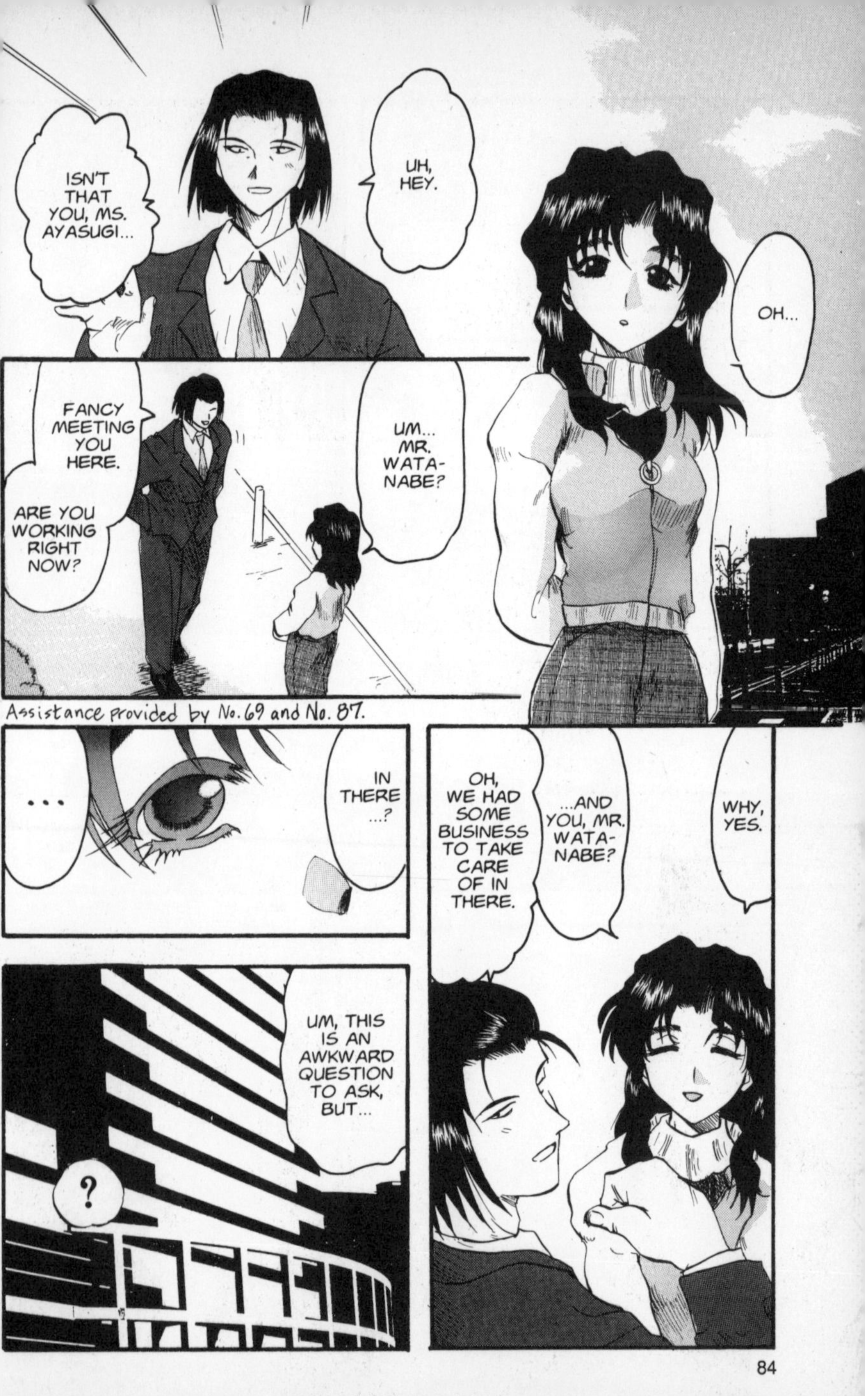
OH...
UH, HEY.
ISN'T THAT YOU, MS. AYASUGI...
UM... MR. WATA-NABE?
FANCY MEETING YOU HERE.
ARE YOU WORKING RIGHT NOW?
Assistance provided by No. 69 and No. 87.
WHY, YES.
...AND YOU, MR. WATA-NABE?
OH, WE HAD SOME BUSINESS TO TAKE CARE OF IN THERE.
IN THERE ...?
...
UM, THIS IS AN AWKWARD QUESTION TO ASK, BUT...
?

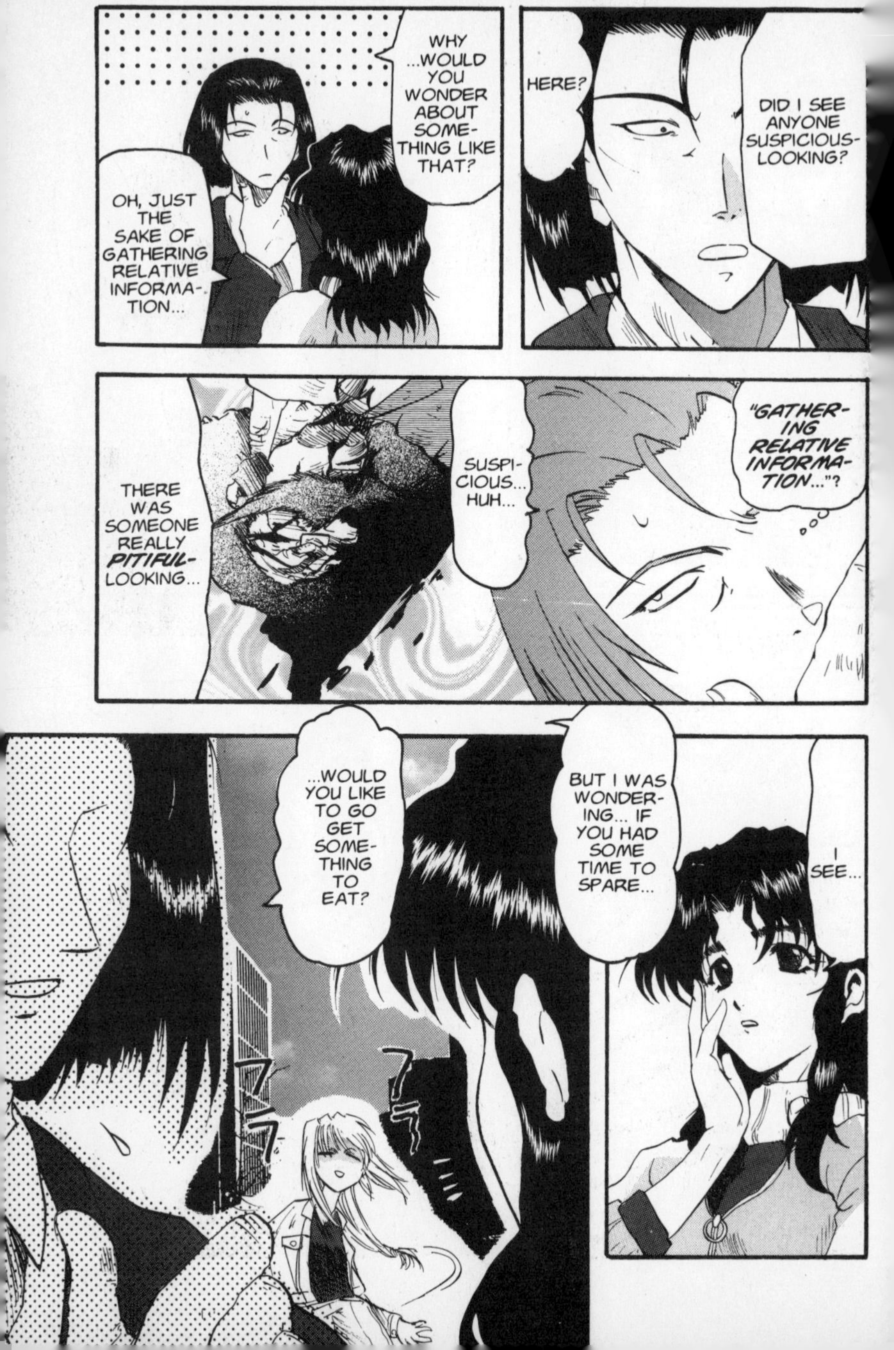
DID I SEE ANYONE SUSPICIOUS-LOOKING?
HERE?
WHY ...WOULD YOU WONDER ABOUT SOME-THING LIKE THAT?
OH, JUST THE SAKE OF GATHERING RELATIVE INFORMA-TION...
"GATHER-ING RELATIVE INFORMA-TION..."?
SUSPI-CIOUS... HUH...
THERE WAS SOMEONE REALLY ***PITIFUL***-LOOKING...
I SEE...
BUT I WAS WONDER-ING... IF YOU HAD SOME TIME TO SPARE...
...WOULD YOU LIKE TO GO GET SOME-THING TO EAT?

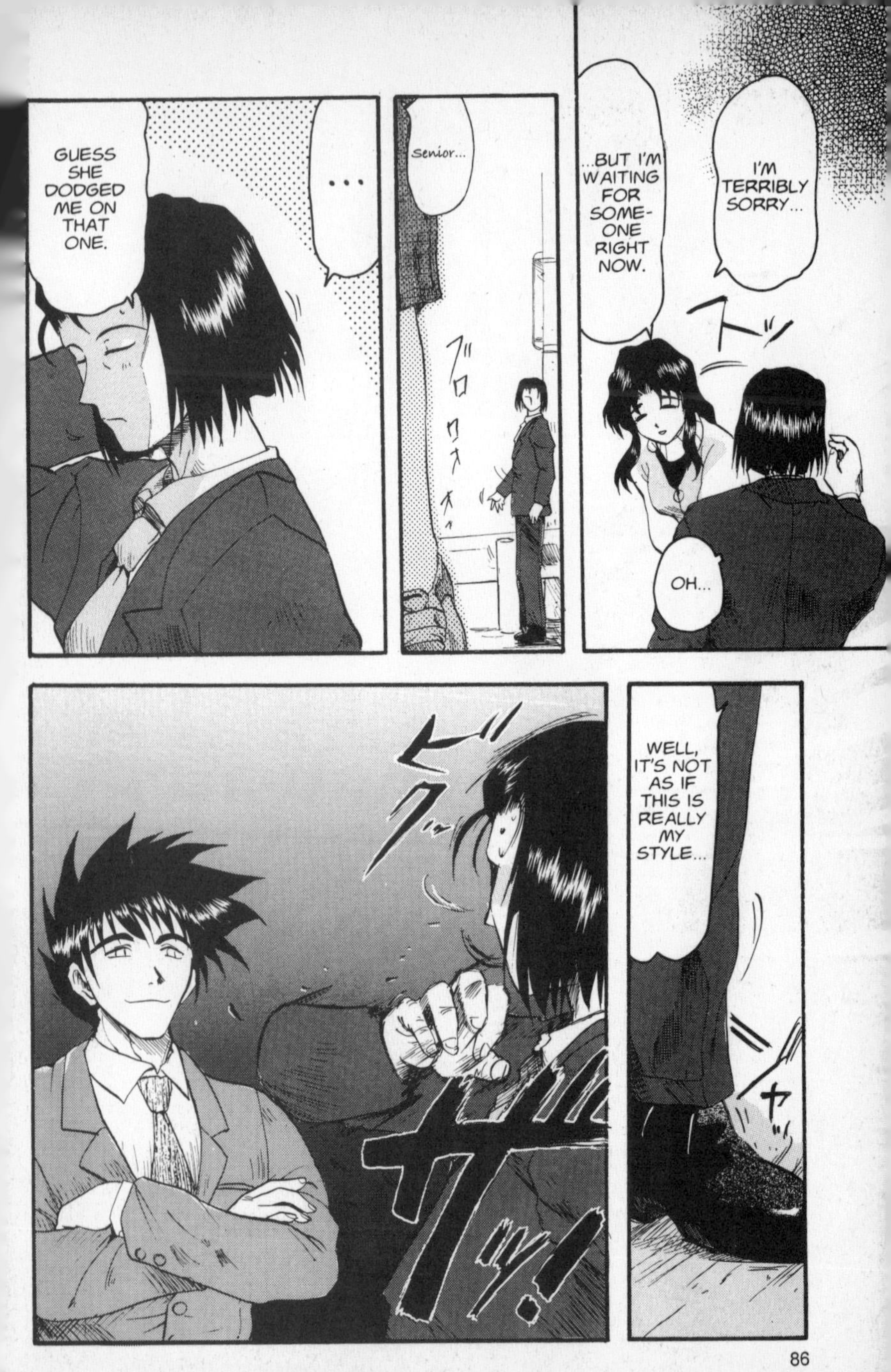
I'M TERRIBLY SORRY...
...BUT I'M WAITING FOR SOMEONE RIGHT NOW.
OH...
Senior...
...
GUESS SHE DODGED ME ON THAT ONE.
WELL, IT'S NOT AS IF THIS IS REALLY MY STYLE...

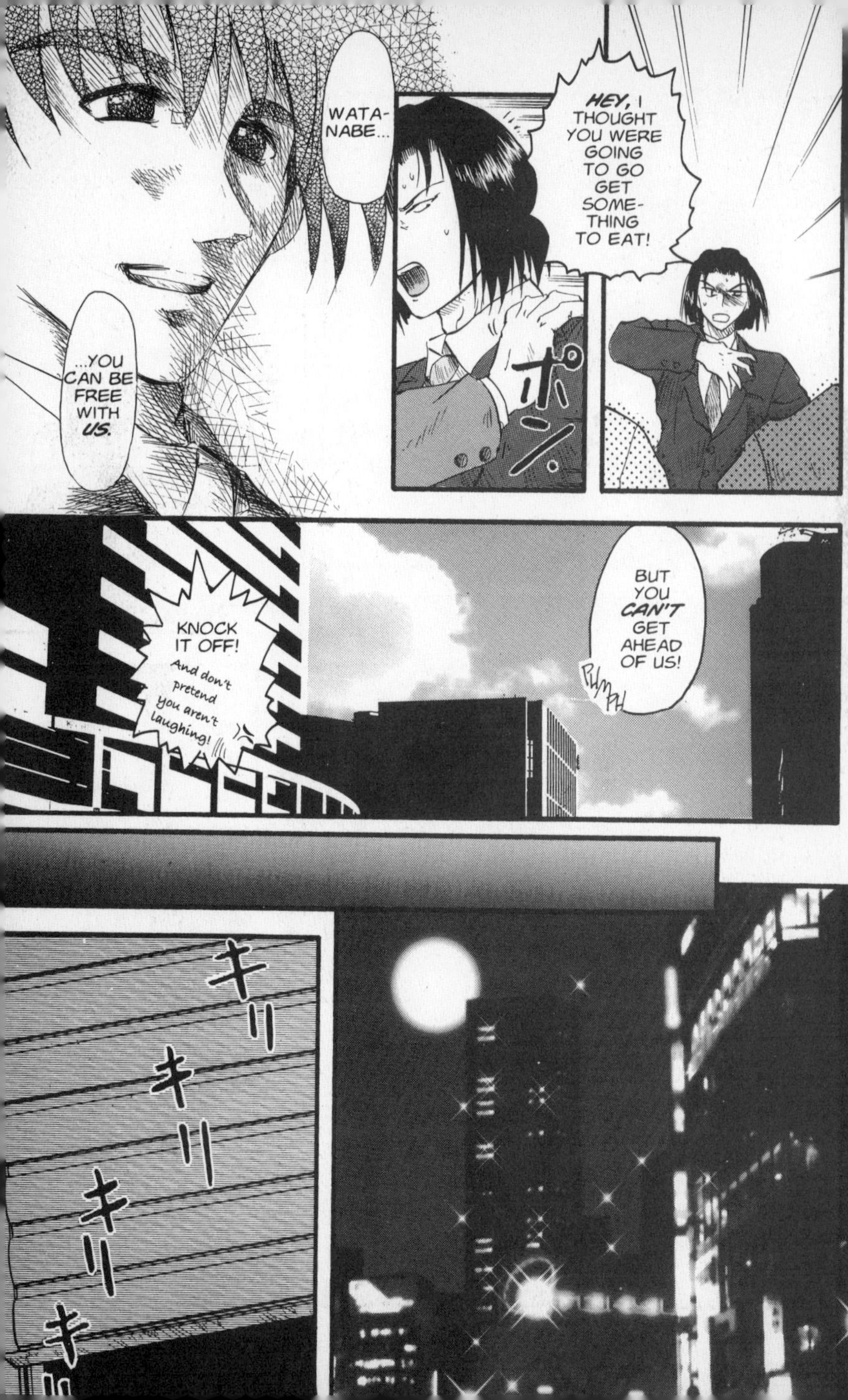
HEY, I THOUGHT YOU WERE GOING TO GO GET SOME-THING TO EAT!
WATA-NABE...
...YOU CAN BE FREE WITH US.
BUT YOU CAN'T GET AHEAD OF US!
PUMPH
KNOCK IT OFF!
And don't pretend you aren't laughing!

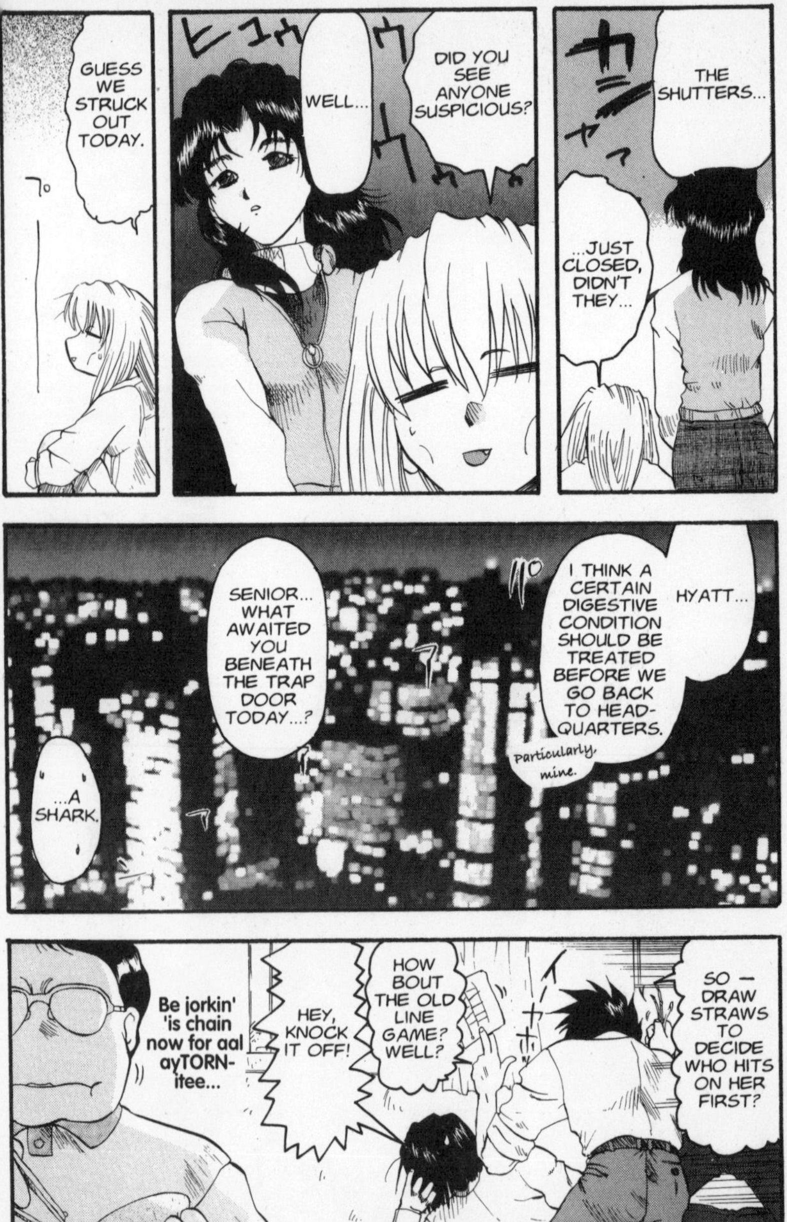
THE SHUTTERS...
...JUST CLOSED, DIDN'T THEY...
DID YOU SEE ANYONE SUSPICIOUS?
WELL...
GUESS WE STRUCK OUT TODAY.
HYATT...
I THINK A CERTAIN DIGESTIVE CONDITION SHOULD BE TREATED BEFORE WE GO BACK TO HEAD-QUARTERS.
Particularly, mine.
SENIOR... WHAT AWAITED YOU BENEATH THE TRAP DOOR TODAY...?
...A SHARK.
SO — DRAW STRAWS TO DECIDE WHO HITS ON HER FIRST?
HOW BOUT THE OLD LINE GAME? WELL?
HEY, KNOCK IT OFF!
Be jorkin' 'is chain now for aal ayTORN-itee...

END MISSION 3

EXCEL SAGA

I'M ABOUT TO GO OUT ON A *DATE!*
I DON'T WANT TO SEE ANY HAIRY-FACED OLD GEEZER!
I APOLOGIZE, DOCTOR — I CAN ASSURE YOU IF THERE WAS *ANYONE ELSE* WHO WAS ON *CALL RIGHT NOW,* I WOULDN'T BE ASKING FOR YOUR ASSISTANCE!
JUST RUB 20ccS OF YOUR SPIT INTO HIS WOUND — THAT OUTTA STABILIZE HIM!
キュッ

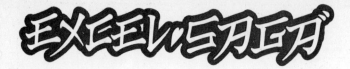

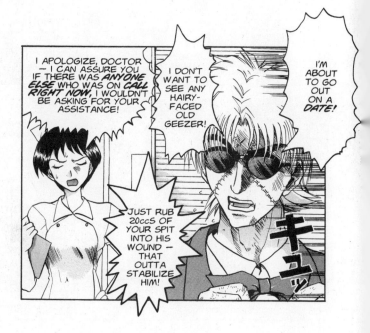

EXCEL SAGA

WHAT!? A HAIRY-FACED OLD GEEZER FROM HIGH UP IN THE CITY ADMINISTRATION?? WELL, WHY DIDN'T YOU SAY SO?
Let the miracle of life
THE VIP PRIVATE ROOM IS VACANT, RIGHT!? GET THE HONOR BAR STOCKED WHILE I'M IN OPS!
Shine brightly!
LOW-LIFE.
カキーーン!

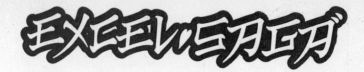

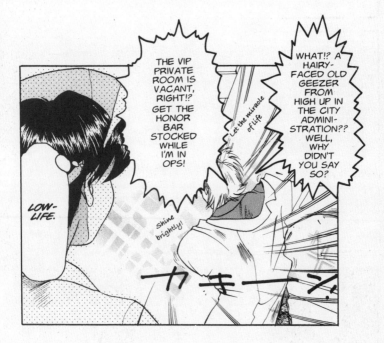

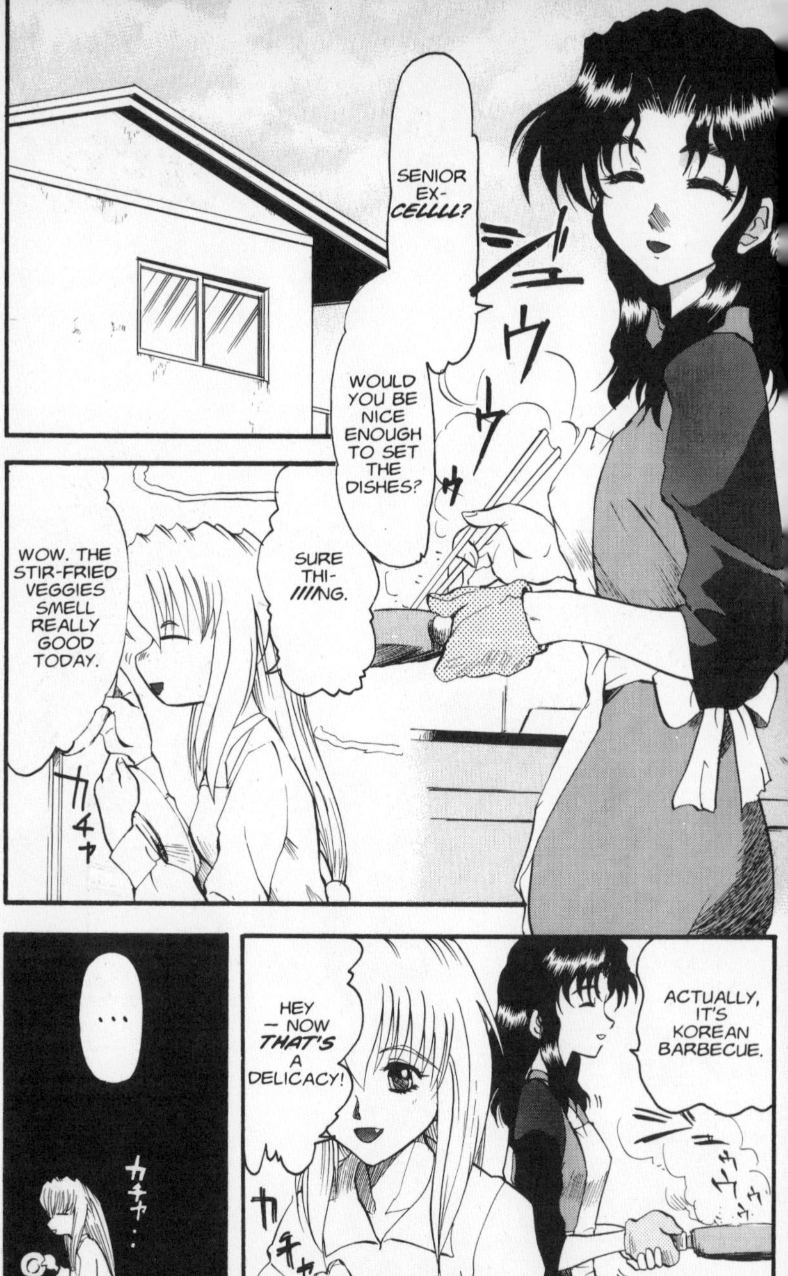
SENIOR EX-*CELLLLL?*
WOULD YOU BE NICE ENOUGH TO SET THE DISHES?
SURE THI-*IIII*NG.
WOW. THE STIR-FRIED VEGGIES SMELL REALLY GOOD TODAY.
ACTUALLY, IT'S KOREAN BARBECUE.
HEY — NOW *THAT'S* A DELICACY!
...

MISSION 4

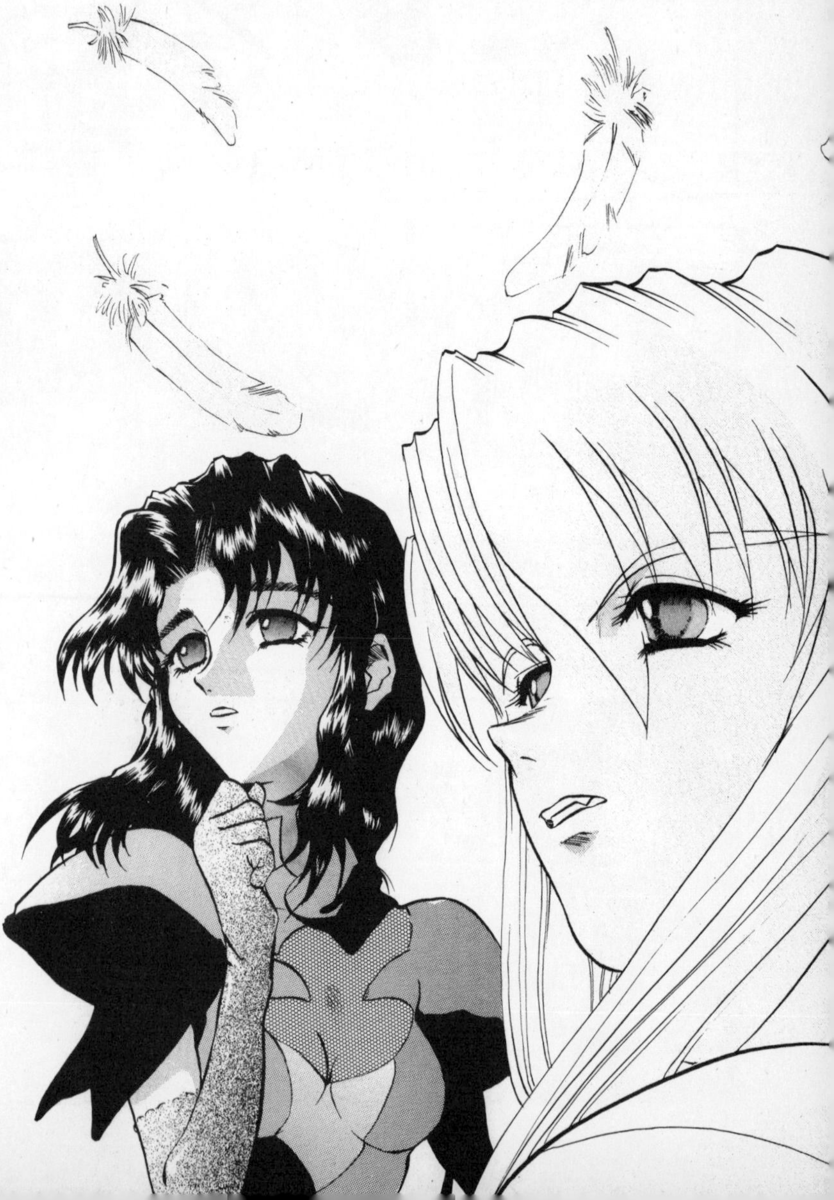

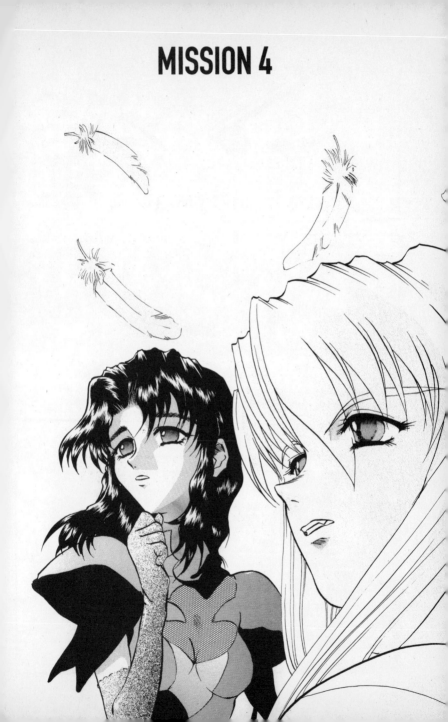

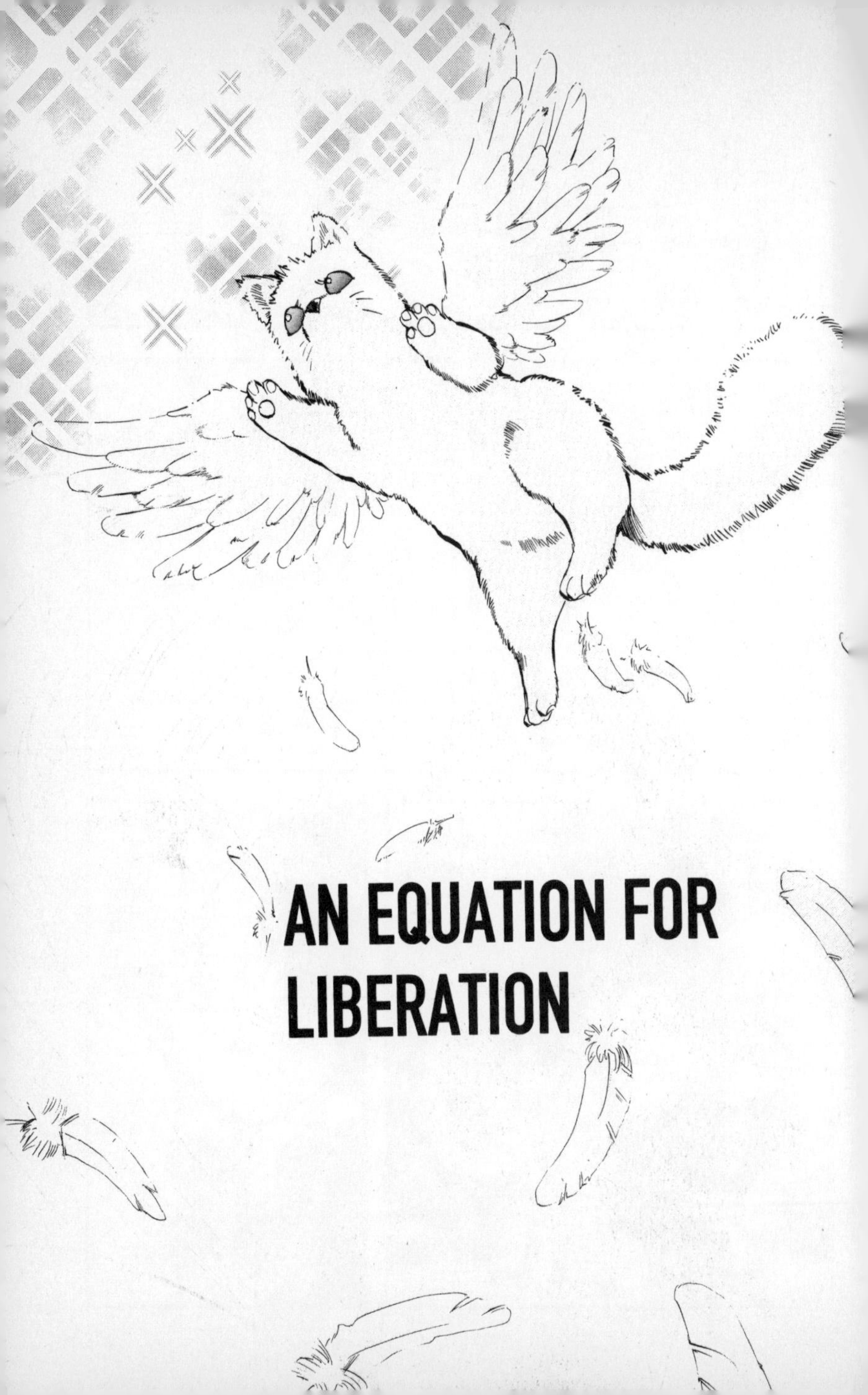

AN EQUATION FOR LIBERATION

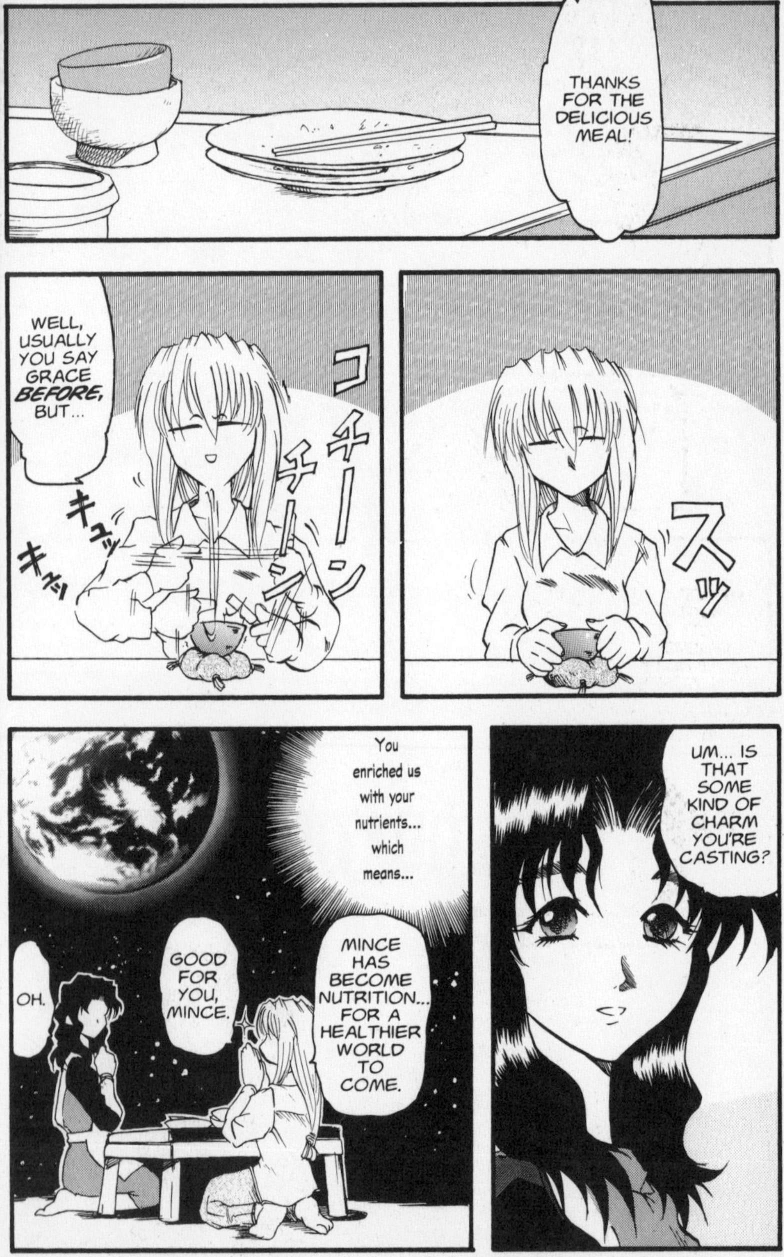
THANKS FOR THE DELICIOUS MEAL!
スッ
WELL, USUALLY YOU SAY GRACE ***BEFORE,*** BUT...
コチーン
チーン
キュッ
キゅッ
UM... IS THAT SOME KIND OF CHARM YOU'RE CASTING?
You enriched us with your nutrients... which means...
MINCE HAS BECOME NUTRITION... FOR A HEALTHIER WORLD TO COME.
GOOD FOR YOU, MINCE.
OH.

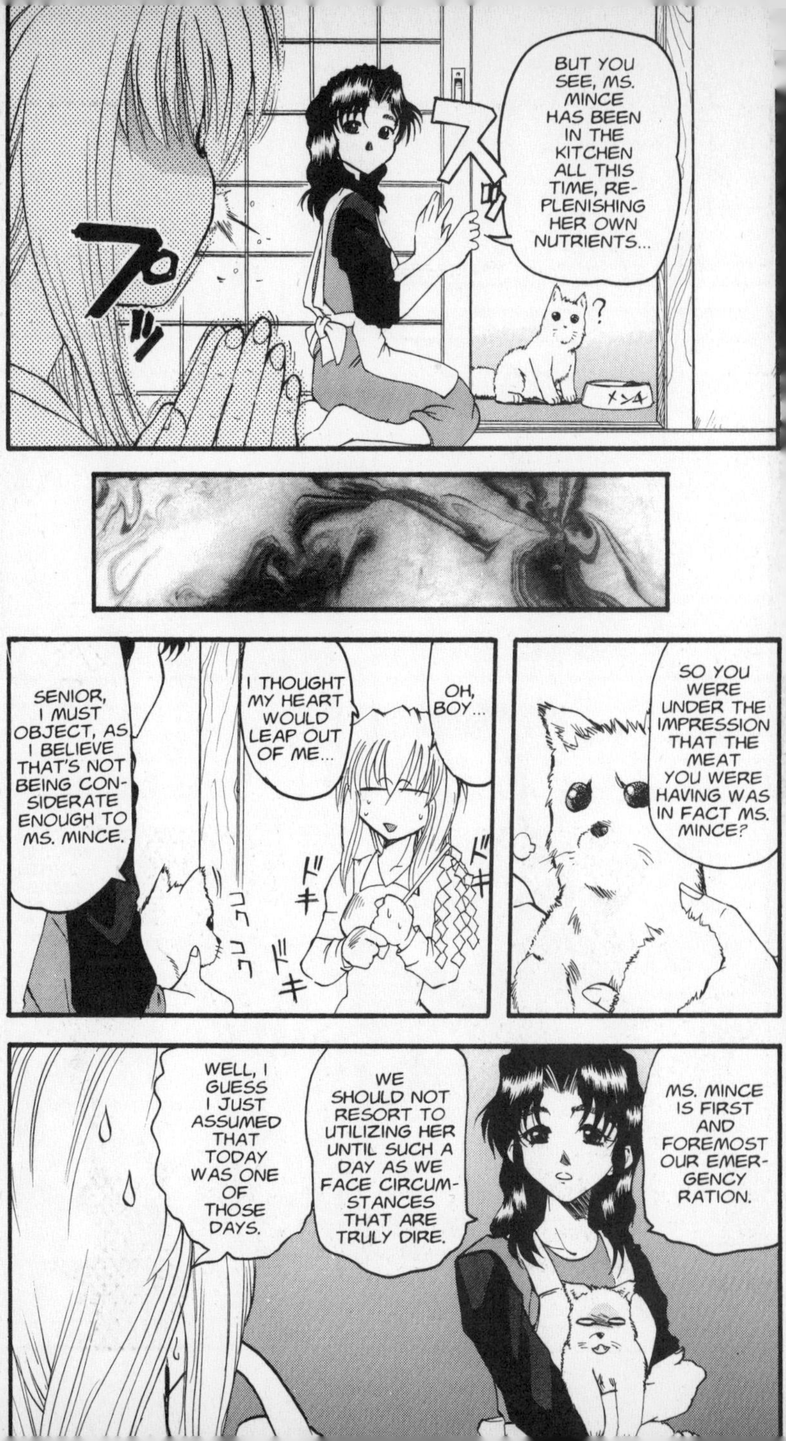
BUT YOU SEE, MS. MINCE HAS BEEN IN THE KITCHEN ALL THIS TIME, RE-PLENISHING HER OWN NUTRIENTS...
スッ
プッ
SO YOU WERE UNDER THE IMPRESSION THAT THE MEAT YOU WERE HAVING WAS IN FACT MS. MINCE?
OH, BOY...
I THOUGHT MY HEART WOULD LEAP OUT OF ME...
ドキドキ
ドキドキ
SENIOR, I MUST OBJECT, AS I BELIEVE THAT'S NOT BEING CON-SIDERATE ENOUGH TO MS. MINCE.
コクコク
MS. MINCE IS FIRST AND FOREMOST OUR EMER-GENCY RATION.
WE SHOULD NOT RESORT TO UTILIZING HER UNTIL SUCH A DAY AS WE FACE CIRCUM-STANCES THAT ARE TRULY DIRE.
WELL, I GUESS I JUST ASSUMED THAT TODAY WAS ONE OF THOSE DAYS.

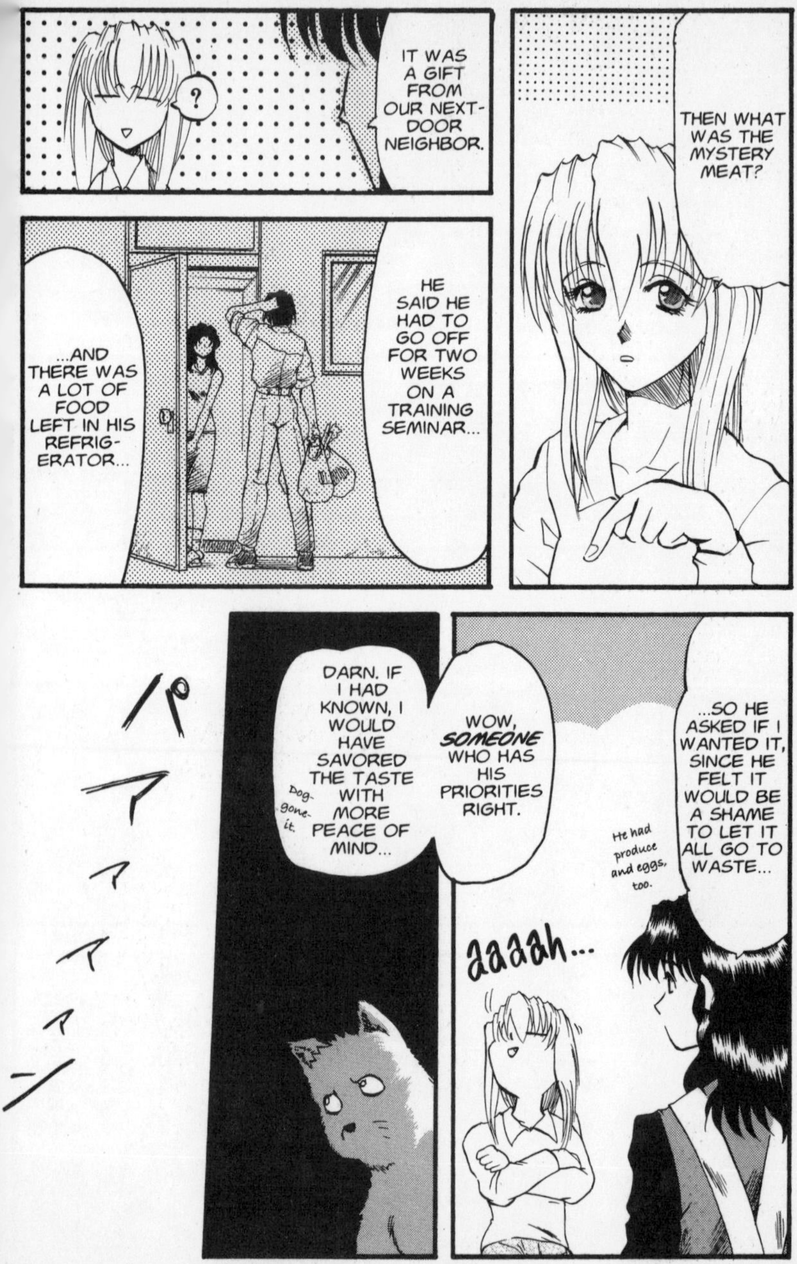
THEN WHAT WAS THE MYSTERY MEAT?
?
IT WAS A GIFT FROM OUR NEXT-DOOR NEIGHBOR.
HE SAID HE HAD TO GO OFF FOR TWO WEEKS ON A TRAINING SEMINAR...
...AND THERE WAS A LOT OF FOOD LEFT IN HIS REFRIGERATOR...
...SO HE ASKED IF I WANTED IT, SINCE HE FELT IT WOULD BE A SHAME TO LET IT ALL GO TO WASTE...
He had produce and eggs, too.
aaaah...
WOW, *SOMEONE* WHO HAS HIS PRIORITIES RIGHT.
DARN. IF I HAD KNOWN, I WOULD HAVE SAVORED THE TASTE WITH MORE PEACE OF MIND...
Dog-gone-it.
パァァァァン

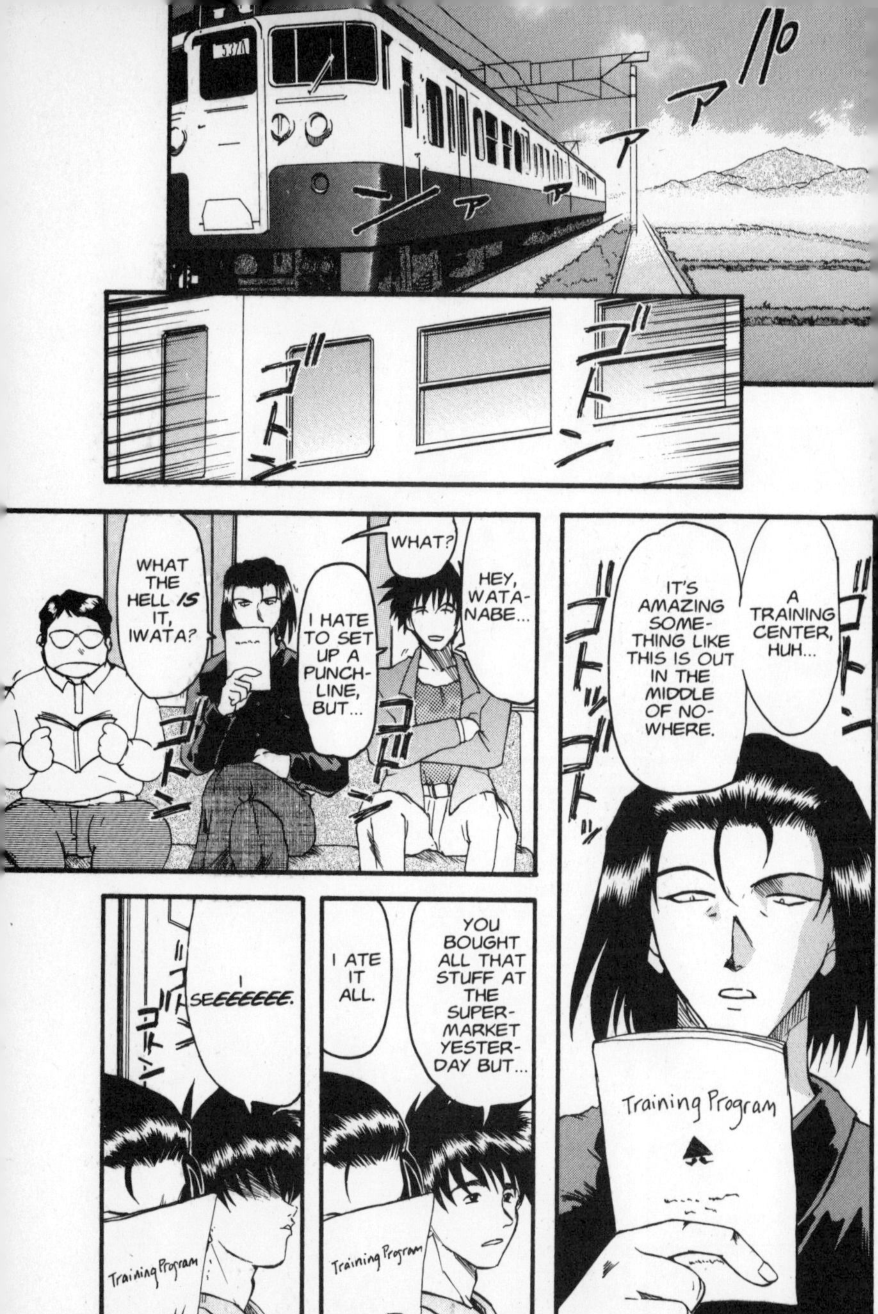
A TRAINING CENTER, HUH...
IT'S AMAZING SOME-THING LIKE THIS IS OUT IN THE MIDDLE OF NO-WHERE.
Training Program
HEY, WATA-NABE...
WHAT?
I HATE TO SET UP A PUNCH-LINE, BUT...
WHAT THE HELL *IS* IT, IWATA?
YOU BOUGHT ALL THAT STUFF AT THE SUPER-MARKET YESTER-DAY BUT...
I ATE IT ALL.
Training Program
I SEEEEEEEE.
Training Program

THANKS. Genkotsudan

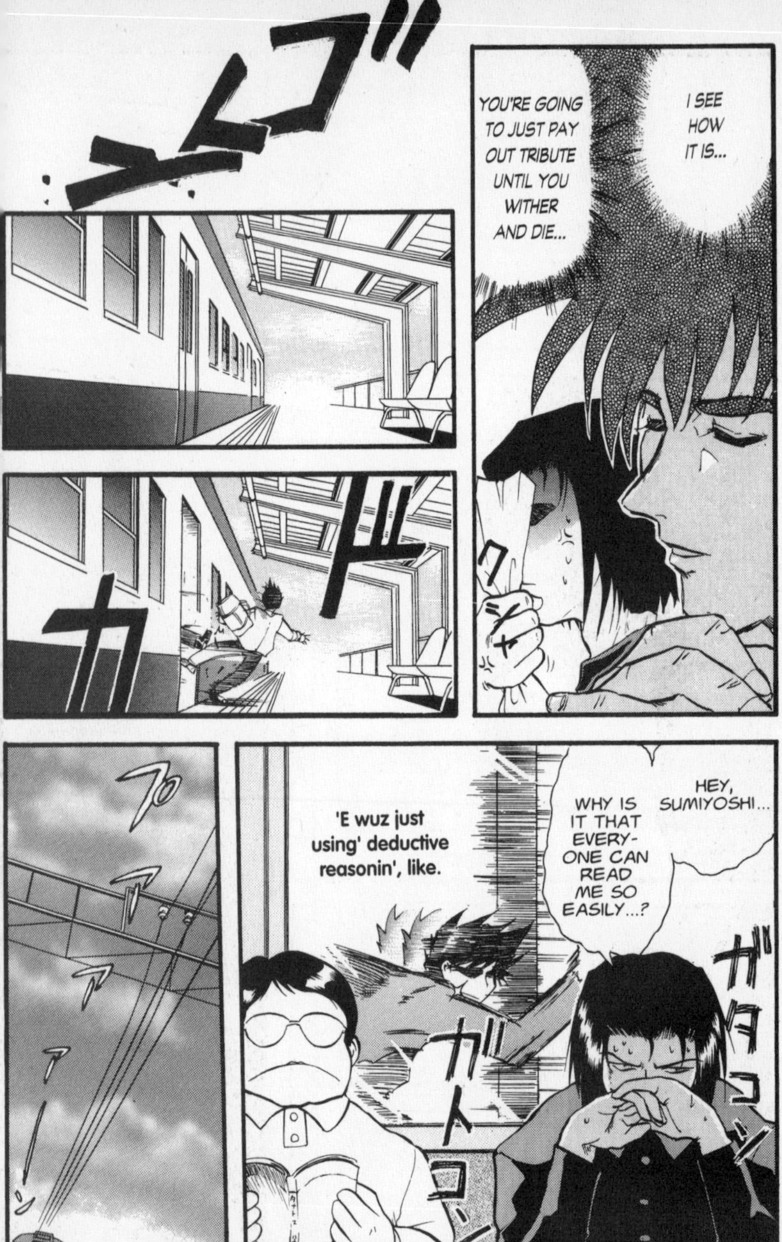
I SEE HOW IT IS...
YOU'RE GOING TO JUST PAY OUT TRIBUTE UNTIL YOU WITHER AND DIE...
HEY, SUMIYOSHI...
WHY IS IT THAT EVERYONE CAN READ ME SO EASILY...?
'E wuz just using' deductive reasonin', like.

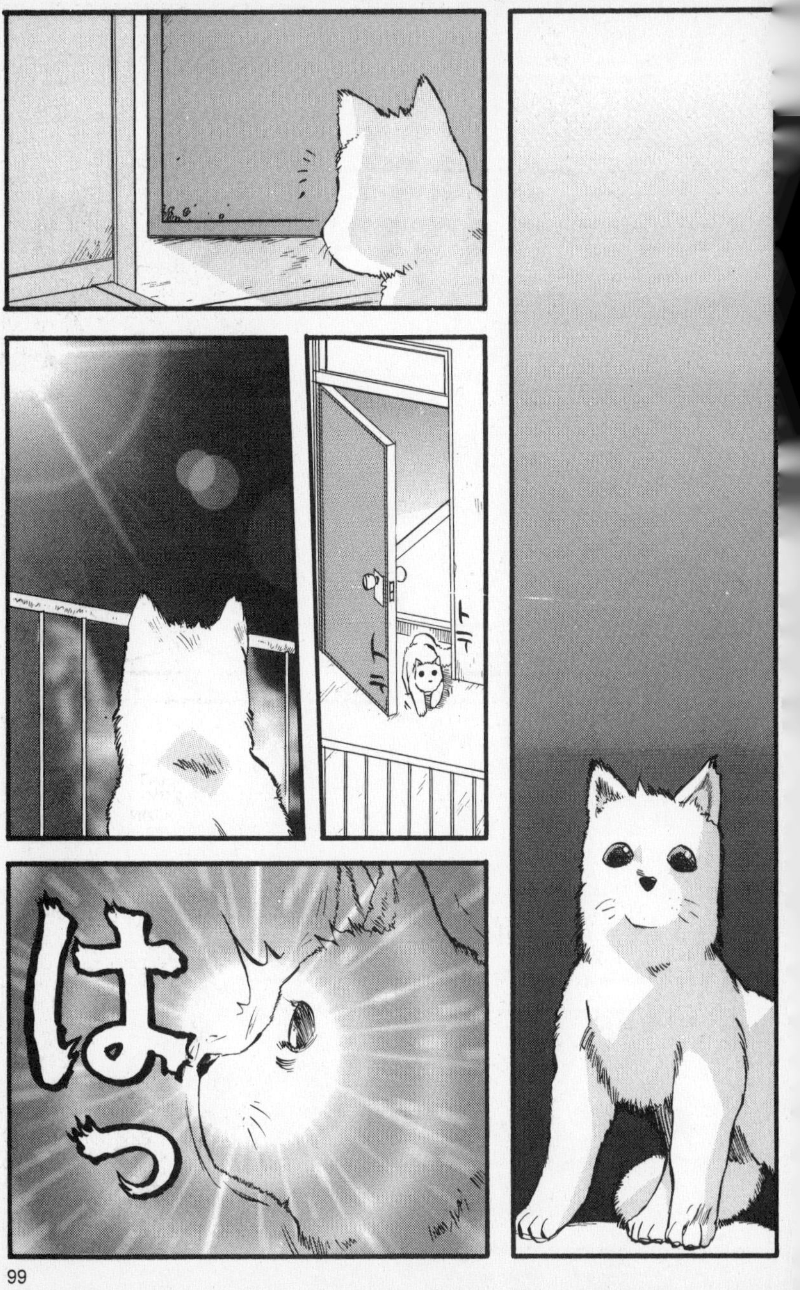
トテ
トテ
はっ

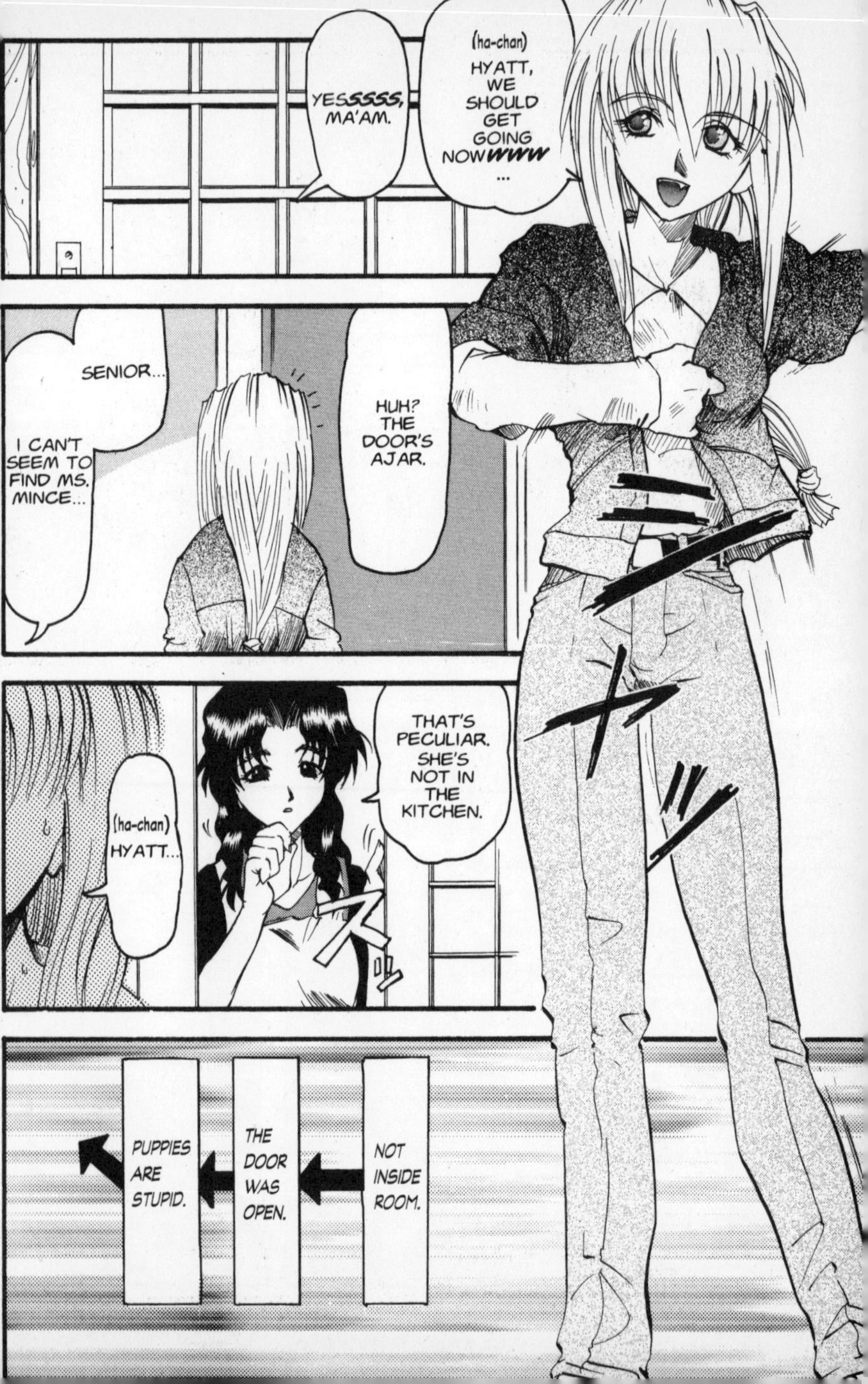
(ha-chan) HYATT, WE SHOULD GET GOING NOWWWW...
YESSSSS, MA'AM.
HUH? THE DOOR'S AJAR.
SENIOR...
I CAN'T SEEM TO FIND MS. MINCE...
THAT'S PECULIAR. SHE'S NOT IN THE KITCHEN.
(ha-chan) HYATT...
NOT INSIDE ROOM.
THE DOOR WAS OPEN.
PUPPIES ARE STUPID.

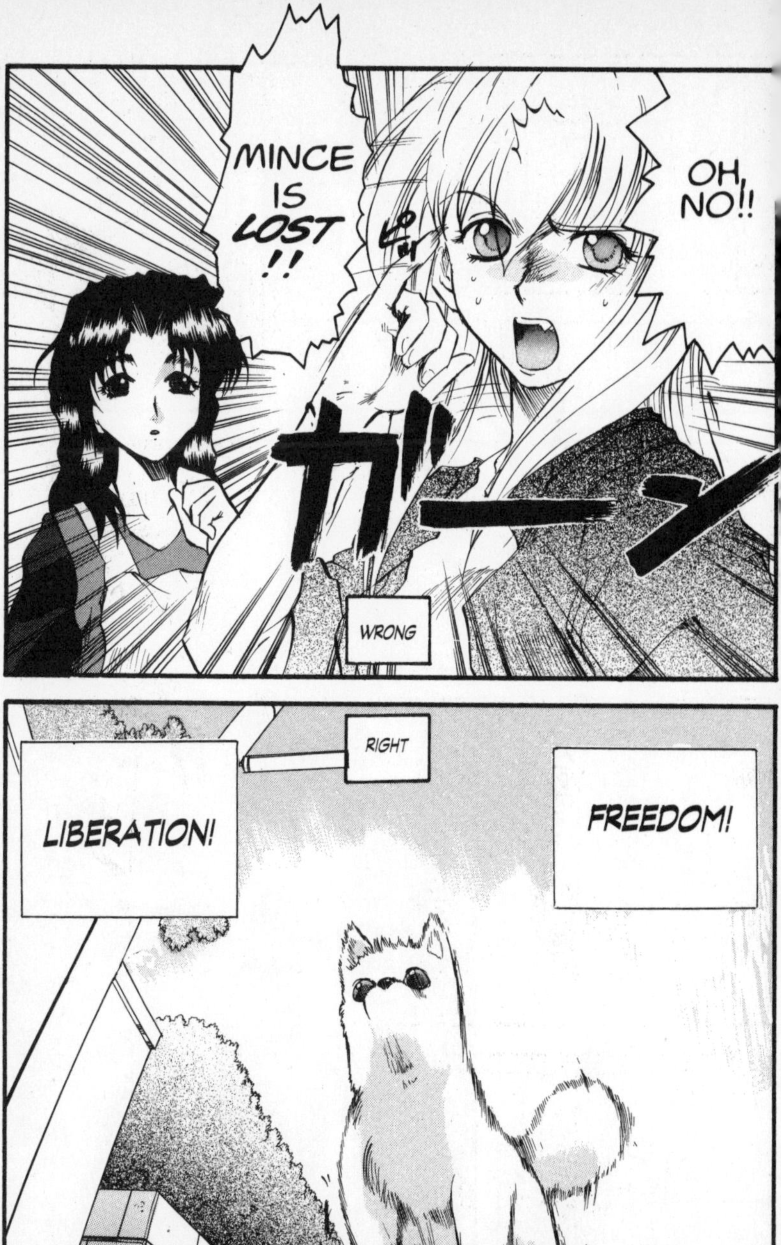
OH, NO!!
MINCE IS LOST!!
ガーン
WRONG
RIGHT
FREEDOM!
LIBERATION!

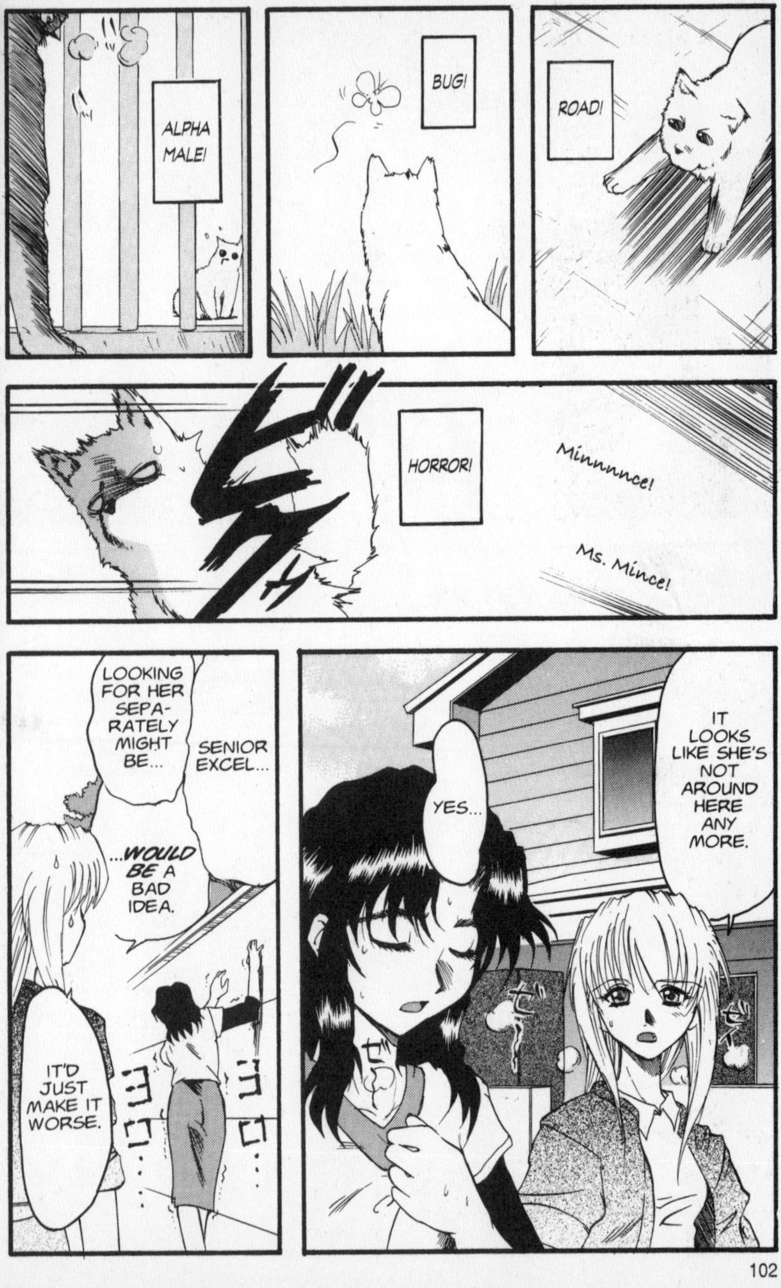
ROAD!
BUG!
ALPHA MALE!
Minnnnnce!
Ms. Mince!
HORROR!
IT LOOKS LIKE SHE'S NOT AROUND HERE ANY MORE.
YES...
SENIOR EXCEL...
LOOKING FOR HER SEPA-RATELY MIGHT BE...
...*WOULD BE* A BAD IDEA.
IT'D JUST MAKE IT WORSE.

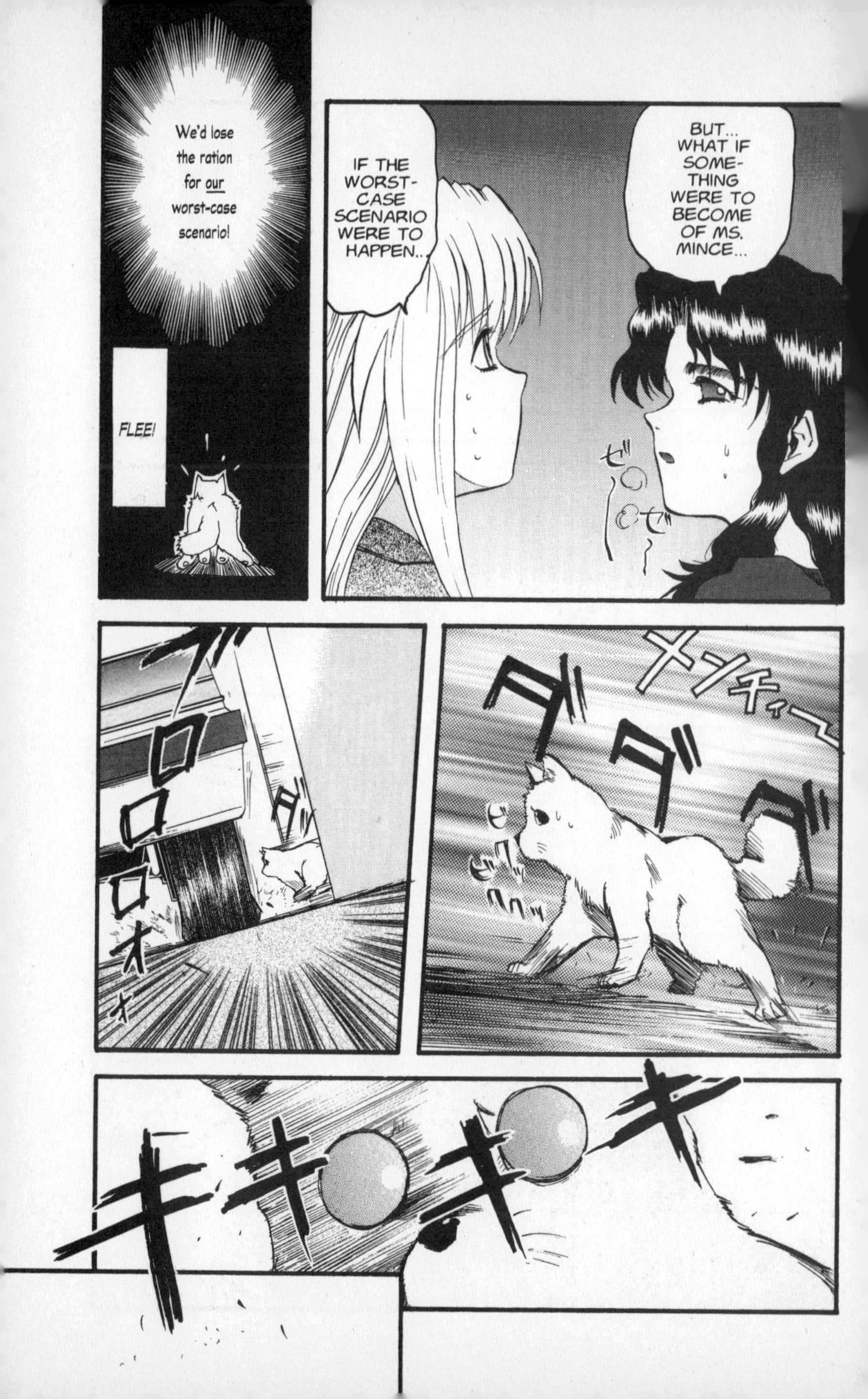
BUT... WHAT IF SOMETHING WERE TO BECOME OF MS. MINCE...
IF THE WORST-CASE SCENARIO WERE TO HAPPEN..
We'd lose the ration for our worst-case scenario!
FLEE!

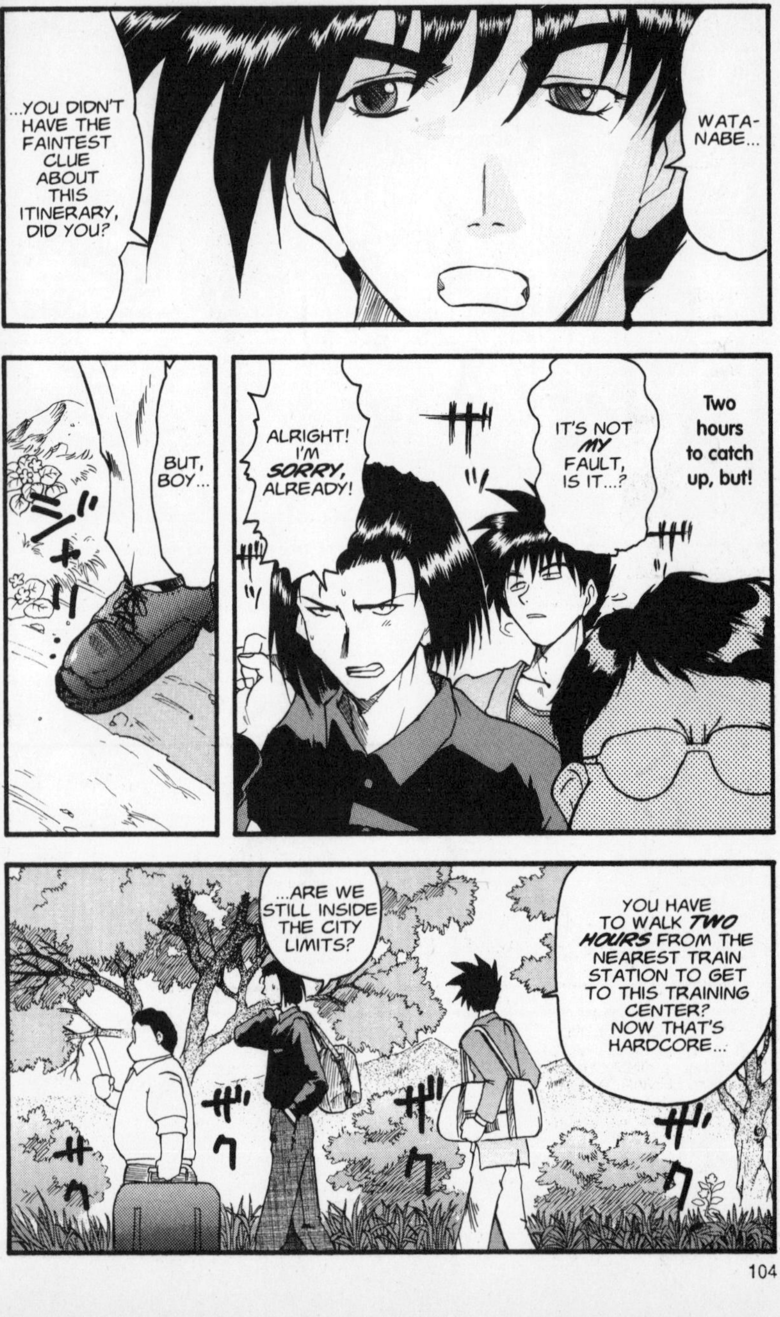

WATA-NABE...
...YOU DIDN'T HAVE THE FAINTEST CLUE ABOUT THIS ITINERARY, DID YOU?
Two hours to catch up, but!
IT'S NOT *MY* FAULT, IS IT...?
ALRIGHT! I'M *SORRY*, ALREADY!
BUT, BOY...
YOU HAVE TO WALK *TWO HOURS* FROM THE NEAREST TRAIN STATION TO GET TO THIS TRAINING CENTER? NOW THAT'S HARDCORE...
...ARE WE STILL INSIDE THE CITY LIMITS?
ザク
ザク
ザク
ザク

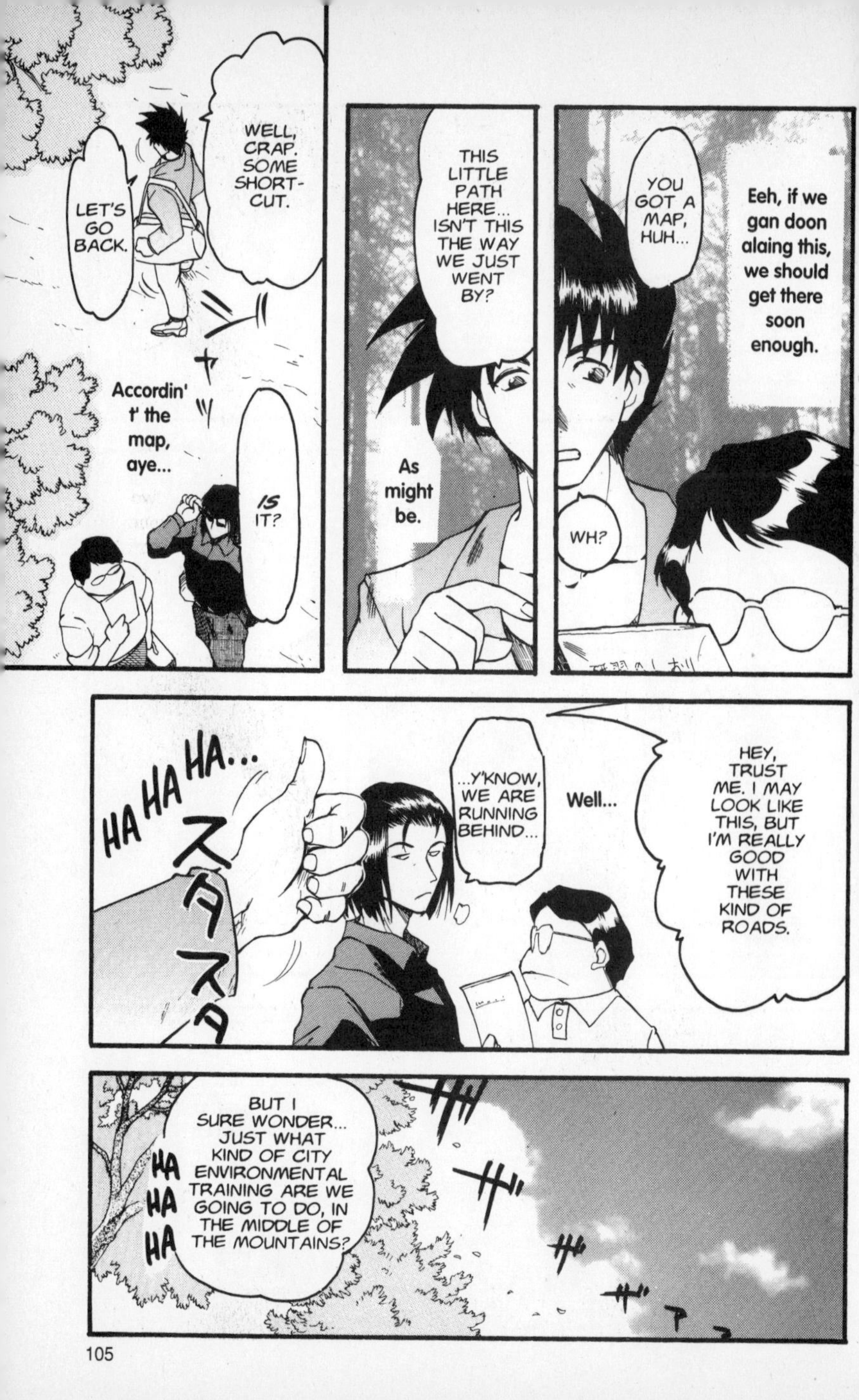
Eeh, if we gan doon alaing this, we should get there soon enough.
YOU GOT A MAP, HUH...
WH?
THIS LITTLE PATH HERE... ISN'T THIS THE WAY WE JUST WENT BY?
As might be.
WELL, CRAP. SOME SHORT-CUT.
LET'S GO BACK.
Accordin' t' the map, aye...
IS IT?
HEY, TRUST ME. I MAY LOOK LIKE THIS, BUT I'M REALLY GOOD WITH THESE KIND OF ROADS.
Well...
...Y'KNOW, WE ARE RUNNING BEHIND...
HA HA HA...
スタスタ
BUT I SURE WONDER... JUST WHAT KIND OF CITY ENVIRONMENTAL TRAINING ARE WE GOING TO DO, IN THE MIDDLE OF THE MOUNTAINS?
HA HA HA

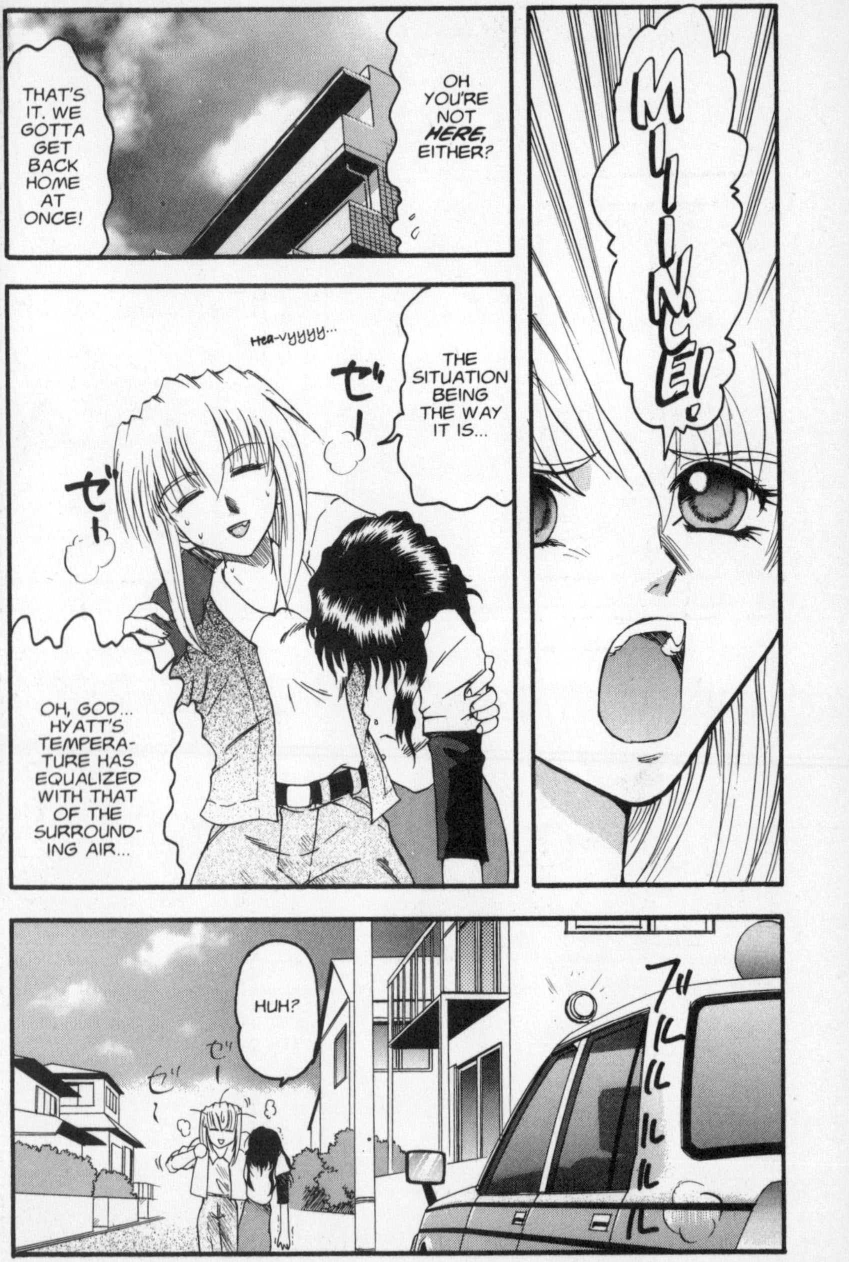
MIIINUE!!
THAT'S IT. WE GOTTA GET BACK HOME AT ONCE!
OH YOU'RE NOT *HERE,* EITHER?
THE SITUATION BEING THE WAY IT IS...
Hea-vyyyy...
ゼー
ゼー
OH, GOD... HYATT'S TEMPERATURE HAS EQUALIZED WITH THAT OF THE SURROUNDING AIR...
ブルルルルル
HUH?
ゼー
ゼー

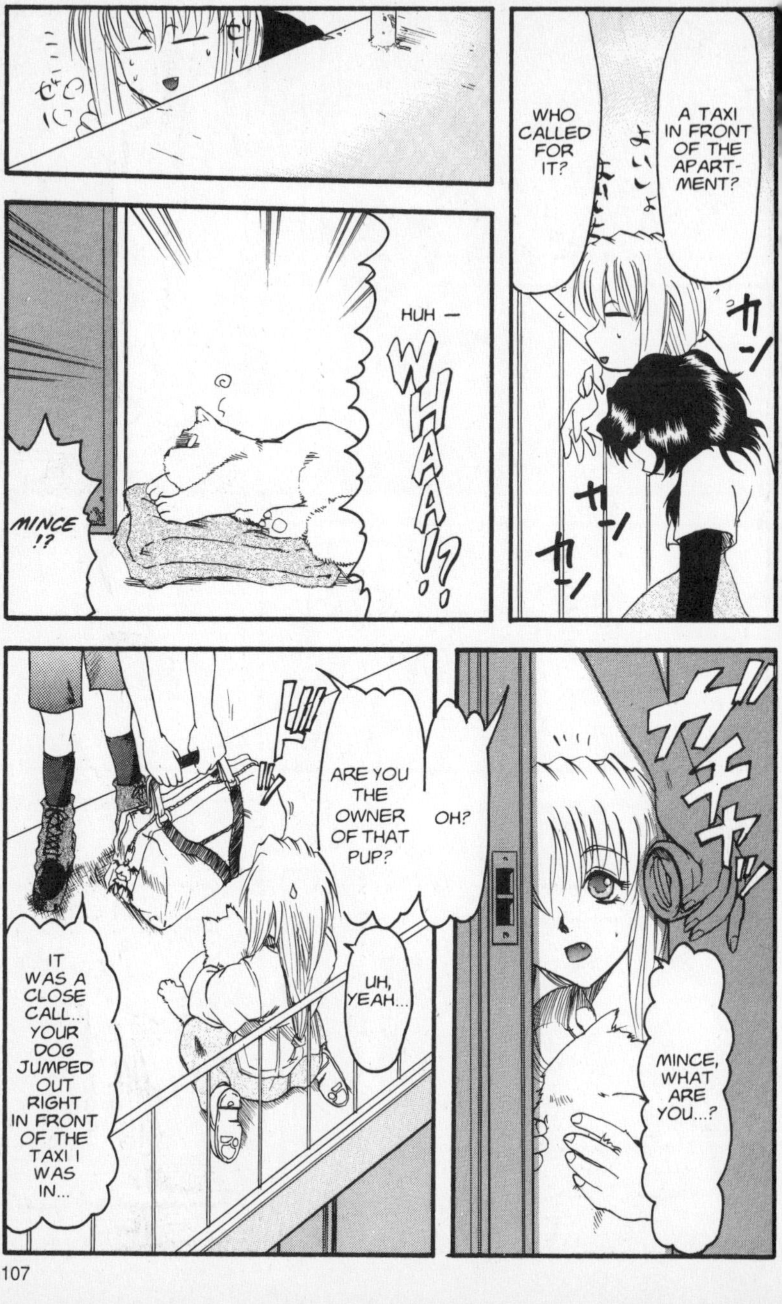
A TAXI IN FRONT OF THE APART-MENT?
WHO CALLED FOR IT?
HUH — WHAAA!!?
MINCE !?
MINCE, WHAT ARE YOU...?
OH?
ARE YOU THE OWNER OF THAT PUP?
UH, YEAH...
IT WAS A CLOSE CALL... YOUR DOG JUMPED OUT RIGHT IN FRONT OF THE TAXI I WAS IN...

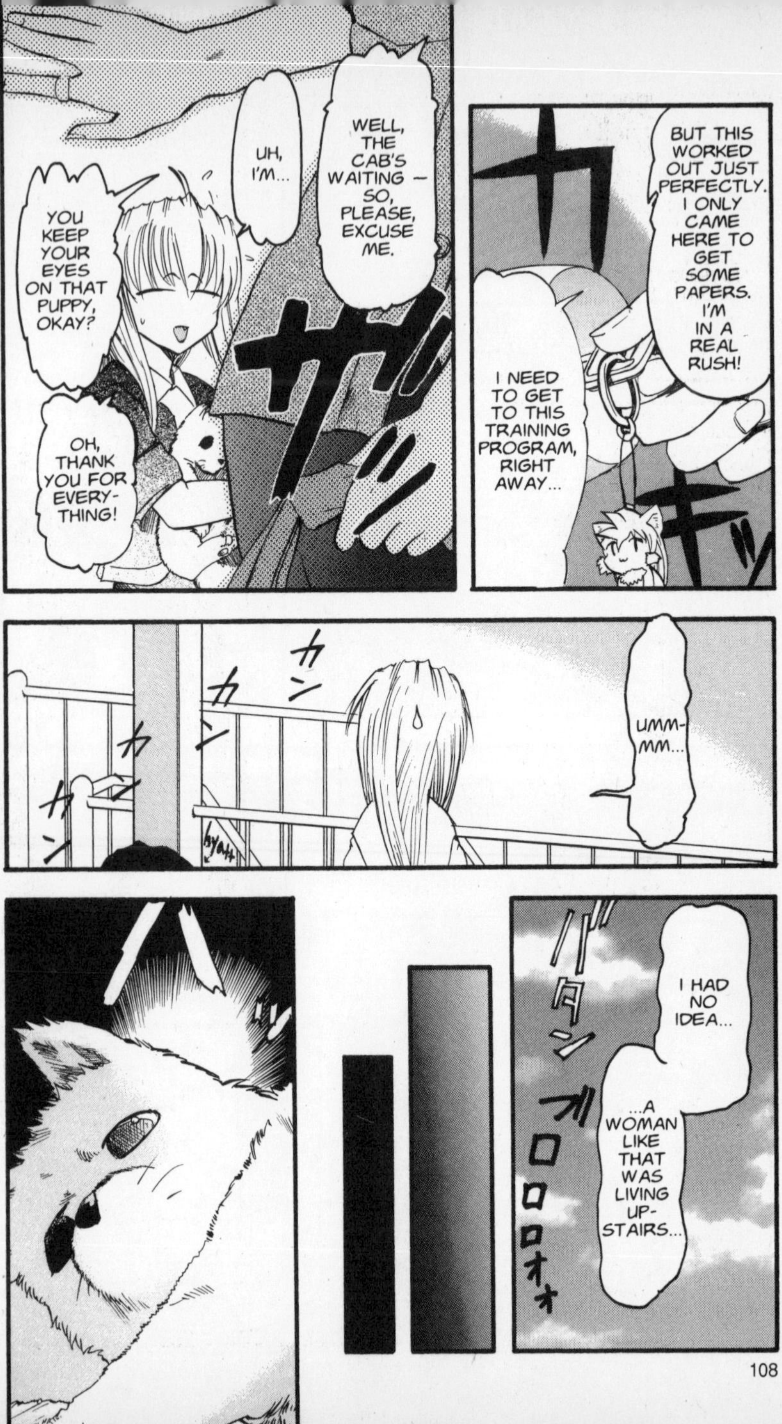
BUT THIS WORKED OUT JUST PERFECTLY. I ONLY CAME HERE TO GET SOME PAPERS. I'M IN A REAL RUSH!
I NEED TO GET TO THIS TRAINING PROGRAM, RIGHT AWAY...
WELL, THE CAB'S WAITING — SO, PLEASE, EXCUSE ME.
UH, I'M...
YOU KEEP YOUR EYES ON THAT PUPPY, OKAY?
OH, THANK YOU FOR EVERY-THING!
UMM-MM...
I HAD NO IDEA...
...A WOMAN LIKE THAT WAS LIVING UP-STAIRS...

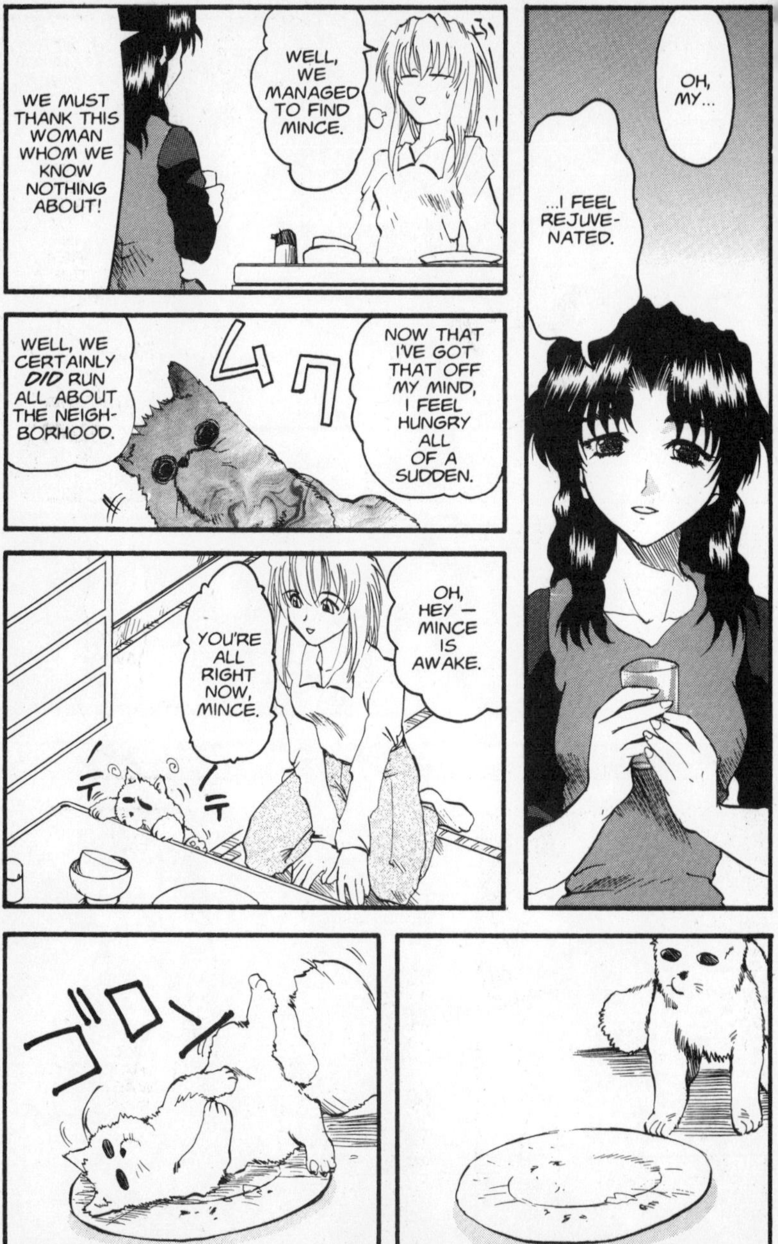
OH, MY...
...I FEEL REJUVENATED.
WELL, WE MANAGED TO FIND MINCE.
WE MUST THANK THIS WOMAN WHOM WE KNOW NOTHING ABOUT!
NOW THAT I'VE GOT THAT OFF MY MIND, I FEEL HUNGRY ALL OF A SUDDEN.
ムク
WELL, WE CERTAINLY *DID* RUN ALL ABOUT THE NEIGHBORHOOD.
OH, HEY — MINCE IS AWAKE.
YOU'RE ALL RIGHT NOW, MINCE.
ゴロン

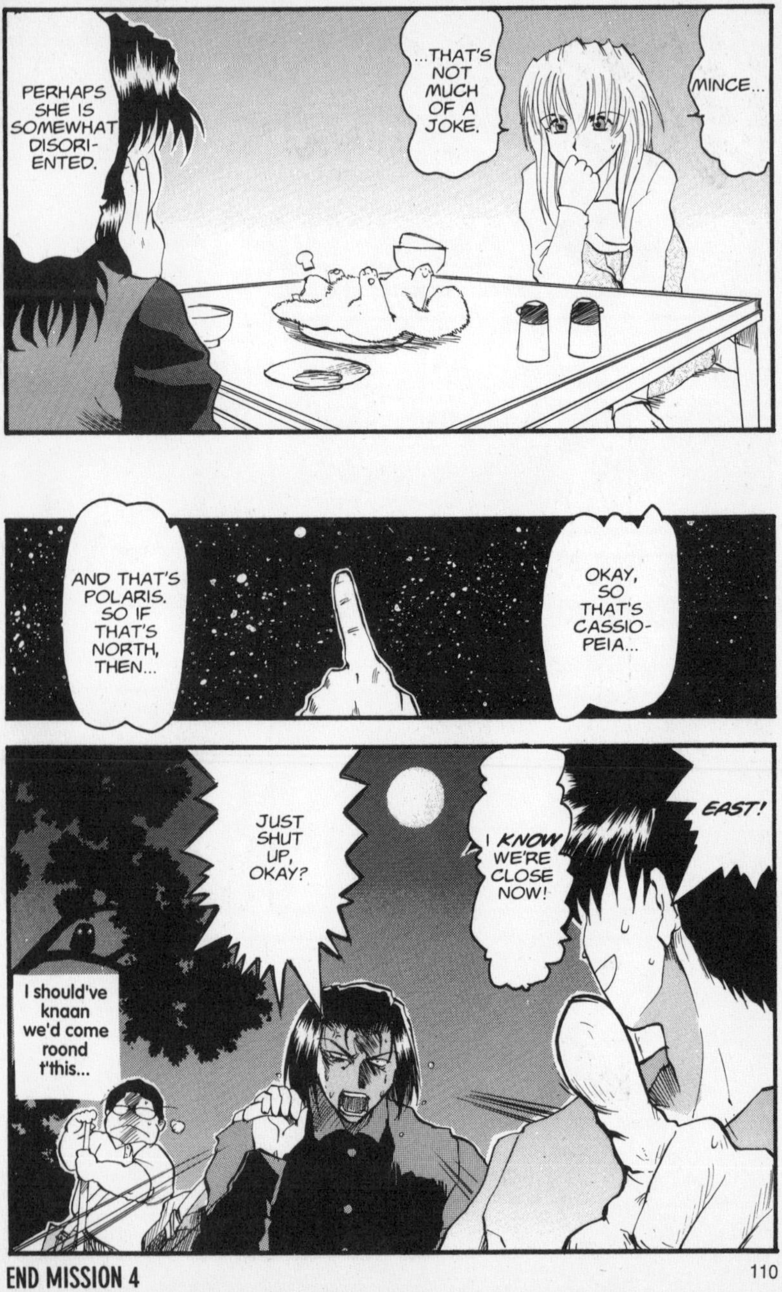
MINCE...
...THAT'S NOT MUCH OF A JOKE.
PERHAPS SHE IS SOMEWHAT DISORIENTED.
OKAY, SO THAT'S CASSIOPEIA...
AND THAT'S POLARIS. SO IF THAT'S NORTH, THEN...
EAST!
I KNOW WE'RE CLOSE NOW!
JUST SHUT UP, OKAY?
I should've knaan we'd come roond t'this...

EXCEL SAGA

SENIOR... PERHAPS I'M READING TOO MUCH INTO THIS, BUT IT SEEMS MS. MINCE'S EYES SHOW A GREAT ESTRANGEMENT...
モキモキ
WELL, THEY SAY INFLICTING STRESS ON AN ANIMAL ENHANCES THE TASTE OF THE LIVER.

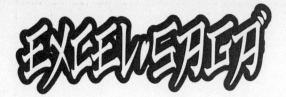

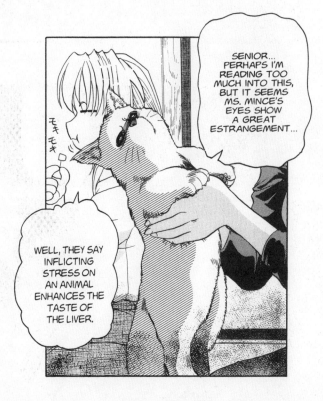

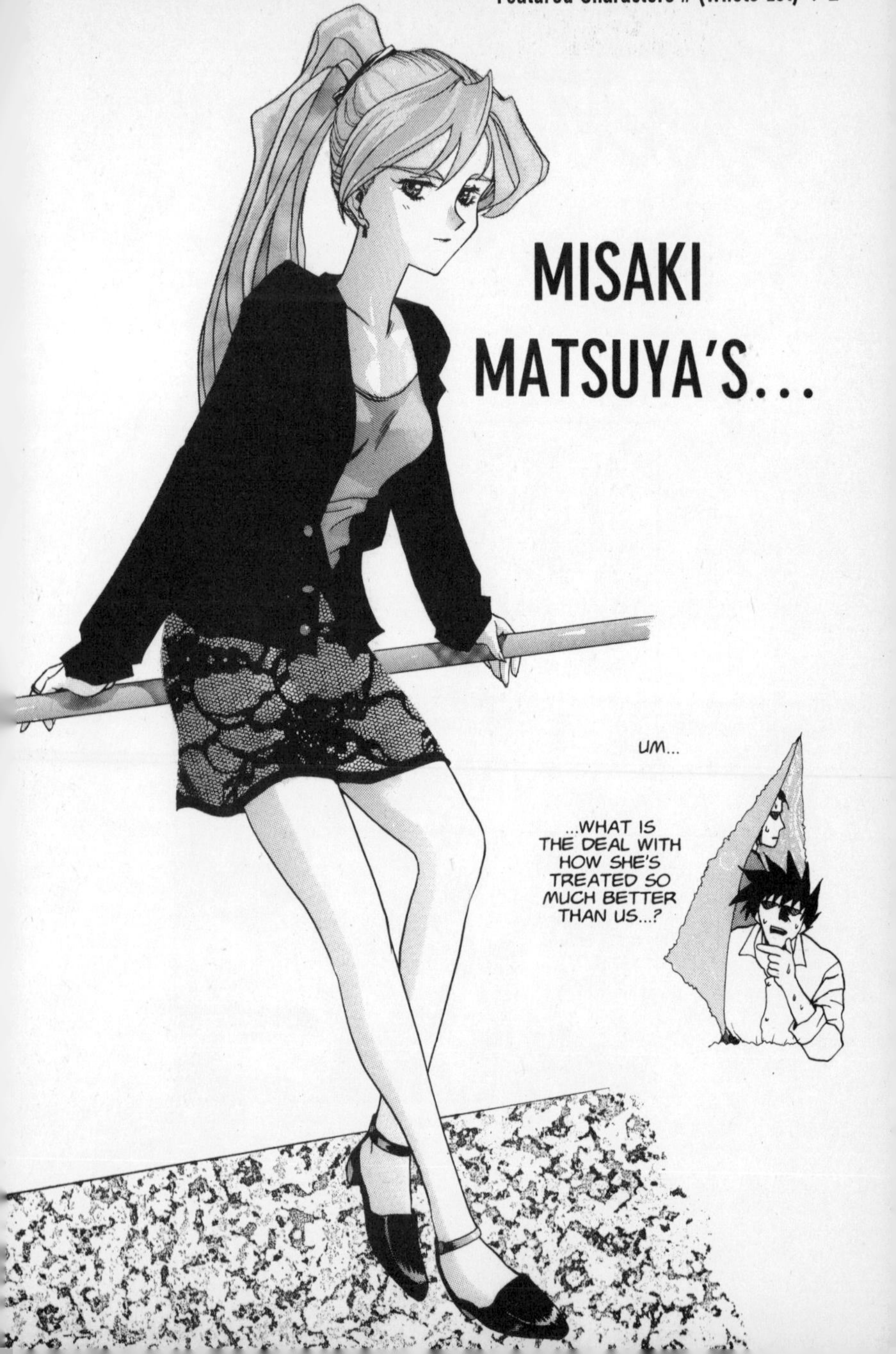
MISAKI MATSUYA'S...
UM...
...WHAT IS THE DEAL WITH HOW SHE'S TREATED SO MUCH BETTER THAN US...?

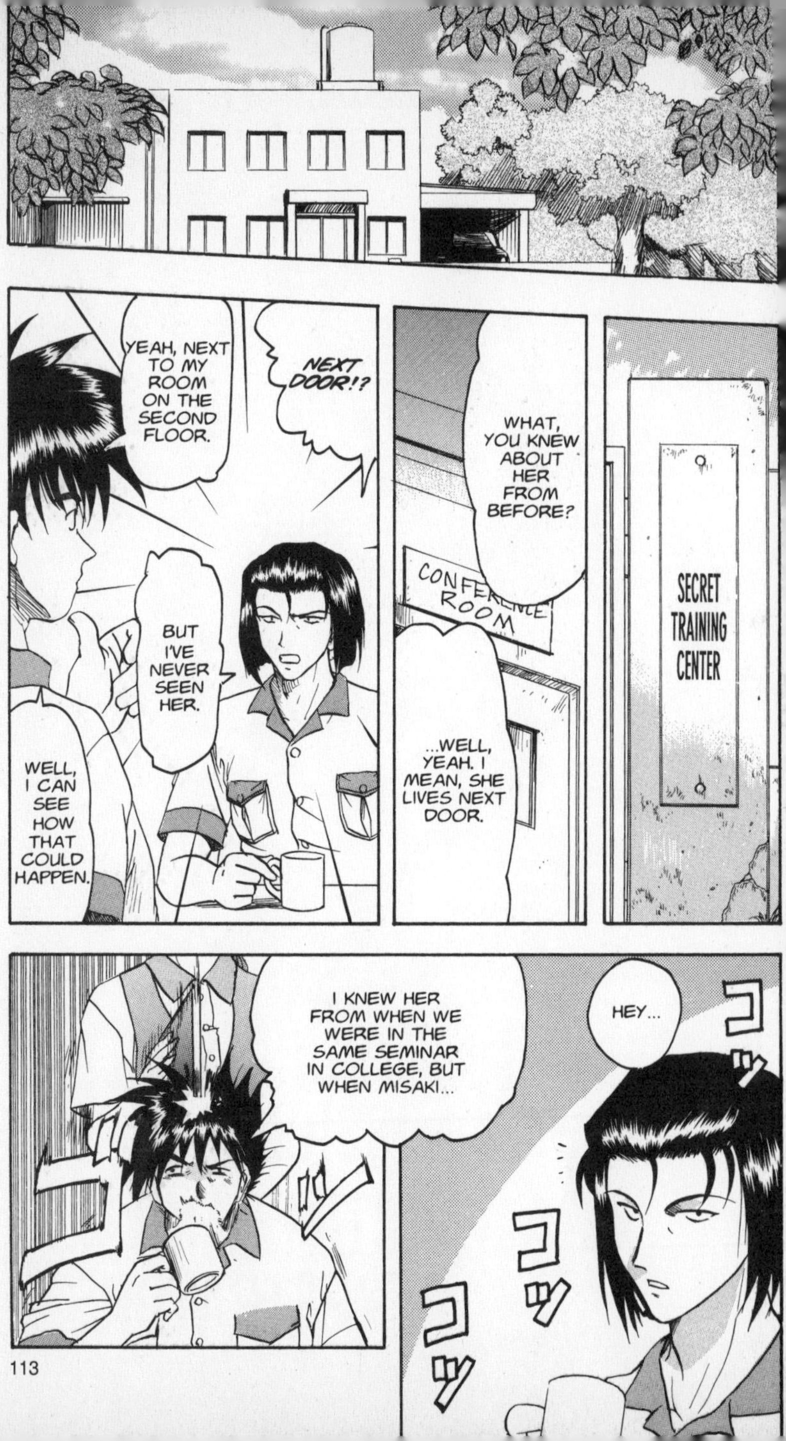

SECRET TRAINING CENTER
WHAT, YOU KNEW ABOUT HER FROM BEFORE?
CONFERENCE ROOM
...WELL, YEAH. I MEAN, SHE LIVES NEXT DOOR.
NEXT DOOR!?
YEAH, NEXT TO MY ROOM ON THE SECOND FLOOR.
BUT I'VE NEVER SEEN HER.
WELL, I CAN SEE HOW THAT COULD HAPPEN.
HEY...
コツ
コツ
コツ
I KNEW HER FROM WHEN WE WERE IN THE SAME SEMINAR IN COLLEGE, BUT WHEN MISAKI...

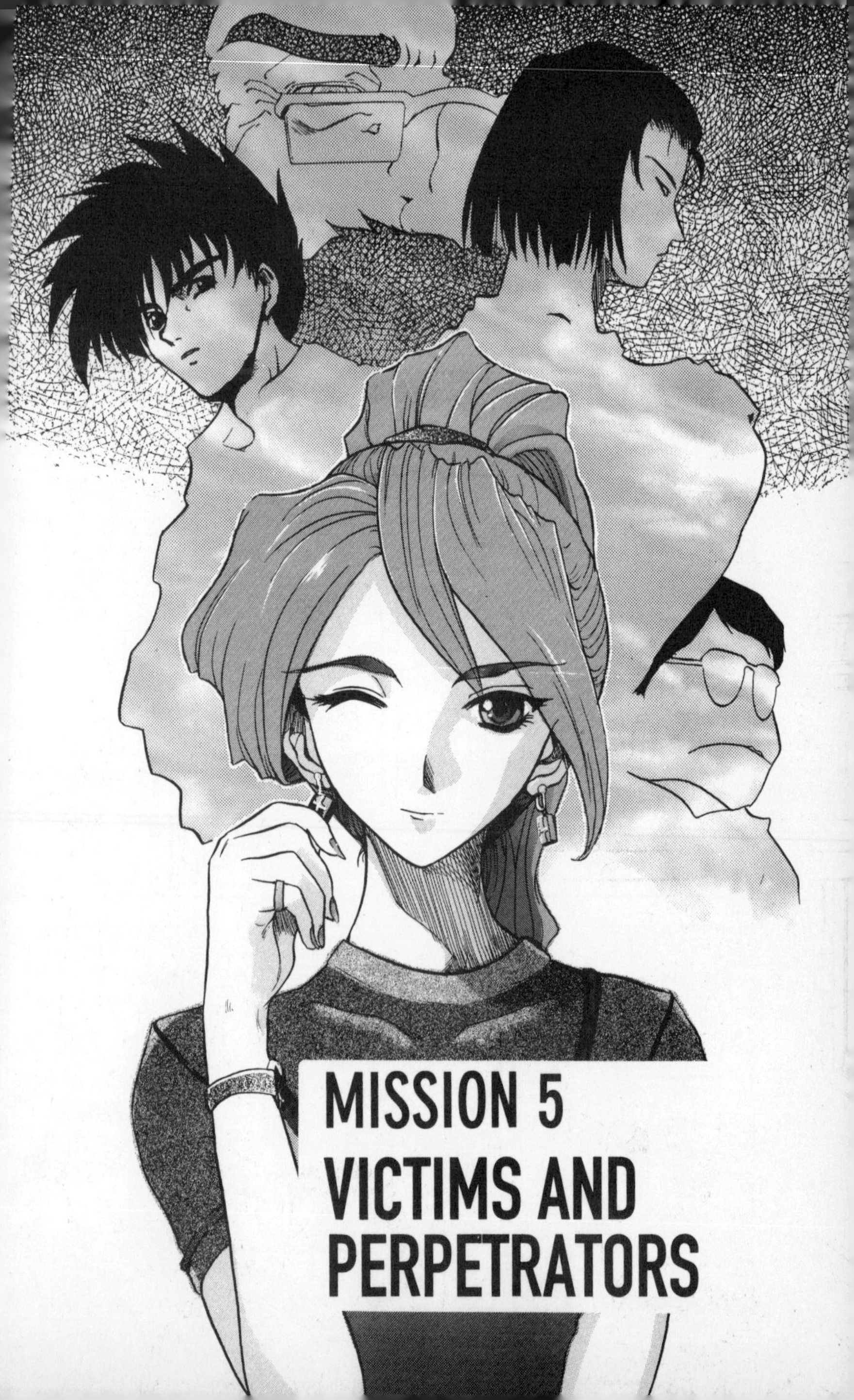
MISSION 5
VICTIMS AND PERPETRATORS

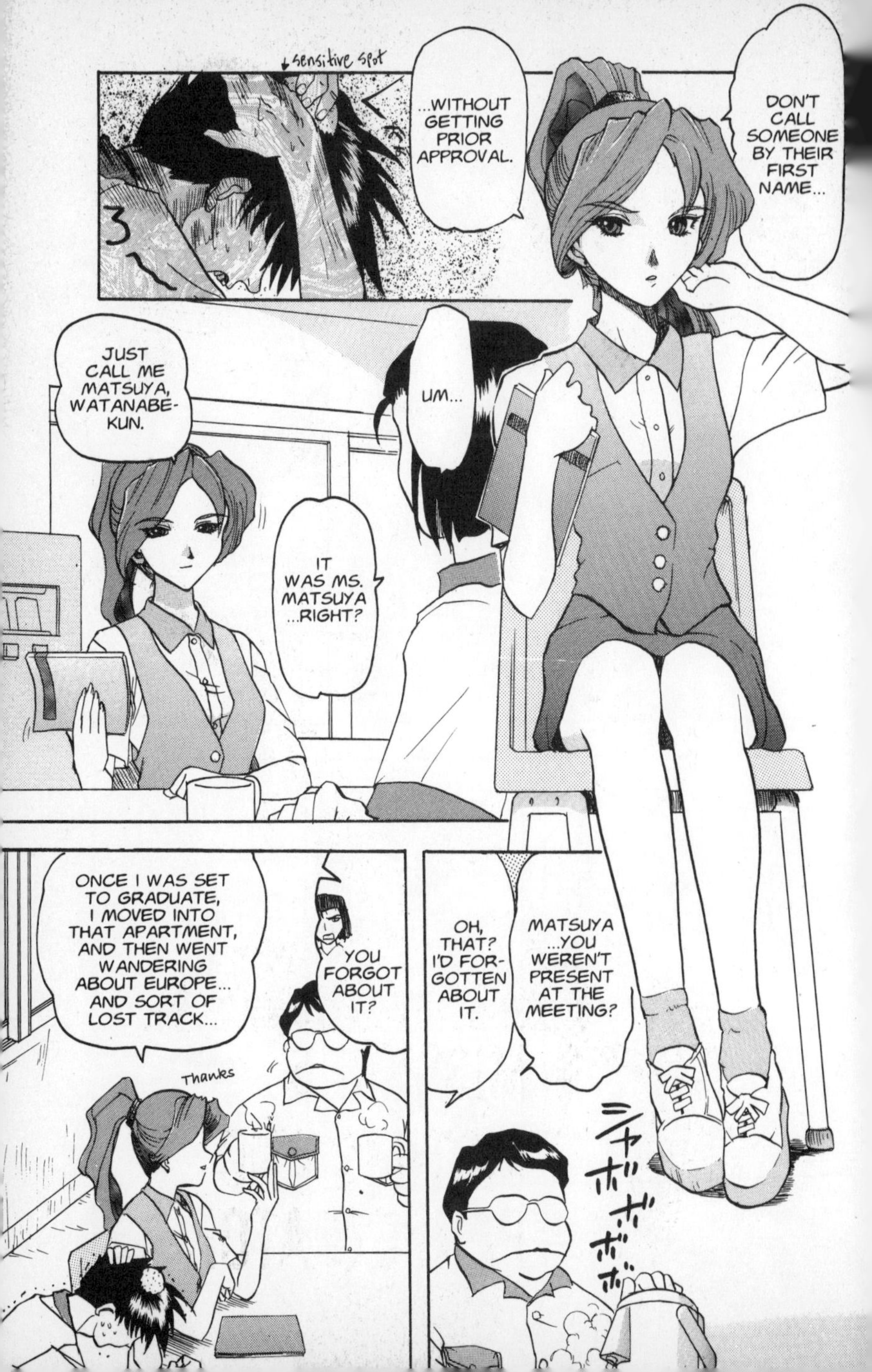
DON'T CALL SOMEONE BY THEIR FIRST NAME...
...WITHOUT GETTING PRIOR APPROVAL.
sensitive spot
UM...
JUST CALL ME MATSUYA, WATANABE-KUN.
IT WAS MS. MATSUYA ...RIGHT?
MATSUYA ...YOU WEREN'T PRESENT AT THE MEETING?
OH, THAT? I'D FORGOTTEN ABOUT IT.
YOU FORGOT ABOUT IT?
ONCE I WAS SET TO GRADUATE, I MOVED INTO THAT APARTMENT, AND THEN WENT WANDERING ABOUT EUROPE... AND SORT OF LOST TRACK...
Thanks

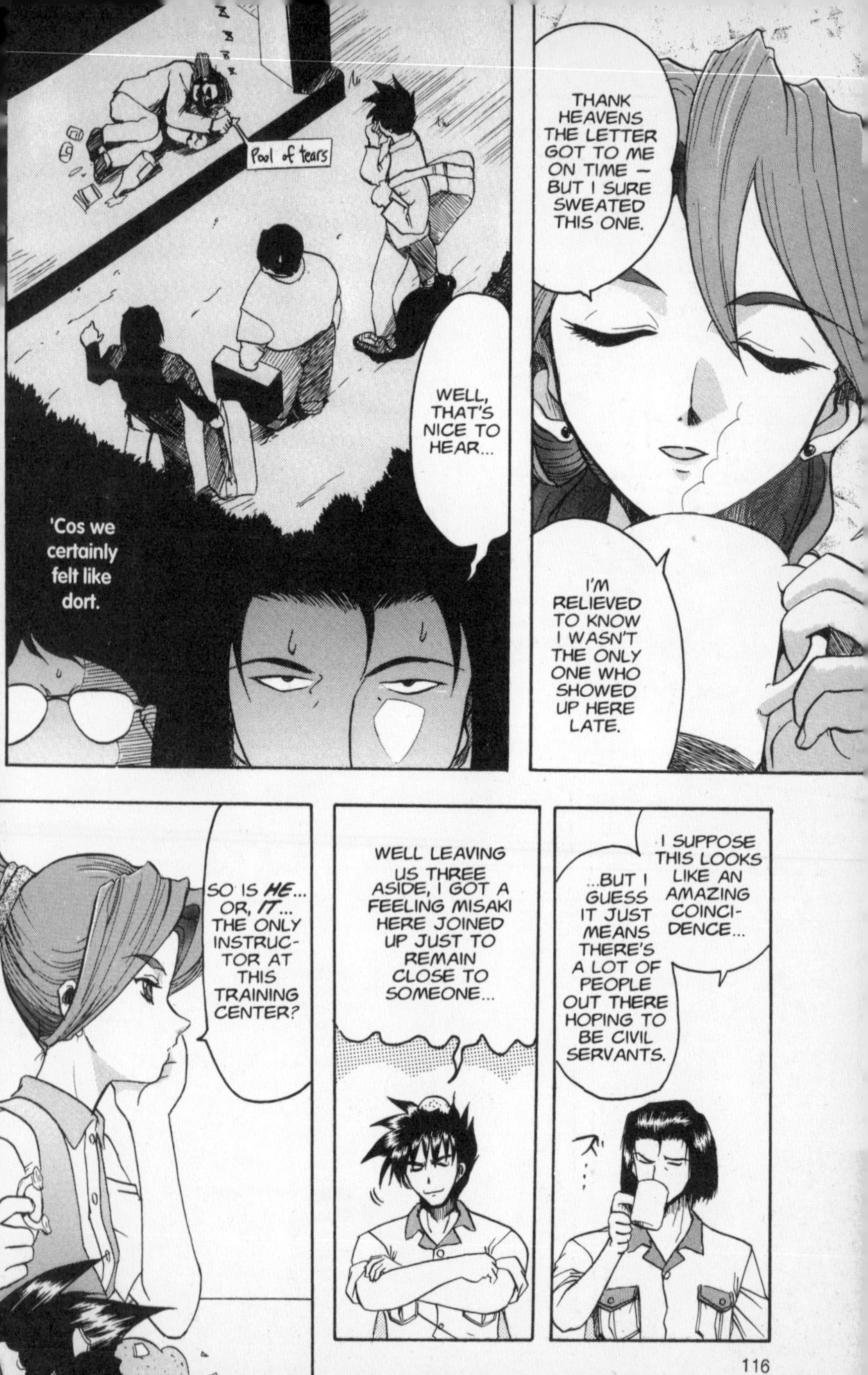
THANK HEAVENS THE LETTER GOT TO ME ON TIME — BUT I SURE SWEATED THIS ONE.
I'M RELIEVED TO KNOW I WASN'T THE ONLY ONE WHO SHOWED UP HERE LATE.
Pool of tears
WELL, THAT'S NICE TO HEAR...
'Cos we certainly felt like dort.
I SUPPOSE THIS LOOKS LIKE AN AMAZING COINCI-DENCE...
...BUT I GUESS IT JUST MEANS THERE'S A LOT OF PEOPLE OUT THERE HOPING TO BE CIVIL SERVANTS.
WELL LEAVING US THREE ASIDE, I GOT A FEELING MISAKI HERE JOINED UP JUST TO REMAIN CLOSE TO SOMEONE...
SO IS *HE*... OR, *IT*... THE ONLY INSTRUC-TOR AT THIS TRAINING CENTER?

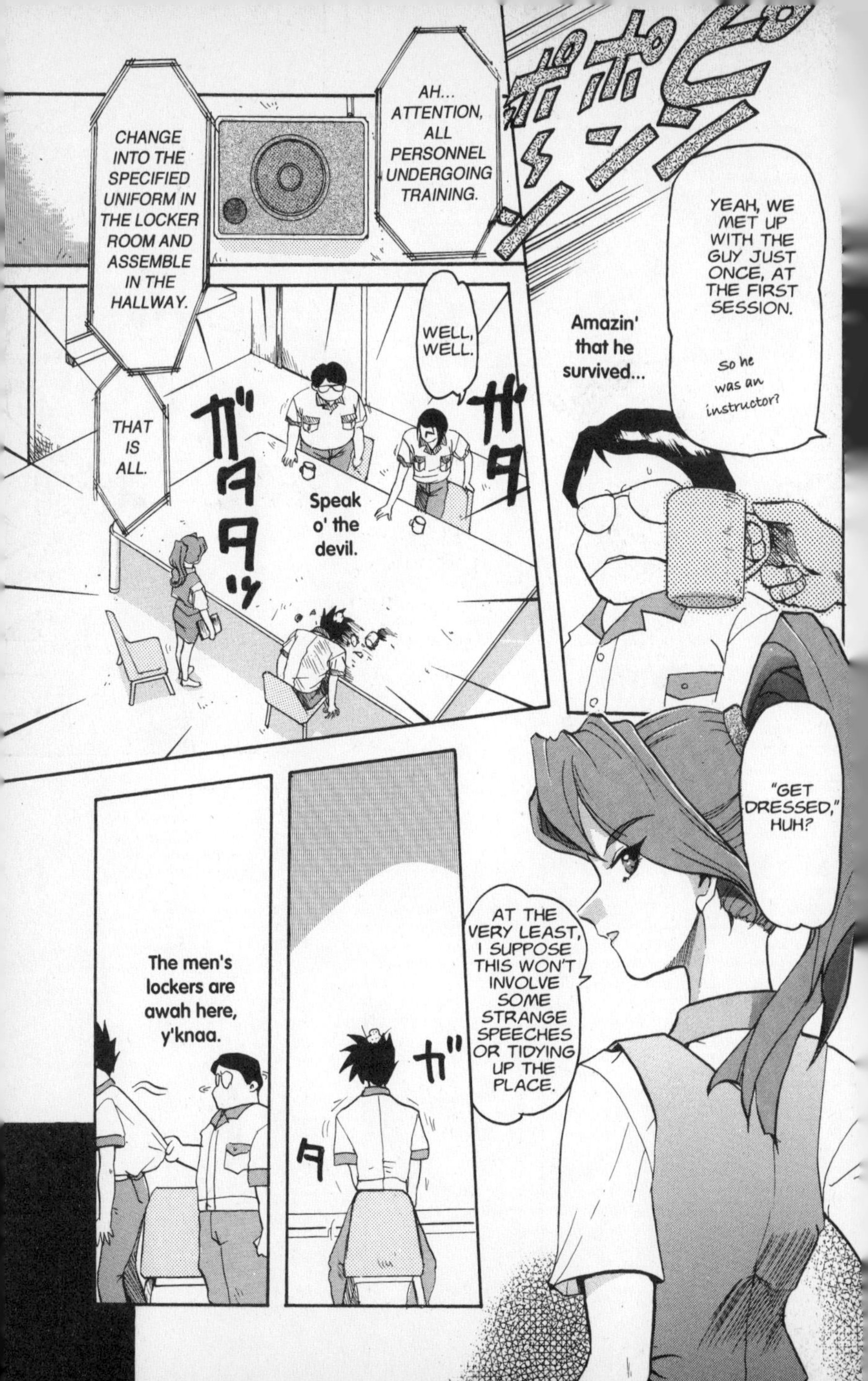
ポポピ〜ン
YEAH, WE MET UP WITH THE GUY JUST ONCE, AT THE FIRST SESSION.
So he was an instructor?
Amazin' that he survived...
AH... ATTENTION, ALL PERSONNEL UNDERGOING TRAINING.
CHANGE INTO THE SPECIFIED UNIFORM IN THE LOCKER ROOM AND ASSEMBLE IN THE HALLWAY.
WELL, WELL.
ガタ
THAT IS ALL.
ガタタッ
Speak o' the devil.
"GET DRESSED," HUH?
AT THE VERY LEAST, I SUPPOSE THIS WON'T INVOLVE SOME STRANGE SPEECHES OR TIDYING UP THE PLACE.
ガ
タ
The men's lockers are awah here, y'knaa.

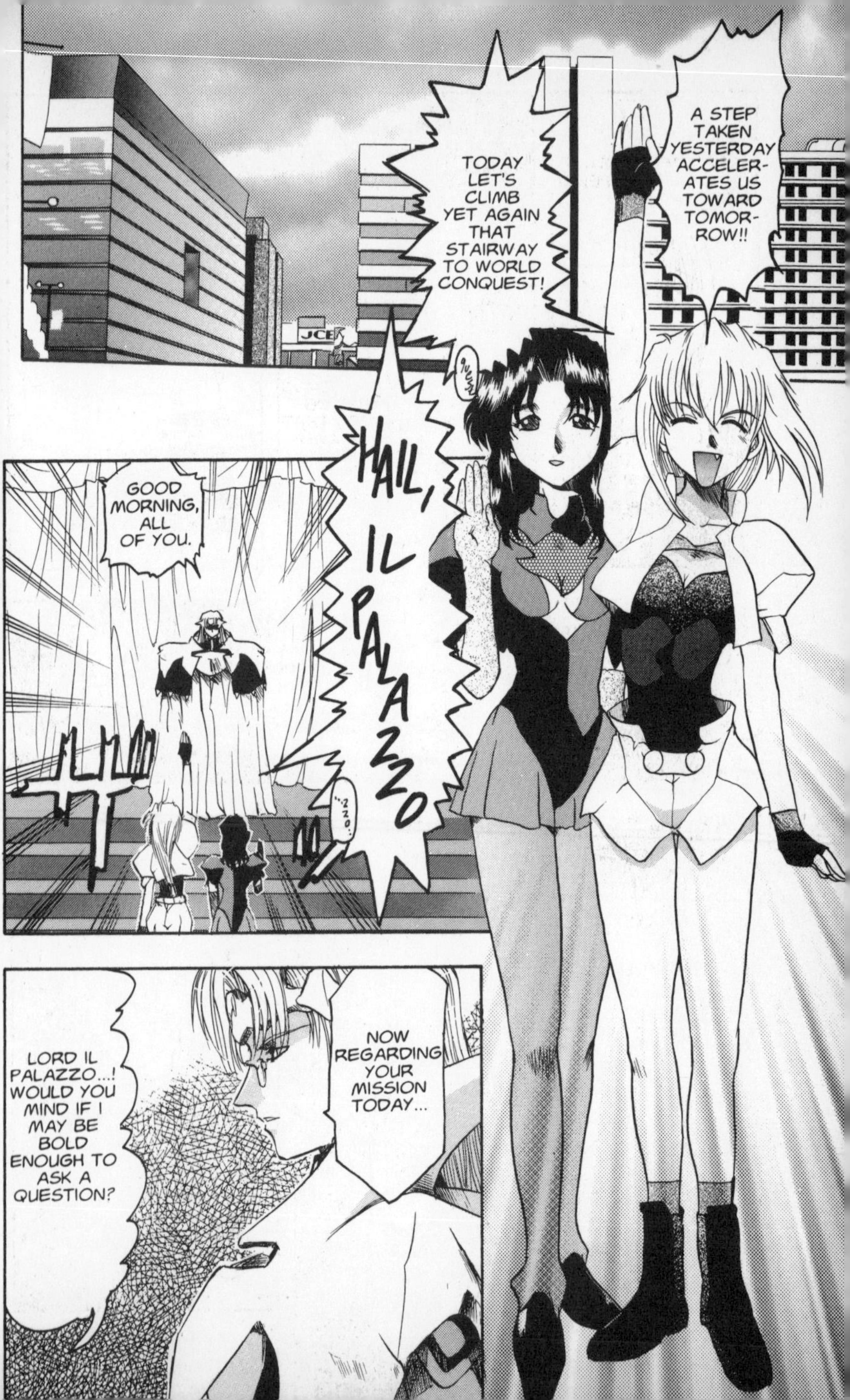
A STEP TAKEN YESTERDAY ACCELERATES US TOWARD TOMORROW!!
TODAY LET'S CLIMB YET AGAIN THAT STAIRWAY TO WORLD CONQUEST!
guess
HAIL, IL PALAZZO
...zzo...
GOOD MORNING, ALL OF YOU.
NOW REGARDING YOUR MISSION TODAY...
LORD IL PALAZZO...! WOULD YOU MIND IF I MAY BE BOLD ENOUGH TO ASK A QUESTION?

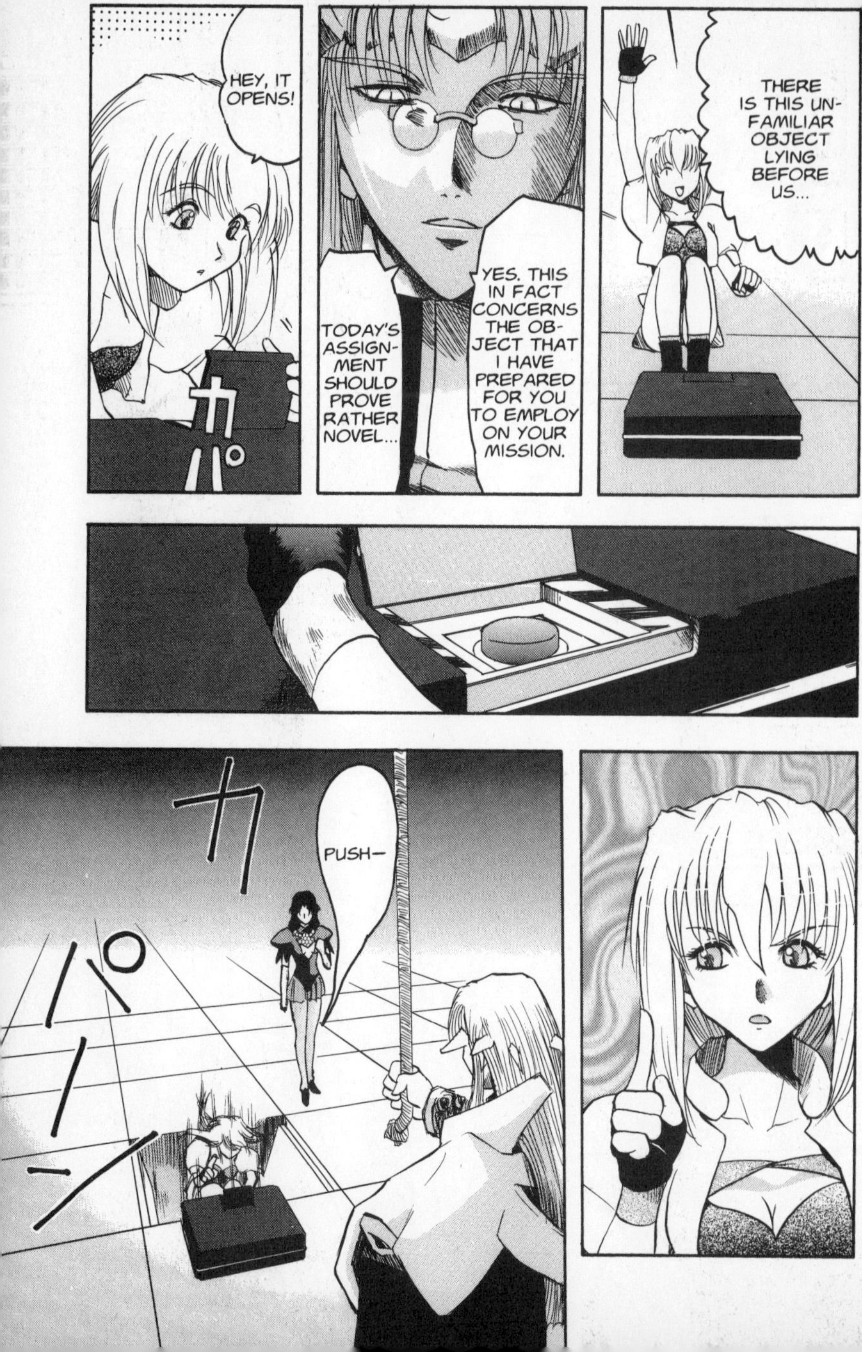
THERE IS THIS UN-FAMILIAR OBJECT LYING BEFORE US...
YES. THIS IN FACT CONCERNS THE OB-JECT THAT I HAVE PREPARED FOR YOU TO EMPLOY ON YOUR MISSION.
TODAY'S ASSIGN-MENT SHOULD PROVE RATHER NOVEL...
HEY, IT OPENS!
カパ
PUSH—
カパーン

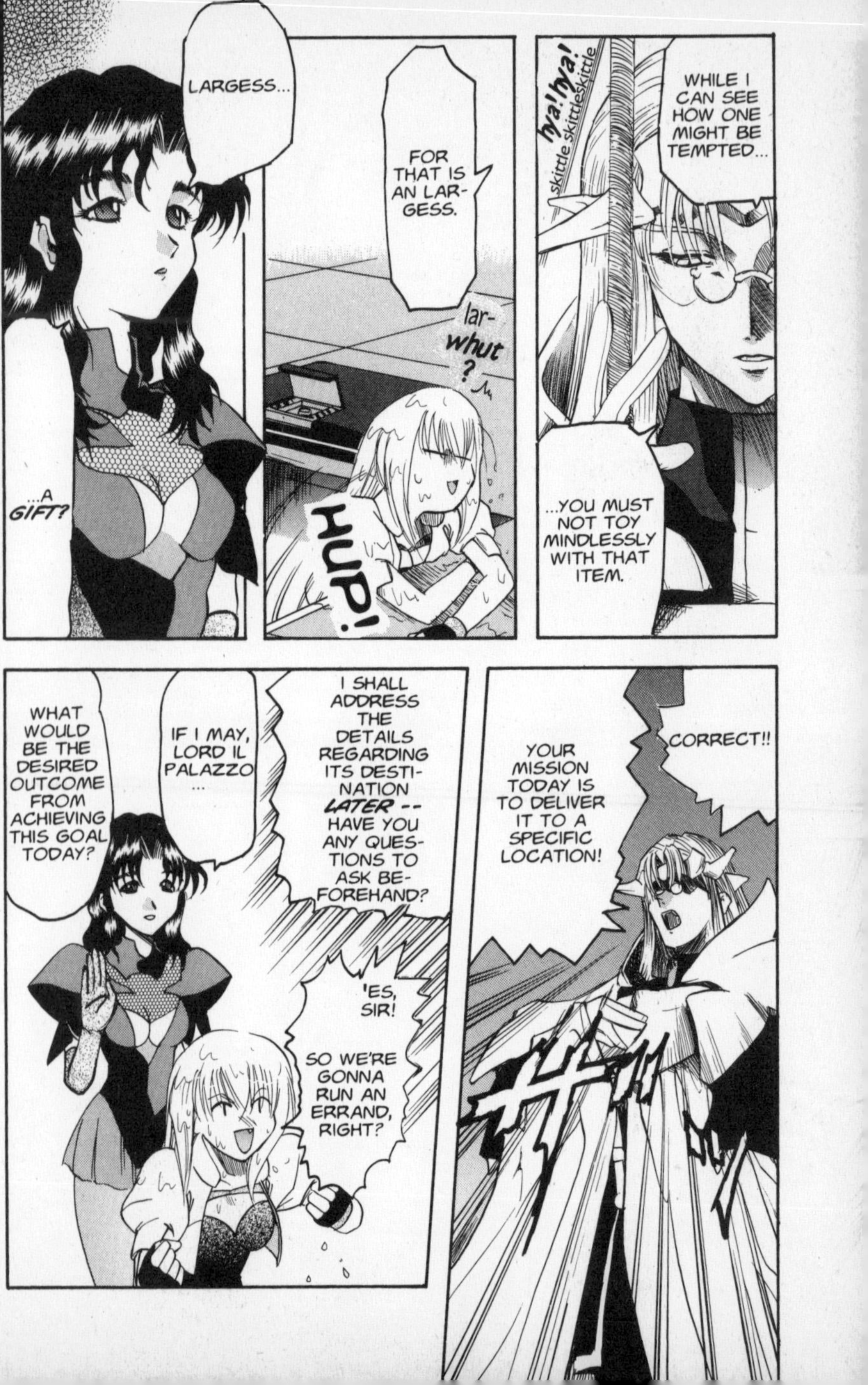

WHILE I CAN SEE HOW ONE MIGHT BE TEMPTED...
hya! hya! skittle skittleskittle
...YOU MUST NOT TOY MINDLESSLY WITH THAT ITEM.
FOR THAT IS AN LARGESS.
lar-whut?
HUP!
LARGESS...
...A GIFT?
CORRECT!!
YOUR MISSION TODAY IS TO DELIVER IT TO A SPECIFIC LOCATION!
I SHALL ADDRESS THE DETAILS REGARDING ITS DESTINATION LATER -- HAVE YOU ANY QUESTIONS TO ASK BEFOREHAND?
'ES, SIR!
SO WE'RE GONNA RUN AN ERRAND, RIGHT?
IF I MAY, LORD IL PALAZZO...
WHAT WOULD BE THE DESIRED OUTCOME FROM ACHIEVING THIS GOAL TODAY?

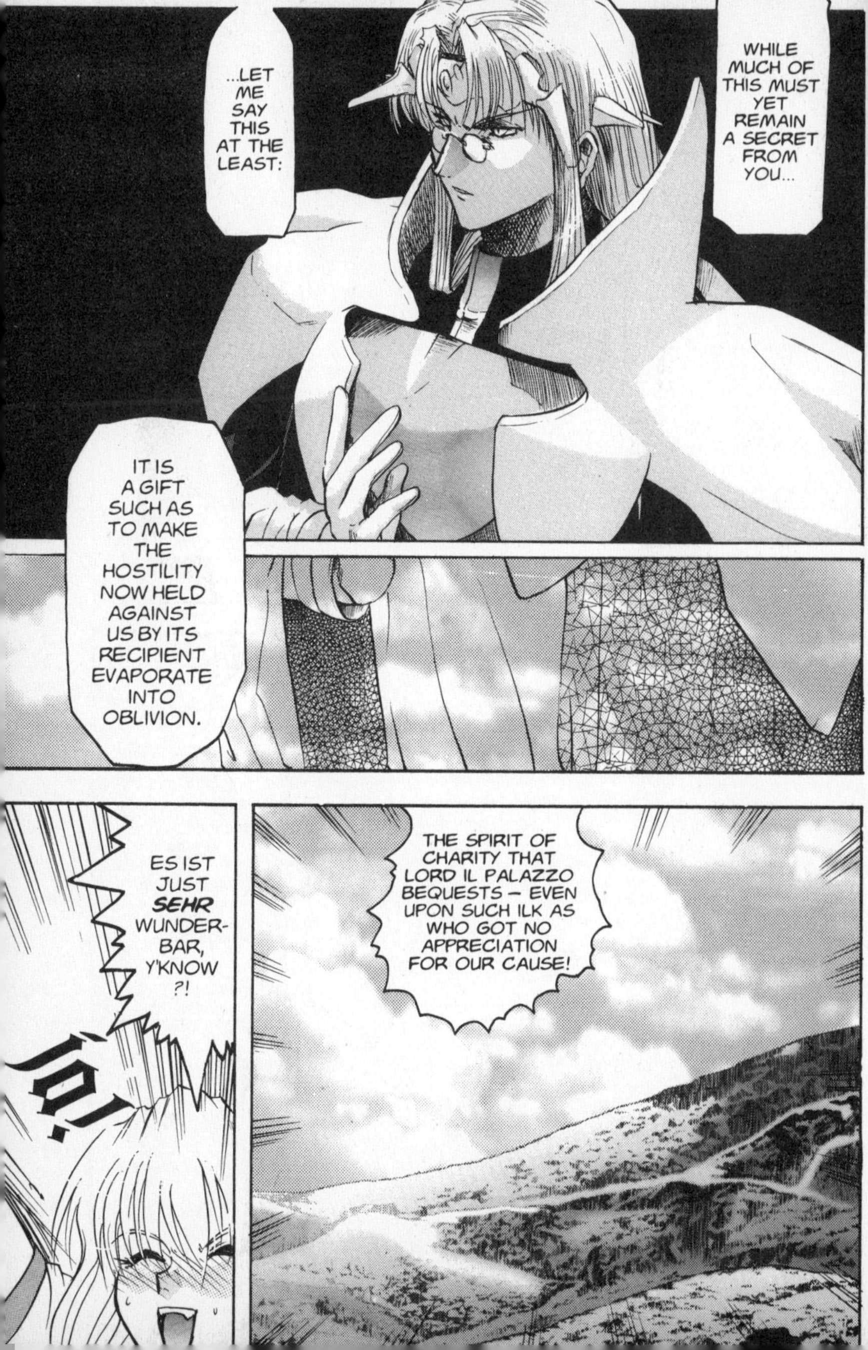
WHILE MUCH OF THIS MUST YET REMAIN A SECRET FROM YOU...
...LET ME SAY THIS AT THE LEAST:
IT IS A GIFT SUCH AS TO MAKE THE HOSTILITY NOW HELD AGAINST US BY ITS RECIPIENT EVAPORATE INTO OBLIVION.
THE SPIRIT OF CHARITY THAT LORD IL PALAZZO BEQUESTS – EVEN UPON SUCH ILK AS WHO GOT NO APPRECIATION FOR OUR CAUSE!
ES IST JUST **SEHR** WUNDER-BAR, Y'KNOW ?!

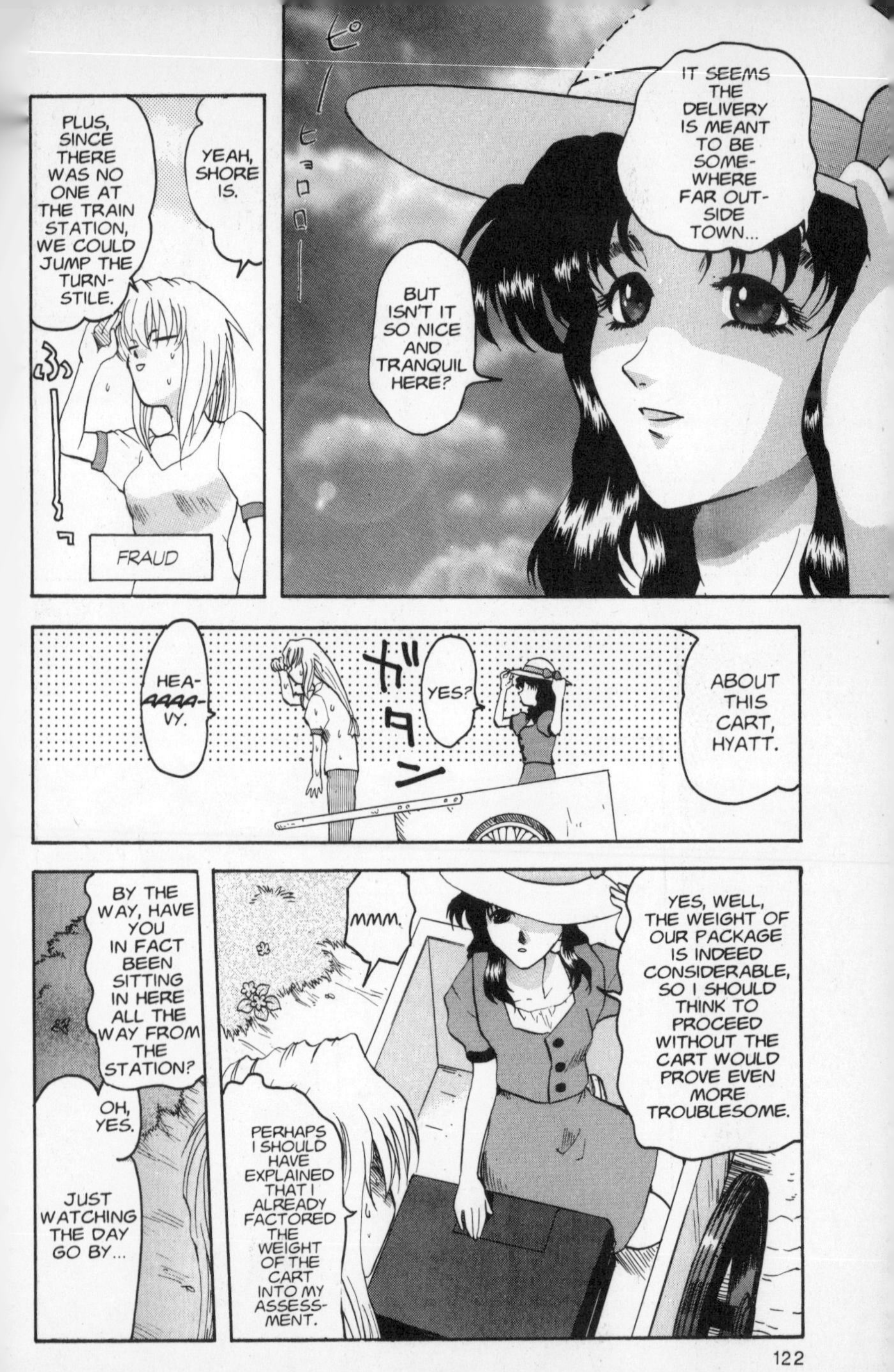
IT SEEMS THE DELIVERY IS MEANT TO BE SOME-WHERE FAR OUT-SIDE TOWN...
ピーヒョロロー
BUT ISN'T IT SO NICE AND TRANQUIL HERE?
YEAH, SHORE IS.
PLUS, SINCE THERE WAS NO ONE AT THE TRAIN STATION, WE COULD JUMP THE TURN-STILE.
FRAUD
ABOUT THIS CART, HYATT.
YES?
ガタン
HEA-AAAA-VY.
YES, WELL, THE WEIGHT OF OUR PACKAGE IS INDEED CONSIDERABLE, SO I SHOULD THINK TO PROCEED WITHOUT THE CART WOULD PROVE EVEN MORE TROUBLESOME.
MMM.
PERHAPS I SHOULD HAVE EXPLAINED THAT I ALREADY FACTORED THE WEIGHT OF THE CART INTO MY ASSESS-MENT.
BY THE WAY, HAVE YOU IN FACT BEEN SITTING IN HERE ALL THE WAY FROM THE STATION?
OH, YES.
JUST WATCHING THE DAY GO BY...

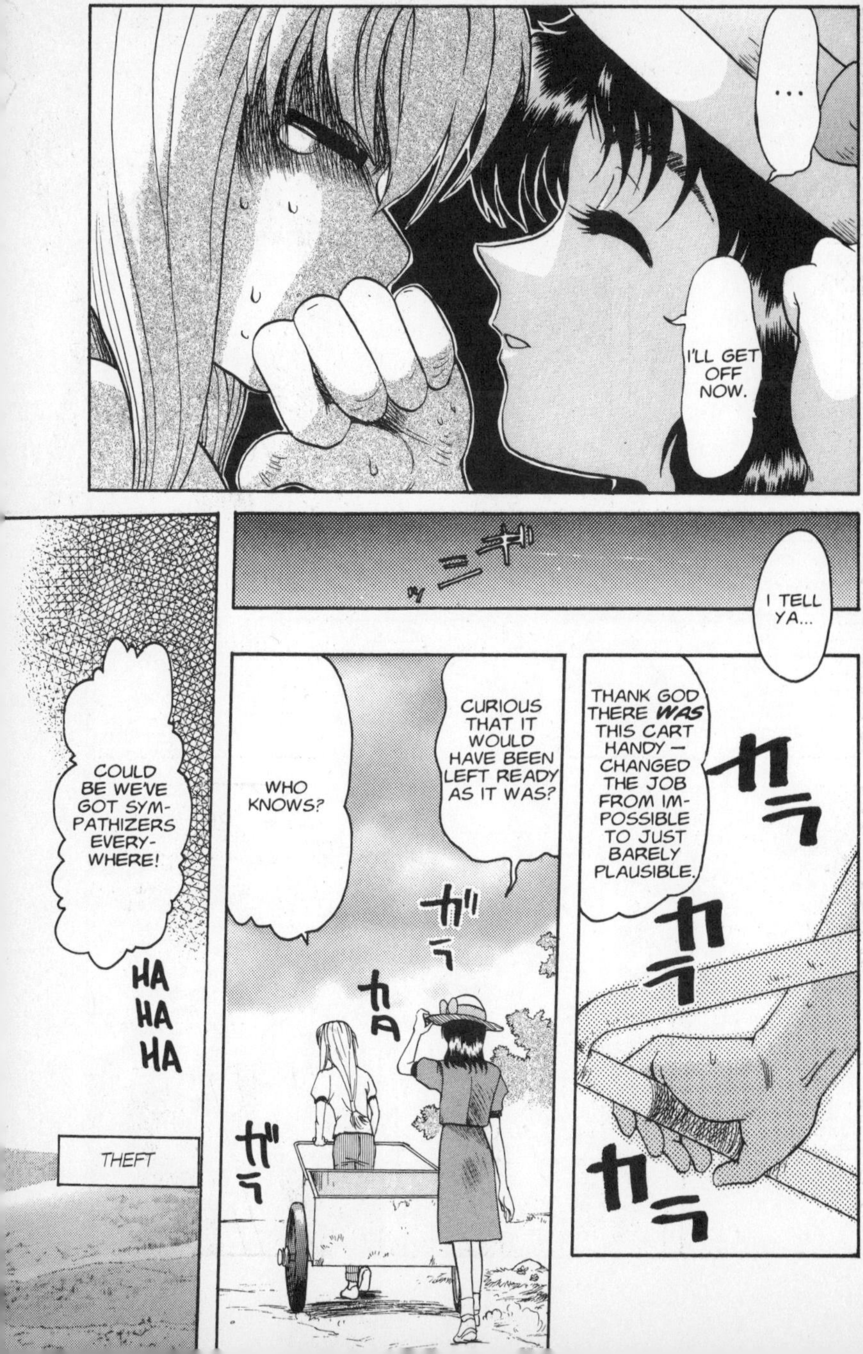

...
I'LL GET OFF NOW.
ギーッ
I TELL YA...
THANK GOD THERE ***WAS*** THIS CART HANDY — CHANGED THE JOB FROM IMPOSSIBLE TO JUST BARELY PLAUSIBLE.
カラ
カラ
カラ
CURIOUS THAT IT WOULD HAVE BEEN LEFT READY AS IT WAS?
WHO KNOWS?
ガラ
カタ
ガラ
COULD BE WE'VE GOT SYMPATHIZERS EVERYWHERE!
HA HA HA
THEFT

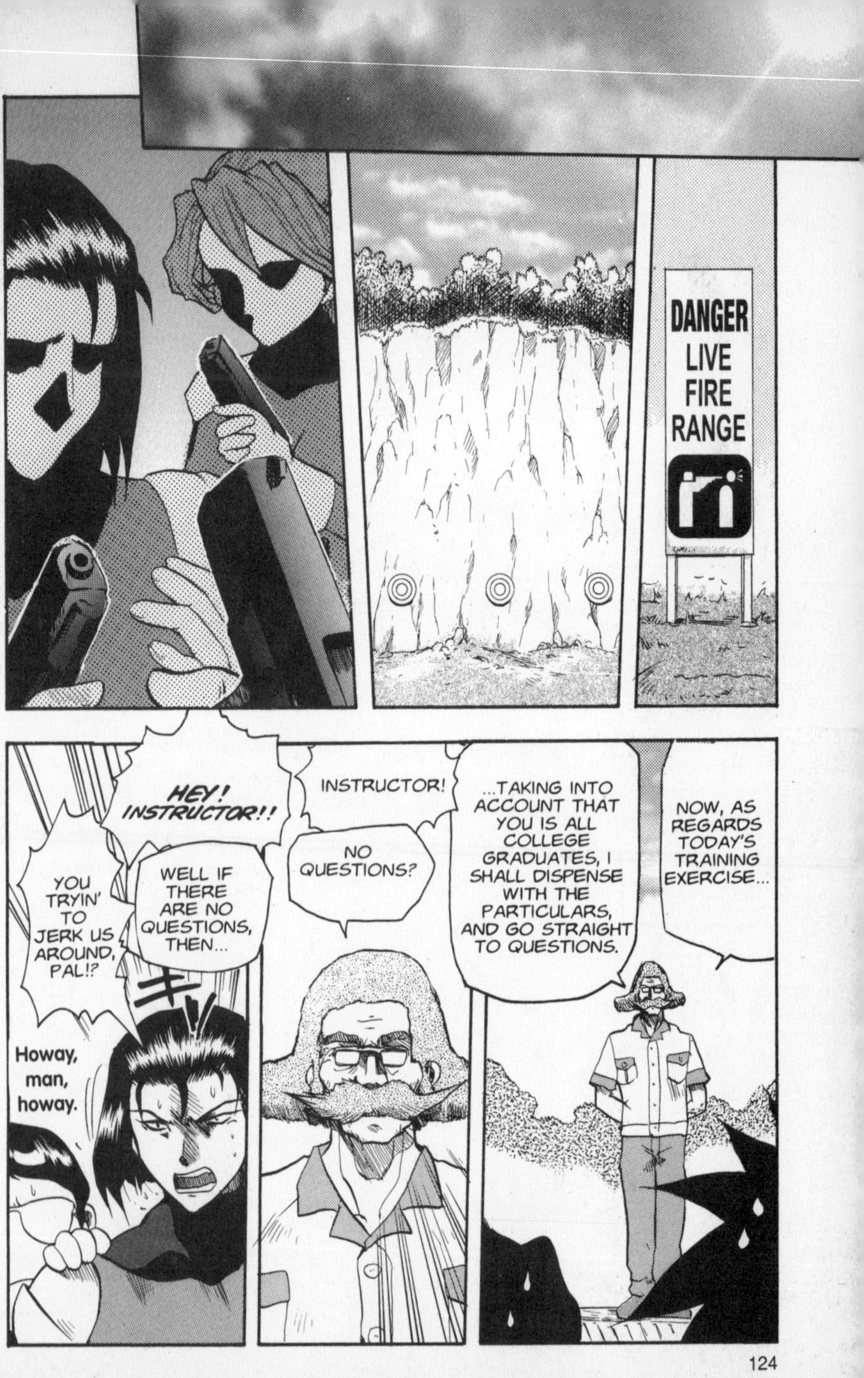
DANGER
LIVE
FIRE
RANGE
NOW, AS REGARDS TODAY'S TRAINING EXERCISE...
...TAKING INTO ACCOUNT THAT YOU IS ALL COLLEGE GRADUATES, I SHALL DISPENSE WITH THE PARTICULARS, AND GO STRAIGHT TO QUESTIONS.
INSTRUCTOR!
NO QUESTIONS?
HEY! INSTRUCTOR!!
WELL IF THERE ARE NO QUESTIONS, THEN...
YOU TRYIN' TO JERK US AROUND, PAL!?
キッ
Howay, man, howay.

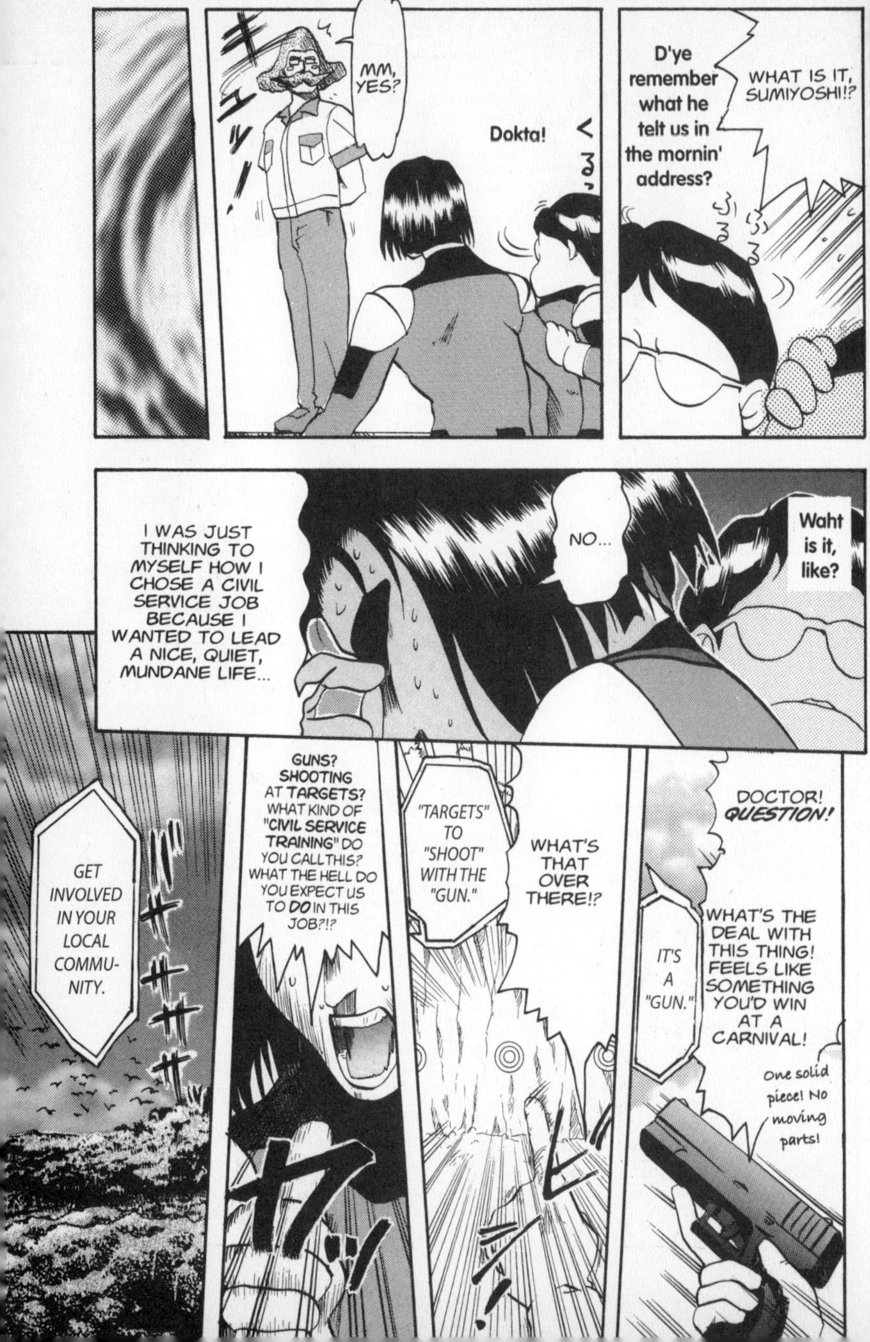
WHAT IS IT, SUMIYOSHI!?
D'ye remember what he telt us in the mornin' address?
Dokta!
MM, YES?
Waht is it, like?
NO...
I WAS JUST THINKING TO MYSELF HOW I CHOSE A CIVIL SERVICE JOB BECAUSE I WANTED TO LEAD A NICE, QUIET, MUNDANE LIFE...
DOCTOR! QUESTION!
WHAT'S THE DEAL WITH THIS THING! FEELS LIKE SOMETHING YOU'D WIN AT A CARNIVAL!
IT'S A "GUN."
One solid piece! No moving parts!
WHAT'S THAT OVER THERE!?
"TARGETS" TO "SHOOT" WITH THE "GUN."
GUNS? SHOOTING AT TARGETS? WHAT KIND OF "CIVIL SERVICE TRAINING" DO YOU CALL THIS? WHAT THE HELL DO YOU EXPECT US TO DO IN THIS JOB?!?
GET INVOLVED IN YOUR LOCAL COMMUNITY.

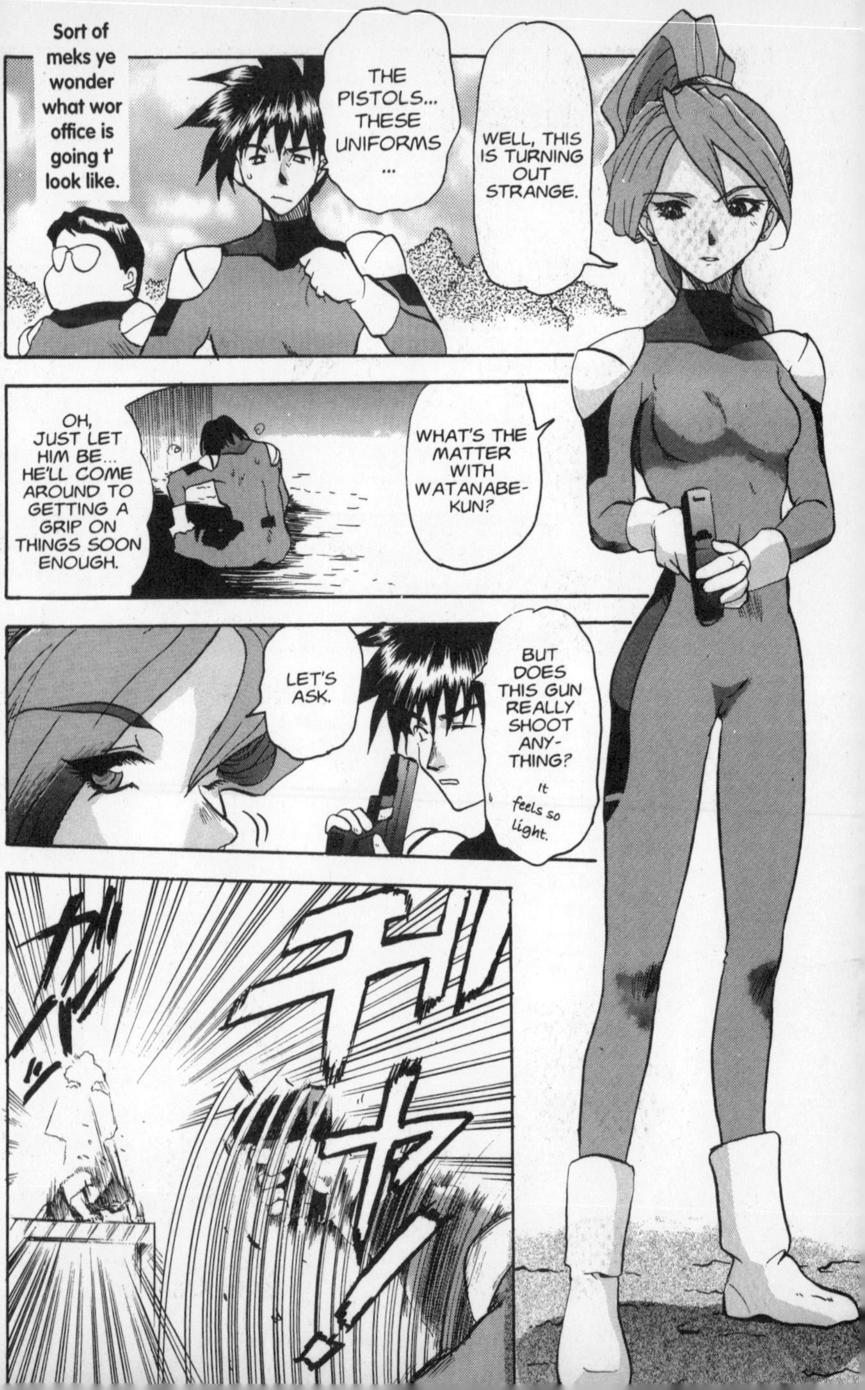
WELL, THIS IS TURNING OUT STRANGE.
THE PISTOLS... THESE UNIFORMS ...
Sort of meks ye wonder what wor office is going t' look like.
WHAT'S THE MATTER WITH WATANABE-KUN?
OH, JUST LET HIM BE... HE'LL COME AROUND TO GETTING A GRIP ON THINGS SOON ENOUGH.
BUT DOES THIS GUN REALLY SHOOT ANYTHING?
It feels so light.
LET'S ASK.

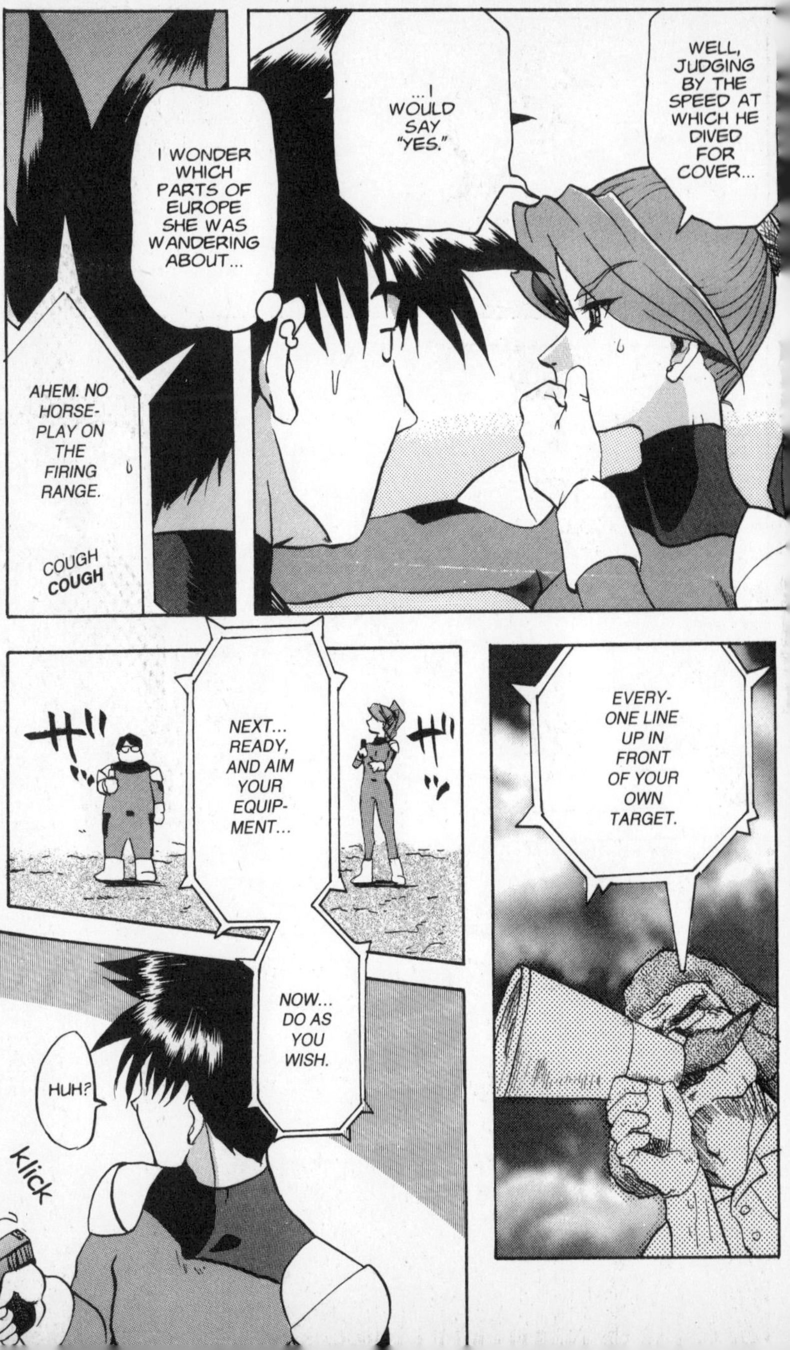
WELL, JUDGING BY THE SPEED AT WHICH HE DIVED FOR COVER...
...I WOULD SAY "YES."
I WONDER WHICH PARTS OF EUROPE SHE WAS WANDERING ABOUT...
AHEM. NO HORSE-PLAY ON THE FIRING RANGE.
COUGH COUGH
EVERY-ONE LINE UP IN FRONT OF YOUR OWN TARGET.
ザッ
NEXT... READY, AND AIM YOUR EQUIP-MENT...
ザッ
NOW... DO AS YOU WISH.
HUH?
klick

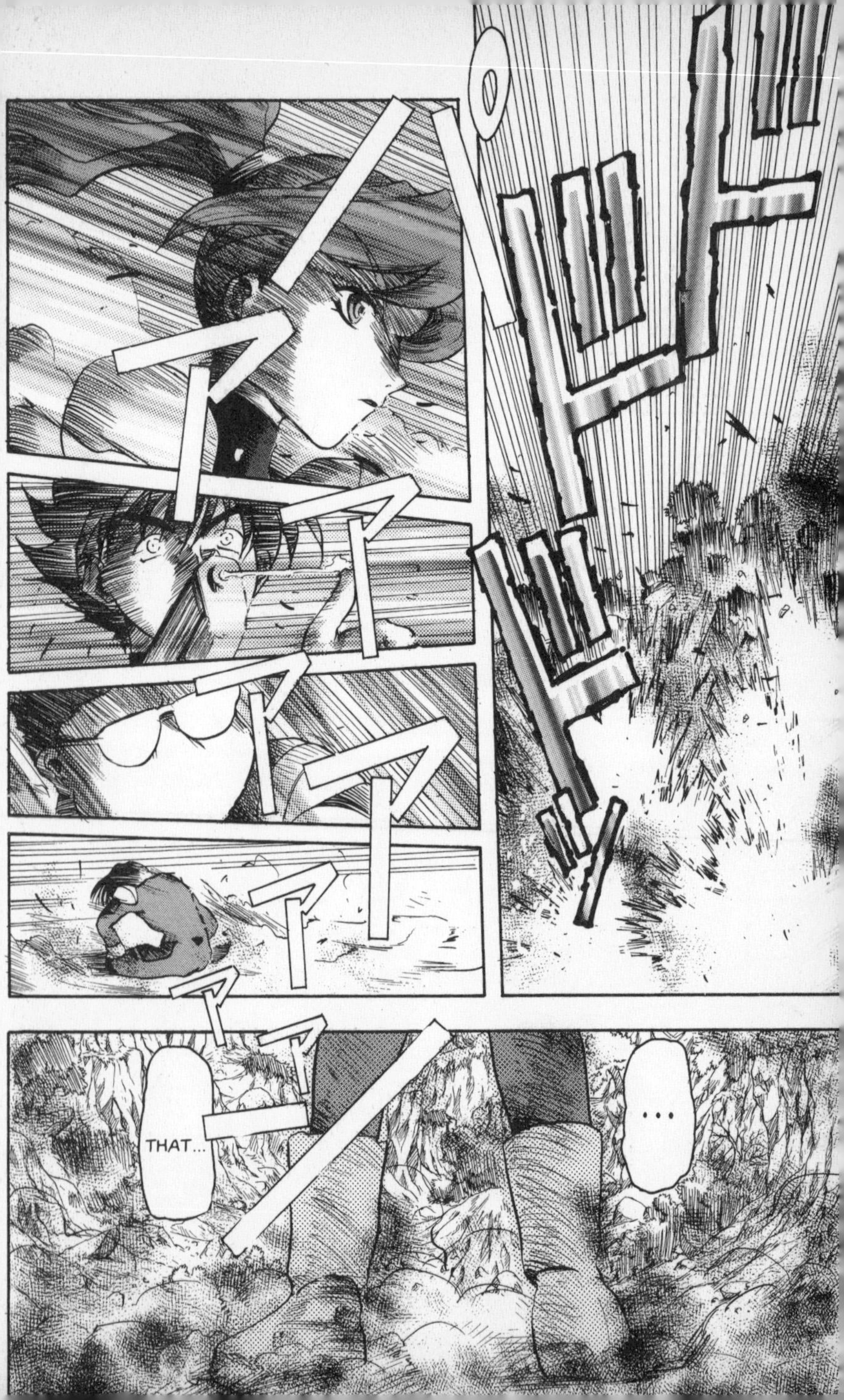
...
THAT...

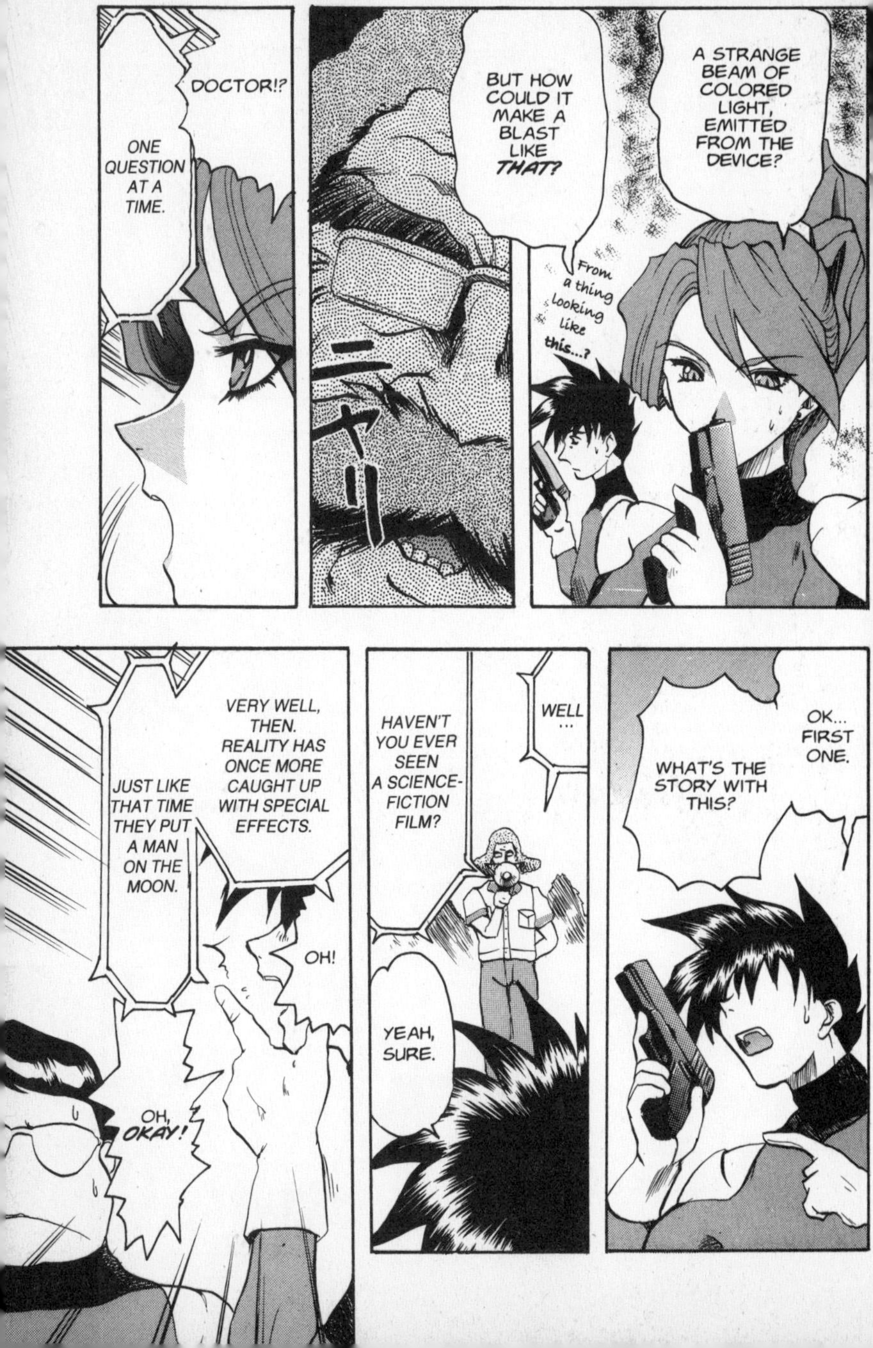
A STRANGE BEAM OF COLORED LIGHT, EMITTED FROM THE DEVICE?
BUT HOW COULD IT MAKE A BLAST LIKE *THAT?*
From a thing looking like **this**...?
ニヤリ
DOCTOR!?
ONE QUESTION AT A TIME.
OK... FIRST ONE.
WHAT'S THE STORY WITH THIS?
WELL ...
HAVEN'T YOU EVER SEEN A SCIENCE-FICTION FILM?
YEAH, SURE.
VERY WELL, THEN. REALITY HAS ONCE MORE CAUGHT UP WITH SPECIAL EFFECTS.
JUST LIKE THAT TIME THEY PUT A MAN ON THE MOON.
OH!
OH, *OKAY!*

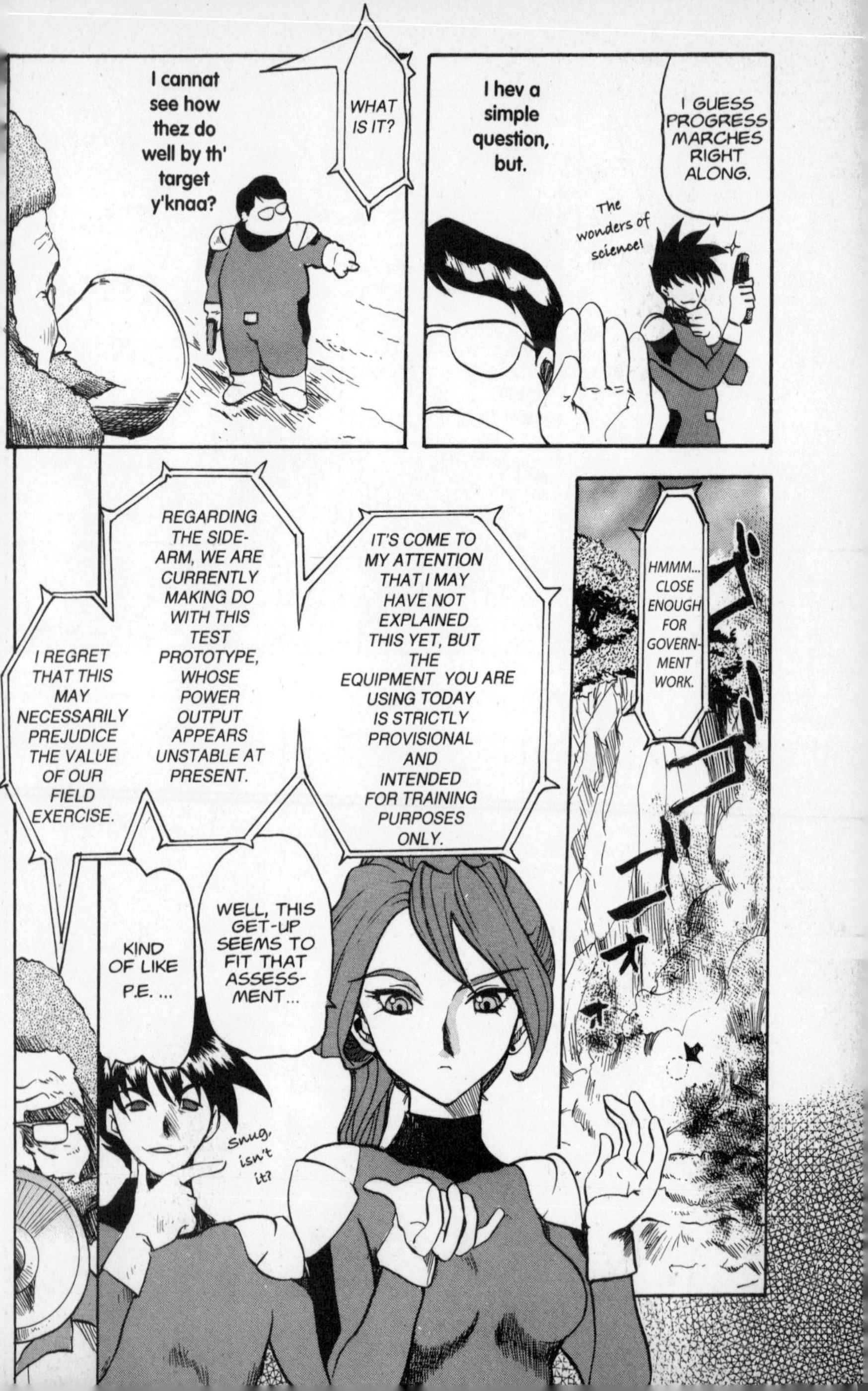
I GUESS PROGRESS MARCHES RIGHT ALONG.
The wonders of science!
I hev a simple question, but.
WHAT IS IT?
I cannat see how thez do well by th' target y'knaa?
HMMM... CLOSE ENOUGH FOR GOVERNMENT WORK.
IT'S COME TO MY ATTENTION THAT I MAY HAVE NOT EXPLAINED THIS YET, BUT THE EQUIPMENT YOU ARE USING TODAY IS STRICTLY PROVISIONAL AND INTENDED FOR TRAINING PURPOSES ONLY.
REGARDING THE SIDE-ARM, WE ARE CURRENTLY MAKING DO WITH THIS TEST PROTOTYPE, WHOSE POWER OUTPUT APPEARS UNSTABLE AT PRESENT.
I REGRET THAT THIS MAY NECESSARILY PREJUDICE THE VALUE OF OUR FIELD EXERCISE.
WELL, THIS GET-UP SEEMS TO FIT THAT ASSESSMENT...
KIND OF LIKE P.E. ...
Snug, isn't it?

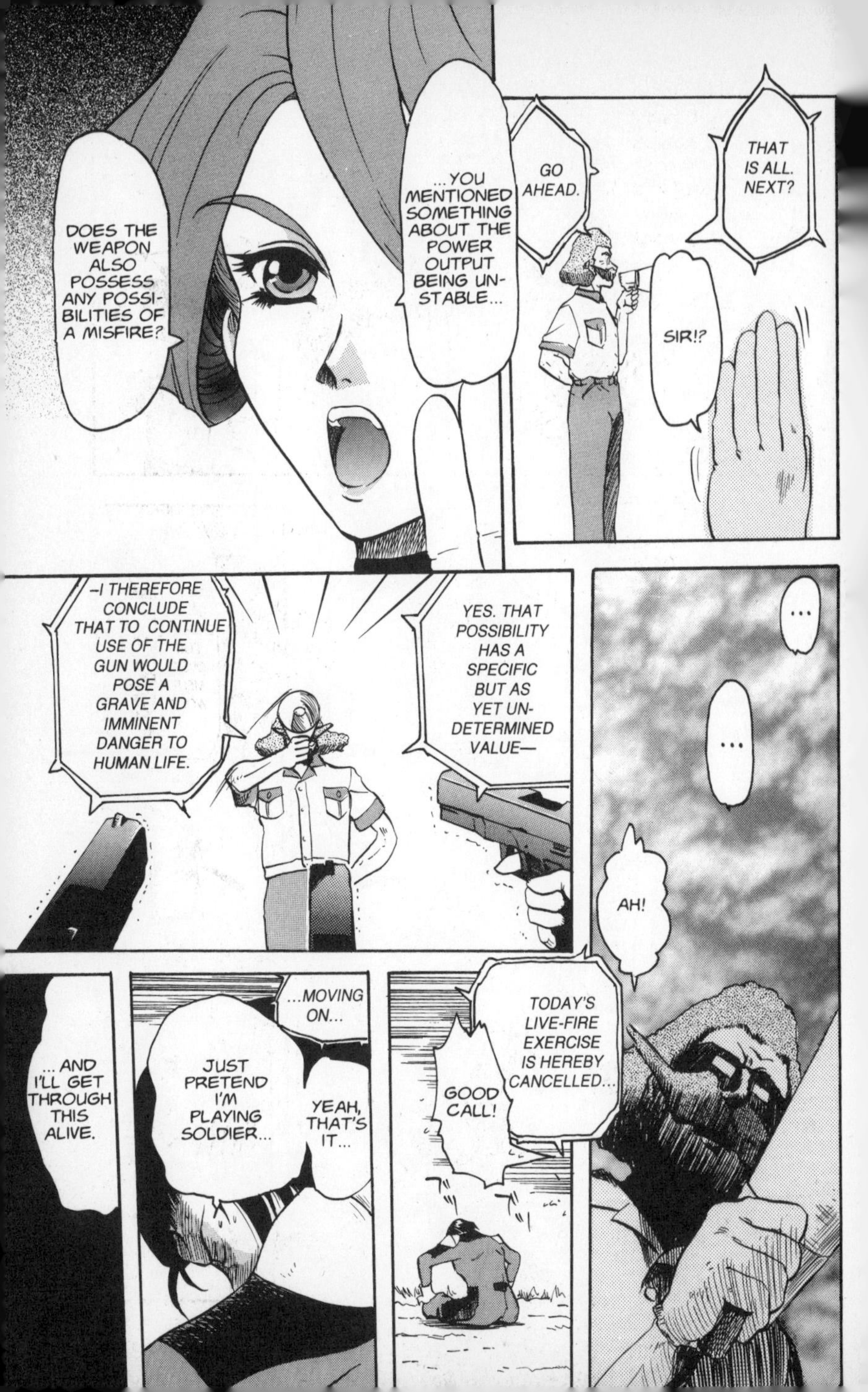
THAT IS ALL. NEXT?
GO AHEAD.
SIR!?
...YOU MENTIONED SOMETHING ABOUT THE POWER OUTPUT BEING UN-STABLE...
DOES THE WEAPON ALSO POSSESS ANY POSSI-BILITIES OF A MISFIRE?
...
...
AH!
YES. THAT POSSIBILITY HAS A SPECIFIC BUT AS YET UN-DETERMINED VALUE—
–I THEREFORE CONCLUDE THAT TO CONTINUE USE OF THE GUN WOULD POSE A GRAVE AND IMMINENT DANGER TO HUMAN LIFE.
TODAY'S LIVE-FIRE EXERCISE IS HEREBY CANCELLED...
GOOD CALL!
...MOVING ON...
YEAH, THAT'S IT...
JUST PRETEND I'M PLAYING SOLDIER...
...AND I'LL GET THROUGH THIS ALIVE.

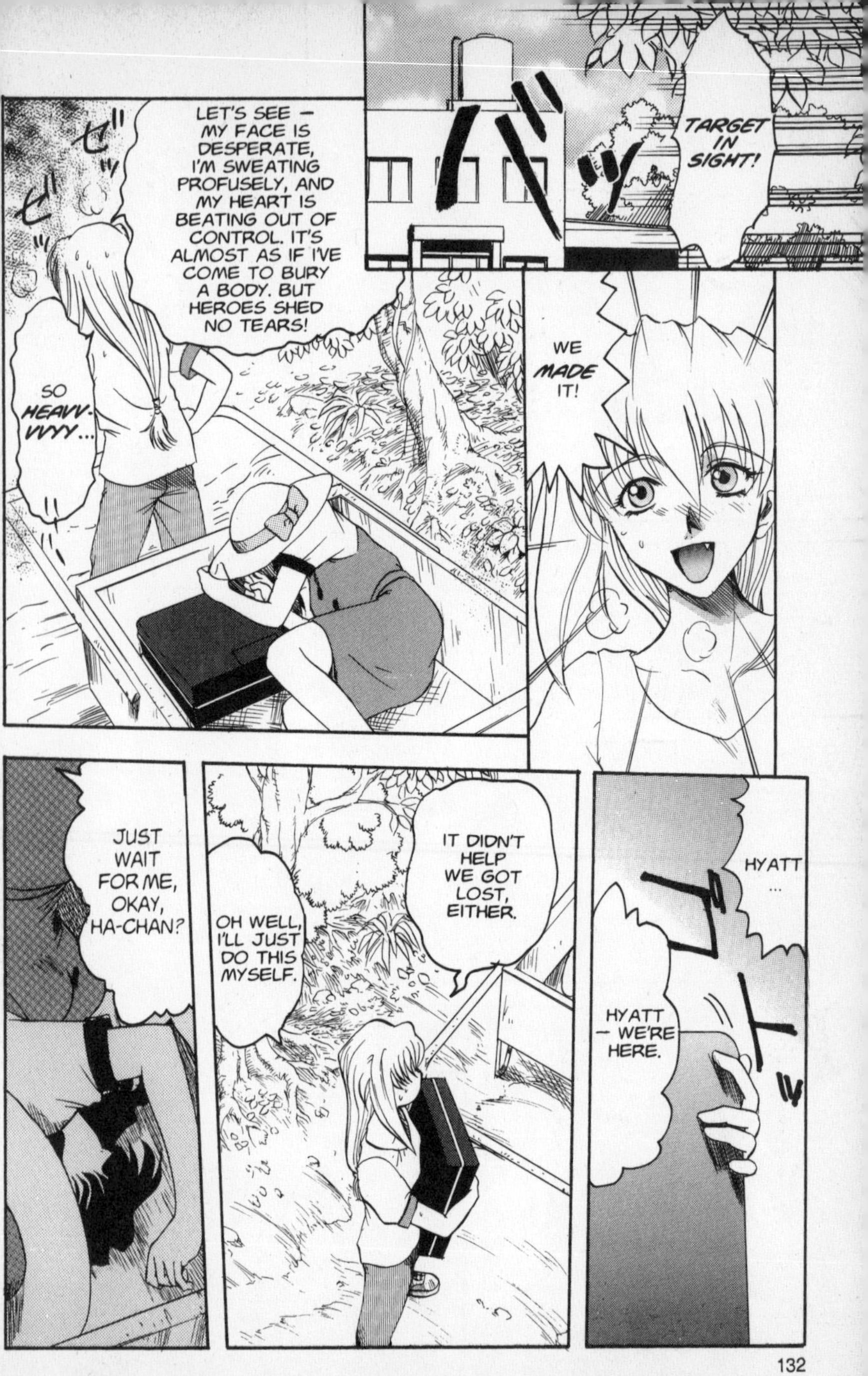
TARGET IN SIGHT!
WE MADE IT!
LET'S SEE — MY FACE IS DESPERATE, I'M SWEATING PROFUSELY, AND MY HEART IS BEATING OUT OF CONTROL. IT'S ALMOST AS IF I'VE COME TO BURY A BODY. BUT HEROES SHED NO TEARS!
SO HEAVV-VVYY...
HYATT ...
HYATT — WE'RE HERE.
IT DIDN'T HELP WE GOT LOST, EITHER.
OH WELL, I'LL JUST DO THIS MYSELF.
JUST WAIT FOR ME, OKAY, HA-CHAN?

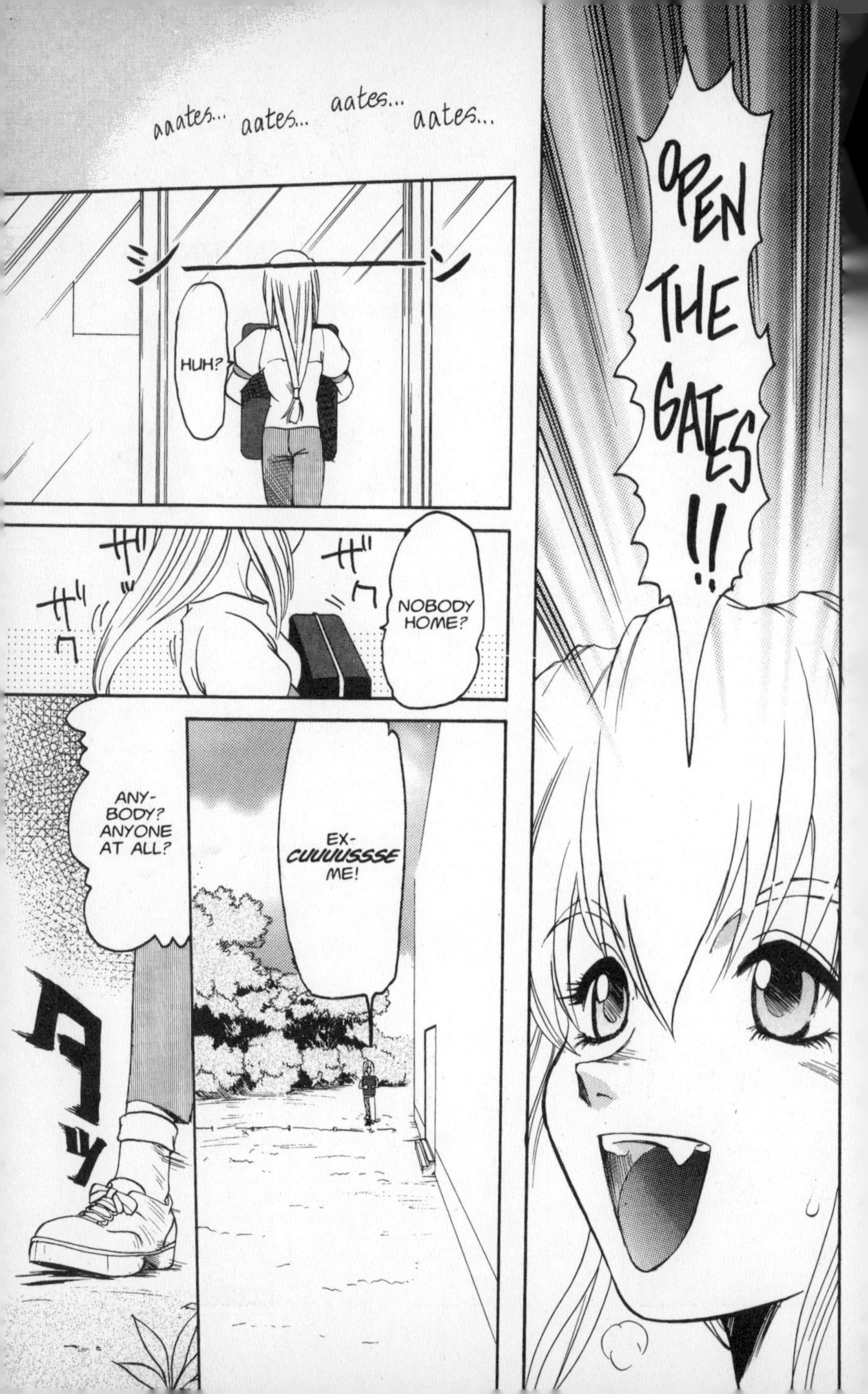
OPEN THE GATES!!
aates... aates... aates... aaates...
HUH?
NOBODY HOME?
EX-CUUUUSSSE ME!
ANY-BODY? ANYONE AT ALL?

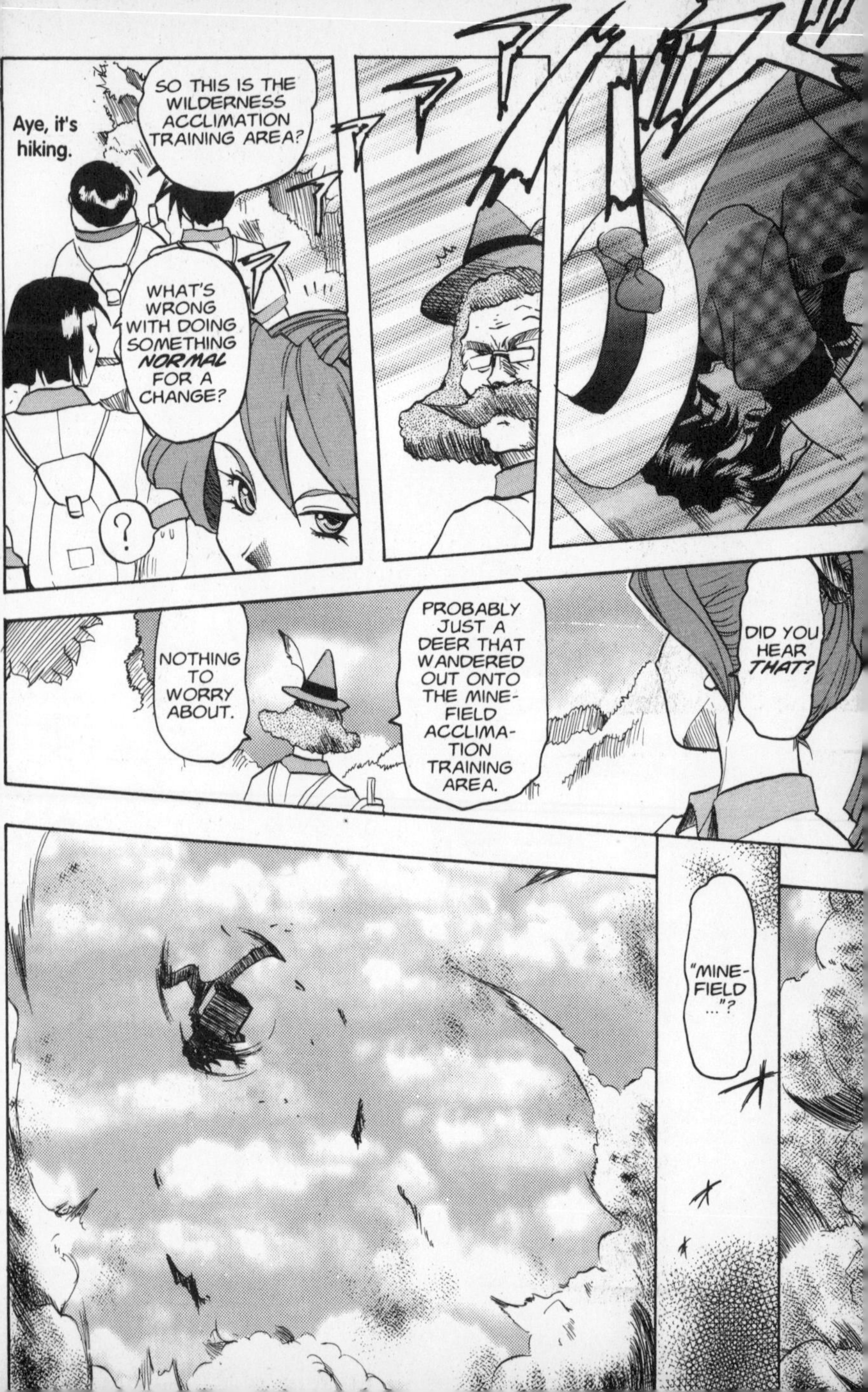
SO THIS IS THE WILDERNESS ACCLIMATION TRAINING AREA?
Aye, it's hiking.
WHAT'S WRONG WITH DOING SOMETHING NORMAL FOR A CHANGE?
?
DID YOU HEAR THAT?
PROBABLY JUST A DEER THAT WANDERED OUT ONTO THE MINE-FIELD ACCLIMA-TION TRAINING AREA.
NOTHING TO WORRY ABOUT.
"MINE-FIELD ..."?

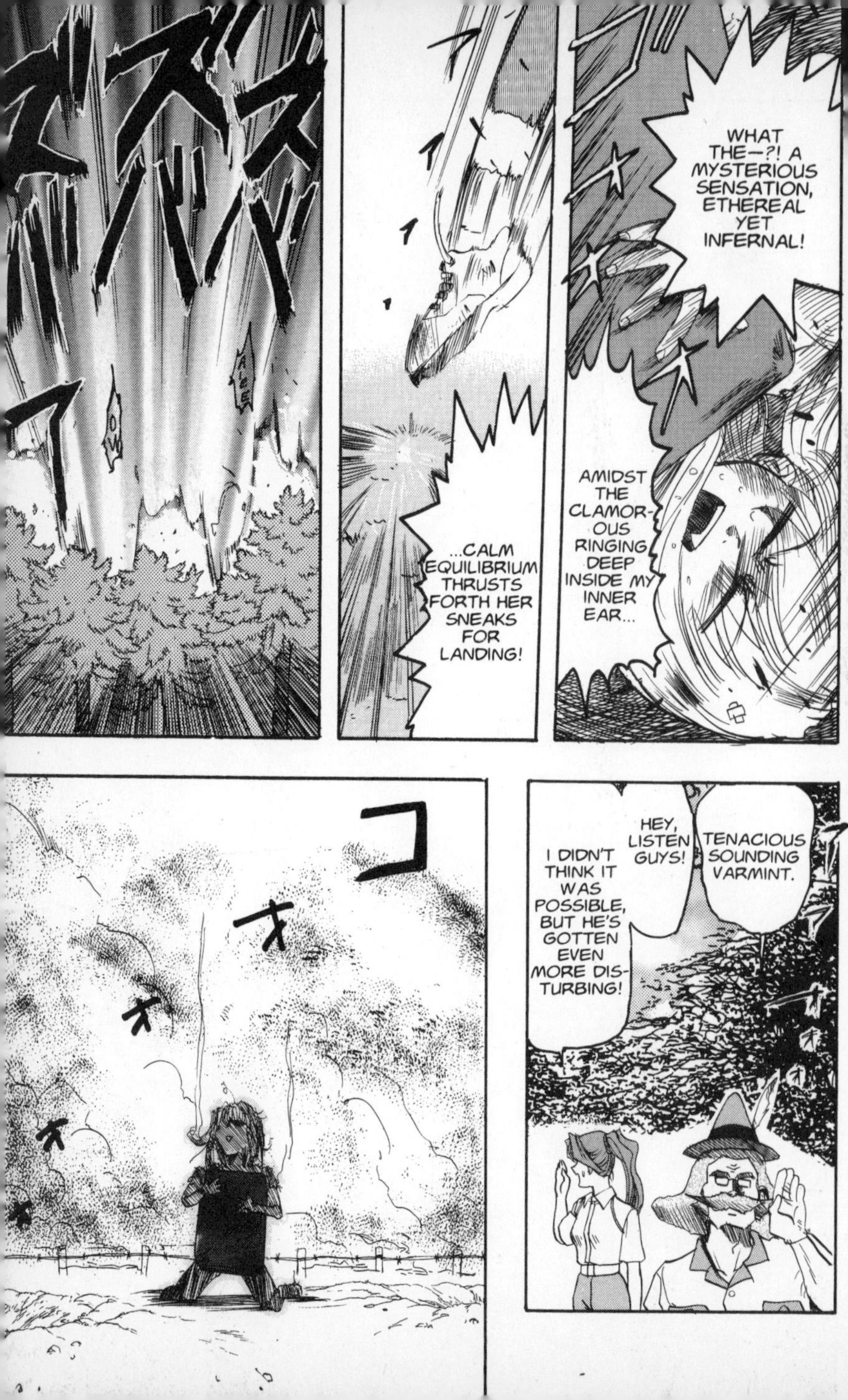
WHAT THE—?! A MYSTERIOUS SENSATION, ETHEREAL YET INFERNAL!
AMIDST THE CLAMOR-OUS RINGING DEEP INSIDE MY INNER EAR...
...CALM EQUILIBRIUM THRUSTS FORTH HER SNEAKS FOR LANDING!
TENACIOUS SOUNDING VARMINT.
HEY, LISTEN GUYS!
I DIDN'T THINK IT WAS POSSIBLE, BUT HE'S GOTTEN EVEN MORE DIS-TURBING!

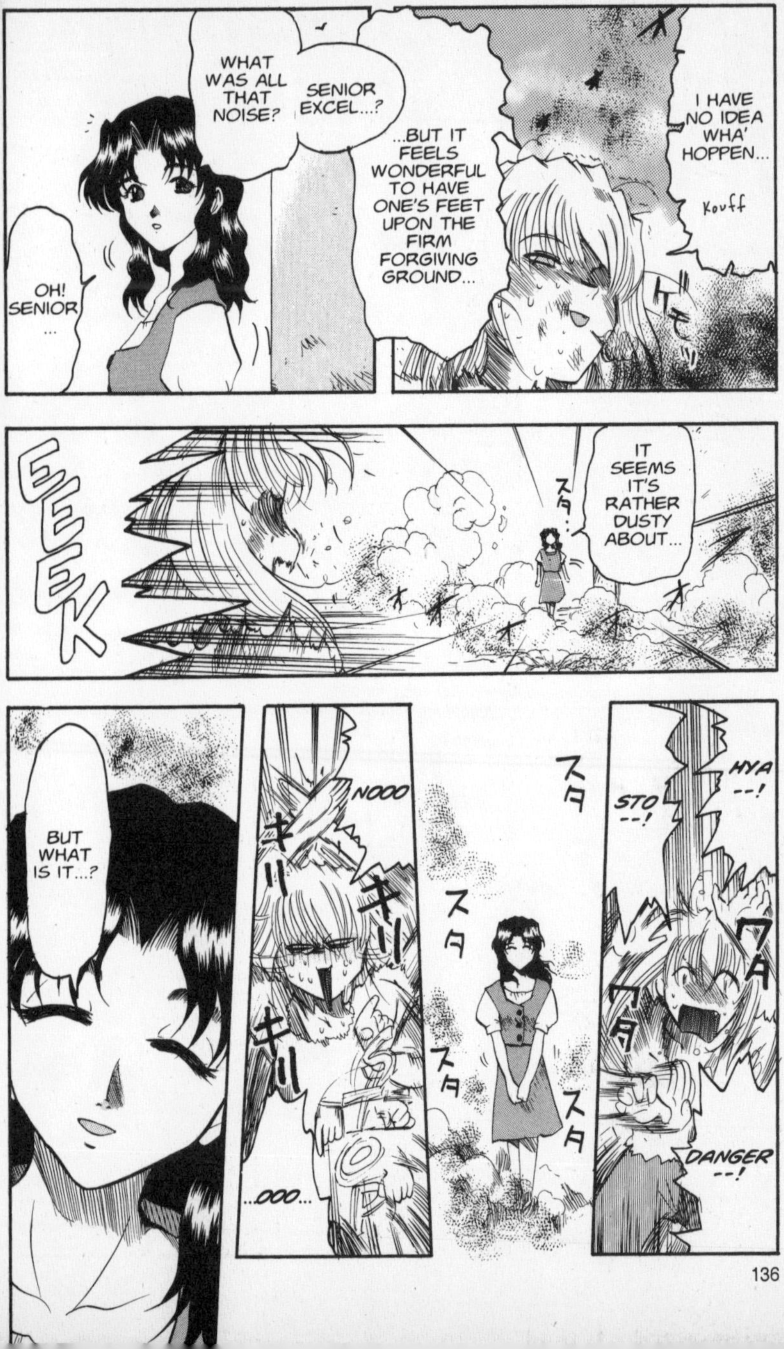
I HAVE NO IDEA WHA' HOPPEN...
Kouff
...BUT IT FEELS WONDERFUL TO HAVE ONE'S FEET UPON THE FIRM FORGIVING GROUND...
WHAT WAS ALL THAT NOISE?
SENIOR EXCEL...?
OH! SENIOR ...
IT SEEMS IT'S RATHER DUSTY ABOUT...
スタ
EEEEK
HYA --!
STO --!
ワタ
ワタ
DANGER --!
スタ
スタ
スタ
スタ
NOOO
キリ
キリ
キリ
...OOO...
BUT WHAT IS IT...?

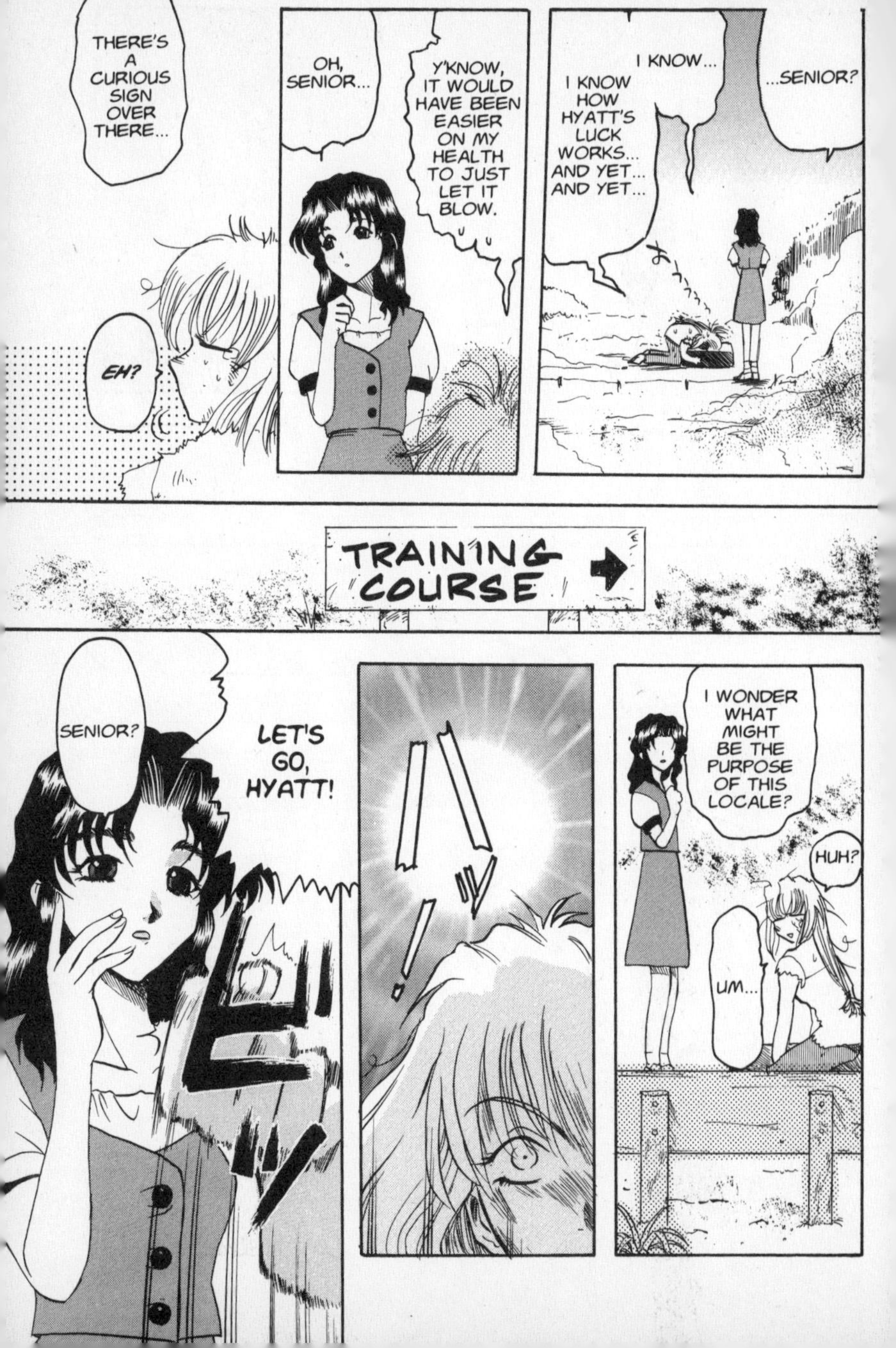
...SENIOR?
I KNOW...
I KNOW HOW HYATT'S LUCK WORKS... AND YET... AND YET...
Y'KNOW, IT WOULD HAVE BEEN EASIER ON MY HEALTH TO JUST LET IT BLOW.
OH, SENIOR...
THERE'S A CURIOUS SIGN OVER THERE...
EH?
TRAINING COURSE
I WONDER WHAT MIGHT BE THE PURPOSE OF THIS LOCALE?
HUH?
UM...
SENIOR?
LET'S GO, HYATT!

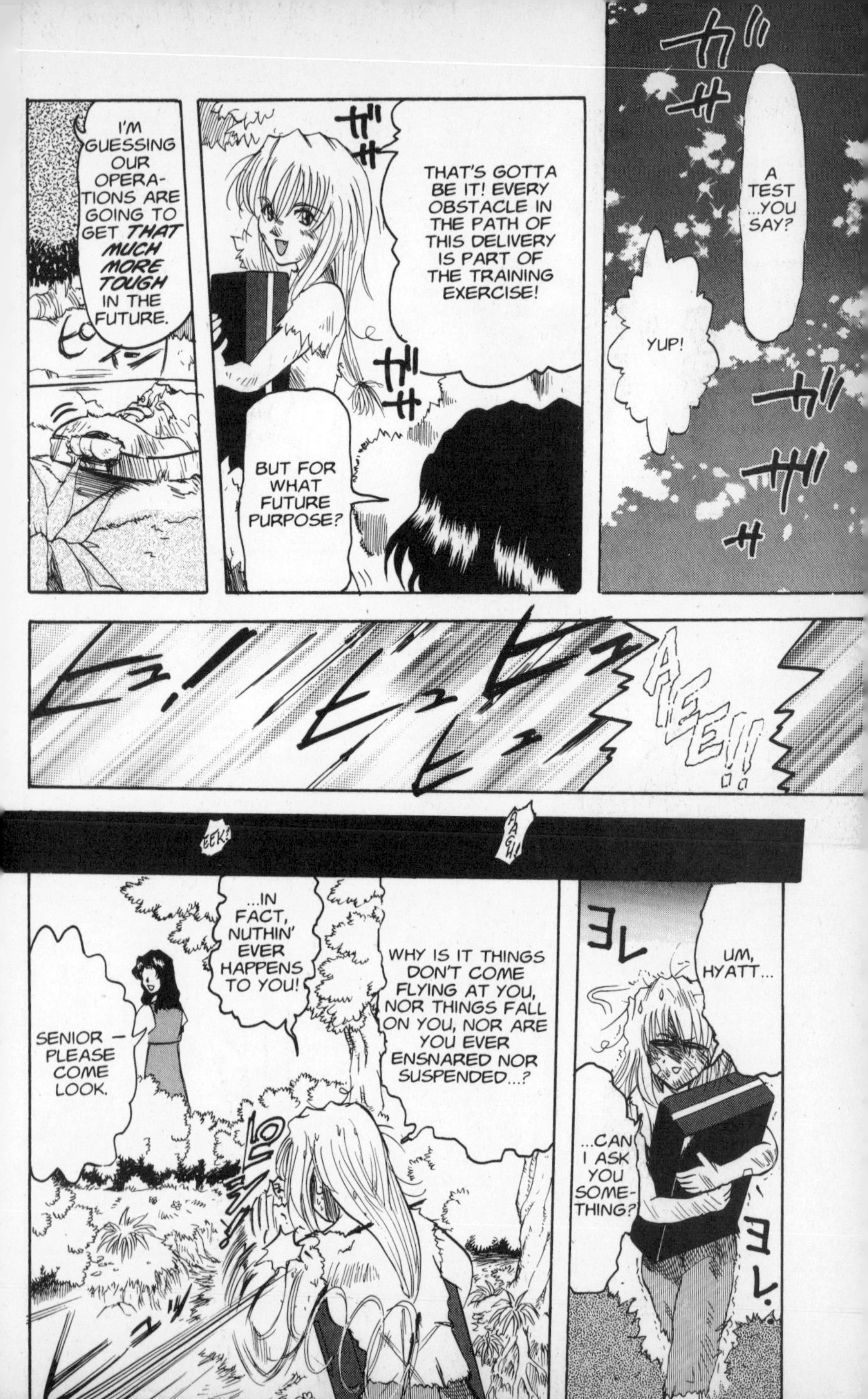
A TEST ...YOU SAY?
YUP!
THAT'S GOTTA BE IT! EVERY OBSTACLE IN THE PATH OF THIS DELIVERY IS PART OF THE TRAINING EXERCISE!
BUT FOR WHAT FUTURE PURPOSE?
I'M GUESSING OUR OPERATIONS ARE GOING TO GET *THAT MUCH MORE TOUGH* IN THE FUTURE.
AIEEE!!
AAGH!
EEK!
UM, HYATT...
...CAN I ASK YOU SOMETHING?
WHY IS IT THINGS DON'T COME FLYING AT YOU, NOR THINGS FALL ON YOU, NOR ARE YOU EVER ENSNARED NOR SUSPENDED...?
...IN FACT, NUTHIN' EVER HAPPENS TO YOU!
SENIOR — PLEASE COME LOOK.

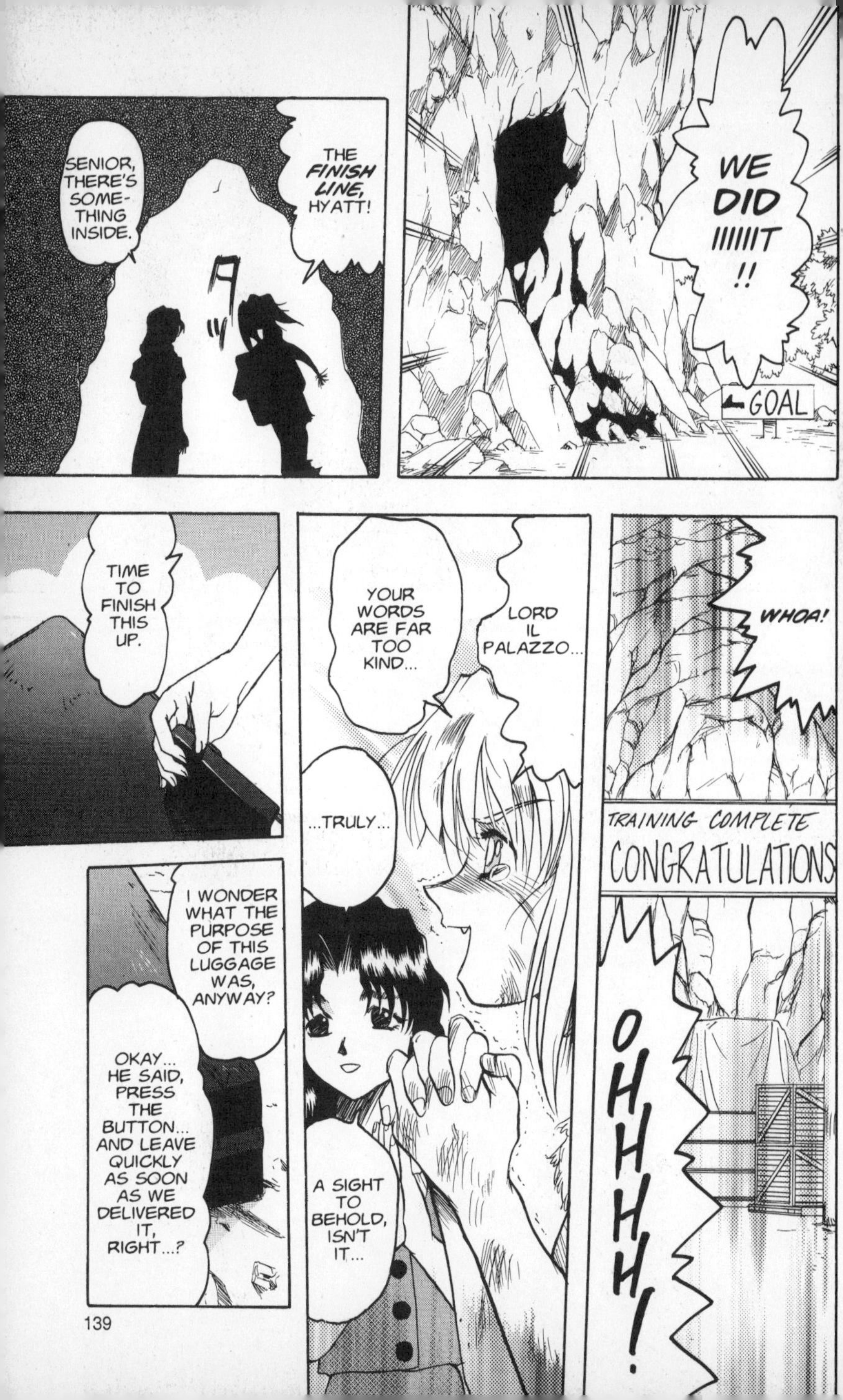
WE DID IIIIIIT!!
GOAL
THE *FINISH LINE*, HYATT!
SENIOR, THERE'S SOME-THING INSIDE.
WHOA!
TRAINING COMPLETE
CONGRATULATIONS
OHHHHH!
LORD IL PALAZZO...
YOUR WORDS ARE FAR TOO KIND...
...TRULY...
A SIGHT TO BEHOLD, ISN'T IT...
TIME TO FINISH THIS UP.
I WONDER WHAT THE PURPOSE OF THIS LUGGAGE WAS, ANYWAY?
OKAY... HE SAID, PRESS THE BUTTON... AND LEAVE QUICKLY AS SOON AS WE DELIVERED IT, RIGHT...?

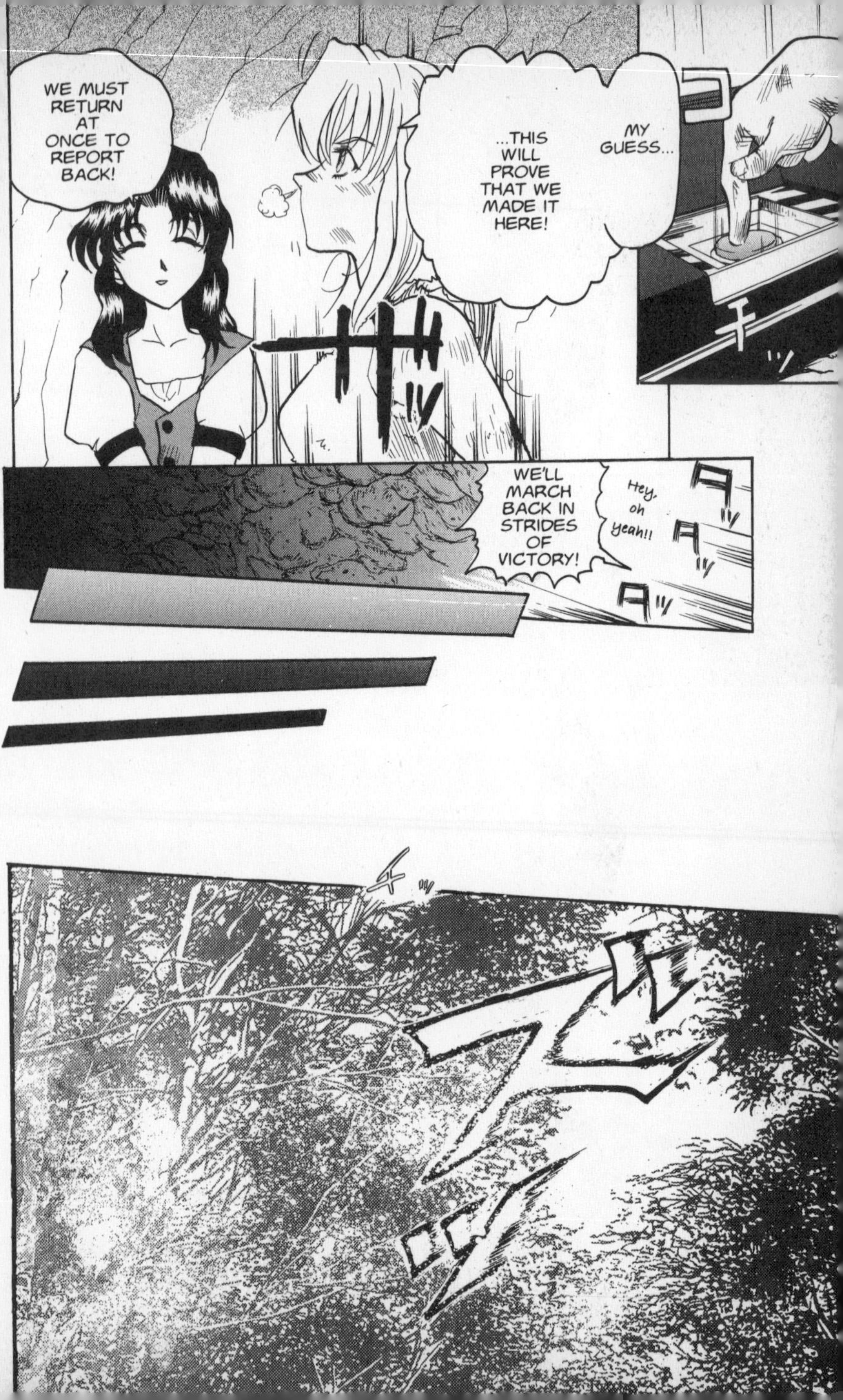
MY GUESS...
...THIS WILL PROVE THAT WE MADE IT HERE!
WE MUST RETURN AT ONCE TO REPORT BACK!
Hey, oh yeah!!
WE'LL MARCH BACK IN STRIDES OF VICTORY!

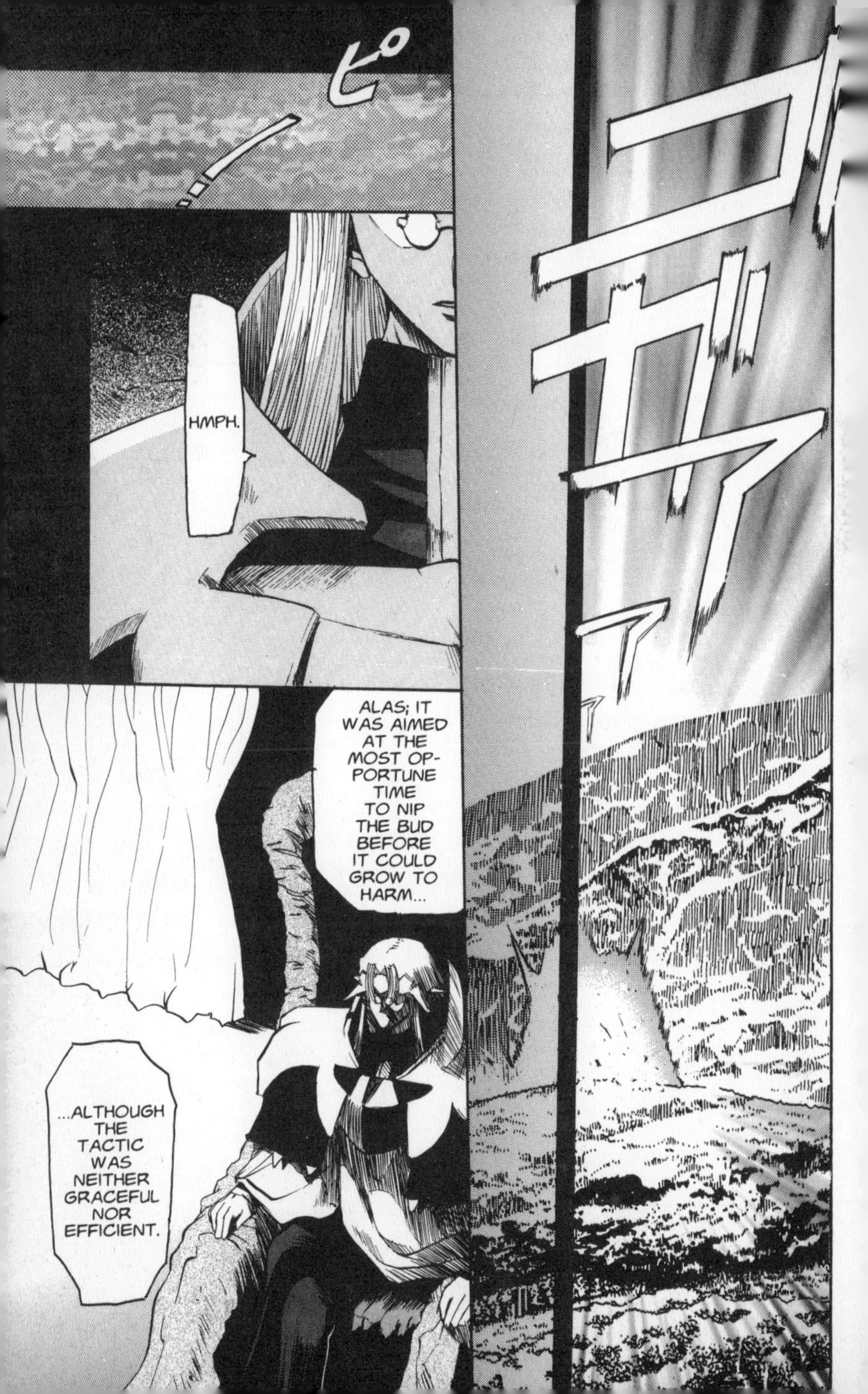
ゴガァァァ
ピ
HMPH.
ALAS; IT WAS AIMED AT THE MOST OP-PORTUNE TIME TO NIP THE BUD BEFORE IT COULD GROW TO HARM...
...ALTHOUGH THE TACTIC WAS NEITHER GRACEFUL NOR EFFICIENT.

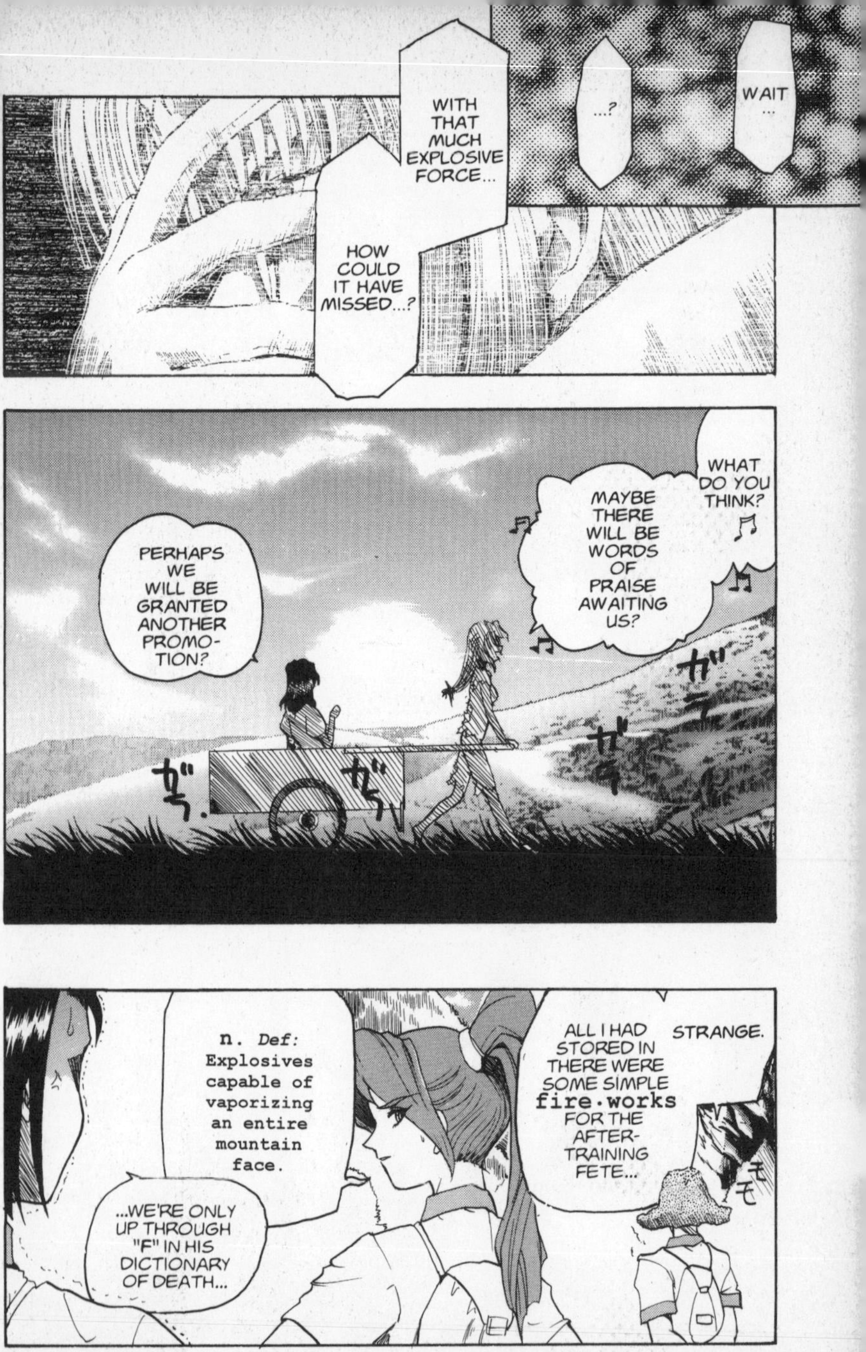
WAIT...
...?
WITH THAT MUCH EXPLOSIVE FORCE...
HOW COULD IT HAVE MISSED...?
WHAT DO YOU THINK?
MAYBE THERE WILL BE WORDS OF PRAISE AWAITING US?
PERHAPS WE WILL BE GRANTED ANOTHER PROMOTION?
ガラ
ガラ
がら
がら.
STRANGE.
ALL I HAD STORED IN THERE WERE SOME SIMPLE fire·works FOR THE AFTER-TRAINING FETE...
モモ
n. *Def:* Explosives capable of vaporizing an entire mountain face.
...WE'RE ONLY UP THROUGH "F" IN HIS DICTIONARY OF DEATH...

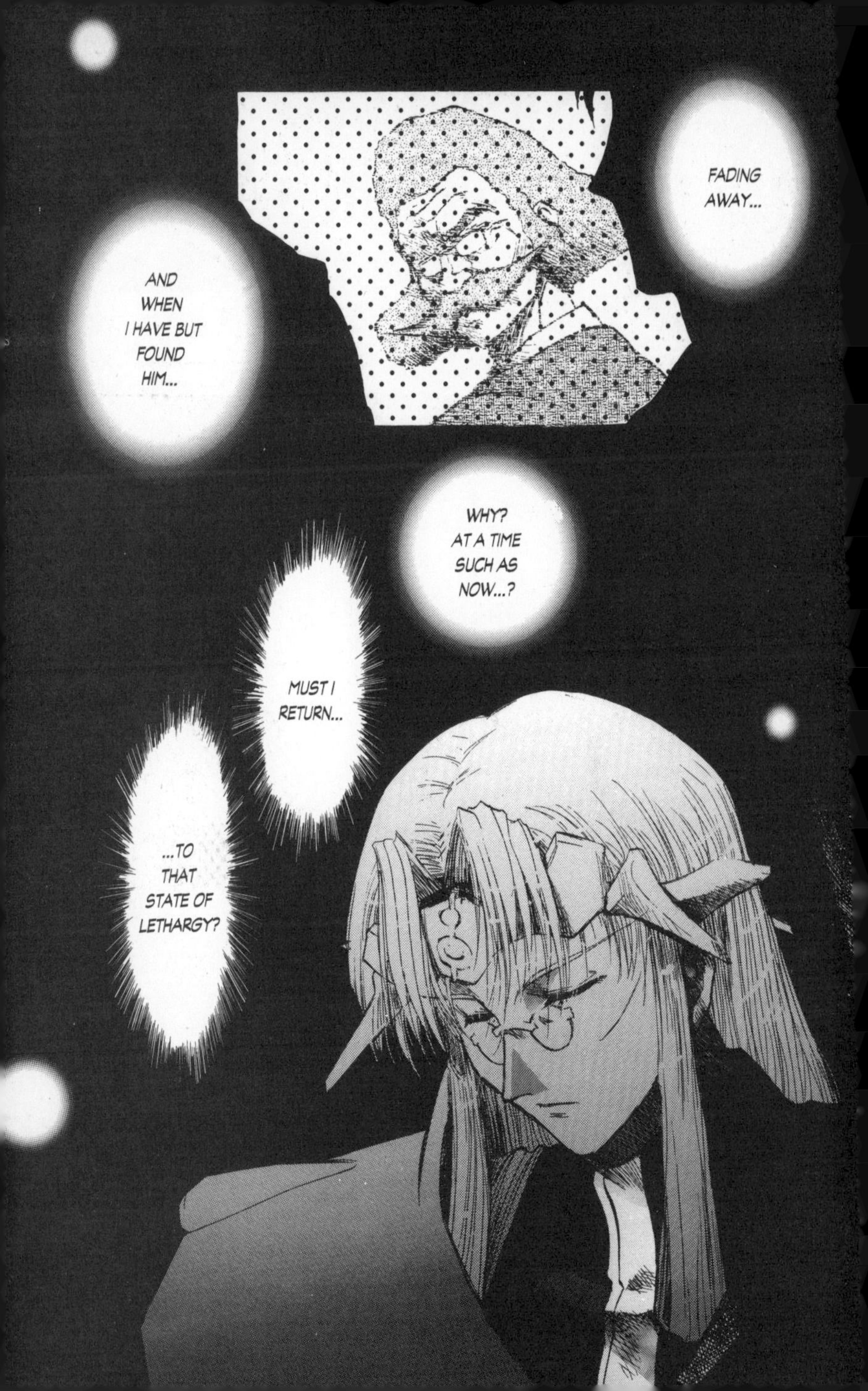
FADING AWAY...
AND WHEN I HAVE BUT FOUND HIM...
WHY? AT A TIME SUCH AS NOW...?
MUST I RETURN...
...TO THAT STATE OF LETHARGY?

MISSION 6
SHIFT IN TACK

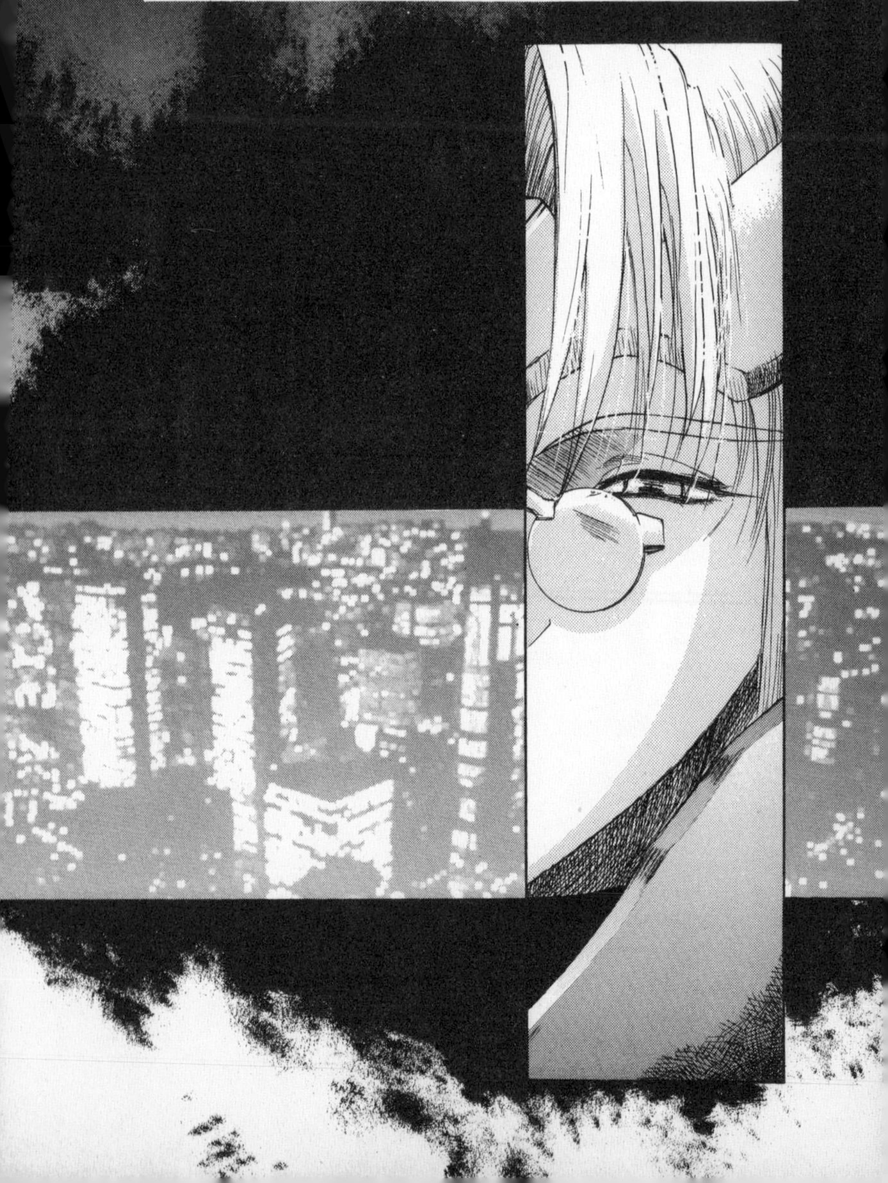

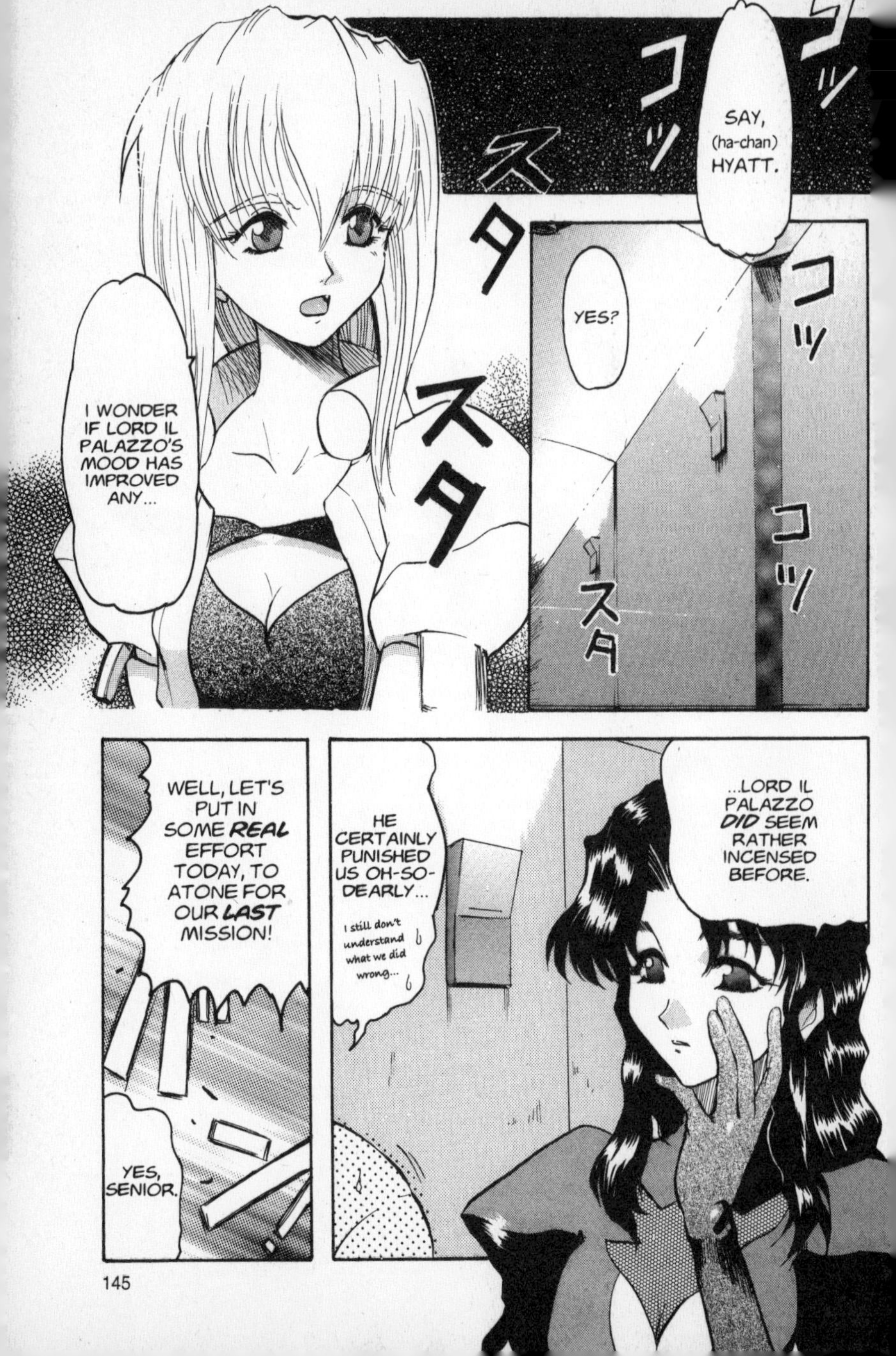

コッ
コッ
SAY, (ha-chan) HYATT.
YES?
コッ
コッ
スタ
スタ
スタ
I WONDER IF LORD IL PALAZZO'S MOOD HAS IMPROVED ANY...
...LORD IL PALAZZO *DID* SEEM RATHER INCENSED BEFORE.
HE CERTAINLY PUNISHED US OH-SO-DEARLY...
I still don't understand what we did wrong...
WELL, LET'S PUT IN SOME ***REAL*** EFFORT TODAY, TO ATONE FOR OUR ***LAST*** MISSION!
YES, SENIOR.

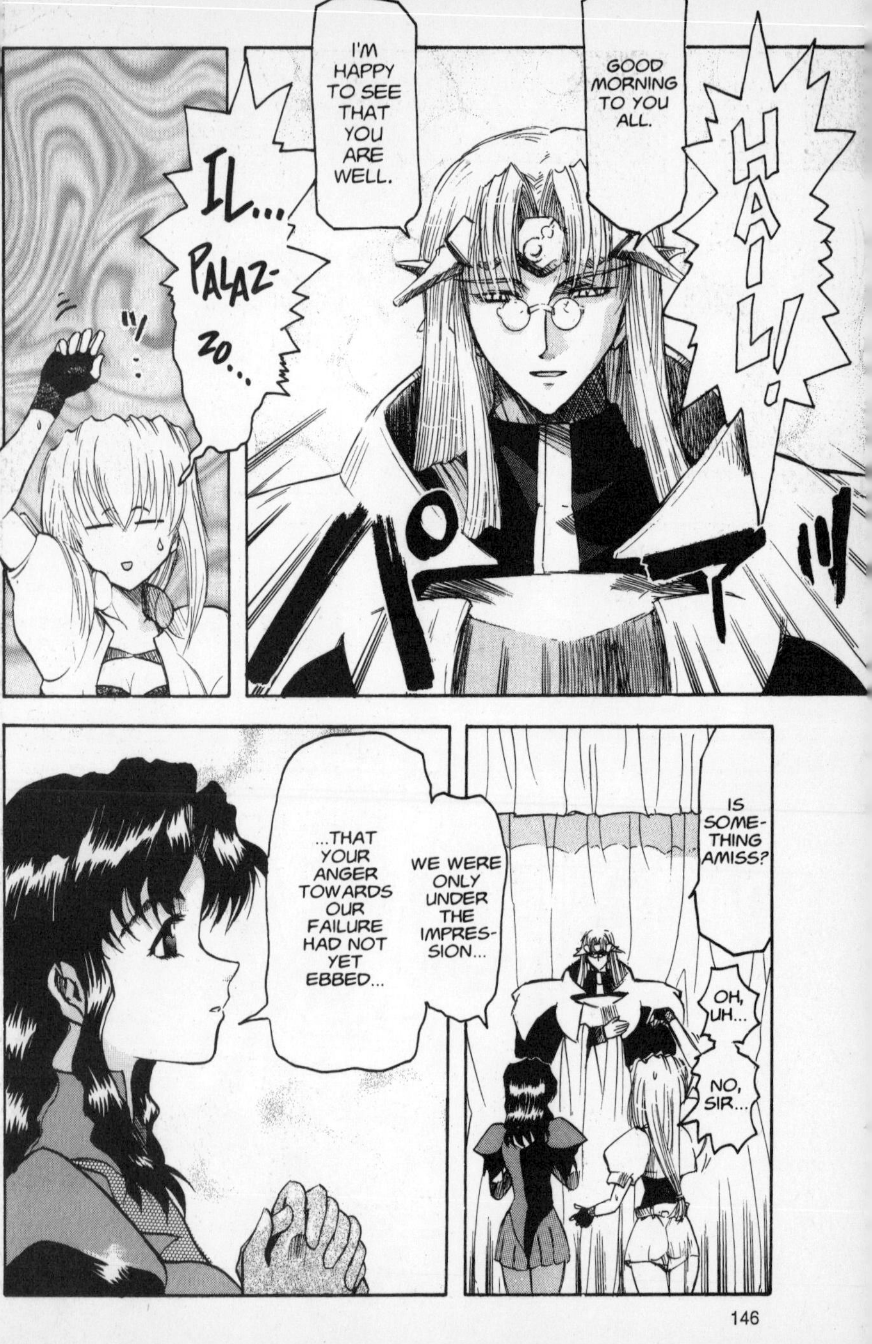
HAIL!
GOOD MORNING TO YOU ALL.
I'M HAPPY TO SEE THAT YOU ARE WELL.
IL... PALAZ-ZO...
IS SOME-THING AMISS?
OH, UH...
NO, SIR...
WE WERE ONLY UNDER THE IMPRES-SION...
...THAT YOUR ANGER TOWARDS OUR FAILURE HAD NOT YET EBBED...

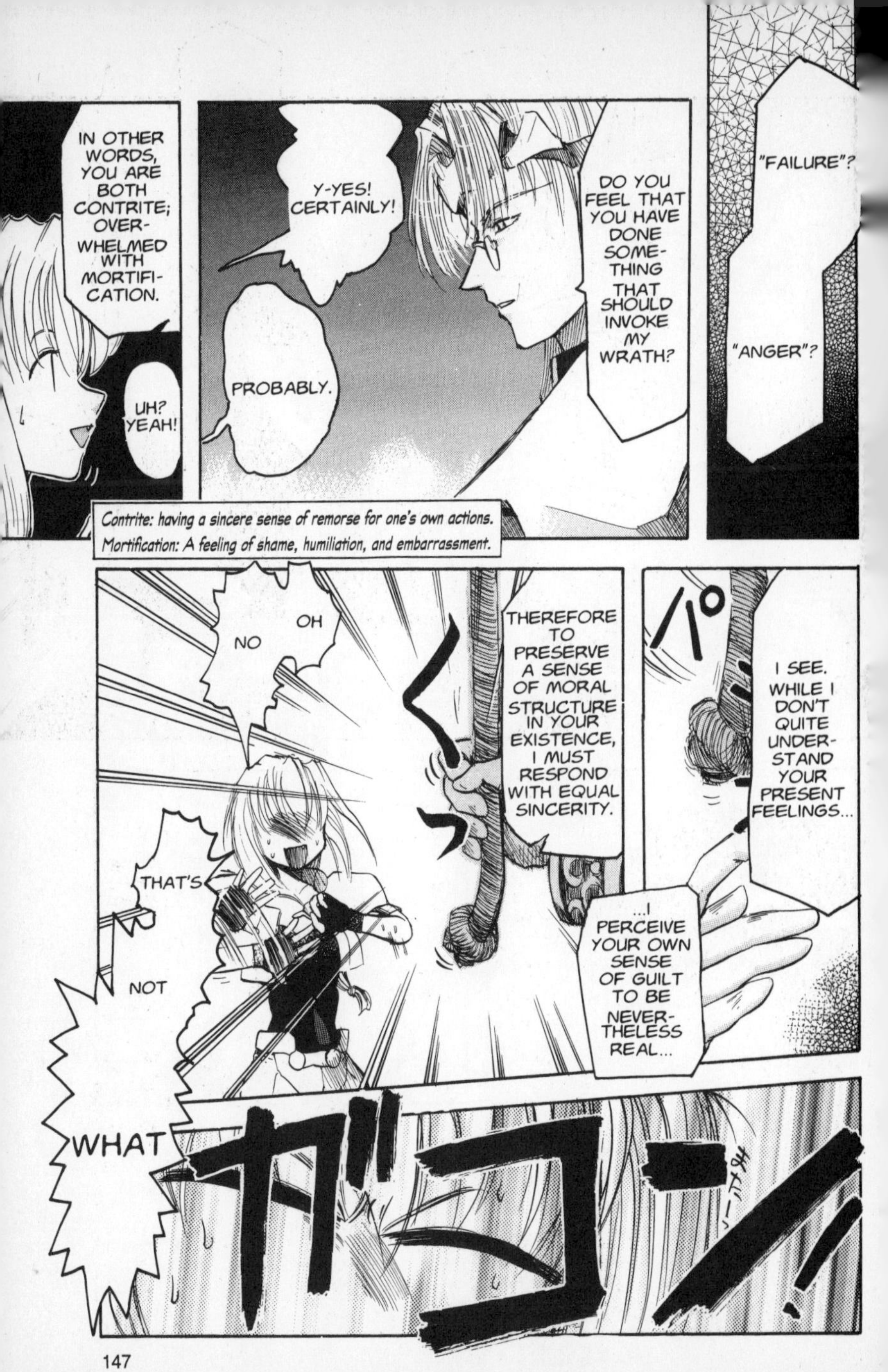

"FAILURE"?
"ANGER"?
DO YOU FEEL THAT YOU HAVE DONE SOMETHING THAT SHOULD INVOKE MY WRATH?
Y-YES! CERTAINLY!
PROBABLY.
IN OTHER WORDS, YOU ARE BOTH CONTRITE; OVERWHELMED WITH MORTIFICATION.
UH? YEAH!
Contrite: having a sincere sense of remorse for one's own actions.
Mortification: A feeling of shame, humiliation, and embarrassment.
パ
I SEE. WHILE I DON'T QUITE UNDERSTAND YOUR PRESENT FEELINGS...
...I PERCEIVE YOUR OWN SENSE OF GUILT TO BE NEVERTHELESS REAL...
THEREFORE TO PRESERVE A SENSE OF MORAL STRUCTURE IN YOUR EXISTENCE, I MUST RESPOND WITH EQUAL SINCERITY.
OH
NO
THAT'S
NOT
WHAT

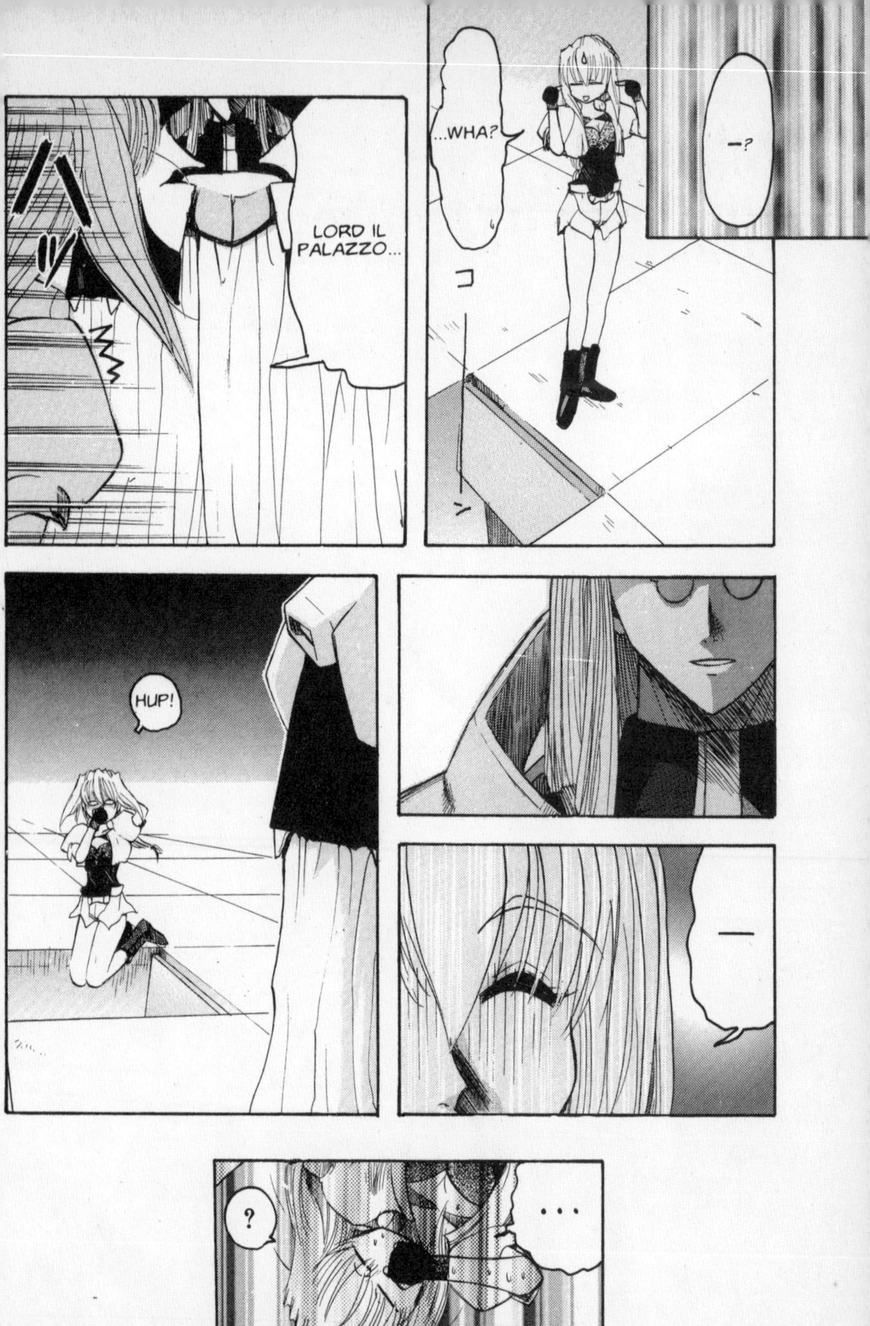
—?
...WHA?
LORD IL PALAZZO...
—
HUP!
...
?

END MISSION 6

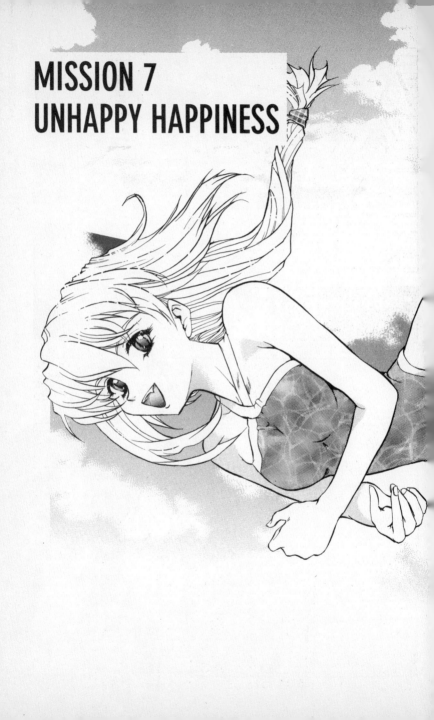

MISSION 7
UNHAPPY HAPPINESS

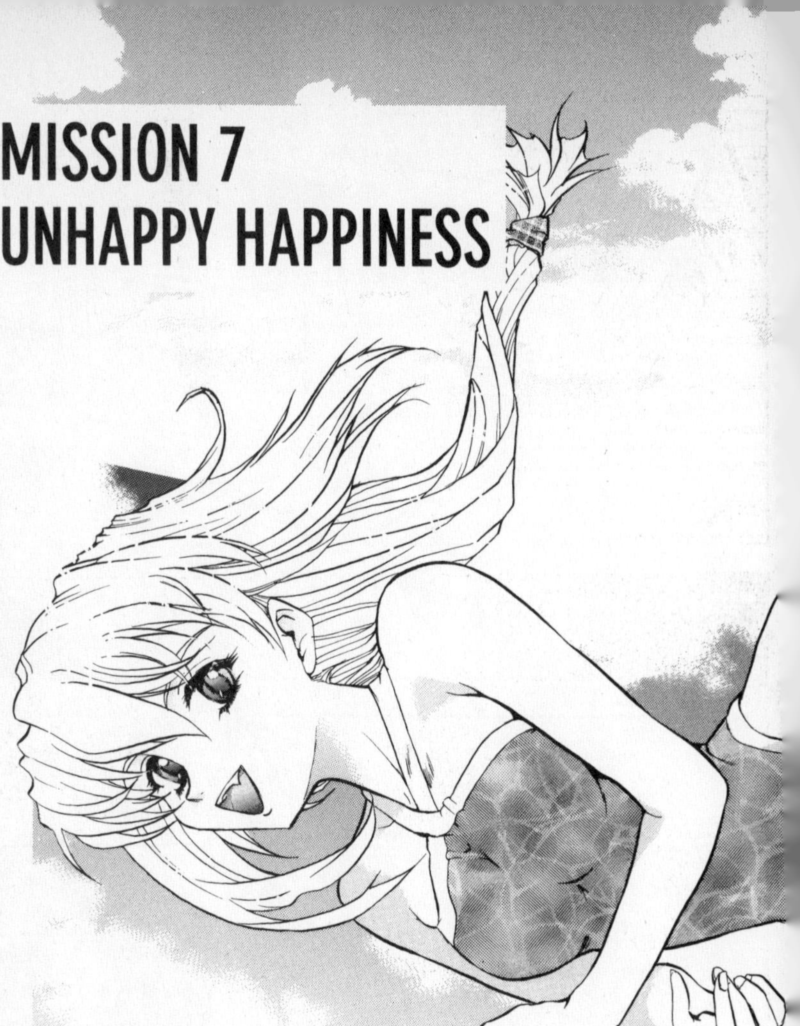

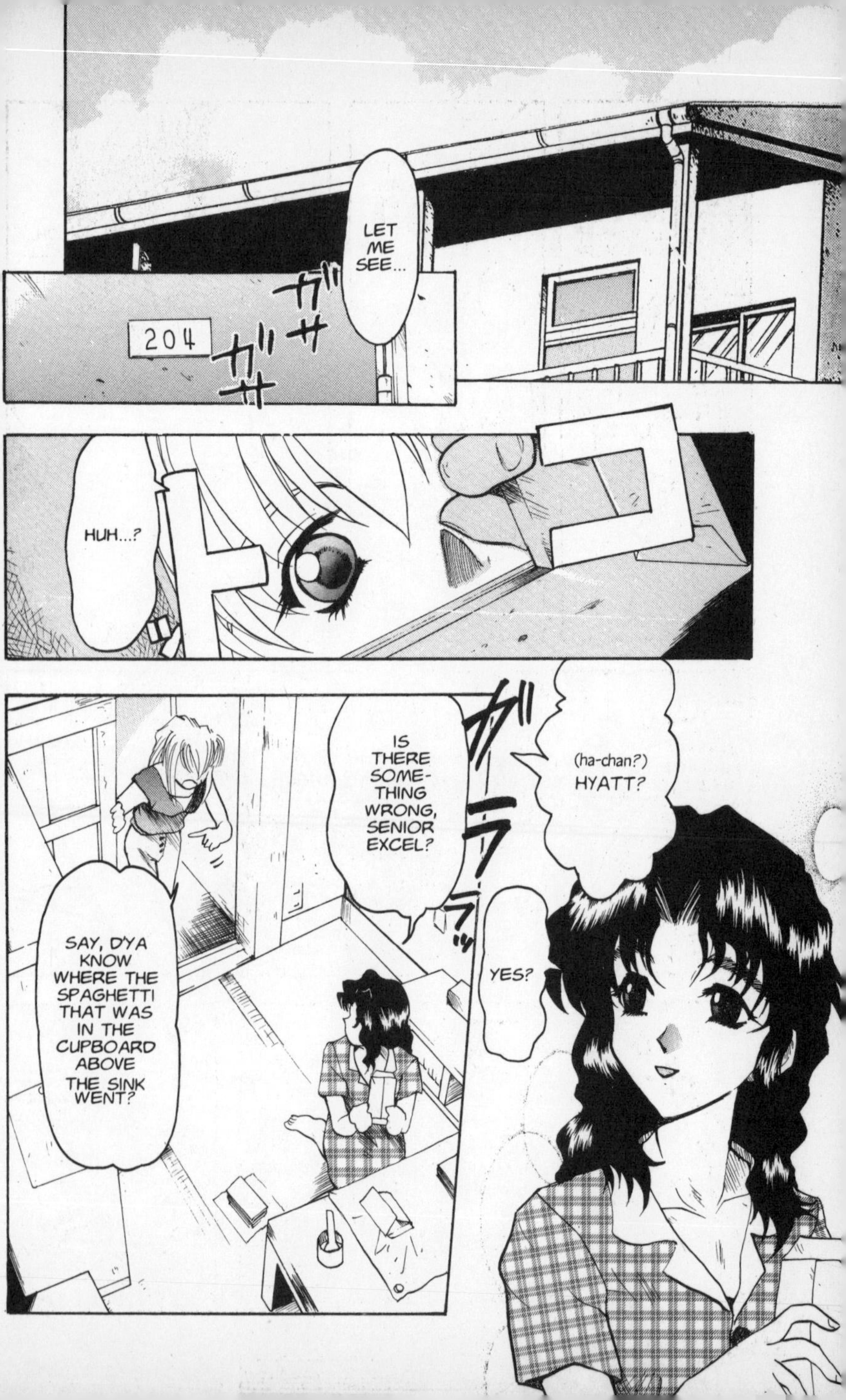
LET ME SEE...
ガサ
ガサ
204
HUH...?
コ
ト
(ha-chan?) HYATT?
ガラーラッ
IS THERE SOMETHING WRONG, SENIOR EXCEL?
YES?
SAY, D'YA KNOW WHERE THE SPAGHETTI THAT WAS IN THE CUPBOARD ABOVE THE SINK WENT?

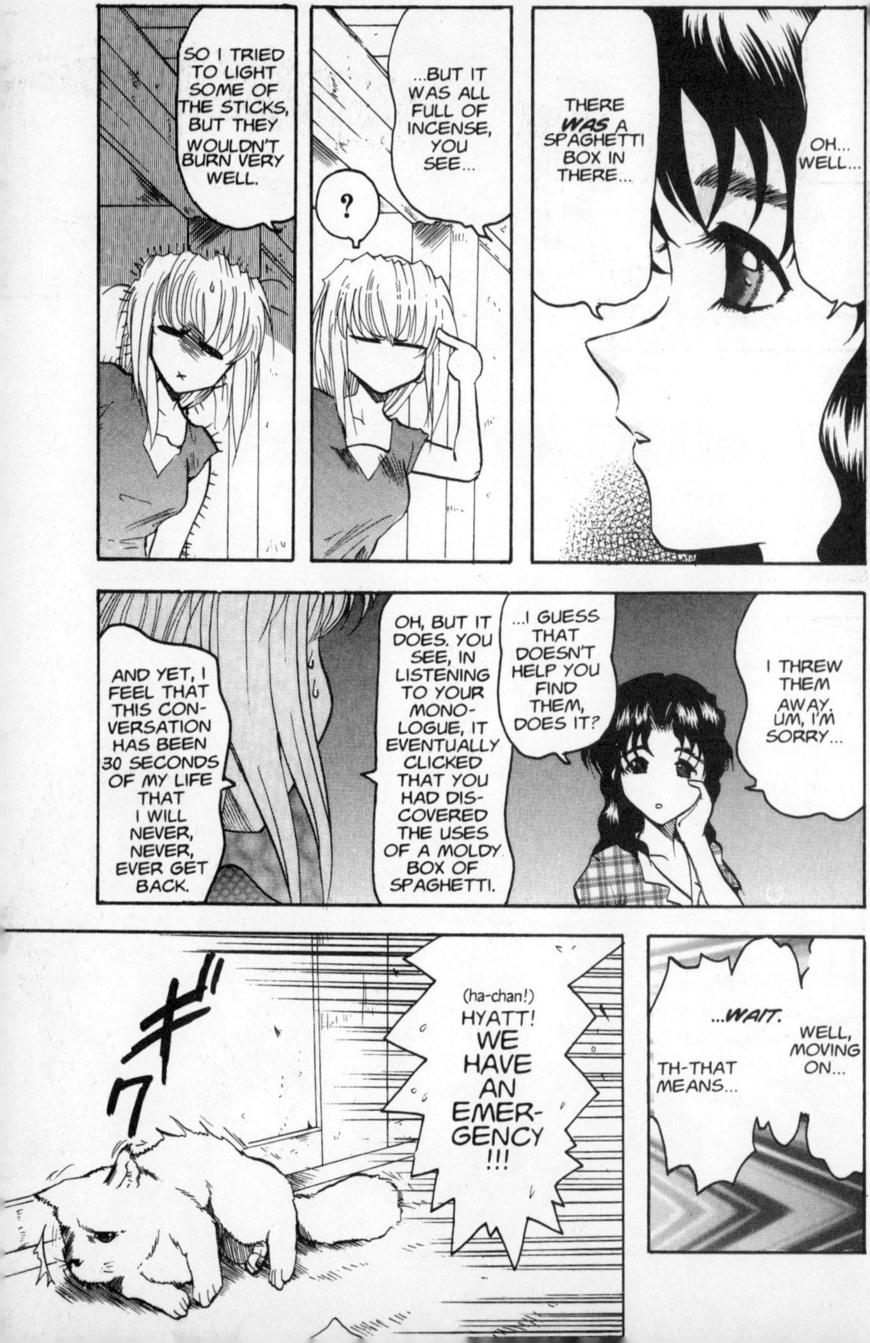
OH... WELL...
THERE *WAS* A SPAGHETTI BOX IN THERE...
...BUT IT WAS ALL FULL OF INCENSE, YOU SEE...
?
SO I TRIED TO LIGHT SOME OF THE STICKS, BUT THEY WOULDN'T BURN VERY WELL.
I THREW THEM AWAY. UM, I'M SORRY...
...I GUESS THAT DOESN'T HELP YOU FIND THEM, DOES IT?
OH, BUT IT DOES. YOU SEE, IN LISTENING TO YOUR MONOLOGUE, IT EVENTUALLY CLICKED THAT YOU HAD DISCOVERED THE USES OF A MOLDY BOX OF SPAGHETTI.
AND YET, I FEEL THAT THIS CONVERSATION HAS BEEN 30 SECONDS OF MY LIFE THAT I WILL NEVER, NEVER, EVER GET BACK.
WELL, MOVING ON...
...*WAIT.*
TH-THAT MEANS...
(ha-chan!) HYATT! WE HAVE AN EMERGENCY!!!
ギク

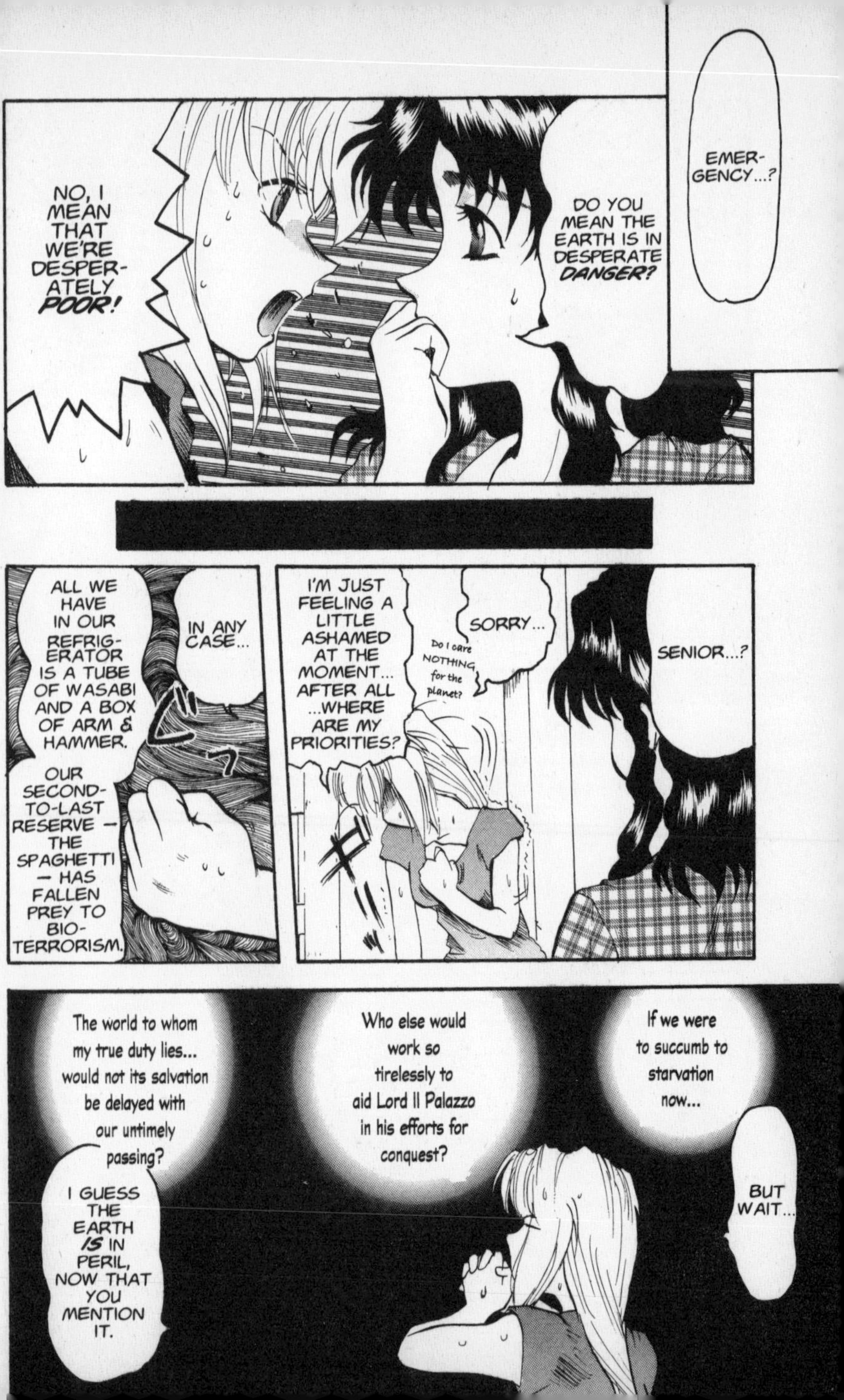
EMERGENCY...?
DO YOU MEAN THE EARTH IS IN DESPERATE *DANGER?*
NO, I MEAN THAT WE'RE DESPERATELY *POOR!*
SENIOR...?
SORRY...
Do I care NOTHING for the planet?
I'M JUST FEELING A LITTLE ASHAMED AT THE MOMENT... AFTER ALL ...WHERE ARE MY PRIORITIES?
IN ANY CASE...
ALL WE HAVE IN OUR REFRIGERATOR IS A TUBE OF WASABI AND A BOX OF ARM & HAMMER.
OUR SECOND-TO-LAST RESERVE — THE SPAGHETTI — HAS FALLEN PREY TO BIO-TERRORISM.
BUT WAIT...
If we were to succumb to starvation now...
Who else would work so tirelessly to aid Lord Il Palazzo in his efforts for conquest?
The world to whom my true duty lies... would not its salvation be delayed with our untimely passing?
I GUESS THE EARTH *IS* IN PERIL, NOW THAT YOU MENTION IT.

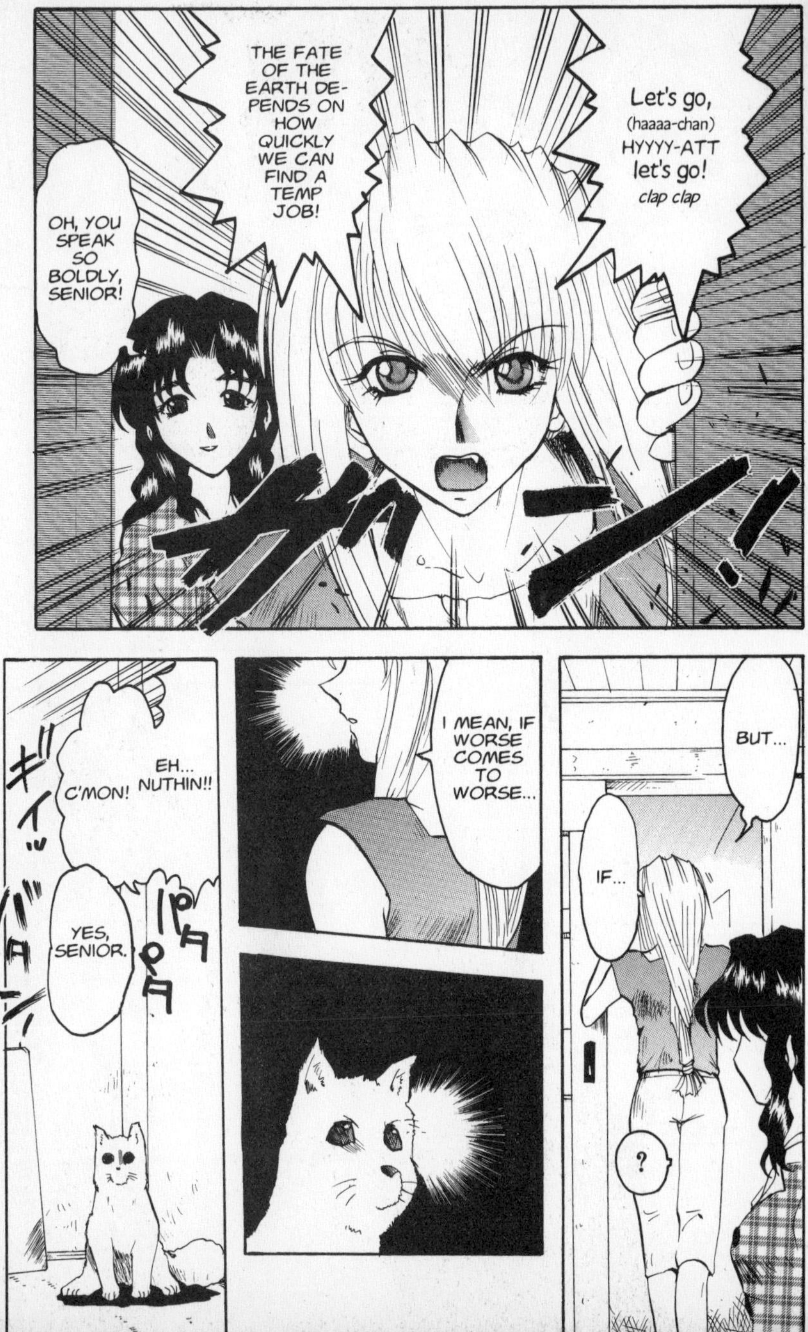
Let's go, (haaaa-chan) HYYYY-ATT let's go! clap clap
THE FATE OF THE EARTH DE-PENDS ON HOW QUICKLY WE CAN FIND A TEMP JOB!
OH, YOU SPEAK SO BOLDLY, SENIOR!
BUT...
IF...
?
I MEAN, IF WORSE COMES TO WORSE...
EH... NUTHIN!!
C'MON!
YES, SENIOR.

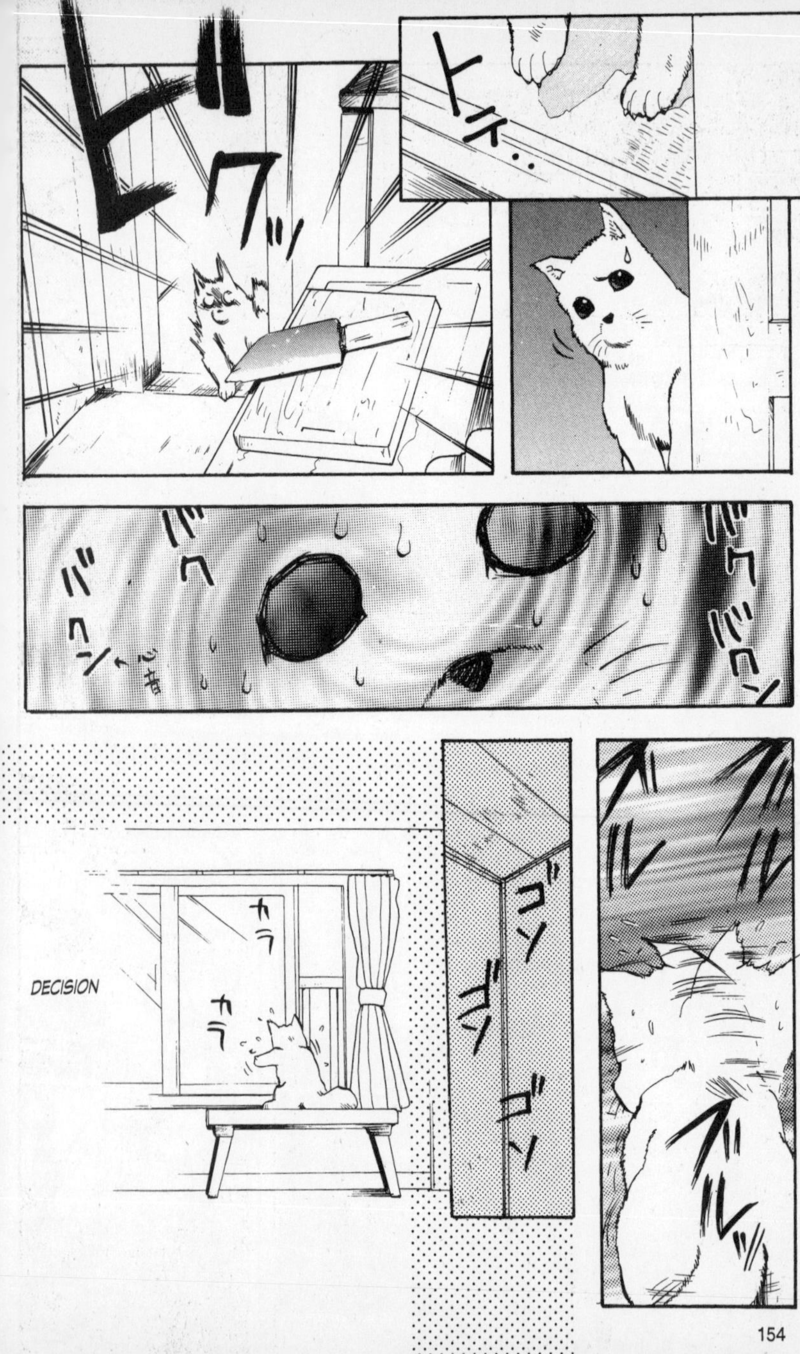
トテ‥
ビクッ
ドクドクン
バクバクン←心音
ブルブル
ゴンゴン
カラカラ
DECISION

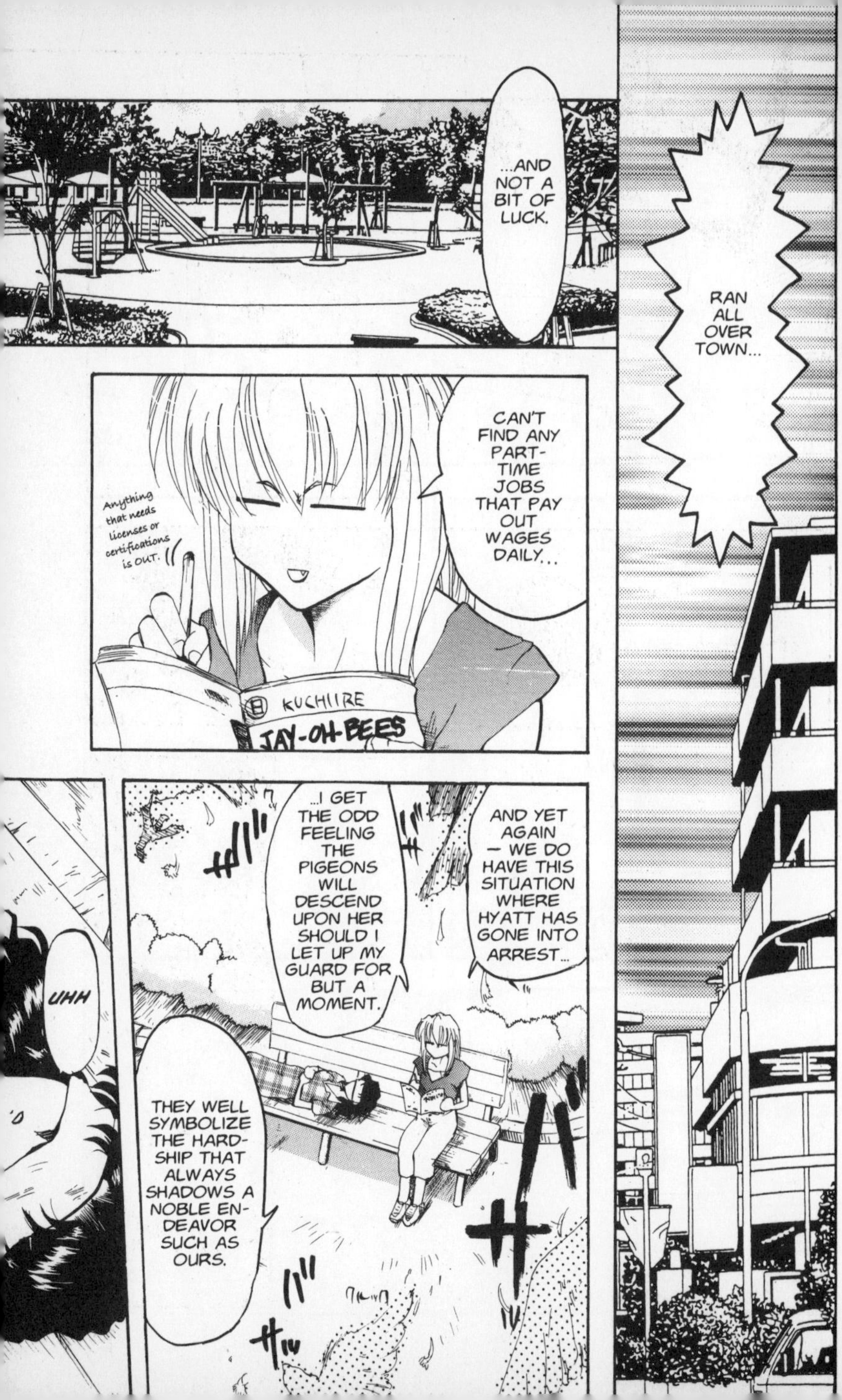
RAN ALL OVER TOWN...
...AND NOT A BIT OF LUCK.
CAN'T FIND ANY PART-TIME JOBS THAT PAY OUT WAGES DAILY...
Anything that needs licenses or certifications is OUT.
KUCHIIRE
JAY-OH-BEES
AND YET AGAIN — WE DO HAVE THIS SITUATION WHERE HYATT HAS GONE INTO ARREST...
...I GET THE ODD FEELING THE PIGEONS WILL DESCEND UPON HER SHOULD I LET UP MY GUARD FOR BUT A MOMENT.
THEY WELL SYMBOLIZE THE HARDSHIP THAT ALWAYS SHADOWS A NOBLE ENDEAVOR SUCH AS OURS.
UHH

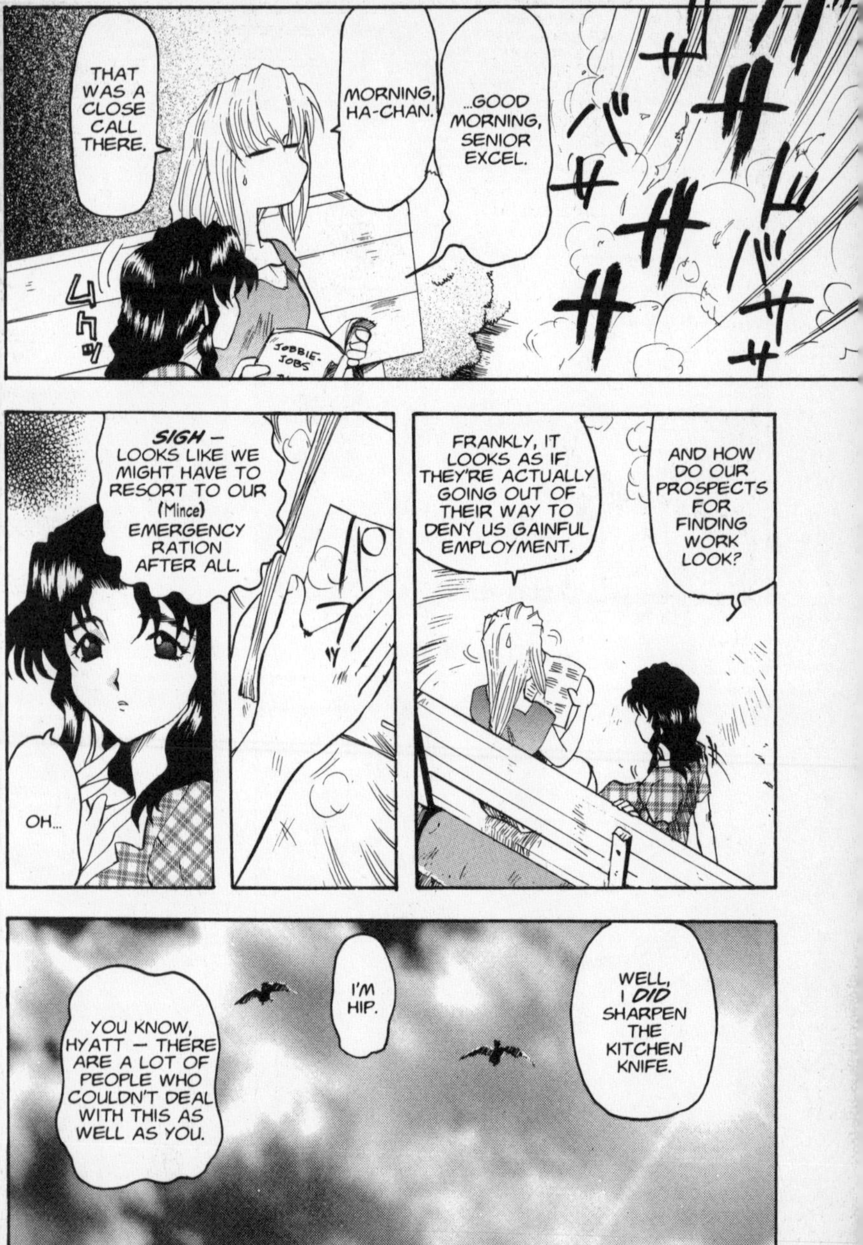
...GOOD MORNING, SENIOR EXCEL.
MORNING, HA-CHAN.
THAT WAS A CLOSE CALL THERE.
JOBBIE-JOBS
AND HOW DO OUR PROSPECTS FOR FINDING WORK LOOK?
FRANKLY, IT LOOKS AS IF THEY'RE ACTUALLY GOING OUT OF THEIR WAY TO DENY US GAINFUL EMPLOYMENT.
SIGH — LOOKS LIKE WE MIGHT HAVE TO RESORT TO OUR (Mince) EMERGENCY RATION AFTER ALL.
OH...
WELL, I *DID* SHARPEN THE KITCHEN KNIFE.
I'M HIP.
YOU KNOW, HYATT — THERE ARE A LOT OF PEOPLE WHO COULDN'T DEAL WITH THIS AS WELL AS YOU.

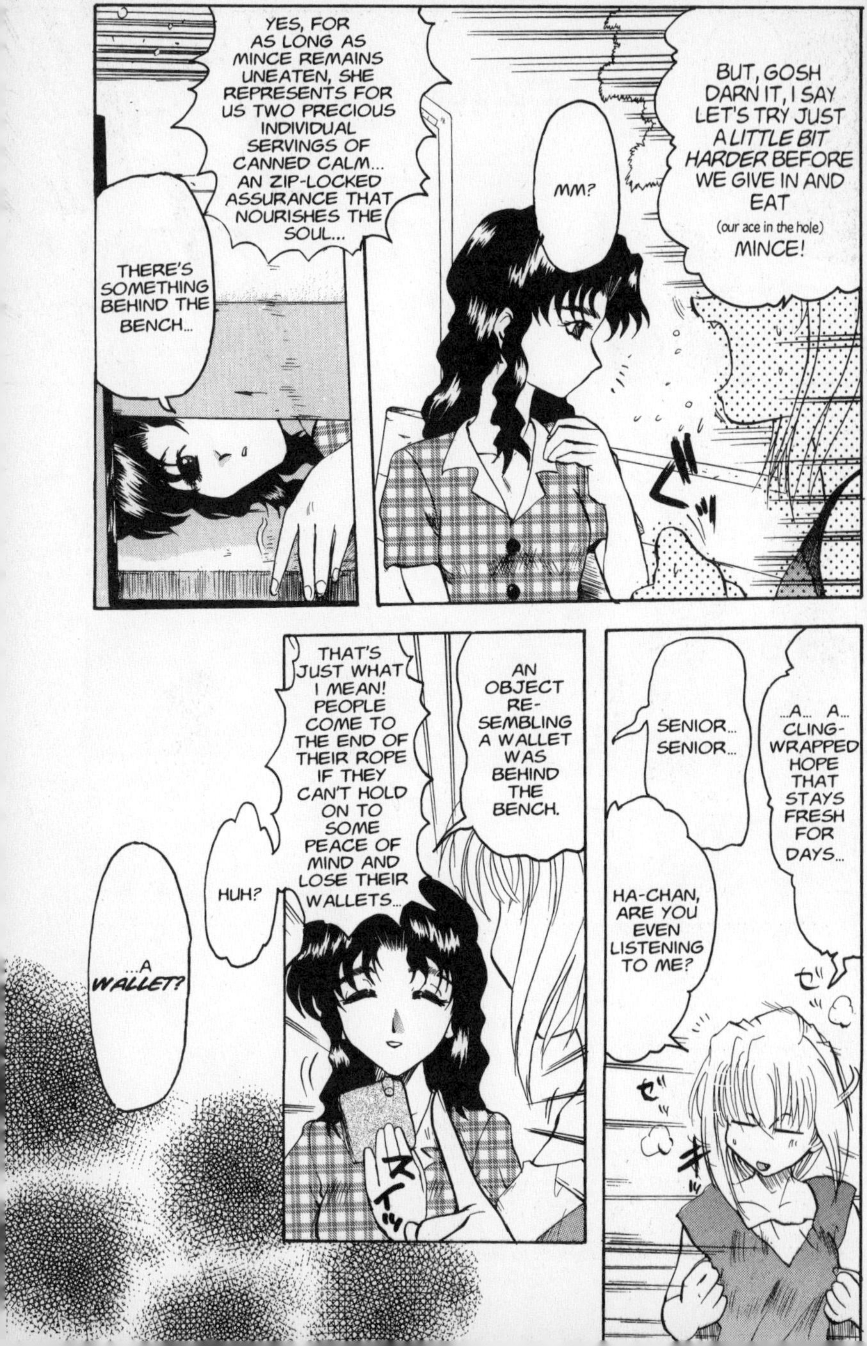
BUT, GOSH DARN IT, I SAY LET'S TRY JUST A LITTLE BIT HARDER BEFORE WE GIVE IN AND EAT (our ace in the hole) MINCE!
MM?
YES, FOR AS LONG AS MINCE REMAINS UNEATEN, SHE REPRESENTS FOR US TWO PRECIOUS INDIVIDUAL SERVINGS OF CANNED CALM... AN ZIP-LOCKED ASSURANCE THAT NOURISHES THE SOUL...
THERE'S SOMETHING BEHIND THE BENCH...
...A... A... CLING-WRAPPED HOPE THAT STAYS FRESH FOR DAYS...
SENIOR... SENIOR...
HA-CHAN, ARE YOU EVEN LISTENING TO ME?
AN OBJECT RE-SEMBLING A WALLET WAS BEHIND THE BENCH.
THAT'S JUST WHAT I MEAN! PEOPLE COME TO THE END OF THEIR ROPE IF THEY CAN'T HOLD ON TO SOME PEACE OF MIND AND LOSE THEIR WALLETS...
HUH?
...A WALLET?

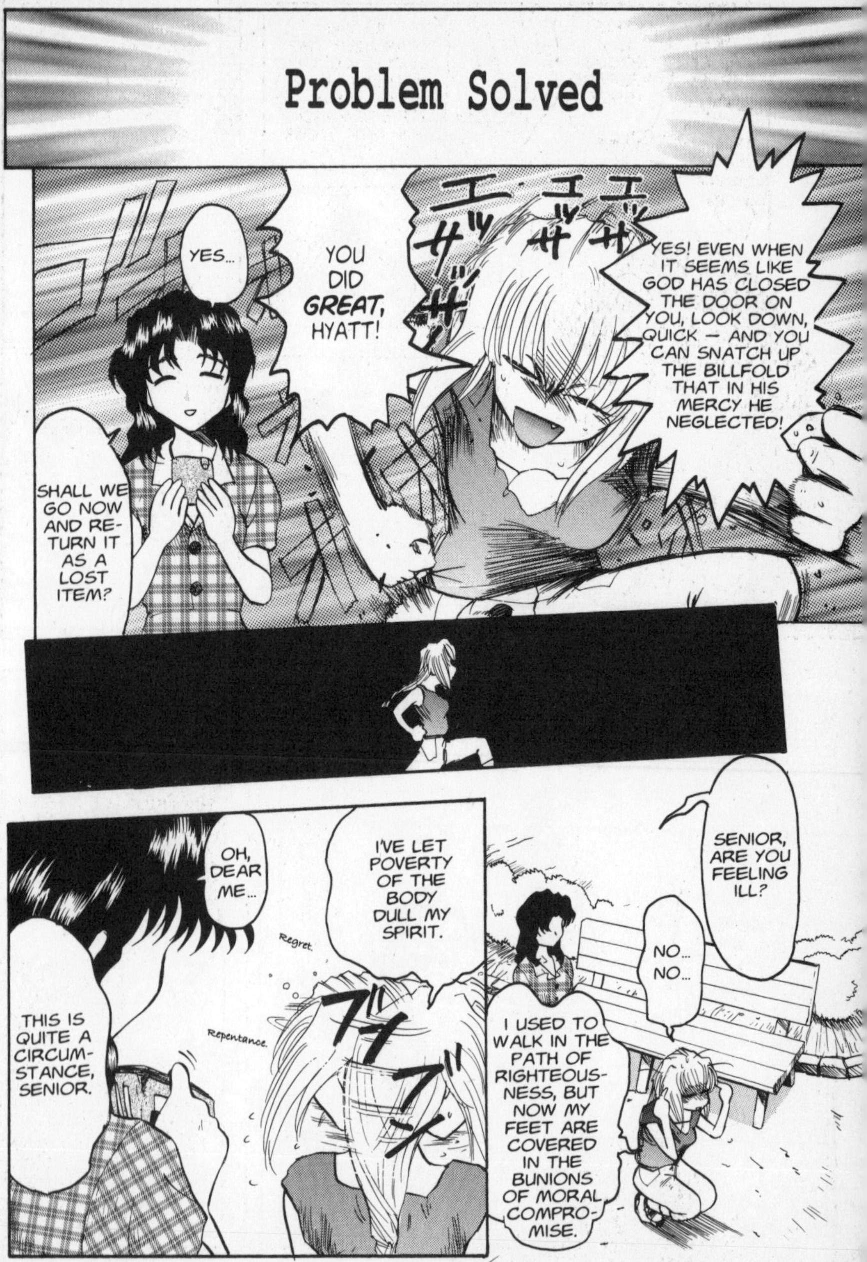
Problem Solved
YES! EVEN WHEN IT SEEMS LIKE GOD HAS CLOSED THE DOOR ON YOU, LOOK DOWN, QUICK — AND YOU CAN SNATCH UP THE BILLFOLD THAT IN HIS MERCY HE NEGLECTED!
YOU DID GREAT, HYATT!
YES...
SHALL WE GO NOW AND RE-TURN IT AS A LOST ITEM?
SENIOR, ARE YOU FEELING ILL?
NO... NO...
I USED TO WALK IN THE PATH OF RIGHTEOUS-NESS, BUT NOW MY FEET ARE COVERED IN THE BUNIONS OF MORAL COMPRO-MISE.
I'VE LET POVERTY OF THE BODY DULL MY SPIRIT.
Regret.
Repentance.
OH, DEAR ME...
THIS IS QUITE A CIRCUM-STANCE, SENIOR.

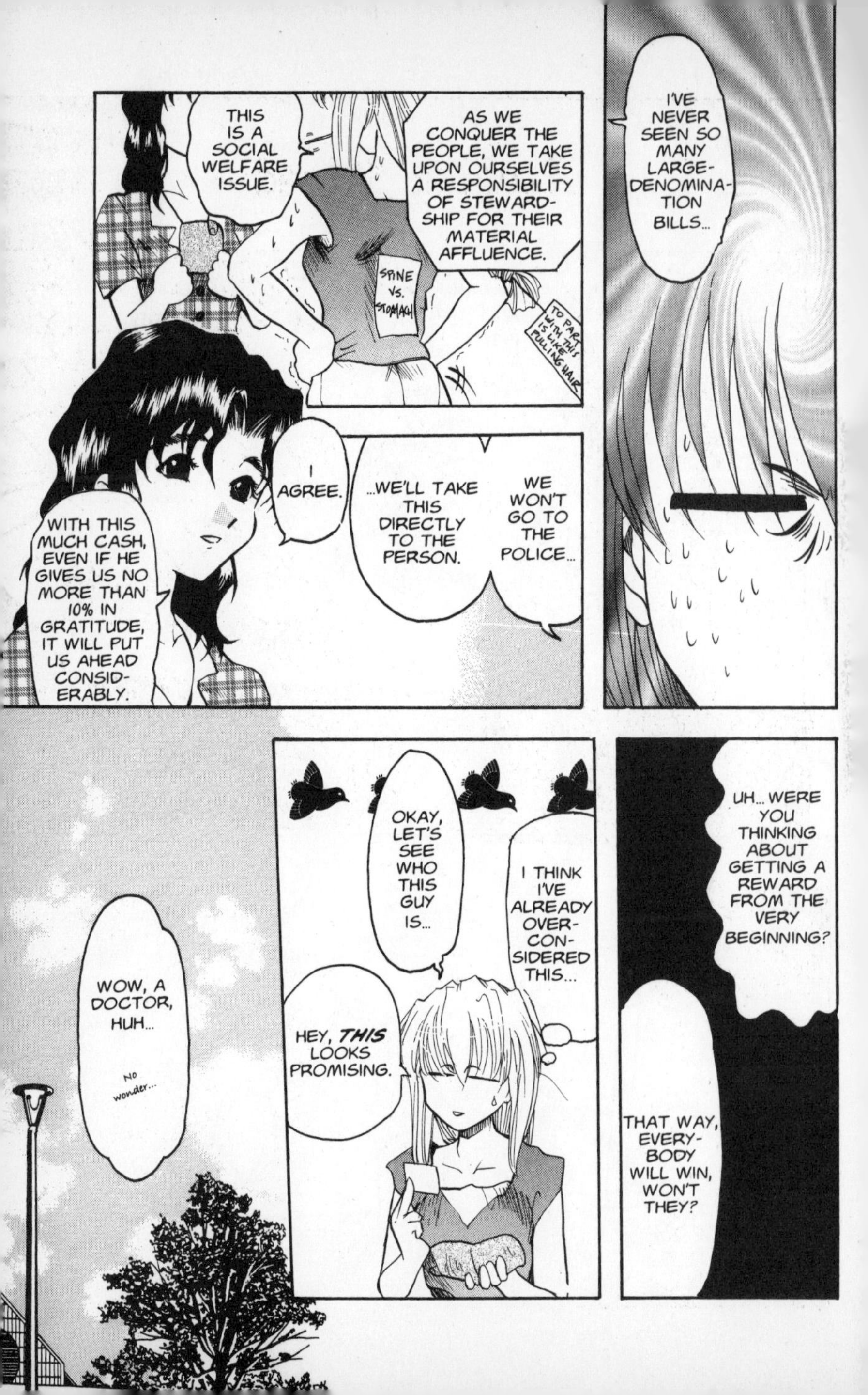

I'VE NEVER SEEN SO MANY LARGE-DENOMINATION BILLS...
AS WE CONQUER THE PEOPLE, WE TAKE UPON OURSELVES A RESPONSIBILITY OF STEWARDSHIP FOR THEIR MATERIAL AFFLUENCE.
THIS IS A SOCIAL WELFARE ISSUE.
TO PART WITH THIS IS LIKE PULLING HAIR
SPINE VS. STOMACH
WE WON'T GO TO THE POLICE...
...WE'LL TAKE THIS DIRECTLY TO THE PERSON.
I AGREE.
WITH THIS MUCH CASH, EVEN IF HE GIVES US NO MORE THAN 10% IN GRATITUDE, IT WILL PUT US AHEAD CONSIDERABLY.
UH... WERE YOU THINKING ABOUT GETTING A REWARD FROM THE VERY BEGINNING?
THAT WAY, EVERYBODY WILL WIN, WON'T THEY?
I THINK I'VE ALREADY OVER-CONSIDERED THIS...
OKAY, LET'S SEE WHO THIS GUY IS...
HEY, *THIS* LOOKS PROMISING.
WOW, A DOCTOR, HUH...
No wonder...

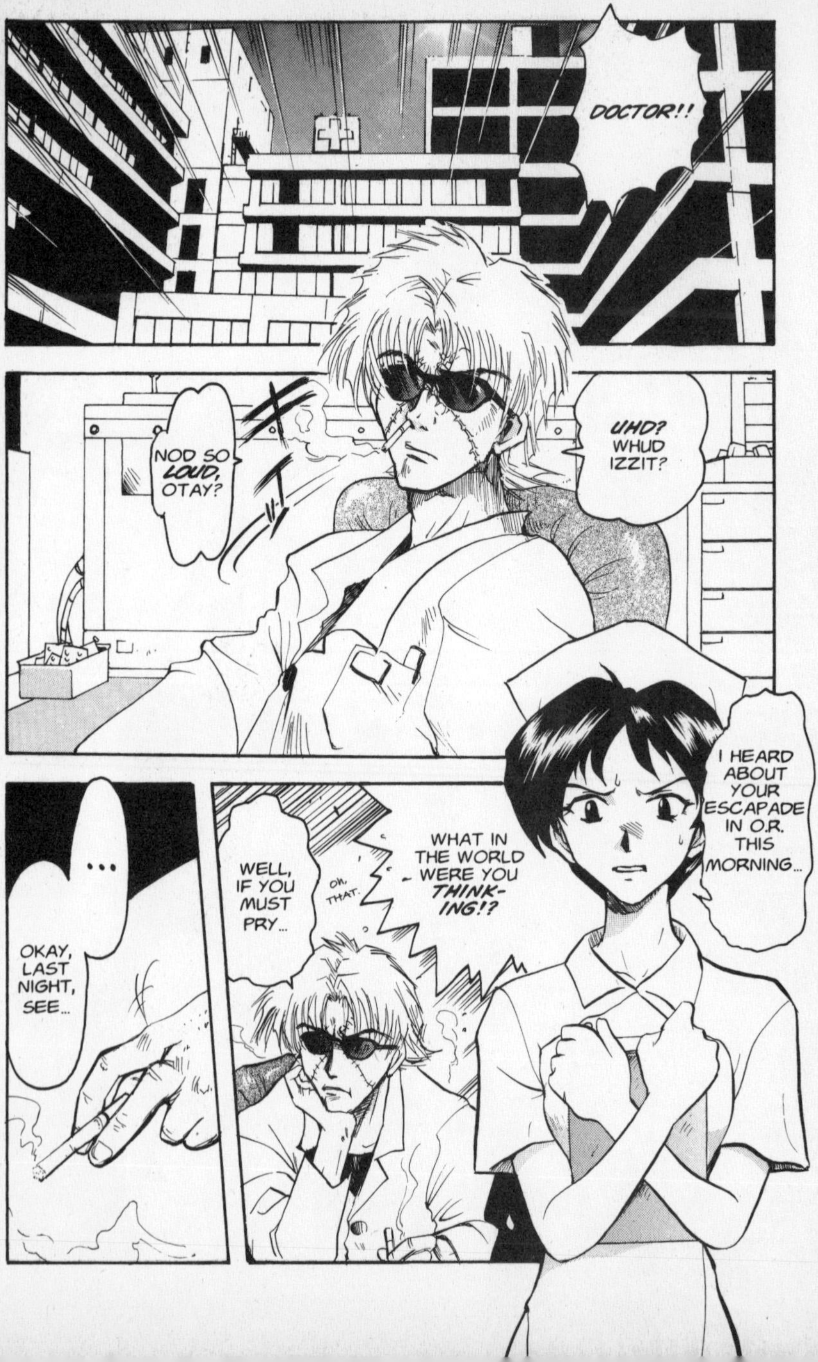
DOCTOR!!
UHD? WHUD IZZIT?
NOD SO LOUD, OTAY?
I HEARD ABOUT YOUR ESCAPADE IN O.R. THIS MORNING...
WHAT IN THE WORLD WERE YOU THINKING!?
oh, THAT.
WELL, IF YOU MUST PRY...
...
OKAY, LAST NIGHT, SEE...

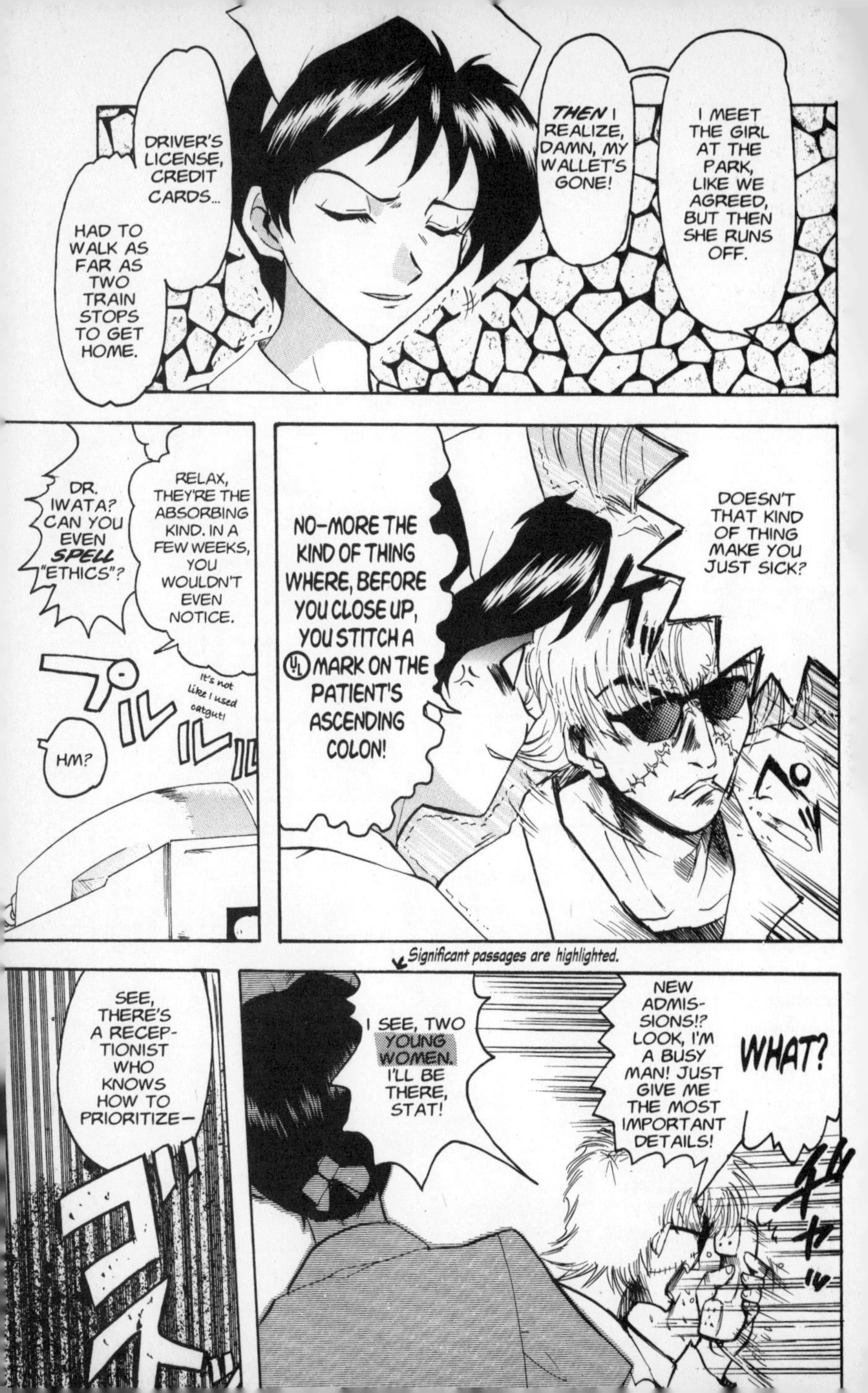
I MEET THE GIRL AT THE PARK, LIKE WE AGREED, BUT THEN SHE RUNS OFF.
THEN I REALIZE, DAMN, MY WALLET'S GONE!
DRIVER'S LICENSE, CREDIT CARDS...
HAD TO WALK AS FAR AS TWO TRAIN STOPS TO GET HOME.
DOESN'T THAT KIND OF THING MAKE YOU JUST SICK?
NO-MORE THE KIND OF THING WHERE, BEFORE YOU CLOSE UP, YOU STITCH A UL MARK ON THE PATIENT'S ASCENDING COLON!
RELAX, THEY'RE THE ABSORBING KIND. IN A FEW WEEKS, YOU WOULDN'T EVEN NOTICE.
DR. IWATA? CAN YOU EVEN SPELL "ETHICS"?
It's not like I used catgut!
プルルル
HM?
Significant passages are highlighted.
WHAT?
NEW ADMISSIONS!? LOOK, I'M A BUSY MAN! JUST GIVE ME THE MOST IMPORTANT DETAILS!
I SEE, TWO YOUNG WOMEN. I'LL BE THERE, STAT!
SEE, THERE'S A RECEPTIONIST WHO KNOWS HOW TO PRIORITIZE—

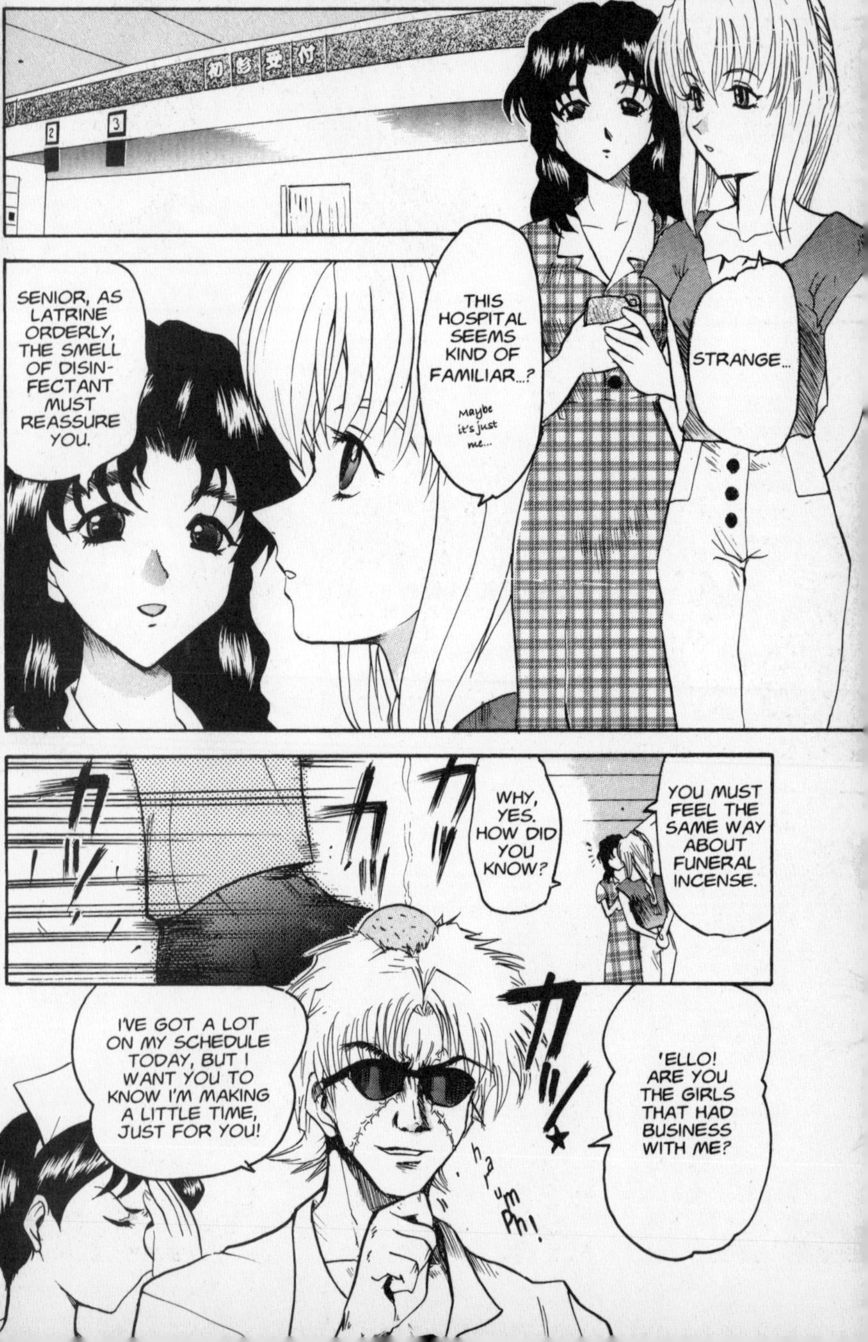
初診受付
3
2
STRANGE...
THIS HOSPITAL SEEMS KIND OF FAMILIAR...?
Maybe it's just me...
SENIOR, AS LATRINE ORDERLY, THE SMELL OF DISIN-FECTANT MUST REASSURE YOU.
YOU MUST FEEL THE SAME WAY ABOUT FUNERAL INCENSE.
WHY, YES. HOW DID YOU KNOW?
'ELLO! ARE YOU THE GIRLS THAT HAD BUSINESS WITH ME?
haumph!
I'VE GOT A LOT ON MY SCHEDULE TODAY, BUT I WANT YOU TO KNOW I'M MAKING A LITTLE TIME, JUST FOR YOU!

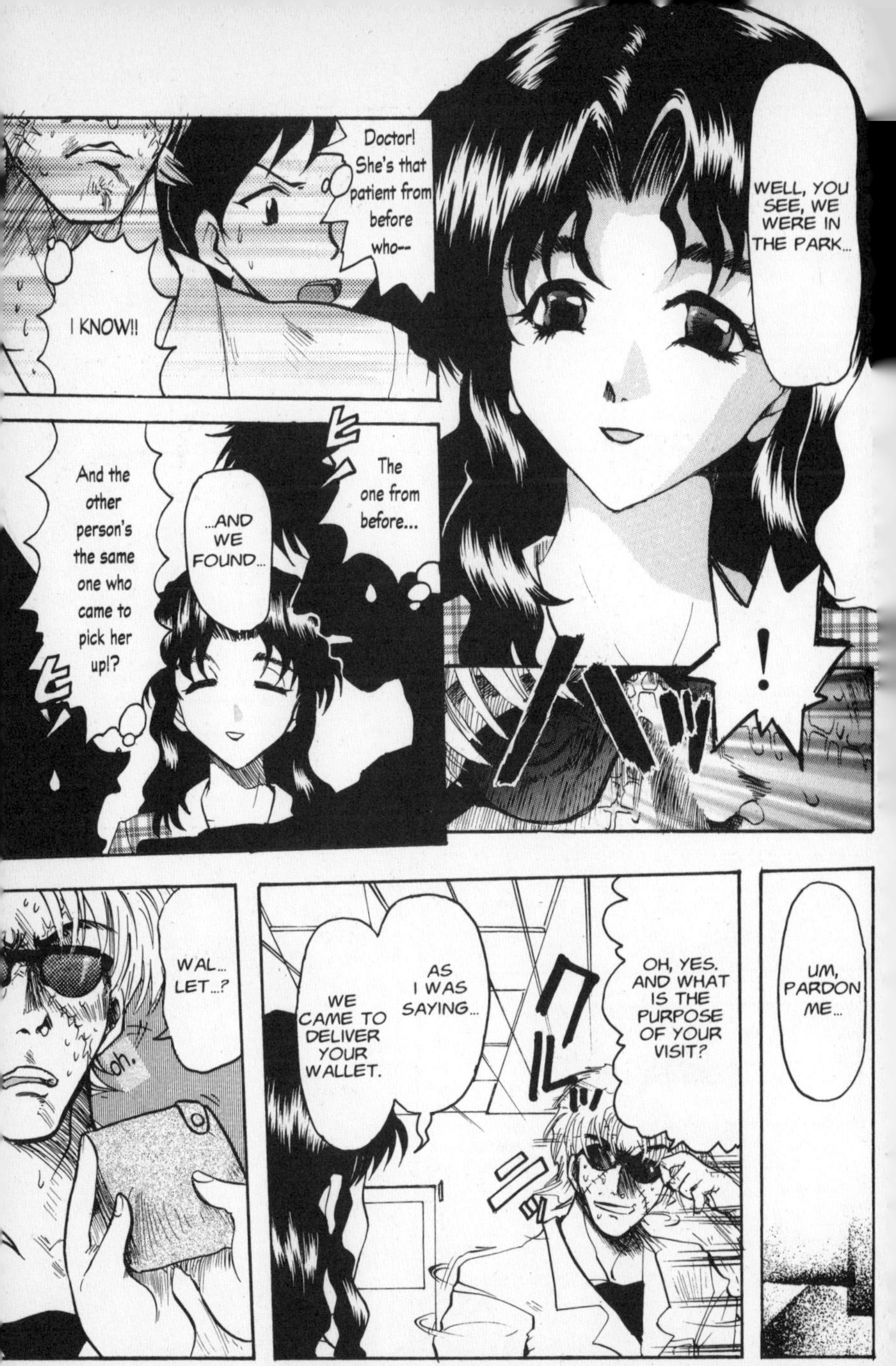
WELL, YOU SEE, WE WERE IN THE PARK...
!
Doctor! She's that patient from before who--
I KNOW!!
The one from before...
...AND WE FOUND...
And the other person's the same one who came to pick her up!?
UM, PARDON ME...
OH, YES. AND WHAT IS THE PURPOSE OF YOUR VISIT?
AS I WAS SAYING...
WE CAME TO DELIVER YOUR WALLET.
WAL... LET...?
oh.

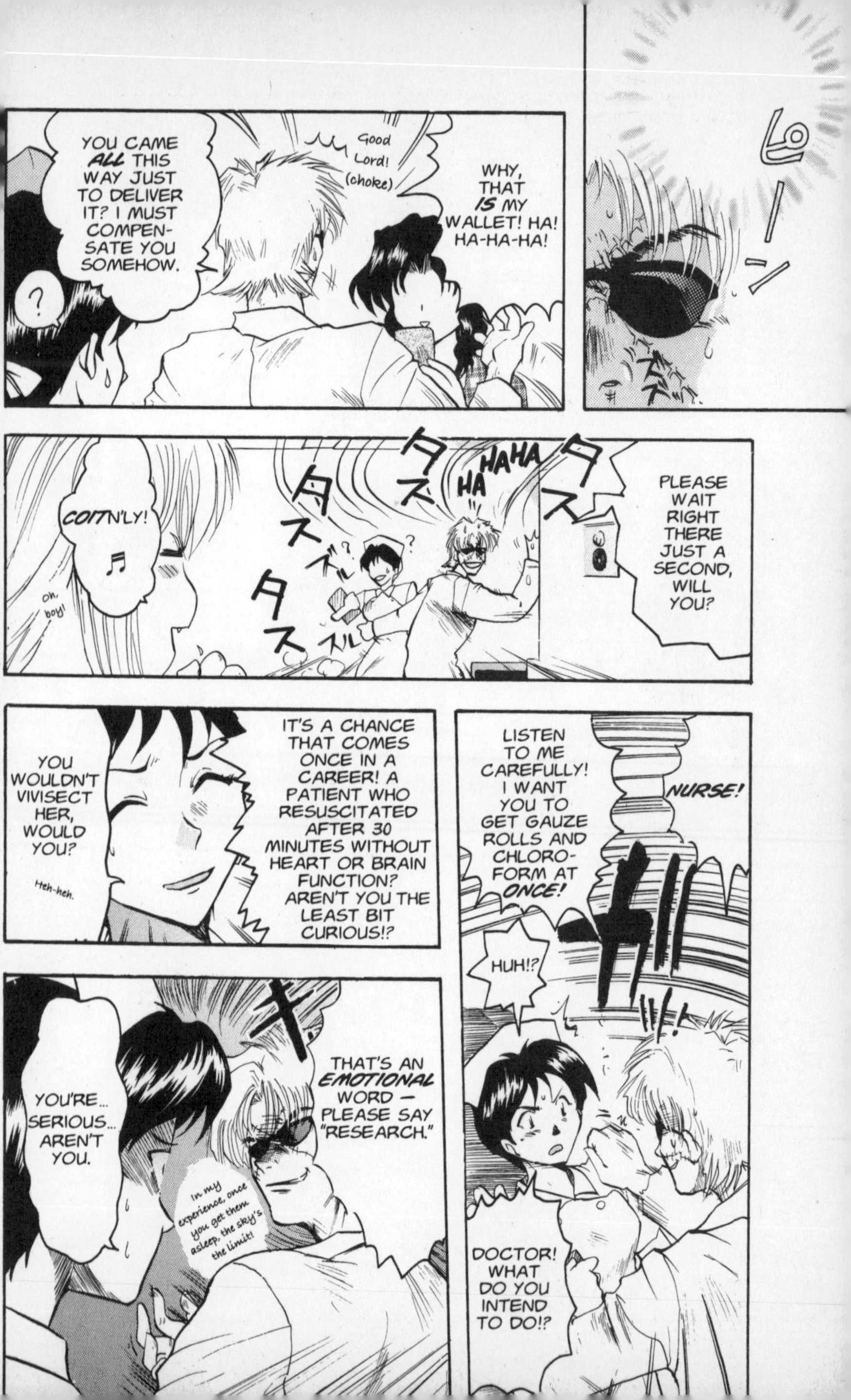
ピーン
WHY, THAT IS MY WALLET! HA! HA-HA-HA!
Good Lord! (choke)
YOU CAME ALL THIS WAY JUST TO DELIVER IT? I MUST COMPEN-SATE YOU SOMEHOW.
?
PLEASE WAIT RIGHT THERE JUST A SECOND, WILL YOU?
HAHA HA
COITN'LY!
♪
oh, boy!
NURSE!
LISTEN TO ME CAREFULLY! I WANT YOU TO GET GAUZE ROLLS AND CHLORO-FORM AT ONCE!
HUH!?
DOCTOR! WHAT DO YOU INTEND TO DO!?
IT'S A CHANCE THAT COMES ONCE IN A CAREER! A PATIENT WHO RESUSCITATED AFTER 30 MINUTES WITHOUT HEART OR BRAIN FUNCTION? AREN'T YOU THE LEAST BIT CURIOUS!?
YOU WOULDN'T VIVISECT HER, WOULD YOU?
Heh-heh.
THAT'S AN EMOTIONAL WORD — PLEASE SAY "RESEARCH."
YOU'RE... SERIOUS... AREN'T YOU.
In my experience, once you get them asleep, the sky's the limit!

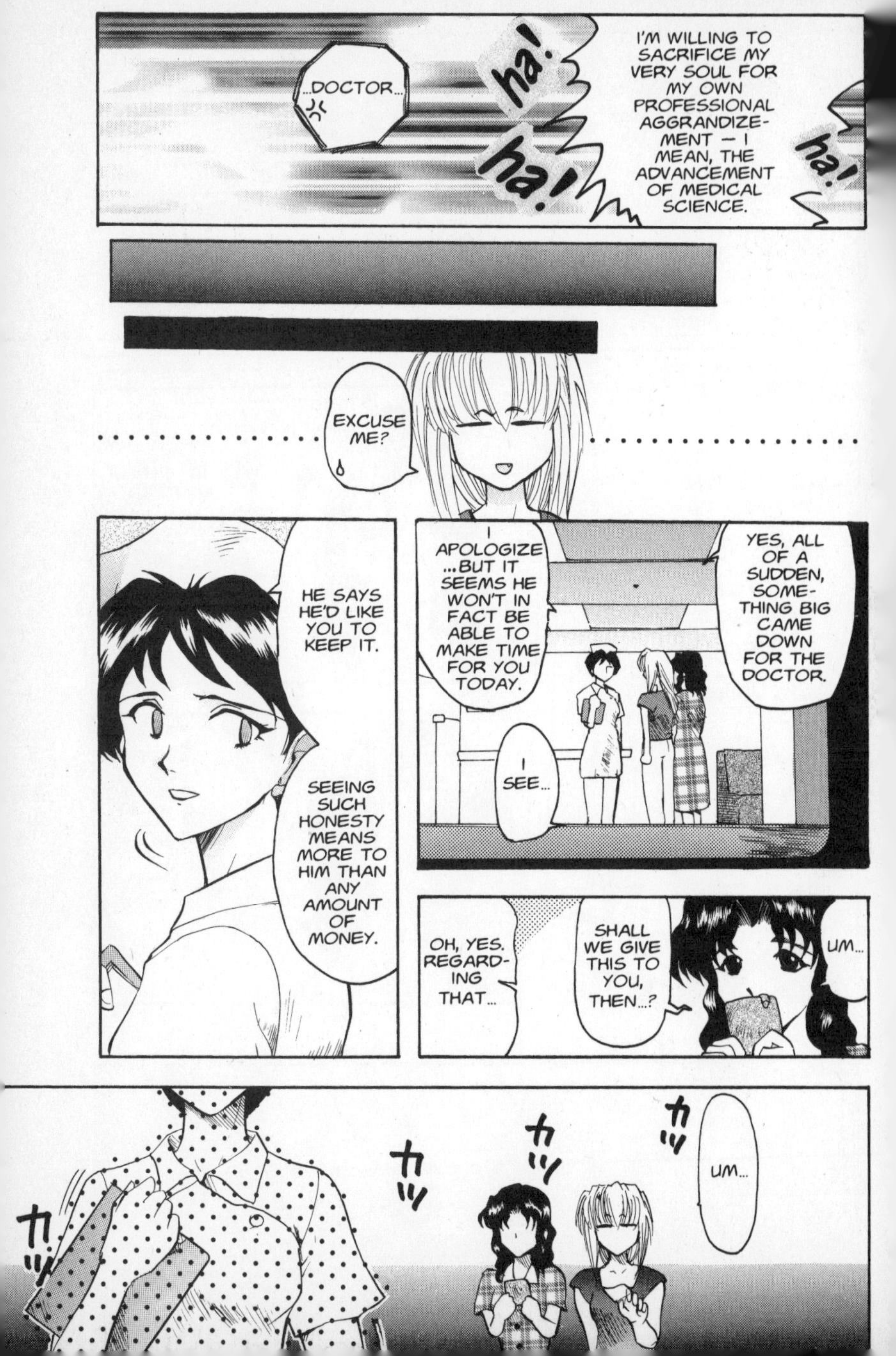
ha!
I'M WILLING TO SACRIFICE MY VERY SOUL FOR MY OWN PROFESSIONAL AGGRANDIZE-MENT — I MEAN, THE ADVANCEMENT OF MEDICAL SCIENCE.
ha! ha!
...DOCTOR...
EXCUSE ME?
YES, ALL OF A SUDDEN, SOME-THING BIG CAME DOWN FOR THE DOCTOR.
I APOLOGIZE ...BUT IT SEEMS HE WON'T IN FACT BE ABLE TO MAKE TIME FOR YOU TODAY.
I SEE...
UM...
SHALL WE GIVE THIS TO YOU, THEN...?
OH, YES. REGARDING THAT...
HE SAYS HE'D LIKE YOU TO KEEP IT.
SEEING SUCH HONESTY MEANS MORE TO HIM THAN ANY AMOUNT OF MONEY.
カッ
UM...
カッ
カッ
カッ

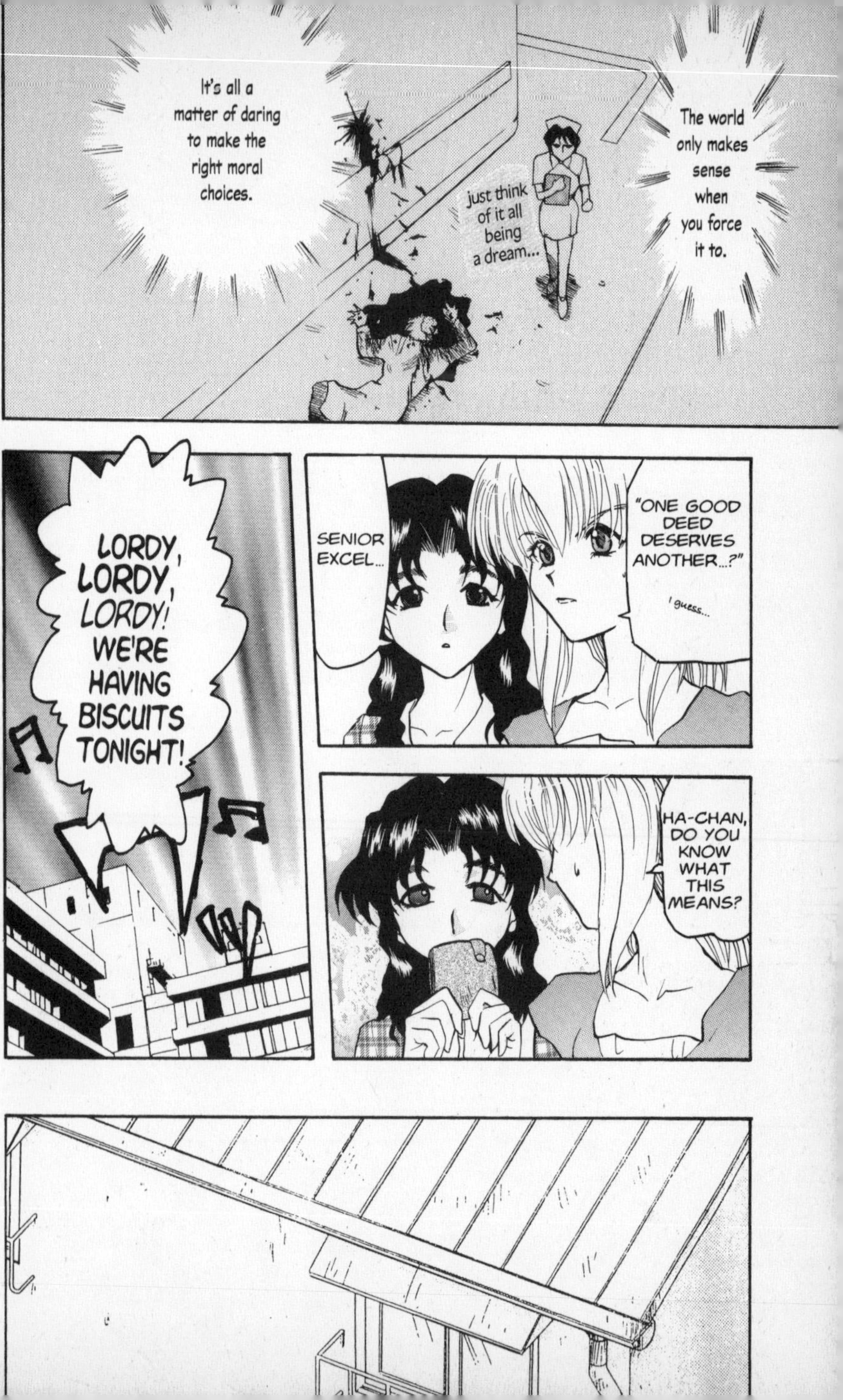
The world only makes sense when you force it to.
just think of it all being a dream...
It's all a matter of daring to make the right moral choices.
"ONE GOOD DEED DESERVES ANOTHER...?"
I guess...
SENIOR EXCEL...
HA-CHAN, DO YOU KNOW WHAT THIS MEANS?
LORDY, LORDY, LORDY! WE'RE HAVING BISCUITS TONIGHT!

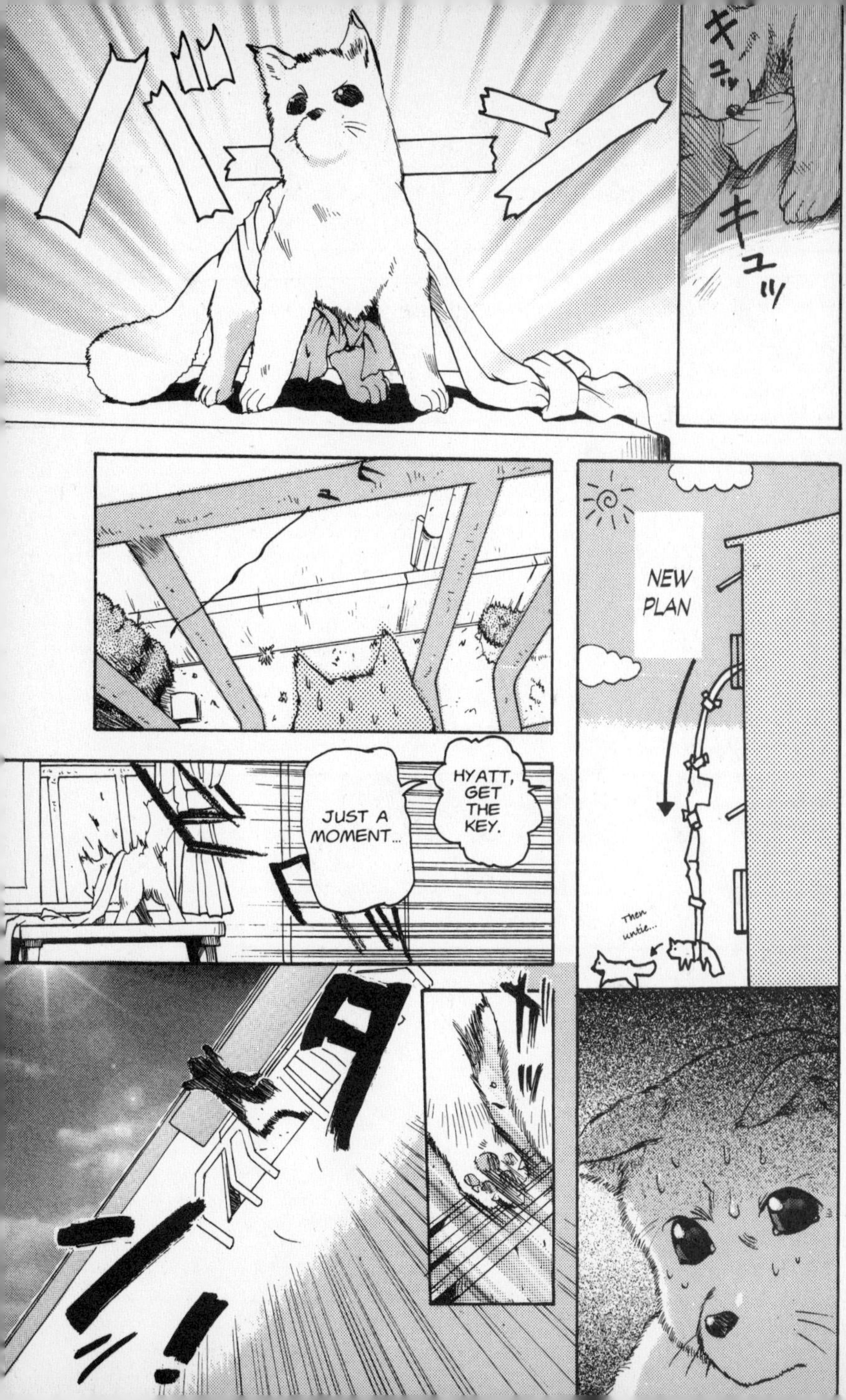
キュッ
キュッ
NEW PLAN
Then untie...
HYATT, GET THE KEY.
JUST A MOMENT...

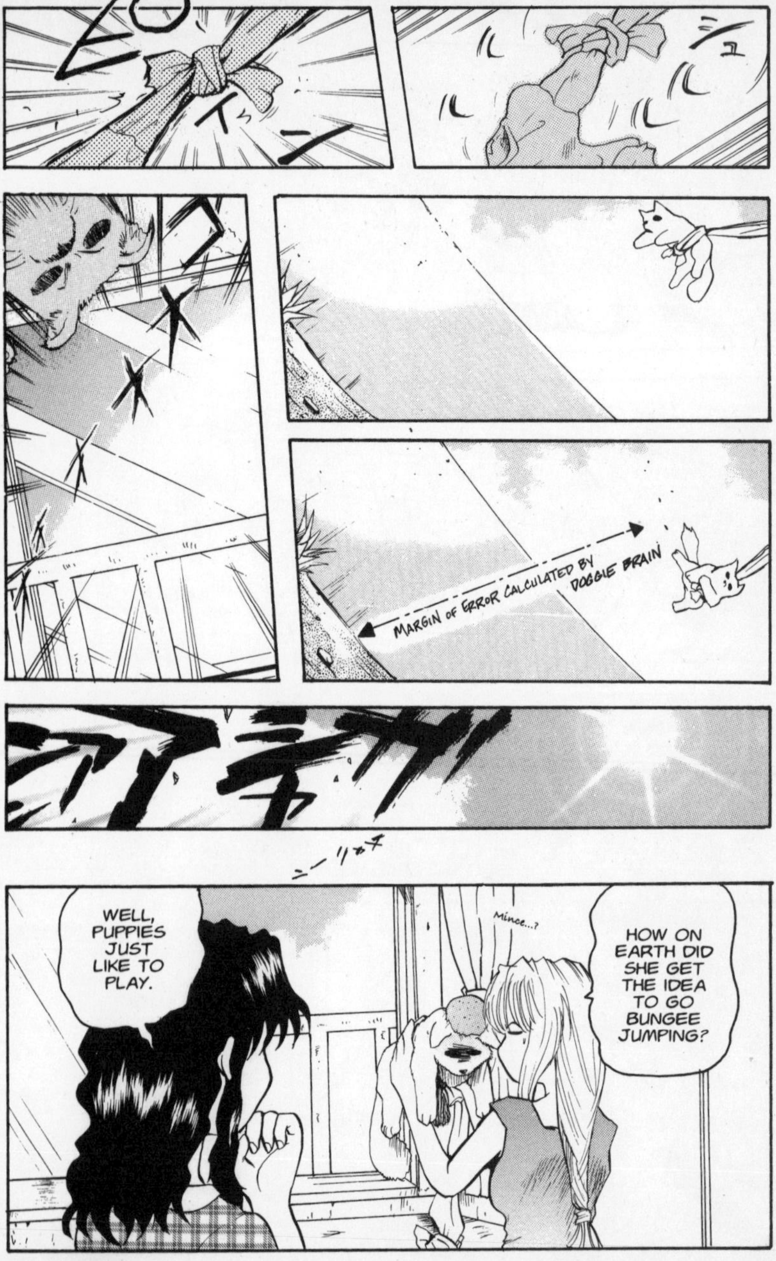
MARGIN OF ERROR CALCULATED BY DOGGIE BRAIN
HOW ON EARTH DID SHE GET THE IDEA TO GO BUNGEE JUMPING?
Mince...?
WELL, PUPPIES JUST LIKE TO PLAY.

EXCEL SAGA

NOT THAT THIS MATTERS...
Eh? What happened, like?
ヒュウ
BUT SUMIYOSHI LIVES DIRECTLY BELOW EXCEL AND HYATT.
It's a meaningless bit of trivia.

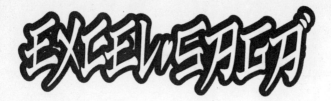

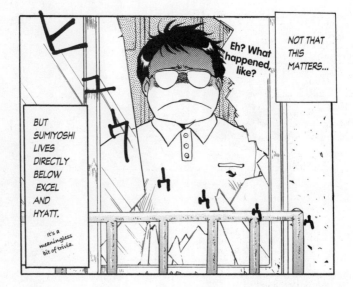

Scenes from the Personal Life of Rikdo Koshi

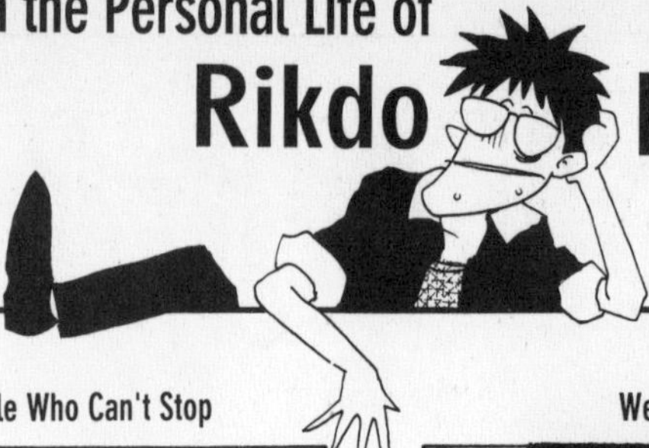

Vol.②

We The Living

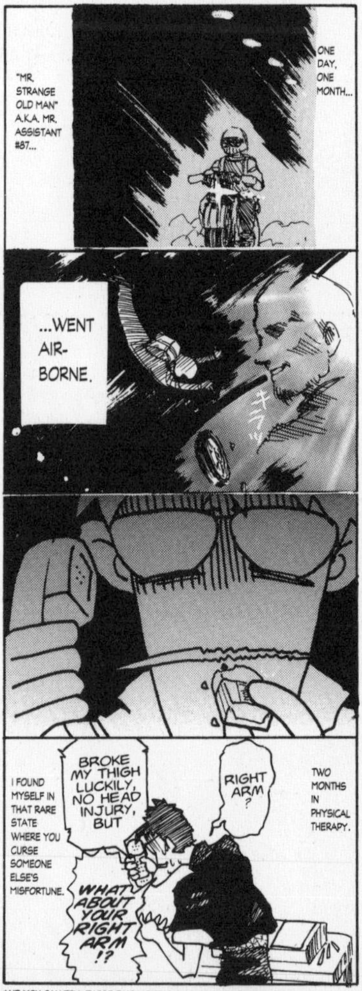

ONE DAY, ONE MONTH...
"MR. STRANGE OLD MAN" A.K.A. MR. ASSISTANT #87...
...WENT AIR-BORNE.
キラッ
TWO MONTHS IN PHYSICAL THERAPY.
RIGHT ARM?
BROKE MY THIGH LUCKILY, NO HEAD INJURY, BUT
I FOUND MYSELF IN THAT RARE STATE WHERE YOU CURSE SOMEONE ELSE'S MISFORTUNE.
WHAT ABOUT YOUR RIGHT ARM!?

AND YOU CAN TELL THOSE TWO MONTHS BY THE AWFUL BACKGROUND ART.

The People Who Can't Stop

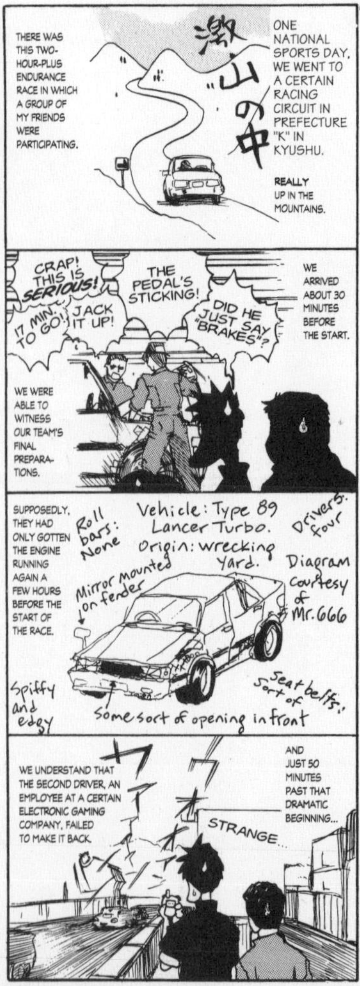

ONE NATIONAL SPORTS DAY, WE WENT TO A CERTAIN RACING CIRCUIT IN PREFECTURE "K" IN KYUSHU.
激山の中
THERE WAS THIS TWO-HOUR-PLUS ENDURANCE RACE IN WHICH A GROUP OF MY FRIENDS WERE PARTICIPATING.
REALLY UP IN THE MOUNTAINS.
WE ARRIVED ABOUT 30 MINUTES BEFORE THE START.
DID HE JUST SAY "BRAKES"?
THE PEDAL'S STICKING!
CRAP! THIS IS SERIOUS!
JACK IT UP!
17 MIN. TO GO!
WE WERE ABLE TO WITNESS OUR TEAM'S FINAL PREPARA-TIONS.
Drivers: four
Vehicle: Type 89 Lancer Turbo.
Origin: wrecking yard.
Roll bars: None
SUPPOSEDLY, THEY HAD ONLY GOTTEN THE ENGINE RUNNING AGAIN A FEW HOURS BEFORE THE START OF THE RACE.
Diagram Courtesy of Mr.666
Mirror mounted on fender
Seat belts: Sort of
Spiffy and edgy
Some sort of opening in front
AND JUST 50 MINUTES PAST THAT DRAMATIC BEGINNING...
STRANGE...
WE UNDERSTAND THAT THE SECOND DRIVER, AN EMPLOYEE AT A CERTAIN ELECTRONIC GAMING COMPANY, FAILED TO MAKE IT BACK.

RESULTS: DEATHS, ZERO. SLIGHT INJURIES, ONE.

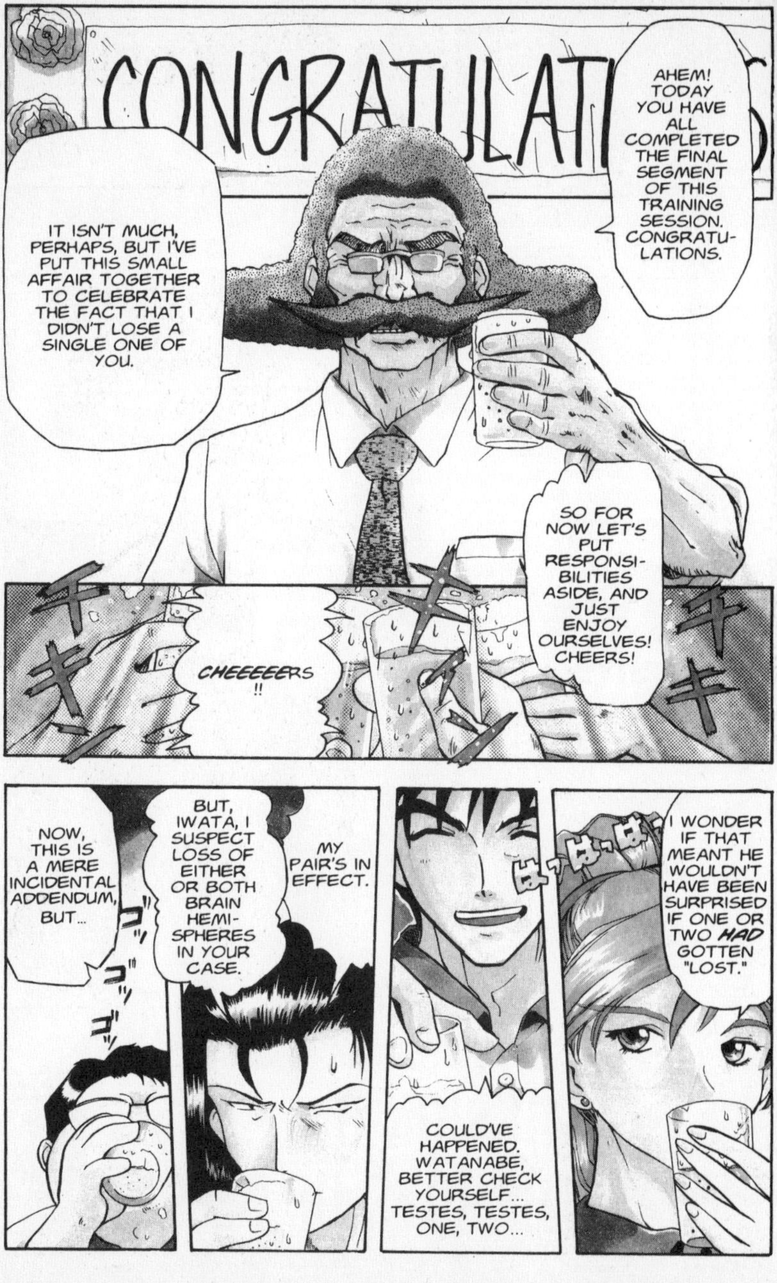
CONGRATULATI
AHEM! TODAY YOU HAVE ALL COMPLETED THE FINAL SEGMENT OF THIS TRAINING SESSION. CONGRATU-LATIONS.
IT ISN'T MUCH, PERHAPS, BUT I'VE PUT THIS SMALL AFFAIR TOGETHER TO CELEBRATE THE FACT THAT I DIDN'T LOSE A SINGLE ONE OF YOU.
SO FOR NOW LET'S PUT RESPONSI-BILITIES ASIDE, AND JUST ENJOY OURSELVES! CHEERS!
CHEEEEERS !!
I WONDER IF THAT MEANT HE WOULDN'T HAVE BEEN SURPRISED IF ONE OR TWO *HAD* GOTTEN "LOST."
COULD'VE HAPPENED. WATANABE, BETTER CHECK YOURSELF... TESTES, TESTES, ONE, TWO...
MY PAIR'S IN EFFECT.
BUT, IWATA, I SUSPECT LOSS OF EITHER OR BOTH BRAIN HEMI-SPHERES IN YOUR CASE.
NOW, THIS IS A MERE INCIDENTAL ADDENDUM, BUT...

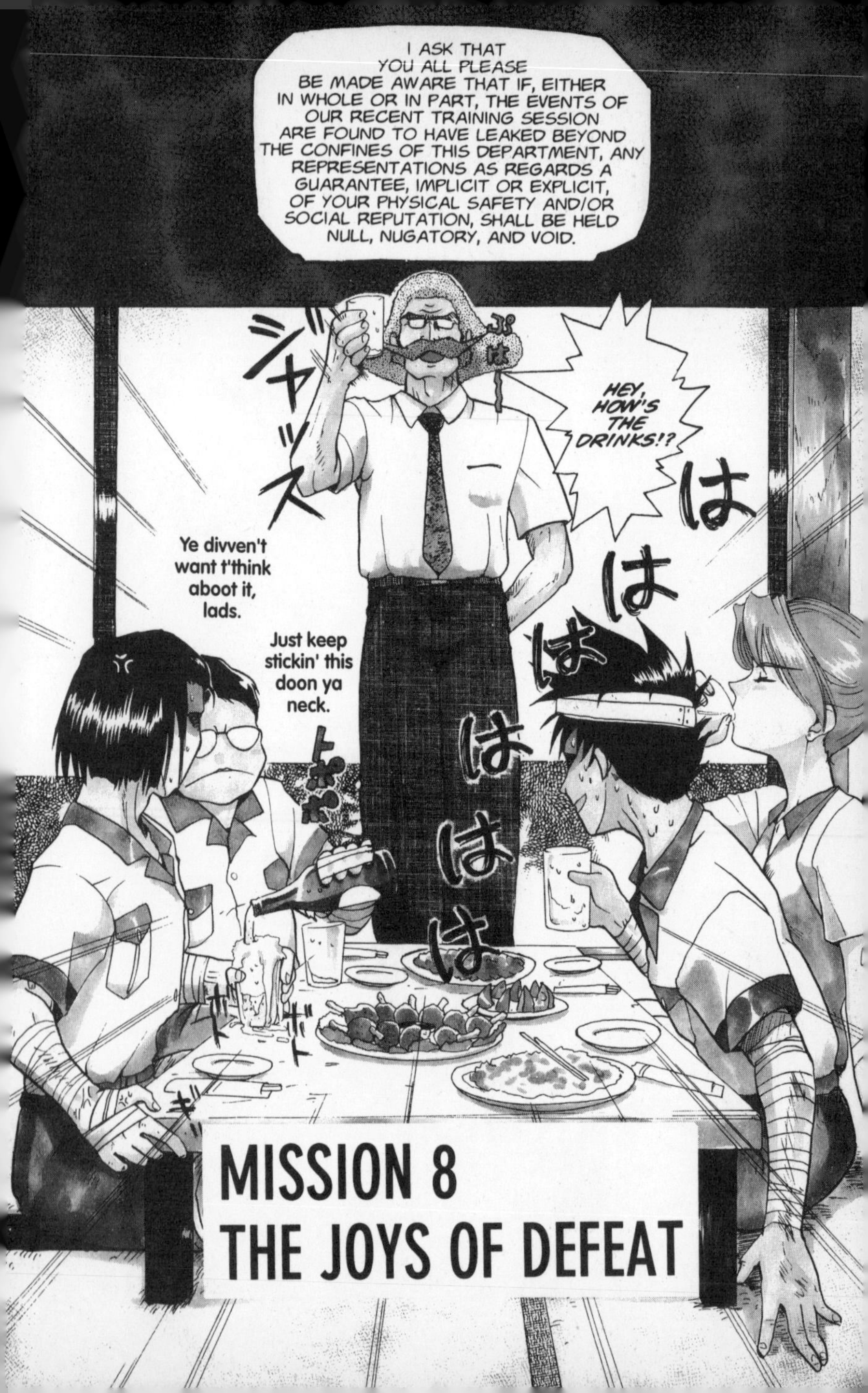
I ASK THAT YOU ALL PLEASE BE MADE AWARE THAT IF, EITHER IN WHOLE OR IN PART, THE EVENTS OF OUR RECENT TRAINING SESSION ARE FOUND TO HAVE LEAKED BEYOND THE CONFINES OF THIS DEPARTMENT, ANY REPRESENTATIONS AS REGARDS A GUARANTEE, IMPLICIT OR EXPLICIT, OF YOUR PHYSICAL SAFETY AND/OR SOCIAL REPUTATION, SHALL BE HELD NULL, NUGATORY, AND VOID.
HEY, HOW'S THE DRINKS!?
はははははは
Ye divven't want t'think aboot it, lads.
Just keep stickin' this doon ya neck.
MISSION 8
THE JOYS OF DEFEAT

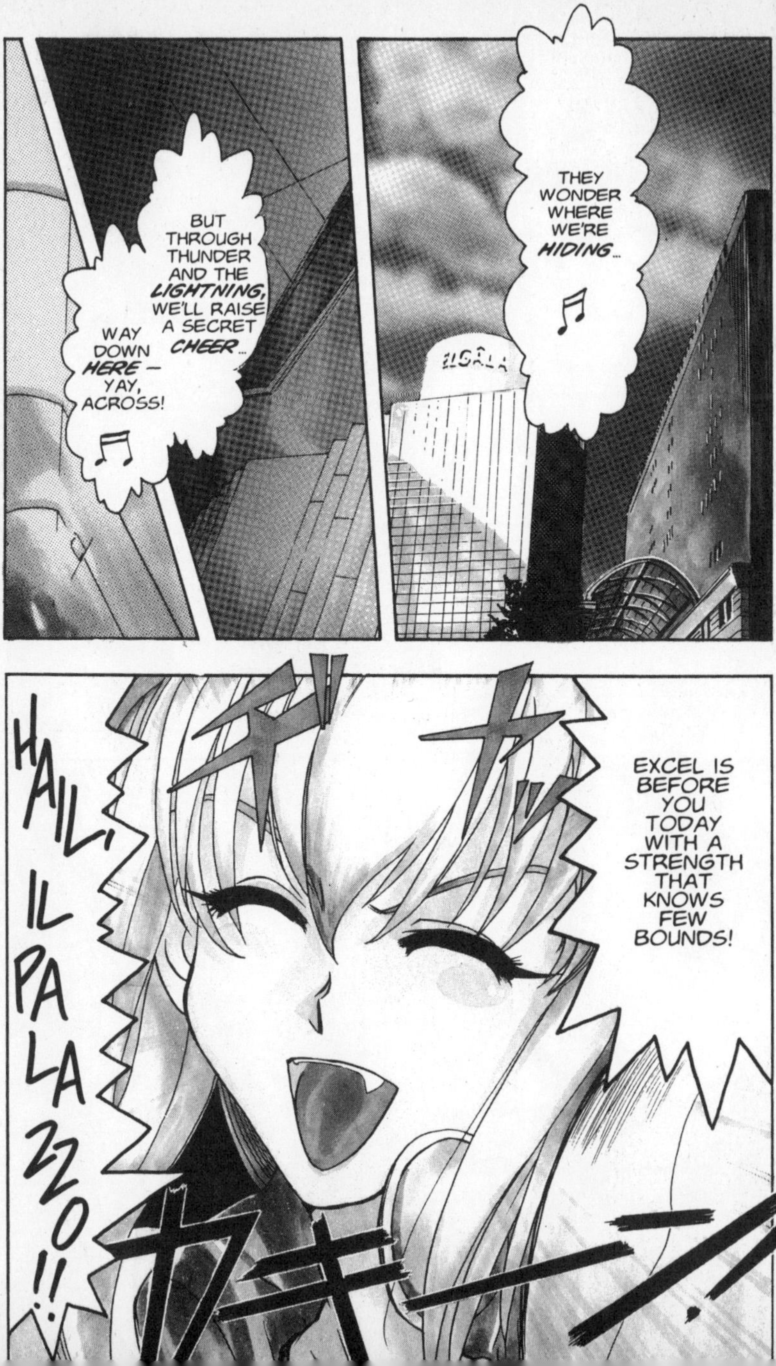
THEY WONDER WHERE WE'RE HIDING...
BUT THROUGH THUNDER AND THE LIGHTNING, WE'LL RAISE A SECRET CHEER...
WAY DOWN HERE—YAY, ACROSS!
EXCEL IS BEFORE YOU TODAY WITH A STRENGTH THAT KNOWS FEW BOUNDS!
HAIL, IL PALAZZO!!

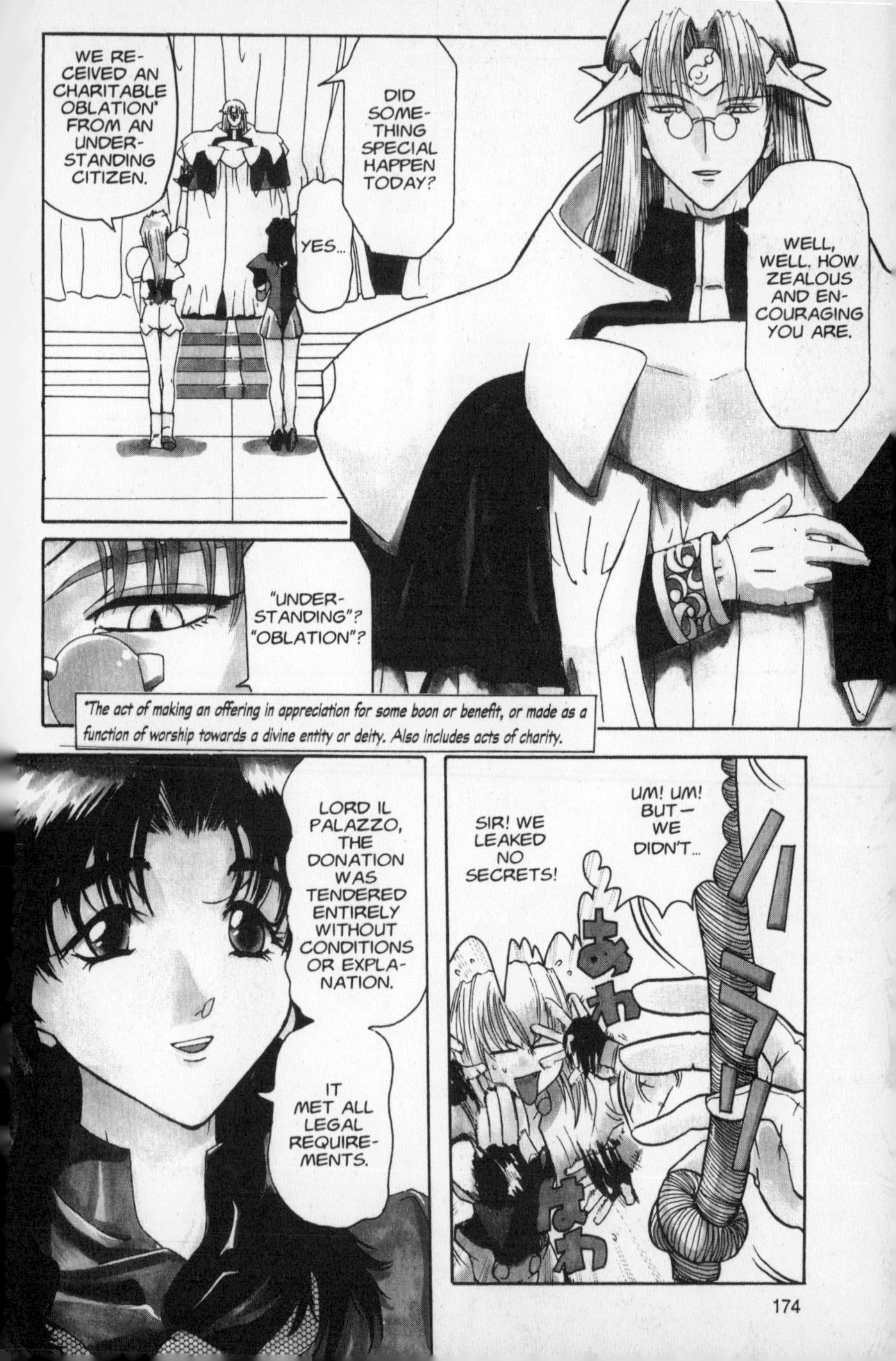
WELL, WELL. HOW ZEALOUS AND EN-COURAGING YOU ARE.
DID SOME-THING SPECIAL HAPPEN TODAY?
YES...
WE RE-CEIVED AN CHARITABLE OBLATION* FROM AN UNDER-STANDING CITIZEN.
"UNDER-STANDING"? "OBLATION"?
UM! UM! BUT— WE DIDN'T...
SIR! WE LEAKED NO SECRETS!
LORD IL PALAZZO, THE DONATION WAS TENDERED ENTIRELY WITHOUT CONDITIONS OR EXPLA-NATION.
IT MET ALL LEGAL REQUIRE-MENTS.

The act of making an offering in appreciation for some boon or benefit, or made as a function of worship towards a divine entity or deity. Also includes acts of charity.

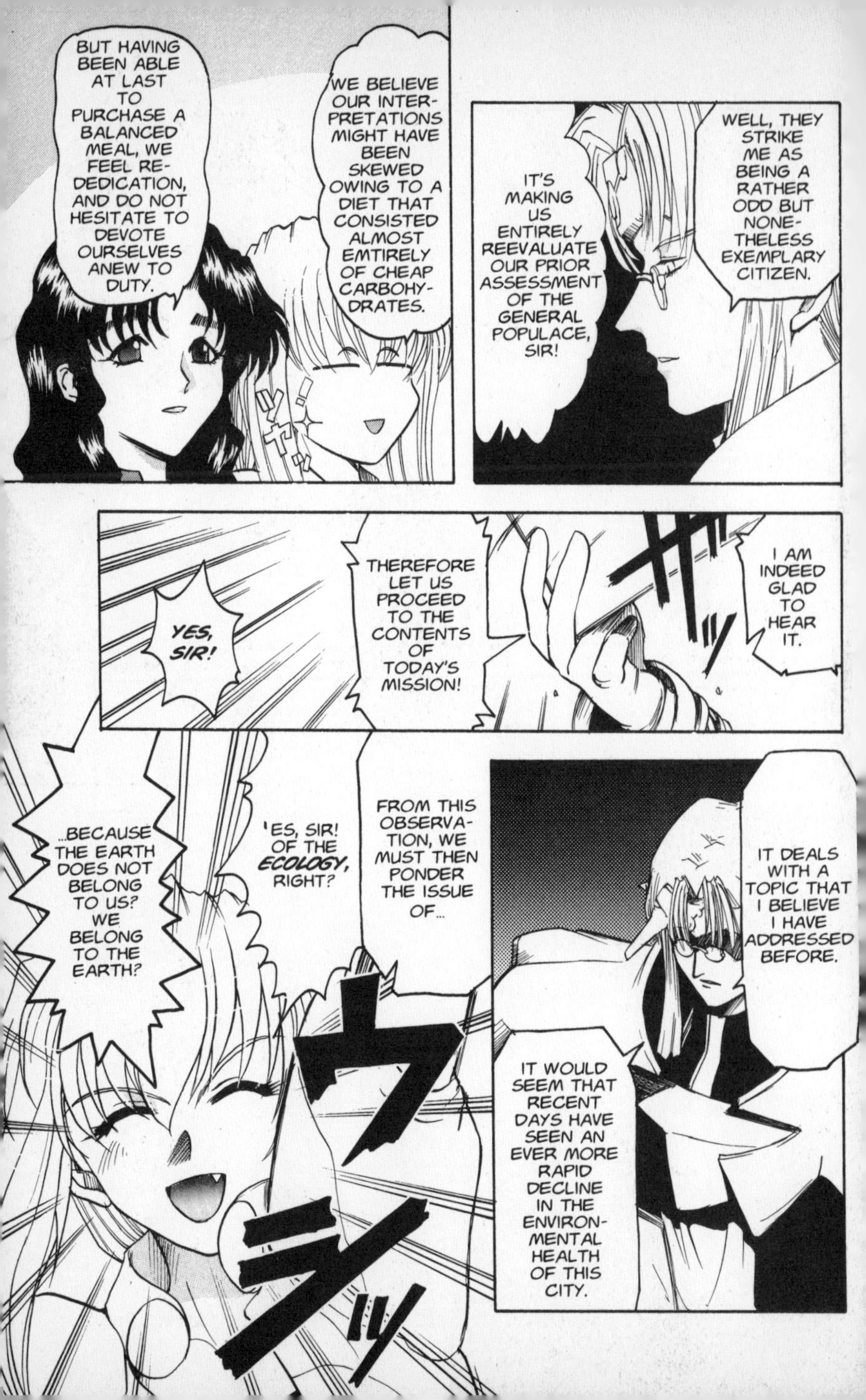

WELL, THEY STRIKE ME AS BEING A RATHER ODD BUT NONE-THELESS EXEMPLARY CITIZEN.
IT'S MAKING US ENTIRELY REEVALUATE OUR PRIOR ASSESSMENT OF THE GENERAL POPULACE, SIR!
WE BELIEVE OUR INTER-PRETATIONS MIGHT HAVE BEEN SKEWED OWING TO A DIET THAT CONSISTED ALMOST EMTIRELY OF CHEAP CARBOHY-DRATES.
BUT HAVING BEEN ABLE AT LAST TO PURCHASE A BALANCED MEAL, WE FEEL RE-DEDICATION, AND DO NOT HESITATE TO DEVOTE OURSELVES ANEW TO DUTY.
I AM INDEED GLAD TO HEAR IT.
THEREFORE LET US PROCEED TO THE CONTENTS OF TODAY'S MISSION!
YES, SIR!
IT DEALS WITH A TOPIC THAT I BELIEVE I HAVE ADDRESSED BEFORE.
IT WOULD SEEM THAT RECENT DAYS HAVE SEEN AN EVER MORE RAPID DECLINE IN THE ENVIRON-MENTAL HEALTH OF THIS CITY.
FROM THIS OBSERVA-TION, WE MUST THEN PONDER THE ISSUE OF...
'ES, SIR! OF THE *ECOLOGY*, RIGHT?
...BECAUSE THE EARTH DOES NOT BELONG TO US? WE BELONG TO THE EARTH?
ウンッ

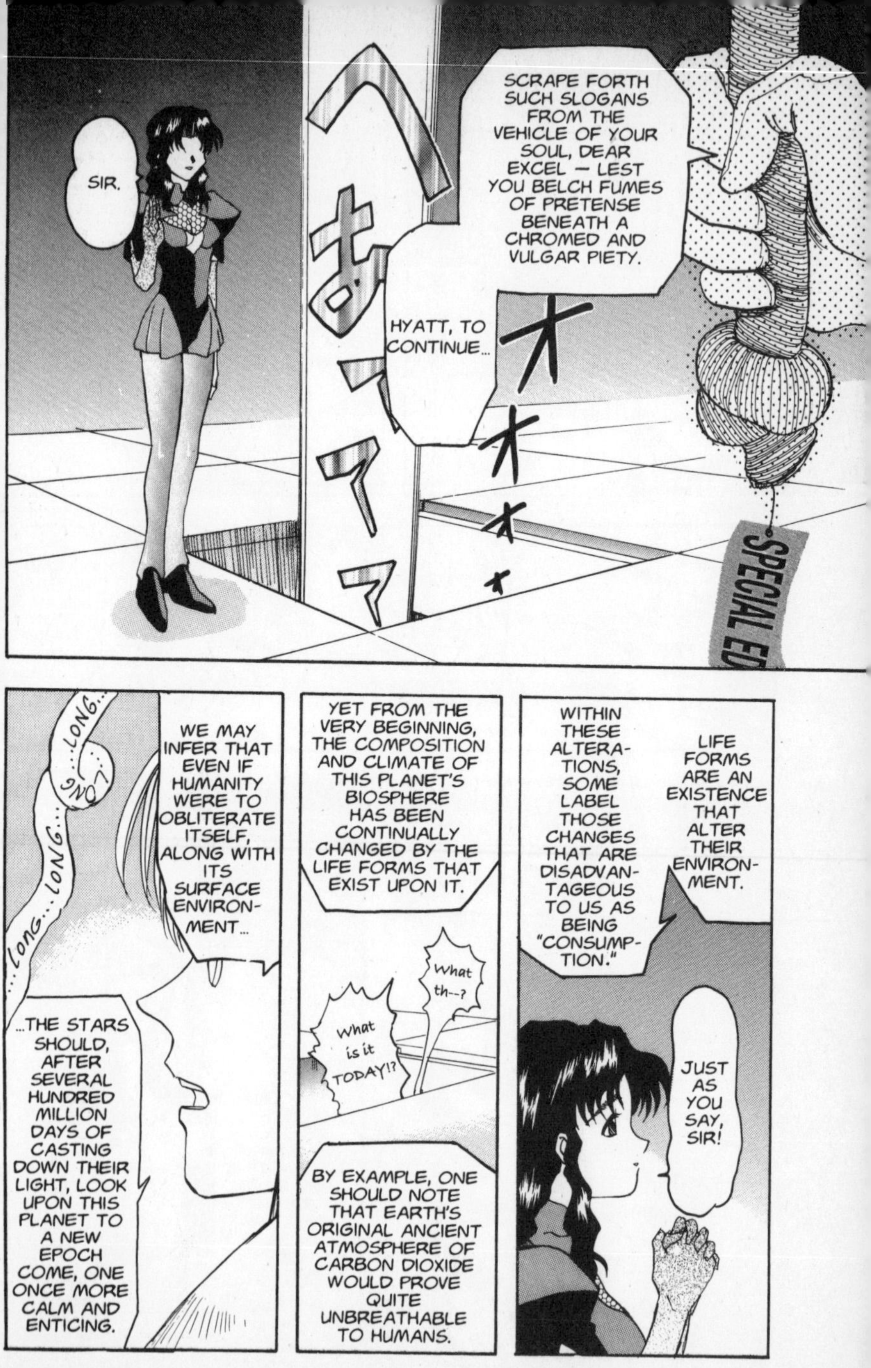
SCRAPE FORTH SUCH SLOGANS FROM THE VEHICLE OF YOUR SOUL, DEAR EXCEL — LEST YOU BELCH FUMES OF PRETENSE BENEATH A CHROMED AND VULGAR PIETY.
HYATT, TO CONTINUE...
SPECIAL ED
SIR.
LIFE FORMS ARE AN EXISTENCE THAT ALTER THEIR ENVIRON-MENT.
WITHIN THESE ALTERA-TIONS, SOME LABEL THOSE CHANGES THAT ARE DISADVAN-TAGEOUS TO US AS BEING "CONSUMP-TION."
JUST AS YOU SAY, SIR!
YET FROM THE VERY BEGINNING, THE COMPOSITION AND CLIMATE OF THIS PLANET'S BIOSPHERE HAS BEEN CONTINUALLY CHANGED BY THE LIFE FORMS THAT EXIST UPON IT.
What th--?
What is it TODAY!?
BY EXAMPLE, ONE SHOULD NOTE THAT EARTH'S ORIGINAL ANCIENT ATMOSPHERE OF CARBON DIOXIDE WOULD PROVE QUITE UNBREATHABLE TO HUMANS.
WE MAY INFER THAT EVEN IF HUMANITY WERE TO OBLITERATE ITSELF, ALONG WITH ITS SURFACE ENVIRON-MENT...
...LONG... LONG... LONG... LONG...
...THE STARS SHOULD, AFTER SEVERAL HUNDRED MILLION DAYS OF CASTING DOWN THEIR LIGHT, LOOK UPON THIS PLANET TO A NEW EPOCH COME, ONE ONCE MORE CALM AND ENTICING.

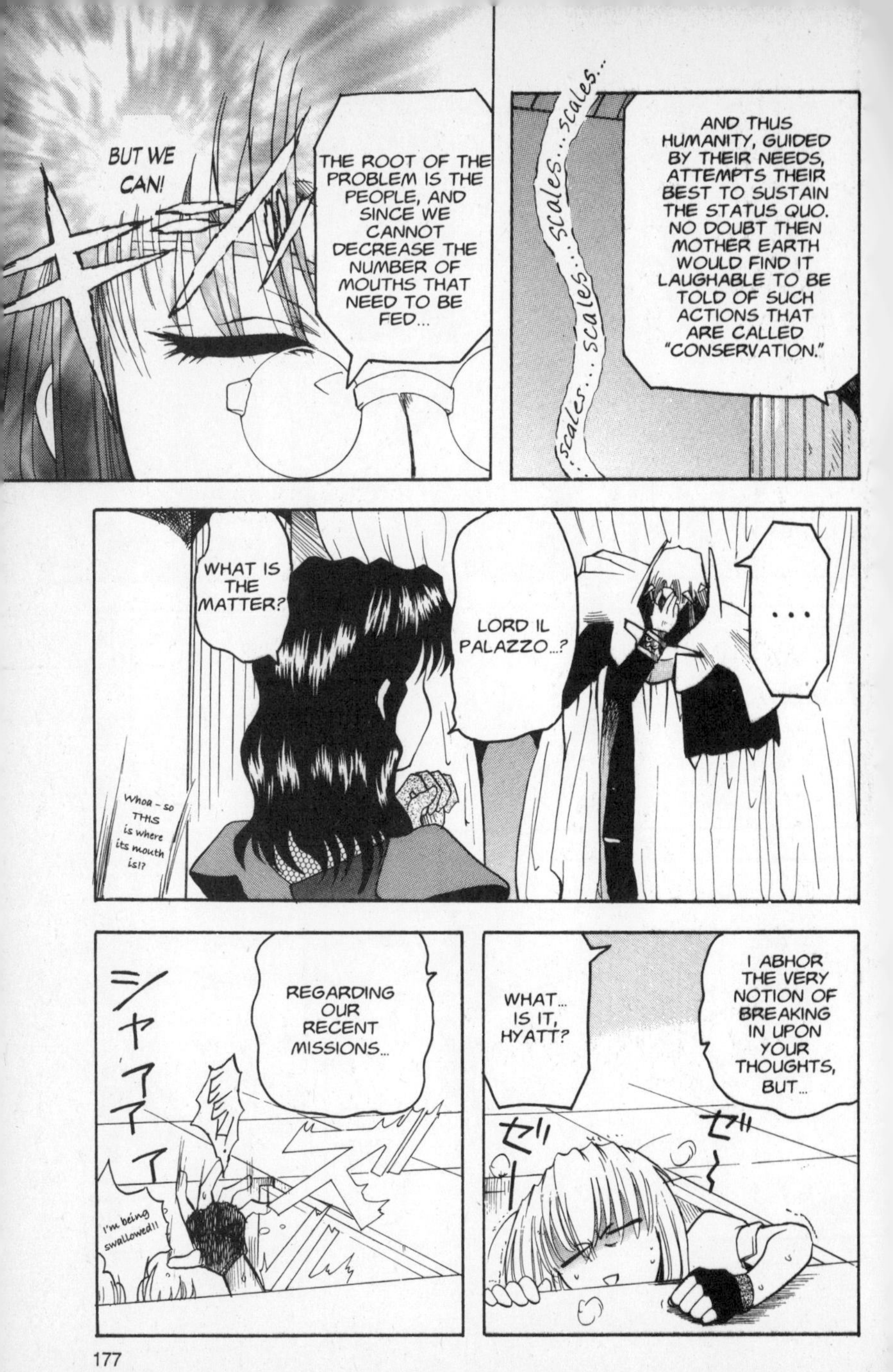
AND THUS HUMANITY, GUIDED BY THEIR NEEDS, ATTEMPTS THEIR BEST TO SUSTAIN THE STATUS QUO. NO DOUBT THEN MOTHER EARTH WOULD FIND IT LAUGHABLE TO BE TOLD OF SUCH ACTIONS THAT ARE CALLED "CONSERVATION."
scales... scales... scales... scales...
THE ROOT OF THE PROBLEM IS THE PEOPLE, AND SINCE WE CANNOT DECREASE THE NUMBER OF MOUTHS THAT NEED TO BE FED...
BUT WE CAN!
...
LORD IL PALAZZO...?
WHAT IS THE MATTER?
Whoa - so THIS is where its mouth is!?
I ABHOR THE VERY NOTION OF BREAKING IN UPON YOUR THOUGHTS, BUT...
WHAT... IS IT, HYATT?
REGARDING OUR RECENT MISSIONS...
I'm being swallowed!!

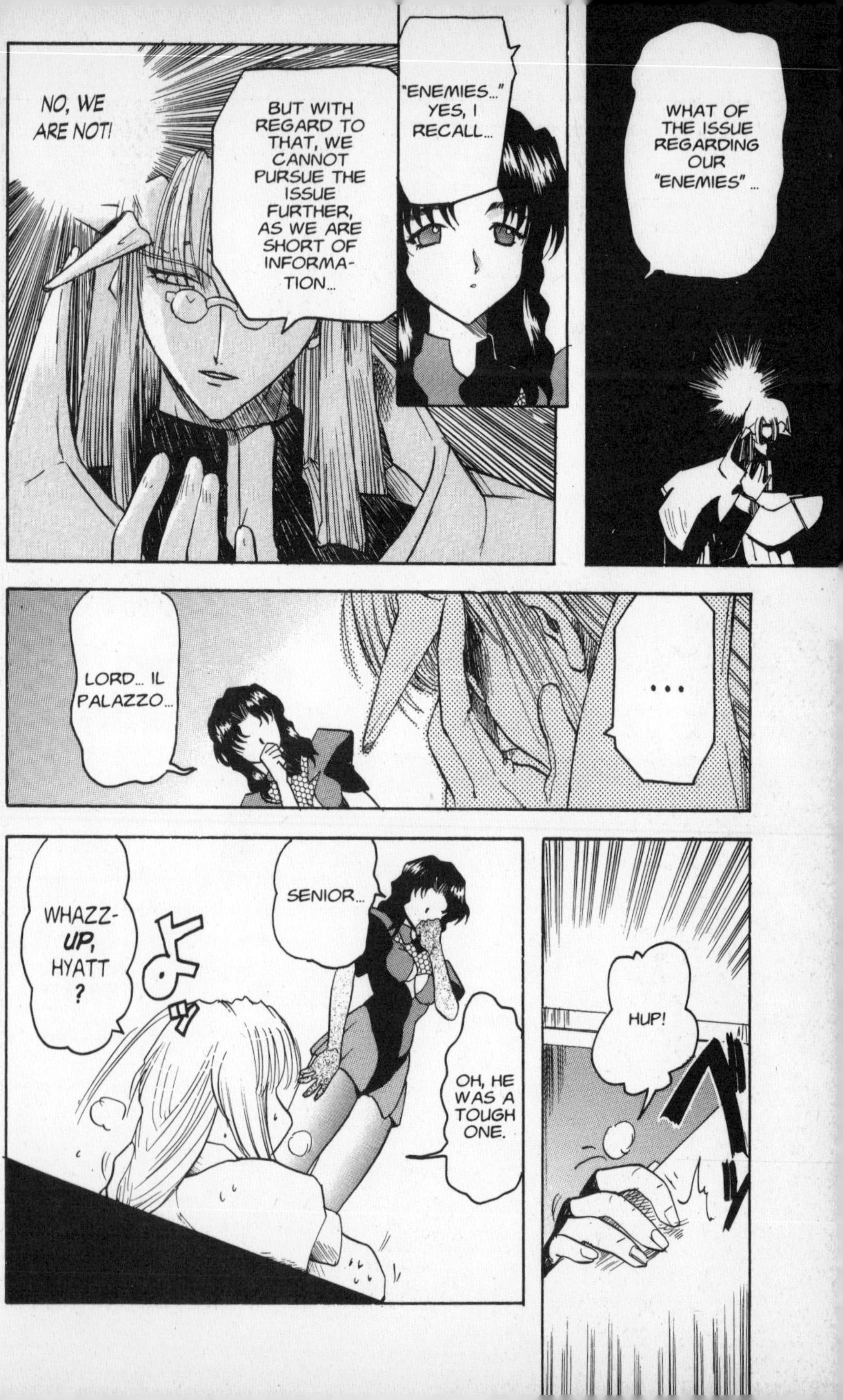

WHAT OF THE ISSUE REGARDING OUR "ENEMIES"...
"ENEMIES..." YES, I RECALL...
BUT WITH REGARD TO THAT, WE CANNOT PURSUE THE ISSUE FURTHER, AS WE ARE SHORT OF INFORMATION...
NO, WE ARE NOT!
...
LORD... IL PALAZZO...
HUP!
SENIOR...
WHAZZ-UP, HYATT?
OH, HE WAS A TOUGH ONE.

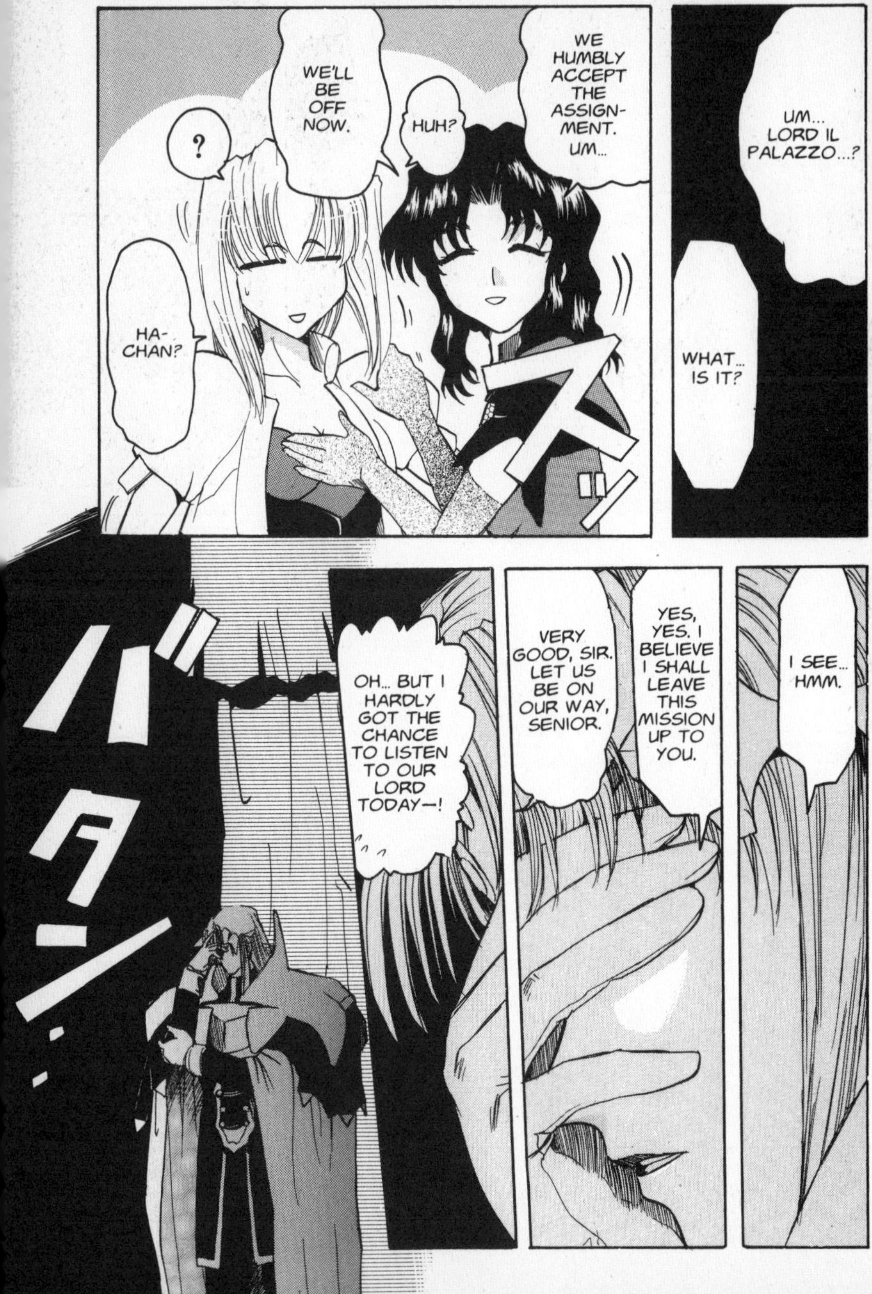
UM... LORD IL PALAZZO...?
WHAT... IS IT?
WE HUMBLY ACCEPT THE ASSIGNMENT. UM...
HUH?
WE'LL BE OFF NOW.
?
HA-CHAN?
I SEE... HMM.
YES, YES. I BELIEVE I SHALL LEAVE THIS MISSION UP TO YOU.
VERY GOOD, SIR. LET US BE ON OUR WAY, SENIOR.
OH... BUT I HARDLY GOT THE CHANCE TO LISTEN TO OUR LORD TODAY—!

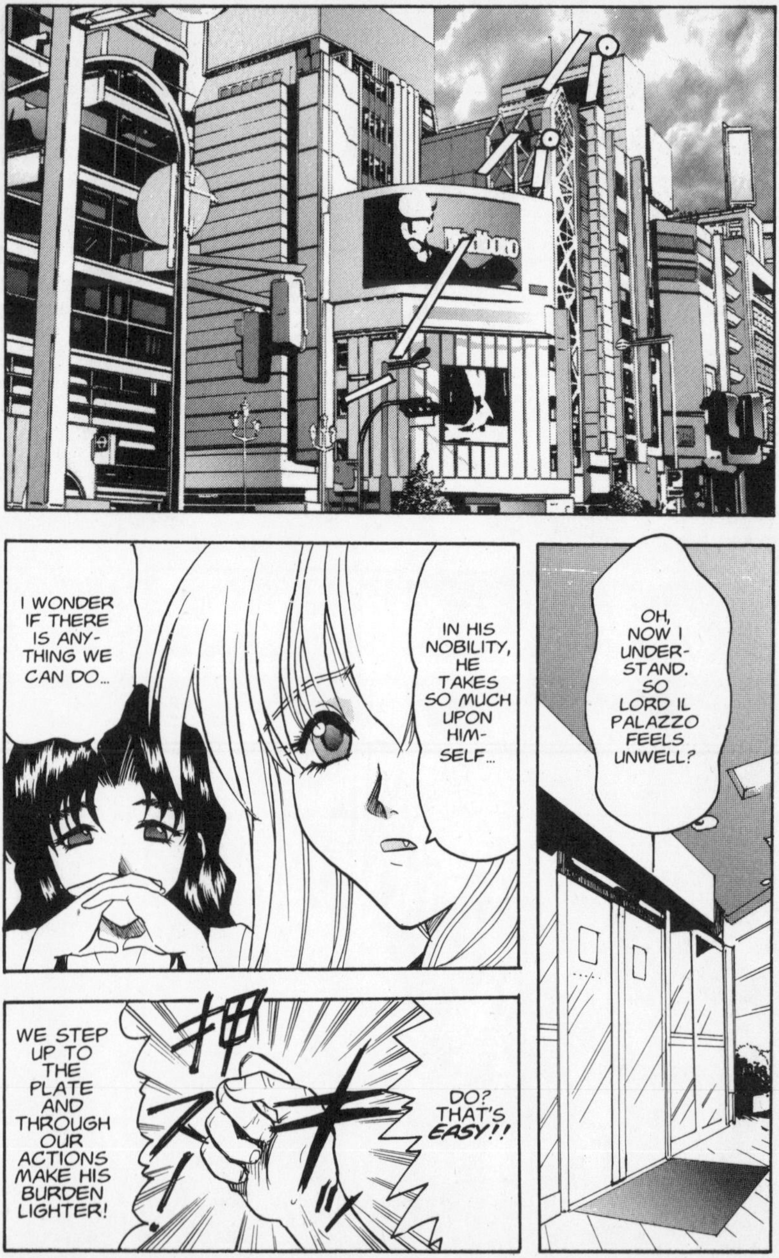
OH, NOW I UNDER-STAND. SO LORD IL PALAZZO FEELS UNWELL?
IN HIS NOBILITY, HE TAKES SO MUCH UPON HIM-SELF...
I WONDER IF THERE IS ANY-THING WE CAN DO...
押
DO? THAT'S *EASY*!!
WE STEP UP TO THE PLATE AND THROUGH OUR ACTIONS MAKE HIS BURDEN LIGHTER!

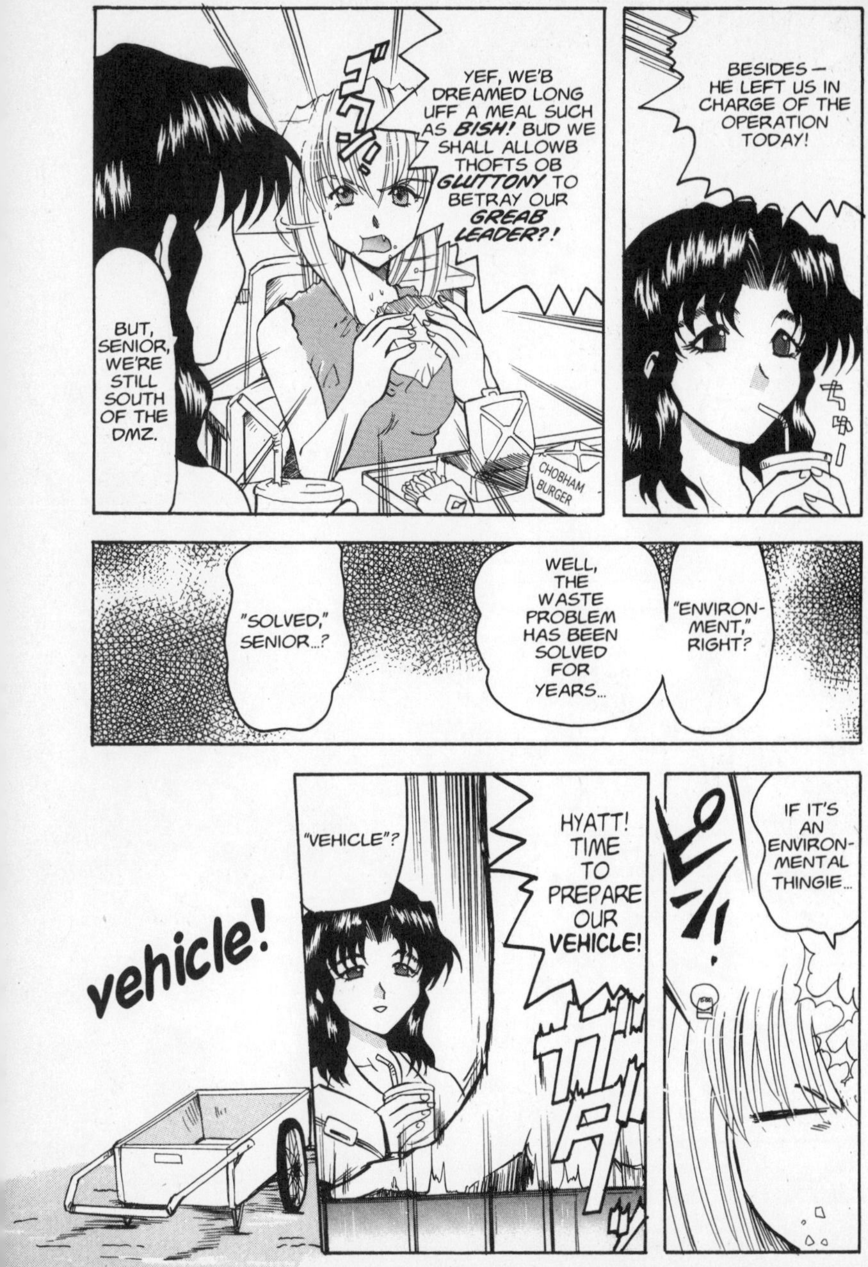
BESIDES—HE LEFT US IN CHARGE OF THE OPERATION TODAY!
YEF, WE'B DREAMED LONG UFF A MEAL SUCH AS BISH! BUD WE SHALL ALLOWB THOFTS OB GLUTTONY TO BETRAY OUR GREAB LEADER?!
CHOBHAM BURGER
BUT, SENIOR, WE'RE STILL SOUTH OF THE DMZ.
"ENVIRON-MENT," RIGHT?
WELL, THE WASTE PROBLEM HAS BEEN SOLVED FOR YEARS...
"SOLVED," SENIOR...?
IF IT'S AN ENVIRON-MENTAL THINGIE...
HYATT! TIME TO PREPARE OUR VEHICLE!
"VEHICLE"?
vehicle!

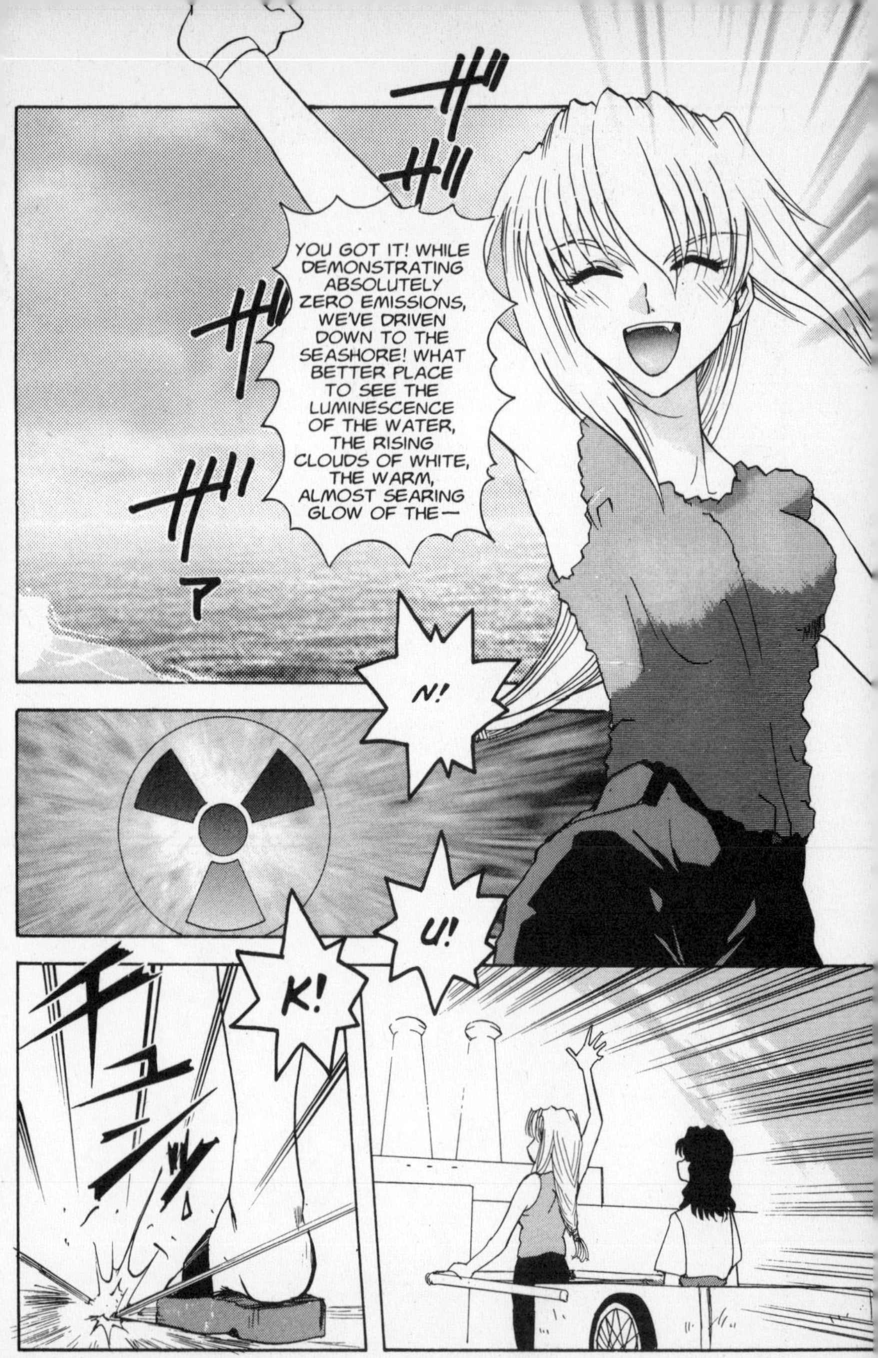
YOU GOT IT! WHILE DEMONSTRATING ABSOLUTELY ZERO EMISSIONS, WE'VE DRIVEN DOWN TO THE SEASHORE! WHAT BETTER PLACE TO SEE THE LUMINESCENCE OF THE WATER, THE RISING CLOUDS OF WHITE, THE WARM, ALMOST SEARING GLOW OF THE—
ザザザザァ
N!
U!
K!
チューン

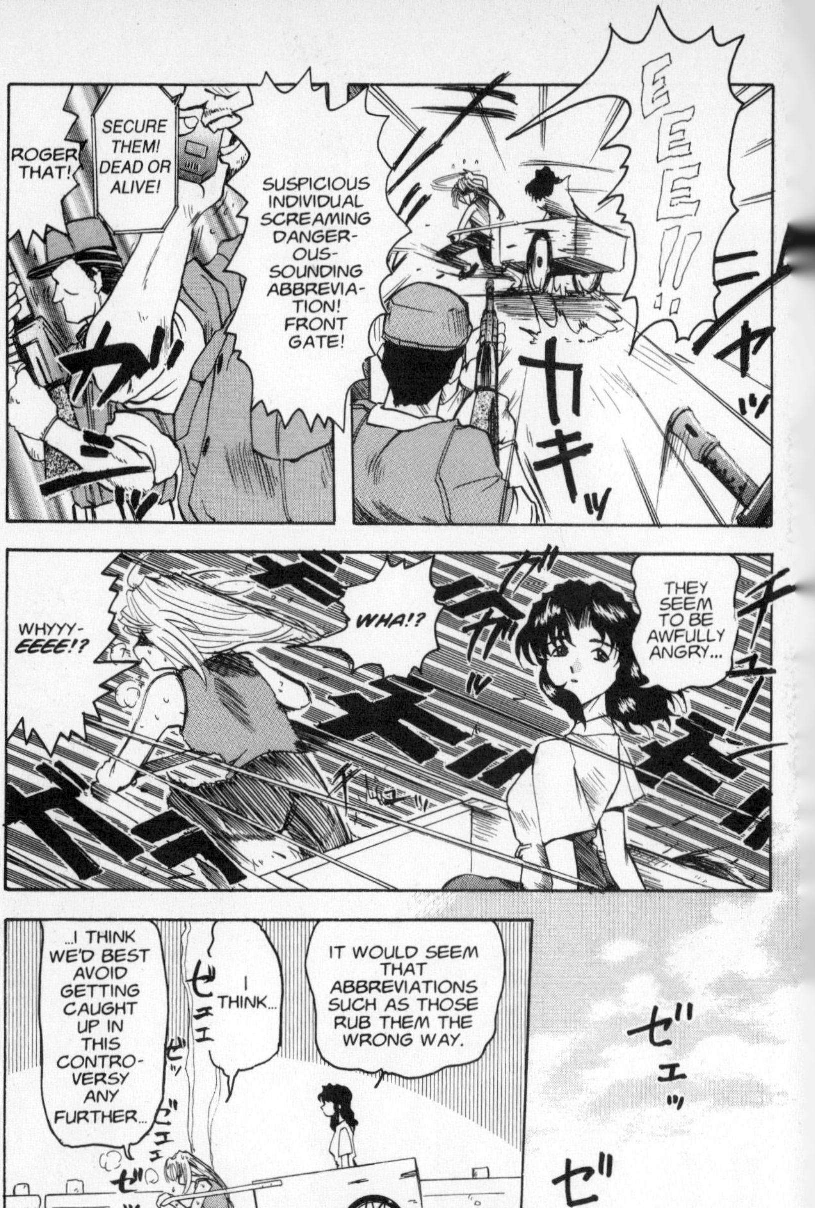
EEE!!
SUSPICIOUS INDIVIDUAL SCREAMING DANGER-OUS-SOUNDING ABBREVIA-TION! FRONT GATE!
SECURE THEM! DEAD OR ALIVE!
ROGER THAT!
THEY SEEM TO BE AWFULLY ANGRY...
WHA!?
WHYYY-EEEE!?
IT WOULD SEEM THAT ABBREVIATIONS SUCH AS THOSE RUB THEM THE WRONG WAY.
I THINK...
...I THINK WE'D BEST AVOID GETTING CAUGHT UP IN THIS CONTRO-VERSY ANY FURTHER...

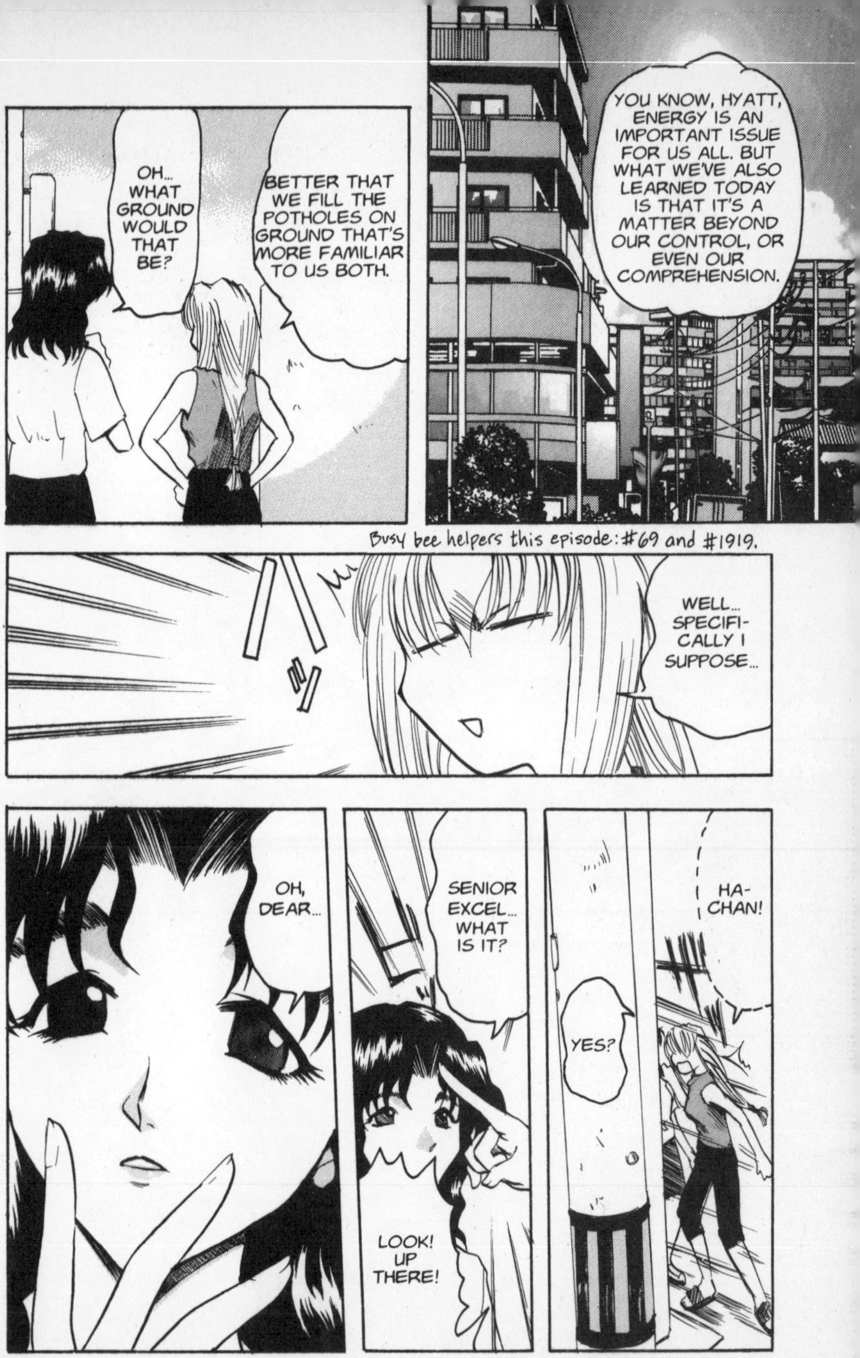

YOU KNOW, HYATT, ENERGY IS AN IMPORTANT ISSUE FOR US ALL. BUT WHAT WE'VE ALSO LEARNED TODAY IS THAT IT'S A MATTER BEYOND OUR CONTROL, OR EVEN OUR COMPREHENSION.
BETTER THAT WE FILL THE POTHOLES ON GROUND THAT'S MORE FAMILIAR TO US BOTH.
OH... WHAT GROUND WOULD THAT BE?
Busy bee helpers this episode: #69 and #1919.
WELL... SPECIFICALLY I SUPPOSE...
HA-CHAN!
YES?
SENIOR EXCEL... WHAT IS IT?
LOOK! UP THERE!
OH, DEAR...

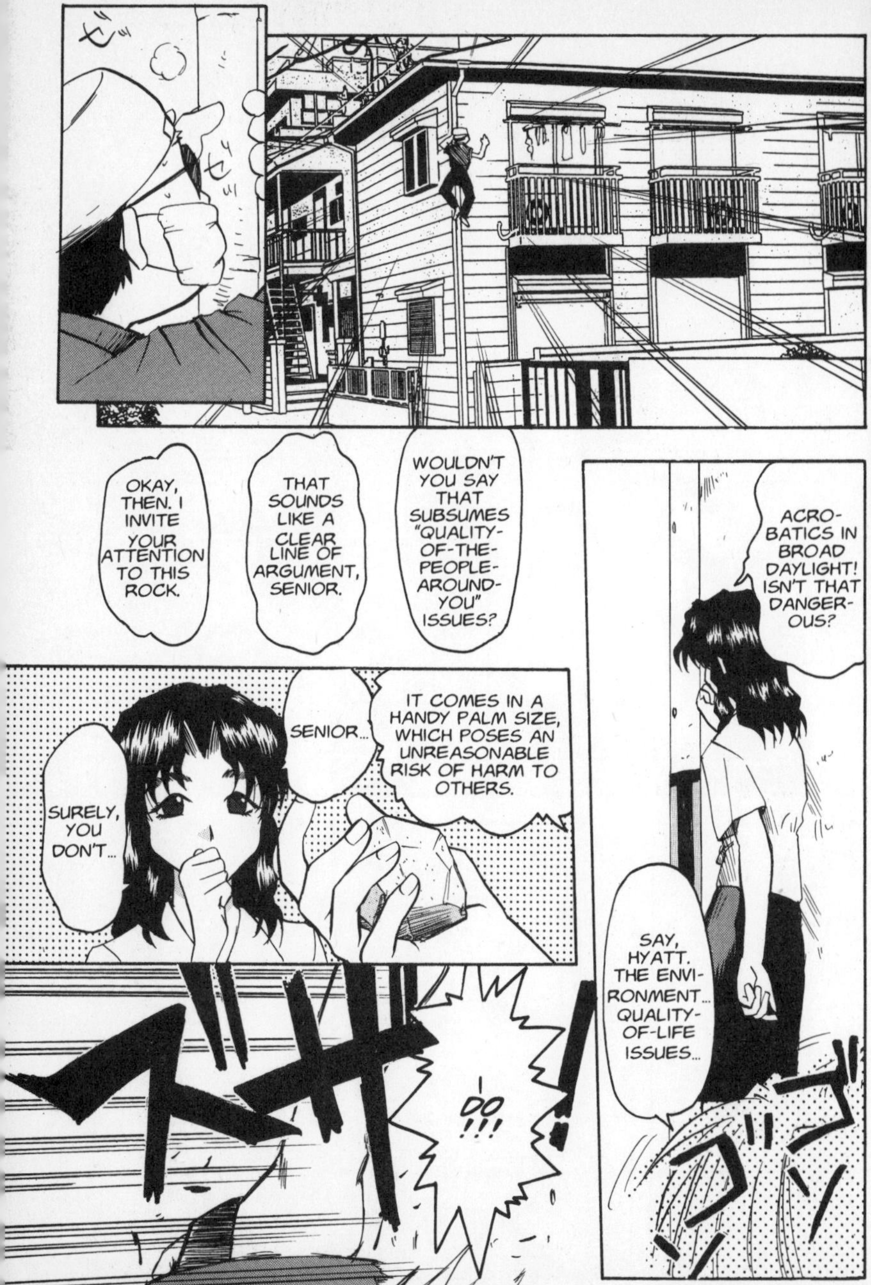
ACRO-BATICS IN BROAD DAYLIGHT! ISN'T THAT DANGER-OUS?
SAY, HYATT. THE ENVI-RONMENT... QUALITY-OF-LIFE ISSUES...
WOULDN'T YOU SAY THAT SUBSUMES "QUALITY-OF-THE-PEOPLE-AROUND-YOU" ISSUES?
THAT SOUNDS LIKE A CLEAR LINE OF ARGUMENT, SENIOR.
OKAY, THEN. I INVITE YOUR ATTENTION TO THIS ROCK.
IT COMES IN A HANDY PALM SIZE, WHICH POSES AN UNREASONABLE RISK OF HARM TO OTHERS.
SENIOR...
SURELY, YOU DON'T...
I DO!!!

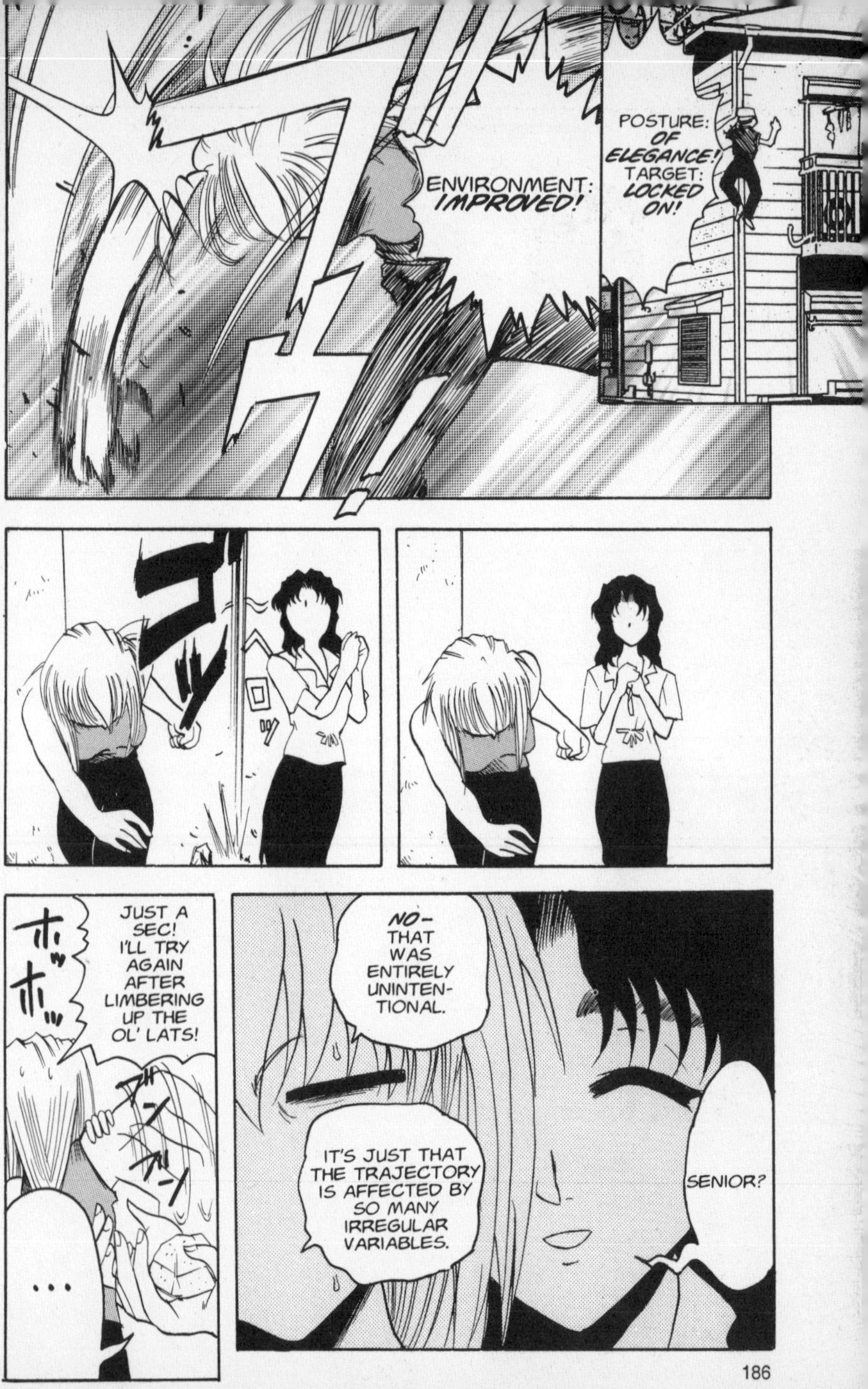
POSTURE: OF ELEGANCE! TARGET: LOCKED ON!
ENVIRONMENT: IMPROVED!
SENIOR?
NO- THAT WAS ENTIRELY UNINTENTIONAL.
IT'S JUST THAT THE TRAJECTORY IS AFFECTED BY SO MANY IRREGULAR VARIABLES.
JUST A SEC! I'LL TRY AGAIN AFTER LIMBERING UP THE OL' LATS!
...

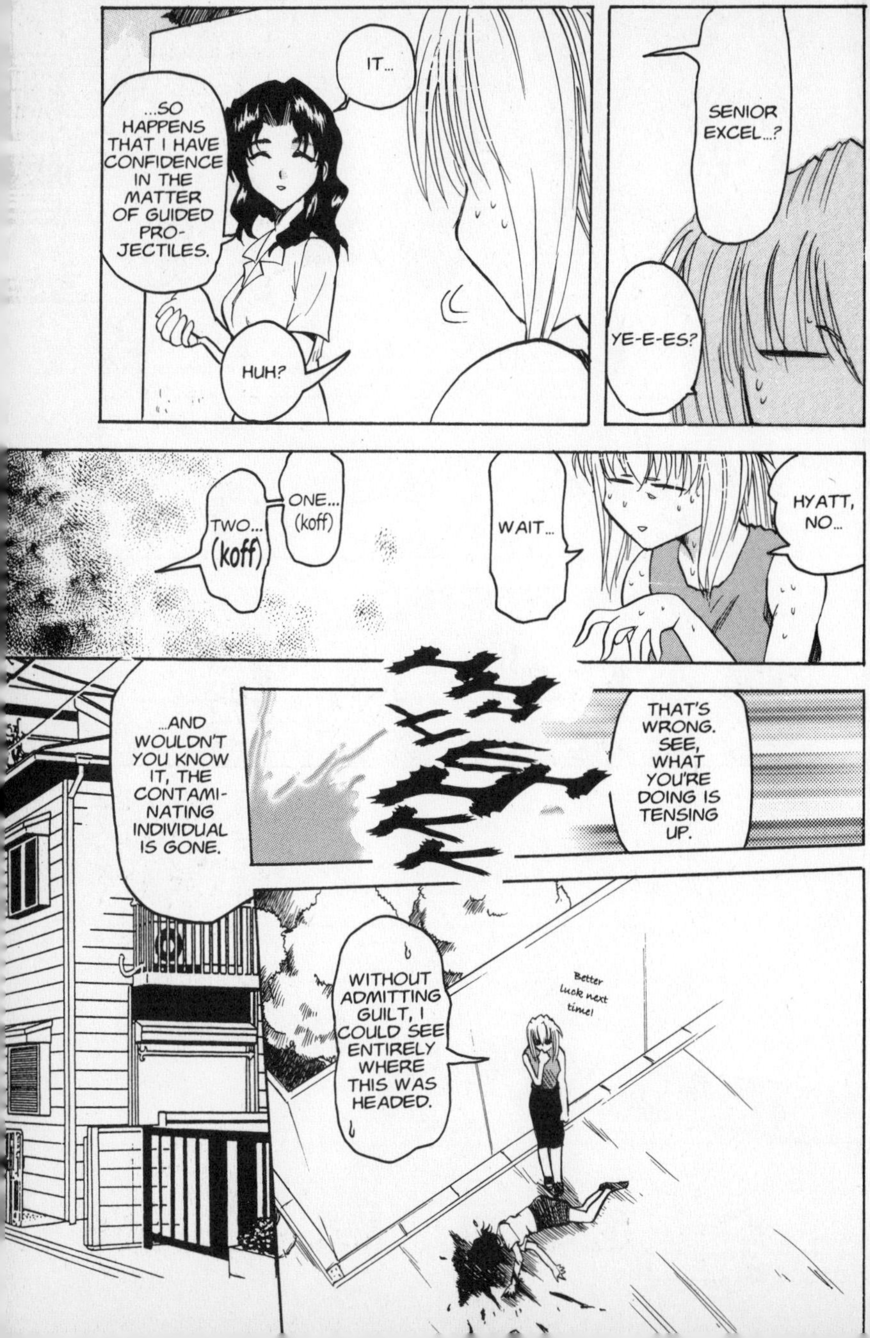
SENIOR EXCEL...?
YE-E-ES?
IT...
...SO HAPPENS THAT I HAVE CONFIDENCE IN THE MATTER OF GUIDED PRO-JECTILES.
HUH?
HYATT, NO...
WAIT...
ONE... (koff)
TWO... (koff)
THAT'S WRONG. SEE, WHAT YOU'RE DOING IS TENSING UP.
...AND WOULDN'T YOU KNOW IT, THE CONTAMI-NATING INDIVIDUAL IS GONE.
Better luck next time!
WITHOUT ADMITTING GUILT, I COULD SEE ENTIRELY WHERE THIS WAS HEADED.

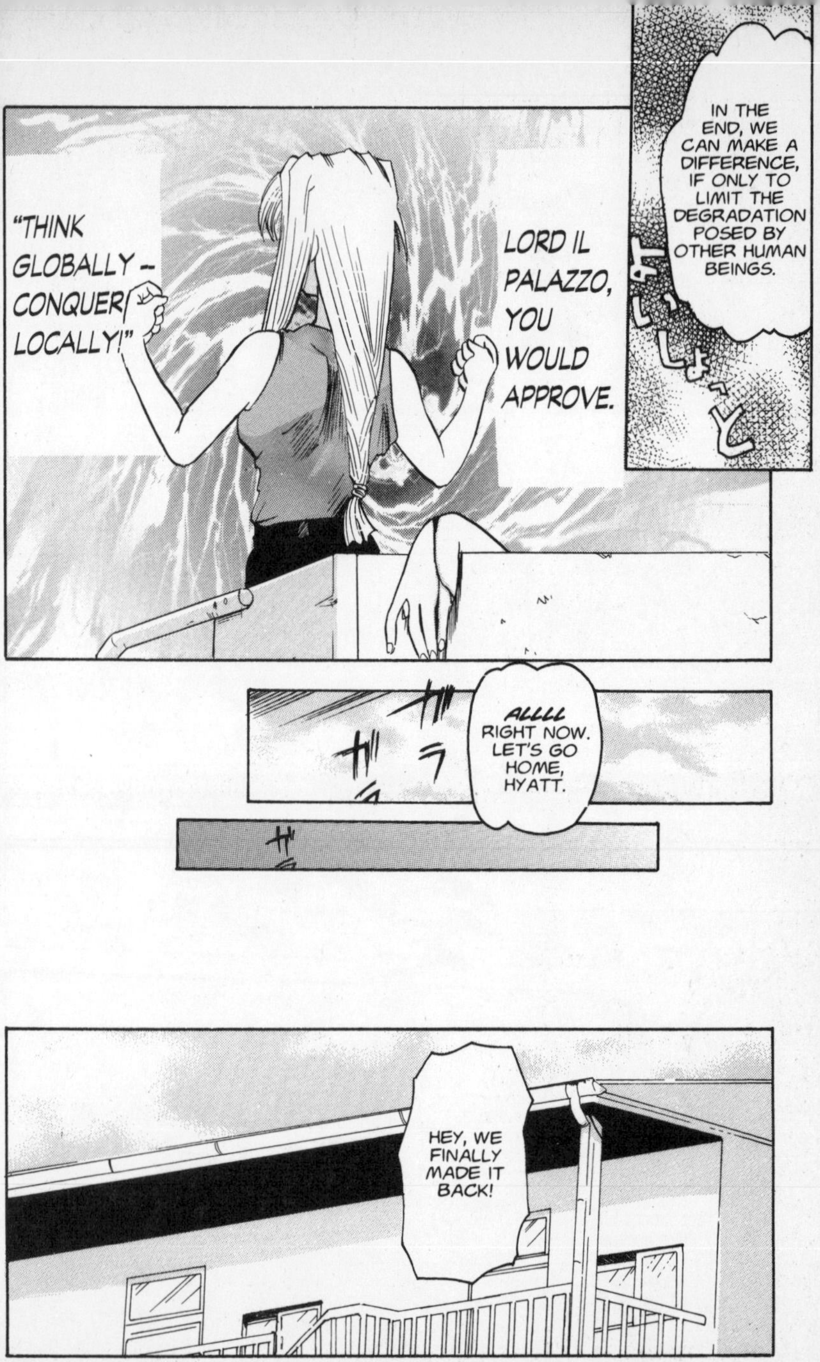
IN THE END, WE CAN MAKE A DIFFERENCE, IF ONLY TO LIMIT THE DEGRADATION POSED BY OTHER HUMAN BEINGS.
LORD IL PALAZZO, YOU WOULD APPROVE.
"THINK GLOBALLY -- CONQUER LOCALLY!"
ALLLL RIGHT NOW. LET'S GO HOME, HYATT.
HEY, WE FINALLY MADE IT BACK!

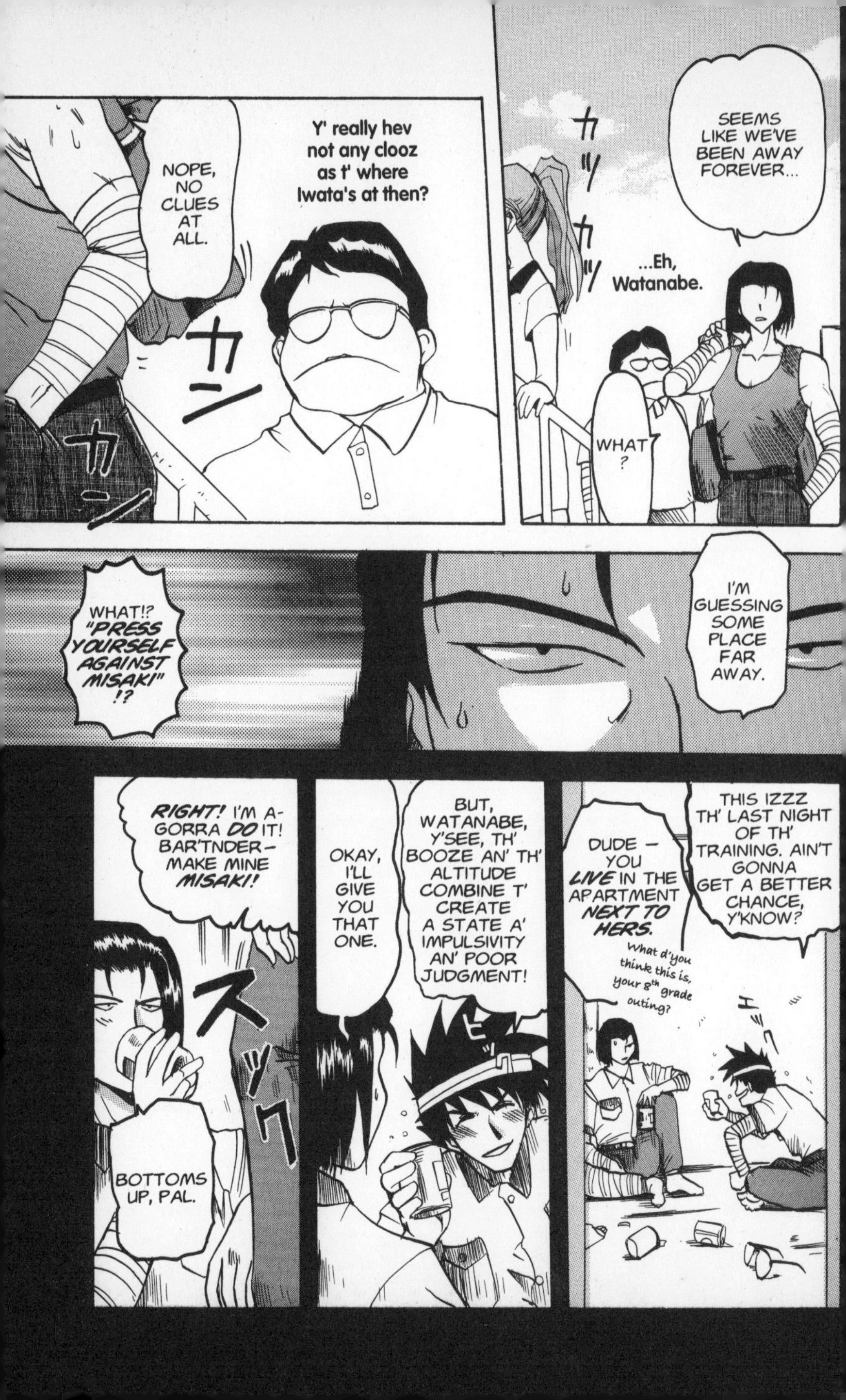
SEEMS LIKE WE'VE BEEN AWAY FOREVER...
カツ カツ
...Eh, Watanabe.
WHAT?
Y' really hev not any clooz as t' where Iwata's at then?
NOPE, NO CLUES AT ALL.
カン カン
I'M GUESSING SOME PLACE FAR AWAY.
WHAT!? "PRESS YOURSELF AGAINST MISAKI" !?
THIS IZZZ TH' LAST NIGHT OF TH' TRAINING. AIN'T GONNA GET A BETTER CHANCE, Y'KNOW?
DUDE — YOU LIVE IN THE APARTMENT NEXT TO HERS.
What d'you think this is, your 8th grade outing?
BUT, WATANABE, Y'SEE, TH' BOOZE AN' TH' ALTITUDE COMBINE T' CREATE A STATE A' IMPULSIVITY AN' POOR JUDGMENT!
OKAY, I'LL GIVE YOU THAT ONE.
RIGHT! I'M A-GORRA DO IT! BAR'TNDER— MAKE MINE MISAKI!
スック
BOTTOMS UP, PAL.

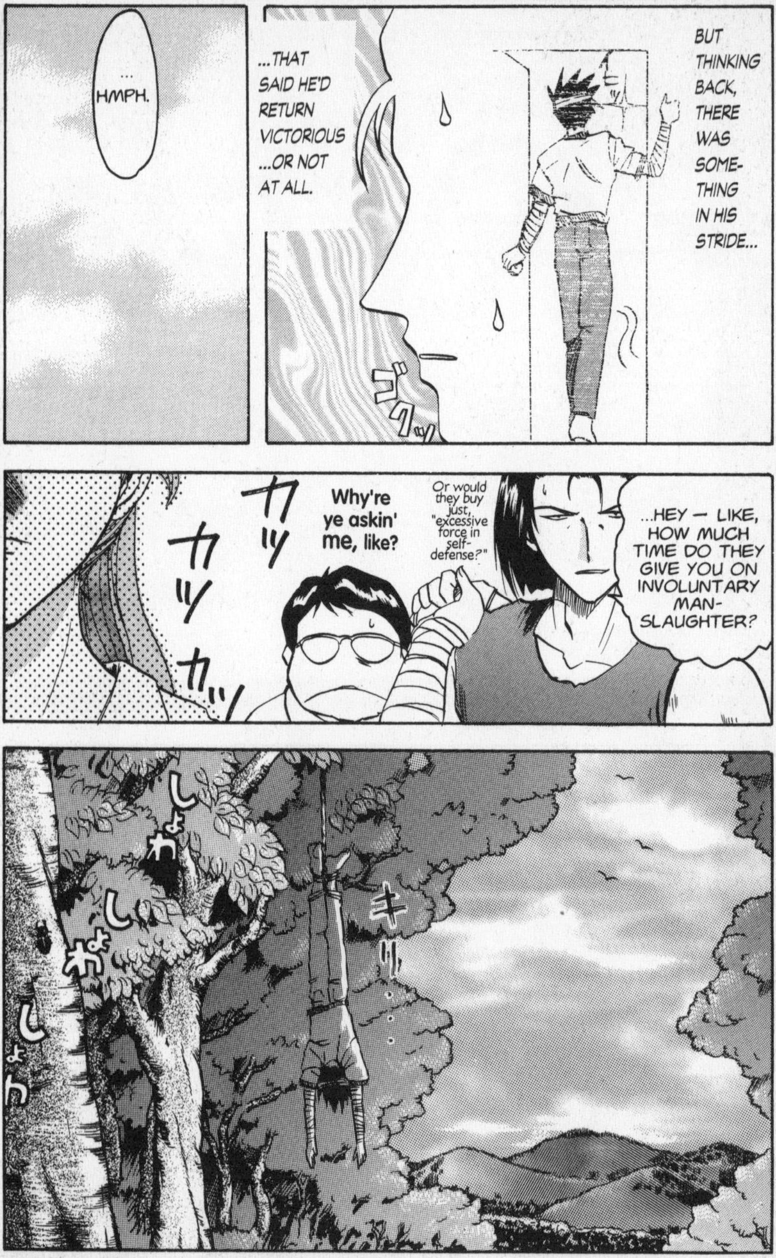
BUT THINKING BACK, THERE WAS SOME-THING IN HIS STRIDE...
...THAT SAID HE'D RETURN VICTORIOUS ...OR NOT AT ALL.
ゴクッ
... HMPH.
...HEY — LIKE, HOW MUCH TIME DO THEY GIVE YOU ON INVOLUNTARY MAN-SLAUGHTER?
Or would they buy just, "excessive force in self-defense?"
Why're ye askin' me, like?
カッ
カッ
カッ

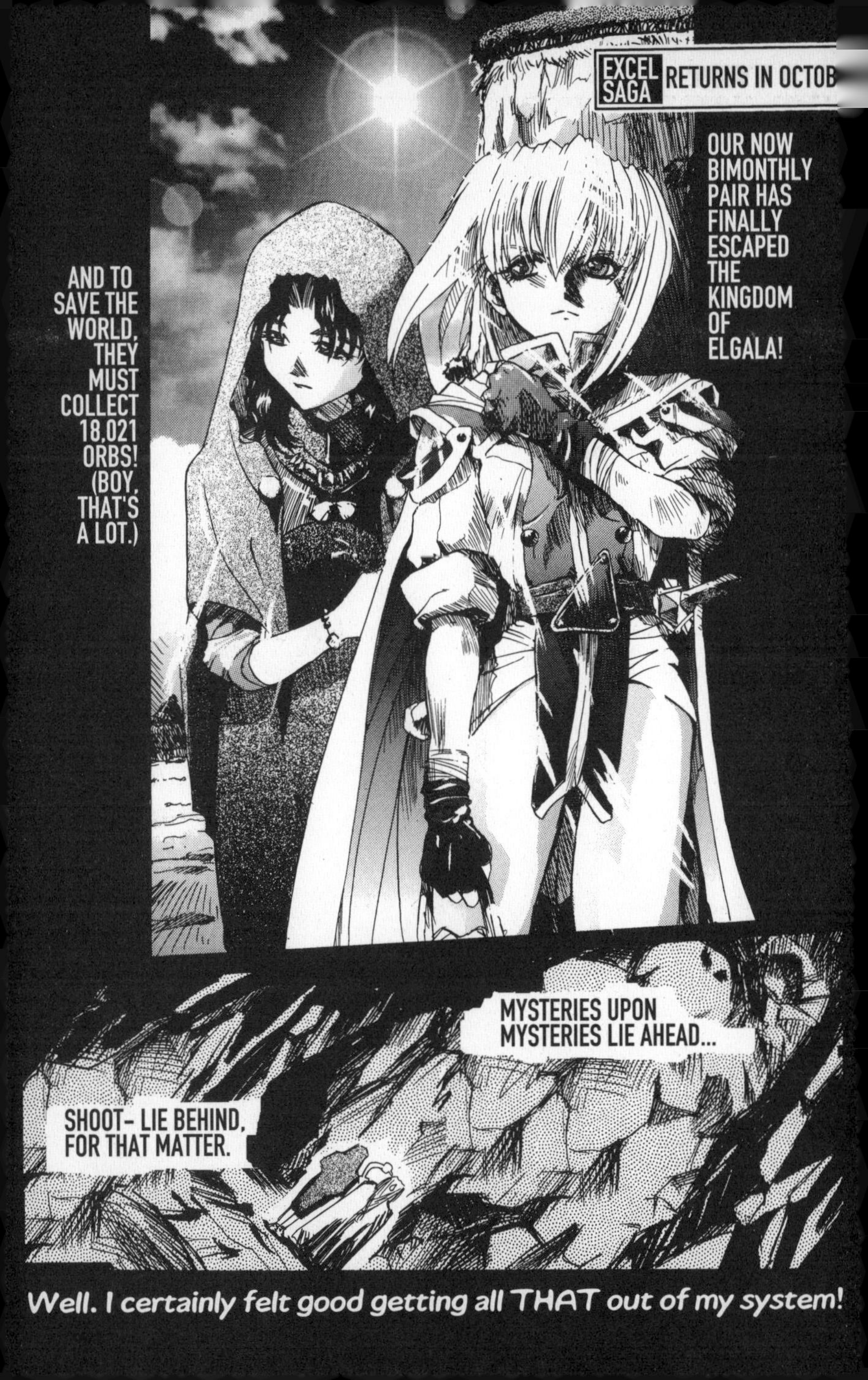
EXCEL SAGA RETURNS IN OCTOB
OUR NOW BIMONTHLY PAIR HAS FINALLY ESCAPED THE KINGDOM OF ELGALA!
AND TO SAVE THE WORLD, THEY MUST COLLECT 18,021 ORBS! (BOY, THAT'S A LOT.)
MYSTERIES UPON MYSTERIES LIE AHEAD...
SHOOT- LIE BEHIND, FOR THAT MATTER.
Well. I certainly felt good getting all THAT out of my system!

GUIDE TO *EXCEL SAGA 02*'s SOUND EFFECTS!

6-4	FX	fssSHHk˙ (shu˙, movement, sliding door opening rapidly)
6-5-1	FX	klak klak (ka˙, sound)
8-1	FX	ho-Humph! (dialog)
8-3-2	FX	ta-DumKk! (ban!, depiction, dramatic)
9-2	FX	zsh˙SHING! (za!, depiction, dramatic)
9-4	FX	Oh oou oh oh oo...oh oh (dialog and depiction, crying)
11-1	FX	ggrip (ki˙, depiction)
11-2	FX	th-THump (giku˙, depiction, becoming alert)
11-3	FX	sh˙SHINGg (bishi˙, depiction)
15-1	FX	glare (ka˙, depiction)
15-3	FX	b˙Thump (bataan!, sound, door closing)
15-4	FX	klok klok klok (ko˙, sound)
15-5	FX	klak klak klak (ka˙, sound)
16-2	FX	kla˙Chak (gachaka˙, sound)
16-3	FX	g˙Thud d˙Thud (doya, depiction, rowdiness -> sound of walking)
16-4	FX	fssk (su˙, movement)
17-3	FX	mnch mnch (moso, depiction, eating without energy)
18-6	FX	gasp (ha˙, depiction)
19-1	FX	qui˙clop (kyupa˙, sound, removing top)
19-2	FX	Kreek Krik (kyu˙, sound, writing with marker)
19-3	FX	thh˙chakk (gasa˙, sound and depiction, moving things about)
19-4-1	FX	zsh˙SHIng! (bishi˙, depiction)
19-4-2	FX	cla˙Chit (sucha, depiction and sound, wearing something)
19-6	FX	ddrip (tsuu˙, depiction, trailing liquid)
20-3	FX	zz˙RK (za˙, movement)
20-5	FX	kla˙kn (karan˙, sound)
21-1	FX	thuk thuk (ton, sound)
21-2	FX	vVmp! (don, sound and depiction, dramatic volume)
21-3	FX	zZ˙SHrk! (zuza˙, sound)
21-4	FX	zSH˙SHINGg (bishi˙, depiction)
21-5	FX	ph˙TiNG! (biku˙, depiction, alarm)
22-2	FX	thh˙chakk thh˙chakk (gasa˙, sound and depiction, moving things about)
22-3-1	FX	ph˙WwooWoo (hyu~, sound, wind blowing)
22-3-2	FX	thh˙chakk (gasa˙, sound and depiction, moving things about)
22-4	FX	th˙thk th˙thk (kasa, sound and depiction,
22-5-1	FX	sh˙ZKk! (bi˙, depiction and movement, making taut)
22-5-2	FX	thh˙chakk (gasa˙, sound and depiction, moving things about)
22-6	FX	p˙TinK (piku, depiction, noticing)
24-2	FX	pLlIrt pLlIrt (purururu˙, sound)
24-3	FX	pLlIrt pLlIr˙tT peep (puru˙pi, sound)
25-1	FX	pip (pi˙, sound)
26-2	FX	Tu–˙t tu–˙t tu–˙t (tsu–˙, sound)
26-3	FX	Tu–˙t tu–˙t (tsu–˙, sound)
26-4	FX	ggrip (gu˙, depiction)
29-1	FX	k˙tnk (katan˙..., sound)
31-1	FX	zZak zZak zZak zZak zZak zZak (zamu, sound)
31-2	FX	gG˙ (do˙, sound and depiction)
31-3	FX	Zsh˙ (za˙, sound and depiction)
31-4	FX	Zsh˙ (za˙, sound and depiction)
31-5	FX	Da-DUMK! (deka˙, depiction, dramatic intro)
32-1	FX	nnn... (shin..., depiction, silence)
32-2	FX	phf˙fffnnnn (kooon, depiction, something lonely and not addressed)
32-3-1	FX	(above) ffsk (su˙, movement)
32-3-2	FX	(below) p˙thump (patamu, sound)
32-4	FX	klonck klonck (kon kon, sound, door knocking)
32-5-1	FX	(white, upper right) ahem (depiction and sound, cough)
32-5-2	FX	(black) Kla˙chak
32-5-3	FX	(white) zVM (nu˙, depiction, sudden appearance)
33-2	FX	p˙thump (patamu, sound)

33-3	FX	ThUP THuD ThUP THuD ThUP (do, sound, somebody running, noisy)
33-4-1	FX	(black) b˙THUmt˙ (baaan!, sound, opening door)
33-4-2	FX	(upper right) spinn (gurin, movement, spinning)
33-4-3	FX	(upper left) flip (kun˙, movement, flipping)
33-4-4	FX	(lower left) fssk (hirari, movement, quick)
33-5	FX	th˙THUDd (da˙tan, sound, feet landing one after another)
34-1	FX	sh˙SHINGg! (gin!, depiction)
34-2-1	FX	(upper) hhGk (gubo˙, dialog)
34-2-2	FX	(middle four in air balloons) WhEEz HuFF hUff HuFF (zee~ haa, sound)
34-2-3	FX	(lower two) krArK SnaP (koki gorin, sound, bone joint sounds)
34-4	FX	g˙THngG˙ d˙THunk (dosasa do˙, sound)
34-5	FX	flap flap flap flap (bara, sound and depiction, flipping through pages)
35-5-1	FX	gGrinG! (gyu˙, movement, fast)
35-5-2	FX	sh˙SHINGg (ba˙shu˙, movement, fast)
35-7-1	FX	tth˙chak! (chyaki˙, sound)
35-7-2	FX	k˙lonk (karaan, sound)
36-1	FX	wHA˙THUD (goka˙, sound)
36-4-1	FX	zVM (nu˙, depiction, deliberate movement)
36-4-2	FX	kla˙CHAnk (kashaan, sound)
37-1	FX	glare (ki˙, depiction)
37-2	FX	thh˙chakk th˙chak (gasa gara, sound and depiction, moving things about)
37-3	FX	fl˙Shak (shaka˙, sound)
37-5	FX	heur~~~~ (ha~, sound, exhale)
38-3	FX	f˙tap (pira, depiction)
39-1	FX	ph˙flip (pi˙, depiction)
39-2	FX	phLAp phLAp (bira˙, movement)
39-4	FX	smile (nika, depiction, assertive grin)
40-1	FX	p˙Thump (pata, sound)
40-4	FX	vW˙phT vW˙phT zW˙phT (baba˙ za˙)
41-5	FX	pip! (pi˙, sound)
42-1	FX	pipip (pipi˙, sound)
42-2	FX	thh˙chakk th˙chak (gasa, sound and depiction, moving things about)
42-3	FX	vG˙REEE (ngaa~, sound, sliding door)
42-4	FX	k˙chank k˙chank (kacha˙n, sound)
42-5	FX	kla˙chak kla˙chak (kacha, sound)
42-6-1	FX	sh˙SHING! (ka˙, depiction)
43-2	FX	zZrak˙ (zu˙, sound)
44-2-1	FX	qui˙clop (kakyu, sound, removing top)
44-2-2	FX	fl˙Shak zl˙Shak (shara zyara, sound)
44-3	FX	wup˙PA~M! (pa˙aan!)
47-2	FX	k˙Thud (do˙, sound)
47-3-1	FX	b˙Tung (buchi˙, sound, cutting a taut line)
47-3-2	FX	thh˙chakk th˙chak (gasa, sound and depiction, moving things about)
47-4	FX	GASP (ha˙, depiction)
47-6	FX	bB˙Rip (bi˙, sound)
48-1	FX	pLlIr (pururu˙, sound)
48-2	FX	pLlIr (pururu˙, sound)
48-3-1	FX	pLlIr pLlIr (pururu˙, sound)
48-3-2	FX	(small) ph˙Thap ph˙Thap (pata pata, depiction of rowdy movement -> sound)
48-4-1	FX	pip˙ (pi˙, sound)
48-4-2	FX	(small) k˙chak (cha˙, sound)

Guide to *Excel Saga* 02's Sound Effects!

Most of Rikdo Koshi's original sound FX are left in their original Japanese in the Viz edition of *Excel Saga*; exceptions being handwritten dialogue and "drawn" notes that have the character of captions (for example, the ACROSS flyer on page 19). We gave some consideration to the idea of translating *nothing at all* in *Excel Saga*, not even the dialogue balloons—in other words, to literally release the original Japanese version to the U.S. market. We would have still charged $9.95 for it, of course, reasoning that by these extra efforts we had made our version of *Excel Saga even more authentic*. Although this concept tested promisingly in the focus groups, we concluded that the market is not quite ready for it just yet, but perhaps in another three weeks. Please contact *Oubliette* c/o Excel Saga, VIZ, LLC, P.O. Box 77064, San Francisco, CA, 94107 with your comments; in eternal remembrance that today's sarcasm is tomorrow's marketing plan.

If, and with obvious difficulty, I may be more serious-er for a few lpi, I just got back from AnimeExpo, which I would like to thank for inviting Rikdo Koshi and his Japanese editor, Mr. Fudetani. If you haven't already heard, they enjoyed their first visit to an American fan convention very much, and Rikdo-san was happy to see that so many people here are already fans of his work. Thank you all for coming out to meet him!—and also, to the translator of both the *Excel Saga* anime and this very manga, Dan Kanemitsu, who acted as interpreter for Rikdo-san. I even saw people cos-playing as Hyatt, Il Palazzo, and of course Excel—this last did her really well, stumbling up to the autograph table and snapping out a "Hail!" to Rikdo-san. Thanks also to Matt Greenfield of ADV Films (home of the *Excel* anime!) for coming by.

Right, the sound FX. Although these sounds are all listed as "FX," they are of two types: onomatopoeia (in Japanese, *giseigo*) where the writing is used in an attempt to imitate the actual sound of something happening, and mimesis (in Japanese, *gitaigo*) where the writing is used to attempt to convey rhetorically a state, mood, or condition. Whereas the first type of FX will invariably be portrayed with *kana* (phonetic script), the second may use *kana* and/or *kanji* (ideogrammatic script). One should note that there is often overlap between these two types. Onomatopoeia notes: *Sound* refers to audible noises being generated somehow. *Movement* refers to the physical movement, or lack of movement, of something; not audible or mostly not audible. *Depiction* refers to the psychological state of something or someone. Remember all numbers are given in the original Japanese reading order: right-to-left—surely, by this point a somewhat superfluous admonition to the reader, who has presumably just read 191 pages of the manga right-to-left, and feels it would have all made just as much sense had it been printed as a double helix.

Page	Type	Effect
82-5-3	FX	(to left) kK'Reek (kiriri, depiction, quick turn)
83-1	FX	RumbLrrumblRumBLgrUMblgrumbl... (gorogorogorogorogoroooo, sound)
83-6	FX	fssk (sui', movement)
85-5	FX	whobble whobble (fura, depiction and movement)
86-1	FX	fsk (sui', movement)
86-2	FX	v'rrom (buroro, sound)
86-4	FX	zz'ak (zya', sound)
86-5-1	FX	th-THUMp (biku', depiction)
86-5-2	FX	zZ'Chak! (za'!, sound)
87-2	FX	pfft (pon, depiction, light tapping)
87-7	FX	kREEk kREEk kREEk kREEk (kiri, sound)
88-1	FX	kIA'CHAnkk (kashaaaan', sound)
88-2	FX	ph'WwooWoo (hyu~, sound, wind blowing, dramatic)
88-3	FX	phf'fffnnnn (pu~~~, depiction, something lonely and not addressed, similar to kooon at 32-2)
88-4	FX	ph'PAAaap (papa—–n, sound, horns or high pitched engine noise)
88-5	FX	Hee hahahha (dialog, maniacal laugh)
89	FX	ggrip (kyu', depiction)
90	FX	sh'SHIIINnG (kakiiiin, depiction, dramatic moment)
91-1	FX	hsSSSS' (zyuu', sound)
91-3	FX	kl'chak k'chak (kacha, sound)
91-4-1	FX	hsSSSS' (zyuu', sound)
91-4-2	FX	kl'chak (kacha, sound)
91-5	FX	kl'chak... (kacha..., sound)
94-2	FX	fsk (su', movement)
94-3-1	FX	k'CHIIIng k'CHIIIng (kochiiin chiiin, sound)
94-3-2	FX	kyu kyu (wsshht, wsshht, crossing sound)
95-1-1	FX	fsk (su', movement)
95-1-2	FX	sputter (pu', sound, plosive bilabial expletive)
95-4-1	FX	th-THUMp th-Thump th-Thump (doki, depiction)
95-4-2	FX	nod nod (koku koku, depiction)
96-6	FX	ph'PAAaaaa (papa—–n, sound, horns or high pitched engine noise)
97-1	FX	ph'PAAaaaa (papa—–n, sound, horns or high pitched engine noise)
97-2	FX	k'ThunKk k'ThunKk (goton, sound)
97-3	FX	k'ThunKk k'ThunK k'Thunk (goton goto', sound)
97-4	FX	k'ThunK k'Thunkn (kodon goton, sound)
97-6	FX	k'ThunK k'Thunk (goton, sound)
98-1	FX	th'chrunch (kusha', sound and depiction)
98-2	FX	gG'ThukK (goton', sound)
98-4	FX	wha'THUD (doka, sound)
98-5	FX	kK'ThukKn kG'Thukonk (gatakon gatokon, sound)
98-6	FX	ph'PAAaaaa (papa—–n, sound, horns or high pitched engine noise)
99-3	FX	ph'thut ph'thut (tote, depiction, walking)
99-5	FX	GASP (ha', depiction)
100-1	FX	(overlay) Ar'aTH (sha', sound, clothing)
100-4	FX	fssk (su', movement)
101-1-1	FX	ph'TING! (pi', depiction)
101-1-2	FX	SHOCK! (GAAN!)
102-3	FX	huff huff (ha', sound)
102-4	FX	th-THUMP! (bikuu', depiction)
102-5	FX	wheeze whEEEz wHEEEz (zei zee~, sound)
102-6	FX	wobble wobble (yoro, depiction)
103-1	FX	whEEEz whEEEz (zee~, sound)
103-3-1	FX	Excel (out of wb) "Mince ~~~ !"
103-3-2	FX	th'THUt th'THUt (dada, movement, fast running)
103-3-3	FX	quiver quiver (biku bikuu, depiction)
103-4-1	FX	th'Thut (ta', movement)
103-4-2	FX	v'rRRom (burororo, sound)
103-5	FX	sKREEEETCH (kikikiki, sound)
104-2	FX	zz'ak zz'ak zz'ak (za', za' za', sound)
104-3	FX	zZ'Chak (zyari', sound)
104-4-1	FX	zZ'ak zZ'ak (sound)
104-4-2	FX	zZ'ak zZ'ak (sound)
105-3	FX	zZ'Chak (zya', sound)
105-4	FX	t'thut t'thut (sutasuta, movement and depiction, walking away)
105-5	FX	th'WwooWooththak (zazaza~, sound, wind blowing and rustling leaves)
106-3	FX	WHEEZE WHEEZE (ze~ ze~ sound)
106-4-1	FX	v'RrRrRr (bururuu, sound, engine running idle)
106-4-2	FX	WHEEZE WHEEZE (ze~ ze~ sound)
107-1-1	FX	UmPH HuMPH (dialog)
107-1-2	FX	klank klank klank (kan, sound, walking on metal surface)
107-2	FX	wheeze wheeze (ze~ ze~ sound)
107-4	FX	kla'chat (gacha', sound)
107-5	FX	d'ThuDd (do', sound)
108-1	FX	k'KliK (kaki', sound, locking)
108-2	FX	zZ'ak (za', movement)
108-3	FX	klank klank klank klank (kan, sound, walking on metal surface)
108-4-1	FX	(white) b'Thump (batan, sound)
108-4-2	FX	v'RORRRRRM (burorororo, sound)
108-7	FX	GASP (ha', depiction)
109-2	FX	Phew (dialog)
109-3	FX	aruth (mukku, movement)
109-4	FX	stagger stagger (note, movement, slow and clumsy movement)
109-6	FX	k'ThunK (igoron, movement, rolling down to be prone)
111	FX	munch munch (moki, depiction, eating)
113-5	FX	klak klak klak (ko', sound, walking, hard soled shoes)
113-6	FX	K'THRAK (go', sound, hard hit)
115-2	FX	'hHurKKK ~~~ (much pain)
115-4	FX	zgl'shshshsh (shabobobobo, sound, water with air mixture being poured out (these things sound like this))
116-3	FX	zu... (sip, sound)
117-1	FX	Ping Pon PoonG (sound, old fashioned PA announcement noise)
117-3-1	FX	k'thunkt (gata, sound, furniture moving in tune to someone standing up)
117-3-2	FX	k'ththunkt (gatata', sound, furniture moving in tune to someone standing up, multiple)
117-5	FX	k'thunkt (gata, sound, furniture moving in tune to someone standing up)
118-3	FX	zssZSHING (depiction and movement, going into pose)
119-3	FX	kla'chank (kapa, depiction (the original FX was for the motion of opening something light, implying that the latch was light and made of plastic. The problem is, it is very difficult to come up with an FX in English just regarding the act of opening something, so I replaced it with an FX regarding the sound created when opening something.)
119-6	FX	kla'chunk (ka'pa-n, see above)
120-4	FX	zssZSHING (za', depiction and movement, going into pose)
121-5	FX	Oh YEAH (dialog)
122-1	FX	trill'iliilt~~~ (pi~hyororo~, sound, innocent sounding bird call of the wild)
122-2	FX	Phew ~~~~ (dialog)
122-3	FX	g'thud (gatan, sound, hard thud)

GUIDE TO *EXCEL SAGA 02*'s SOUND EFFECTS!

48-5	FX	sh'SHINGg! (pishi˚, depiction, taut pose)
48-6	FX	v'bup puup puup (bupu˚ pu–, sound, the phone sound after being hung up)
48-7	FX	puup puup (sound, the phone sound after being hung up)
49-5	FX	vGRGGGRRRGR (gogogoooo, sound, smoldering)
50-1	FX	t'DuTH (da˚, movement, dashing movement)
50-2	FX	zthh'chakk zth'chak (zara˚, sound and depiction, moving things about)
50-3	FX	zZraTH'chaKK zZrath'aKK (dozasa doza, sound)
50-4	FX	ph'pht ph'pht ph'pht ph'pht (poi, movement, lightly tossing things in)
50-5-1	FX	(small) humph numph humph (ho˚ ho˚ ho˚, sound, expletive accompanying physical movement)
50-5-2	FX	(upper, large) k'THkk't
50-5-3	FX	(lower, large) vV'Zagth vV'Zagthth (boto bototo, sound and depiction, raking it in)
51-3	FX	k'thakk (gasa, sound)
51-5-1	FX	tiling–ling (pinpoon, sound, someone entering the store)
51-5-2	FX	k'thakk thakK (gasa, sound)
51-6	FX	nnn~~~ (shiiin, silence)
52-2	FX	ph'VLupVLu~~~p (dodo~, sound, water pouring down)
53-1	FX	fphNnnng (suu…., depiction, opening eyes)
54-1	FX	zsh'SHINGg! (babi˚, depiction)
54-2	FX	glare (ka˚, depiction)
55-4	FX	ph'thrath (fasa˚, sound, clothing)
55-5	FX	ffsk (fu˚, movement)
56-1-2	FX	wheeze wHEEz (ze–, sound)
56-2	FX	z'Rathh (basa˚, sound)
56-4	FX	klak klak klak (ka˚, sound)
56-4/5	FX	b'THUndd (bataan, sound)
56-5	FX	klak klak (sound)
57-1	FX	klak klak klak klak (sound)
57-2-1	FX	klak klak (sound)
57-2-2	FX	(out of wrd balloon, h–w) Brrr, so cold…
57-4	FX	vNnNNNN (ooo, sound, dramatic space)
58-1	FX	fphNnnng (suu…., depiction, opening eyes)
58-2	FX	vNnNNNN (ooo, sound, dramatic space)
59-1	FX	ph'shaaaa (saaa, depiction, soft tone)
59-2	FX	v'VRRRRMnnn (kooo, depiction, hazy and vast space)
60	FX	GASP (ha˚, depiction)
61-2	FX	k'reek (kyu, depiction)
61-3	FX	k'sheuk k'sheuk (shun, sound, boiling water in kettle)
62-2	FX	munch munch (moki, depiction)
62-3	FX	munch munch (moki, depiction)
62-5	FX	um'pah (paa˚, sound, exhale expletive)
63-2	FX	ffskk fssk (shu˚, movement)
63-3	FX	ggrip (kyu˚, depiction, taut)
63-6	FX	breezzz (sara˚, depiction, nonchalant –> breezy tone, with ease)
64-1	FX	kk'kreek (kukiriri, depiction, tightening)
64-2	FX	kla'chat (gacha, sound)
64-3	FX	p'am p'am (pamu, sound)
64-4	FX	ggr'kreek (gishi, sound, taut and creaking)
64-5	FX	g'THUDd (goto, sound)
65-4	FX	kla'chat (gacha, sound)
66-1	FX	cough (geho, sound)
67-1	FX	shock (gabyo~n, depiction, shocked, comic twist)
67-4-1	FX	kla'chat (gacha, sound)
67-4-2	FX	klak klak klak klak (gan, gan, gan, gan, sound)
70-1	FX	g'THuDd (gatan, sound)

70-2	FX	zZINGg˚ (bi˚, depiction and movement, fast movement followed by sudden stop)
70-2 /3	FX	sh'SHIIINnG (kakiiin, depiction, dramatic moment)
70-5	FX	Oh~~~~ (kuka–, dialog, frustration expletive)
71-5	FX	sh'CHAKK! (za!, depiction and movement, posing)
72-2	FX	kk'GrGRuBlllLLLGll (kukogogegege, sound)
72-3	FX	GrumbLgrumblGrumBLgrUMblgrumbl… (gorogorogorogorogorooooo, sound)
72-4	FX	hK'GrBruMbllLL gg'GrumBlegrumblegrumble (goro gorogoron gorogoro gorooooon, sound)
72-5	FX	glare (ka˚, depiction)
73-1-1	FX	whUP˚ (da˚, sound, first part to a "splash")
73-1-2	FX	'Plashsss (paaaan, sound)
73-2	FX	thr'plash (pashan, sound)
73-3-1	FX	thr'plash (pashan, sound)
73-3-2	FX	thr'plash Sur'plash (pash˚ basha˚, sound)
73-4-1	FX	zya'Plash (zyapu˚, sound)
73-4-2	FX	thr'PLAzzsh (zyapu˚, sound)
73-5-1	FX	thr'plash (basha˚, sound)
73-5-2	FX	Sur'plash (pasha˚, sound)
73-6-1	FX	thr'plash thr'plash (basha˚, sound)
73-6-2	FX	zya'PlashG'Plash (zyabupo~n, sound)
74-2	FX	zss'ZSH'ZZSSHIN (za, depiction, dramatic reinforcement)
74-3	FX	Z'SHING (za˚,)
75-5	FX	phf'fffnnnn (kooon, depiction, something lonely and unaddressed)
75-6	FX	pph'p (fu, depiction, light being lit or turned off)
76-1	FX	pph'P (pa, depiction, light being turned on or off)
76-2	FX	ThUP ThuD ThUP THuD ThUP (do, sound, somebody running, noisy)
76-3	FX	ThUP THuD ThUP THuD ThUP (do, sound, somebody running, noisy)
76-4	FX	ThuD kK'RekK! (do, sound) (gukii, depiction, twisting something)
76-5/6	FX	gG'THRAGgSH! (gu'shaaa, sound)
77-1	FX	pph'Pph (pa, depiction, light being turned on or off)
77-4	FX	ph'Krek (piku, movement, minute)
77-5	FX	Umph (dialog)
77-6	FX	kKRREk (kin…., sound)
78-2	FX	g'Thudd (goto˚, sound)
78-5-1	FX	(black) b'THUmt (baaan!, sound, opening door)
78-5-2	FX	(upper right) spinn (gurin, movement, spinning)
78-5-3	FX	(upper left) flip (kun˚, movement, flipping)
78-5-4	FX	(lower left) fssk (hirari, movement, quick)
79-1	FX	klak klak klak (kotsu, sound)
80-4-1	FX	ph'PAAaap (papa——–n, sound, horns or high pitched engine noise)
80-4-2	FX	v'VROOM (borororo, sound)
80-5	FX	rustle rustle rustle rustle (zawa, depiction)
81-5	FX	phVEEP VOOP (peepoo, sound, sirens)
81-6	FX	phVEEP VOOP phVEEP VOOP (peepoo, sound, sirens)
82-1-1	FX	(upper) v'ROOM (sound)
82-1-2	FX	(lower) phVEEP VOOP phVEEP VOOP (peepoo, sound, sirens)
82-2	FX	phVEEP VOOP phVEEP VOOP (peepoo, sound, sirens)
82-3-1	FX	(small) ph'WheeZ (fuko–, sound, breathing)
82-3-2	FX	phVEEP VOOP phVEEP VOOP (peepoo, sound, sirens)
82-3-3	FX	(small) ph'WheeZ (fuko–, sound, breathing)
82-4	FX	growlgrowlgrowl (˚ooon, sound)
82-5-1	FX	(upper) GrumbLgrumblGrumBLgrUMblgrumbl… (gorogorogorogorogorogorooooo, sound)
82-5-2	FX	(to right) z'Thud (zudo˚, depiction, the sinking feeling in the stomach)

156-3	FX	pfft (pafu¨, sound, fluffy sensation)
157-1	FX	ggrip (gu¨, depiction)
157-3–1	FX	wheez (ze¨, sound)
157-3-2	FX	wheez (ze¨, sound)
157-3-3	FX	glare (ki¨, depiction, expression tightening in anger)
157-4	FX	shpp (sui, sound)
158-2	FX	Yeah baby, yeah baby, yeah baby, oh yeah baby! (dialog, see footnotes for more)
158-5	FX	SHAKE SHAKE (bun, movement)
160-2	FX	kreek (ki¨, sound)
161-2–1	FX	humph! (ke¨, depiction, disgust)
161-2-2	FX	ph'pooie (pe¨, sound, spitting)
161-3	FX	p'RINGRINGRING (purururu, sound)
161-4	FX	kla'chak (zya¨, sound)
161-5	FX	wh'ThunGk! (gosu¨, sound, dull impact)
162-4	FX	klak klak klak (ka¨, sound)
162-5	FX	klak (sound)
163-2	FX	GASP (ha¨, depiction)
163-4	FX	whisper whisper (hiso, hiso depiction)
163-6-1	FX	KrK (kuru¨, movement, quick turn)
163-6-2	FX	grin (ni¨, depiction)
164-1-1	FX	ph'TING! (pi-n¨, depiction, idea popping up or something clicking inside your mind)
164-1-2	FX	zsni'ZNIFF (zuzu, sound, sniffing)
164-3-1	FX	ph'tat ph'tat ph'tat ph'tat (tasu, sound, deliberate walking, odd)
164-3-2	FX	z'Zrk z'Zrk (zuru suru, depiction and sound, being dragged out)
164-4	FX	k'grip (ga¨, sound and depiction, sudden grabbing of something/someone)
164-6	FX	GLARE (ki¨, tightening expression)
165-8	FX	klak klak klak klak (katsu, sound)
166-4	FX	Wee~~~ (wa¨, depiction, overwhelming outburst of elation)
167-1	FX	grik grik (gyu, depiction, fastening something tight or closing a grip on something)
167-2	FX	ta–DAH (ba–n¨, depiction, dramatic)
167-4	FX	ph'WwooWoo (hyu~, sound, wind blowing, dramatic)
167-5	FX	ph'TING! (biku, depiction, unwelcome news)
167-6	FX	g'thk (ga¨, movement and depiction, kicking action)
167-7	FX	wVMm (tan!, movement, jumping in midair)
168-1	FX	ph'thrlthrlthrl (shururu, depiction, unraveling)
168-2	FX	k'THINC (peen, depiction, something going taut)
168-5	FX	vVVVVVrm (kuoo, depiction, inclosing)
168-6	FX	K'CRASHsh (gashaaa, sound)
168-7	FX	tinglingling (chariin, sound, bell ringing)
169	FX	ph'WwooWoo (hyu~, sound, wind blowing, dramatic)
170-2	FX	shine (kira¨, depiction, sparkling teeth)
170-8-1	FX	v'VRROM (vuooon, sound)
170-8-2	FX	eREEEE (kaaaan, sound, high rpm)
170-8-3	FX	p'BAng p'BAng (pan, sound, misfire)
171-3	FX	clink clink clink (chiki kiin chikin, sound)
171-4	FX	Hah hah hah hah (dialog, dry laugh most likely by Kabapu)
171-7	FX	glug glug glug (go¨, depiction and sound)
172-1-1	FX	p'phew (p'uha~, sound, exhaling following drinking)
172-1-2	FX	sh'CHAkkIT! (zya'su, depiction and movement, posing)
172-1-3	FX	Hahahahaha (dialog)
172-1-4	FX	t'LupLupLup (topopo, sound, pouring)
172-1-5	FX	ph'VLupVLup (boto, sound, pouring out, hard)
172-1-6	FX	ggrip (giri, depiction)
173-4-1	FX	sh'CHAkk! (zya¨, depiction and movement, posing)
173-4-2	FX	sh'SHIIInG (kakiiin, depiction, dramatic moment)
174-4-1	FX	ph'fwing (harai, depiction, something light being dangled)
174-4-2	FX	panic panic (awa hawa, depiction, mental state)

175-2	FX	shine (tsuya, depiction, a health shine)
175-3	FX	sh'ZHAkk! (za¨, depiction and movement, posing)
175-5	FX	Ah–hAAA (dialog)
176-1-1	FX	vRRRRR (ooo, sound, residual)
176-1-2	FX	hwaAAAieee (HEAaaa, dialog)
177-2	FX	sk'KREEKk (kishi¨, sound and depiction, some type of stress sound)
177-4	FX	wheeze wheeze (ze~¨, sound)
177-5-1	FX	sh'lunGe (zuru¨, being pulled in)
177-5-2	FX	hissss (shaaa¨, sound, snake hiss)
177-5-3	Excel	I'm being swallowed!!
178-5	FX	bl'chat (be¨, sound, wet contact sound)
178-6	FX	Umph! (dialog)
179-2	FX	fssk (su¨, movement and depiction, quiet and deliberate)
179-6	FX	b'THUmp (batan, sound, door closing)
180-1	FX	ph'PAAaap (papa——n, sound, horns or high pitched engine noise)
180-4-1	FX	GGRIP (ki¨, depiction, taut mind -> changed to clinched fist)
180-4-2	FX	OSU! [¨push!" The Sumo wrestlers say this]
181-1	FX	sch'lrrp (chu~¨, sound, sucking sound)
181-2	FX	hg'gnk! (gokun!, sound, swallowing)
181-4	FX	ph'TING! (pin!, depiction, something clicking)
181-5	FX	gk'thungkt (gada, sound, furniture moving in tune to someone standing up)
182-2	FX	z'thrsh z'thrsh z'thrsh z'thrshsh (za zaa, sound, waves)
182-5	FX	k'CHIng! (chun, sound, bullet whisking by)
183-1-1	FX	kl'chak (zya¨, sound)
183-1-2	FX	clack't (kaki¨, sound, cocking sound)
183-1-3	FX	krkreekrk (kriri¨, sound and movement, sudden turn)
183-2	FX	zaklack't (gashi¨, sound)
183-3-1	FX	k'CHIng! (chun¨, sound, bullet whisking by)
183-3-2	FX	(large text) kg'REEK kg'reek k'REEK [repeat as needed] (gara kara gara, sound, cart pulling sounds)
183-3-3	FX	(next to Hyatt's head) v'VLAMVLAM
183-3-4	FX	(small, lower middle) k'CHINg! (chun¨, sound, bullet whisking by)
183-4	FX	whEEz whEEz (zee¨, sound)
183-5	FX	whEEEz whEEz whEEEEz whEEz (zee¨ zeee, sound)
184-3	FX	GASP (ha¨, depiction)
184-4	FX	z'zrk (za¨, sound)
184-6	FX	sh'ZKk! (bi¨, depiction and movement, pointing)
185-2	FX	Hmph Hmph (ze¨, sound, here excitement)
185-3	FX	thh'chakk th'chakk (goso, sound and depiction, moving things about)
185-6	FX	Z'ZZRK (zuza!, sound)
186-2	FX	ph'VMmph! (buu!, sound and movement)
186-4-1	FX	(white) f'wobble (hero¨, depiction, faltering wobble)
186-4-2	FX	(black) G'THUD!
186-6-1	FX	(upper) humph humph (dialog)
186-6-2	FX	ph'vmph (bun, sound and movement)
187-4	FX	gK'cOaUGHh (gobu¨, sound, coughing up something)
188-1	FX	Humph (dialog)
188-3/4	FX	k'REEK k'reek k'REEK [repeat as needed] (gara kara gara, sound, cart pulling sounds)
189-1	FX	tnk tnk (ka, ka sound)
189-2	FX	klank klank (kan, sound, walking on metal surface)
189-4	FX	hck¨ (e'ku, dialog)
189-5	FX	hhck¨ (hi'ku, dialog)
189-6	FX	ArUth (su'ku, movement, getting up)
190-1	FX	hg'gnk (goku¨, sound, swallowing)
190-3	FX	klak klak klak (ka¨¨ ka¨ ka¨, sound)
190-4-1	FX	kk'reek (kiri... sound)
190-4-2	FX	sh'chreek sh'chreek sh'chreek (showa, sound, a type of cicadas make this noise)

GUIDE TO *EXCEL SAGA* 02'S SOUND EFFECTS!

123-2	FX	creek (gishi', sound)
123-3	FX	k'reek k'reek k'reek (kara, sound, cart pulling sounds)
123-4	FX	k'REEK k'REEK k'REEK (gara kara gara, sound, cart pulling sounds. Technically not just creaking, but the aggregate of noises made by the cart—this FX is used for many mechanical processes).
124-7	FX	glare (ki', depiction, expression tightening in anger)
125-1	FX	shake shake (furu, movement, shaking head)
125-2-1	FX	twrl (kuru, movement)
125-2-2	FX	sshreek' (kyu'!, movement, fast turn with creaking of shoes)
125-6	FX	sh'shinGG (bishi!, movement and depiction, pointing at something)
125-7	FX	da-DUM!! (ka', depiction, moment of truth like dramatic FX)
125-8	FX	wv'vlffvluffvluff (basasasasa', sound, birds taking flight)
126-5-1	FX	sh'CHAK! (zya!, movement)
126-5-2	FX	ARUTHh' (gaba', movement, ducking of cover (in this case)
127-4-1	FX	zzrk (za', sound, gravel under foot)
127-4-2	FX	zzrk (za', sound, gravel under foot)
128-1	FX	vl'BlaG BAnG BaM (dododo', sound, explosions)
128-2/6	FX	VREEEEEENnnn (paaan, sound, light beam emission)
129-2	FX	GRIN (niyari, depiction)
130-3	FX	vGRGGGRRRGR (gogogoooo, sound, smoldering)
131-5	FX	mutter sputter (butsu, depiction)
132-1	FX	va'VUMP! (ba', depiction, dramatic introduction (adaptation of mimesis of clothing moving rapidly)
132-3-1	FX	wheeze wheeze (ze, sound)
132-3-2	FX	hahh hahh (haa, haa, sound)
132-4	FX	k'thunk (goto, sound)
133-3	FX	nnnnn (shi-n, depiction, silence)
133-4	FX	zzqak zzak zzqak (zaku za' zaku, sound, walking about)
133-6	FX	t'thut (ta, sound)
134-1/3	FX	wA'BOOOOM (ZUBAaaaaa, sound)
134-5	FX	'rR rR uR (ooo, sound, residual sound)
135-1	FX	bBVvvmmm (goooo, sound, reinforcement of fire's power)
135-2	FX	'rR rR uR (aaaa, sound, residual sound)
135-3	FX	wha'BANG wha'BANG wha'BANGg (zuba zuba zubaa, sound, explosion)
135-4	FX	a'rR rRa uraR (aaooo, sound, residual sound)
135-5	FX	ph'rrroarrrr rr rrr (koooo, sound, residual calm returning after massive noise)
136-1-1	FX	rR rr roar urar (ooo, sound, residual)
136-1-2	FX	kouff (dialog)
136-3-1	FX	t'thut (suta, sound and depiction, walking)
136-3-2	FX	rR rr roar urar (ooo, sound, residual)
136-4	FX	flap flap (wata, movement and depiction, panic)
136-5	FX	t'thut t'thut t'thut t'thut (suta, sound and depiction, walking)
136-6	FX	eEEEK! EEEK!! EEK!! (kiri, depiction, state of high anxiety and tension)
137-1	FX	ohhhhh . . . (ooooo, moaning sound)
137-6	FX	GASP (ha', depiction)
137-7	FX	zZINGg' (bi', depiction and movement, fast movement followed by sudden stop)
138-1	FX	thh'ash th'ach t'thash (gasa gazasa, sound and depiction, moving things about)
138-2	FX	thh'ash t'thash (gasa gasa, sound and depiction, moving things about)
138-3	FX	p'KRINK (pieen, sound, tripping something)
138-4	FX	th'ffsk th'fsk th'fssk th'fsk (hyu!, sound and depiction, fast and quiet projectile)
138-6	FX	hobble hobble (yore, movement and depiction)
138-7-1	FX	wap! (pishi, sound)

138-7-2	FX	th'fsk (hyu', sound and depiction, fast and quiet projectile)
139-1	FX	thmp (ta', sound)
140-1	FX	ka'clik (kochi, sound)
140-2	FX	zzrak! (za', sound, getting up quickly)
140-3	FX	t'thut t'thut t'thut (ta', sound)
140-7-1	FX	ff'ick (chi', sound, gentle click sound)
140-7-2	FX	vWA' (zu', sound, start of explosion)
141-1	FX	vBGRAAAANGgg (gogaaa, sound, explosion)
141-3	FX	beeeeep (pi—~, sound, electronic)
142-3	FX	k'REEK k'reek k'REEK k'reek (gara, sound, cart pulling sounds)
142-4	FX	vrvrvr (mo, sound, residual)
145-1	FX	klak klak (ko', sound, walking, hard soled shoes)
145-2	FX	klak klak f'that (ko' ko' suta, sounds walking)
145-3	FX	f'that f'that (suta, sound and depiction, standard walking)
145-5	FX	b'thump (ban!, sound, door opening)
146-1	FX	ph'pha~~ (pa', depiction, radiant appearance)
146-2	FX	...? (tsu, depiction, taken back at something not being right, the sound of cold sweat running down)
147-4	FX	s'swing (paran, depiction, something light being dangled)
147-5	FX	yank (ku, movement, pulling)
147-6-1	FX	kla'CHUNK (gakon!, sound)
148-2	FX	phf'fffnnnn (kooon, depiction, something lonely and unaddressed)
148-3	FX	GASP (ha', depiction)
150-2	FX	thh'chakk th'chakk (gasa, sound and depiction, moving things about)
150-3	FX	K'THUNK (koto', sound, opening sliding door and such)
150-5	FX	kR'claclacla (garara, sound, opening sliding door resting on bearings)
151-6	FX	thu-thump! (giku, depiction, unwelcome recognition of unfolding threat or eventuality, i.e. the instant where you fear your wife is catching on to your infidelity)
152-4	FX	urrK (giri', depiction, mental tension resulting from anguish, etc. Original [core] meaning of giri' is something being tightened.)
152-5	FX	ggrip (gu' sound)
153-1	FX	ta-THMP! (zan!, depiction, dramatic)
153-5-1	FX	rustle rustle (pata, depiction, moving about to get ready)
153-5-2	FX	kreek (gei', sound)
153-5-3	FX	b'thmp (batan!, sound, door closing)
154-1	FX	t-thut. . . (tote . . ., depiction and movement)
154-3	FX	ph'TING! (biku', depiction, unwelcome news. Biku and giku (151-6) are very similar. Giku is a sense of alarm that's more cerebral, while biku is more instinctual. Because this FX was to be followed by the pounding of Mince's heart, I chose another option.
154-4	FX	b'Thud b'Thud b'Thud b'Thud (baku bakun, depiction, heartbeats)
154-5	FX	SHAKE SHAKE SHAKE (buru, movement, shaking head violently)
154-6	FX	thh'chakk th'chakk (gasa, sound and depiction, moving things about)
154-7	FX	klaklakla (karakara, sound, window opening)
155-4-1	FX	wv'vlff (basa, sound)
155-4-2	FX	coo (ku-, sound)
155-4-3	FX	co' (ku', sound)
155-4-4	FX	wv'vluff (basa, sound)
155-4-5	FX	(lower right) wv'vluff (basa, sound)
155-4-6	FX	(lower middle) c'coo (curu'ku, sound)
155-4-7	FX	wv'vluff (basa, sound)
156-1	FX	wv'vluffVLUFFvluffvluff (dobasasa basasasa basa basa, sound)
156-2	FX	arath' (muku, movement, getting up)

54-5-1: Excel is alluding to the Japanese (especially in Kansai, the region of Osaka, Kobe, and Kyoto) humor construct of *boke* and *tsukkomi*. One person makes a stupid or "out-there" remark or simply plays dumb, and thus presents the *boke*, and another person points out the fallacy or the ridiculousness of the situation, the *tsukkomi*. While that describes the mechanics of this routine, which is often performed as a two-person stand-up act ("Beat" Takeshi Kitano, who played the teacher in *Battle Royale* and is best known in the West for his dramatic roles, first became famous as part of such an act, "The Two Beats"—and believe it or not, he was the *boke*) one has to note that the words *boke* and *tsukkomi* have significance on their own. *Boke* is a variation on the word *boketa/houkeru*, the verb form of *boke*. *Bokeru/houkeru* means "to be (or act) absent-minded" and/or "being senile" and the elongated version of the word, *bou~*, is commonly employed as mimesis for a person that's gazing out to space. In other words, both Excel and Hyatt can play the part of *boke*: Excel can do so by making remarks as a result of her overactive imagination; and Hyatt can do so by being the person she always is. The word *tsukkomi* is actually the noun form of the verb *tsukkomu*, which means "to insert," "plug-up," or "to become entrenched," as in the phrase *tsukkonda hanashiai*, an deeply engaging conversation. The typical physical action undertaken by the *tsukkomi* against the *boke* is a slight batting action with the back of the hand, but it need not be limited to this, i.e. the infamous xx-ton mallet swung around by Kaori in *City Hunter* is an example of a *tsukkomi*. Many Americans might be surprised to be told the *boke/tsukkomi* routine is readily found in US entertainment—the Skipper and his hat in *Gilligan's Island* is probably a classic example, but many of the road trip movies featuring Dean Martin and Jerry Lewis feature this as well. One of the preferred instrument of *tsukkomi* in Japan is the *harisen*, a large piece of cardboard paper folded into a fan form, so that it makes a loud noise when hit. Furthermore, many jokes have been constructed around the semantic undertone of "sexual insertion" that can be easily associated to the word *tsukkomi*.

63-4-1: The Coming of Age Day, *Shiki-Jitsu* (the same *Shiki-Jitsu* from which *Neon Genesis Evangelion* creator Hideaki Anno's second feature-length live-action film, released in 2000, takes its name) is a national holiday in Japan where on the second Monday in January of each year, all of those that turned 20 in the prior 12 month period celebrate becoming "full-fledged adults." While many rights are granted at the age of 18 (i.e. the right to obtain a driver's license, etc.) the right to vote and the right to drink are only granted at the age of 20. The Japanese legal system stipulates that a person can only be considered a full adult after turning the age of 20.

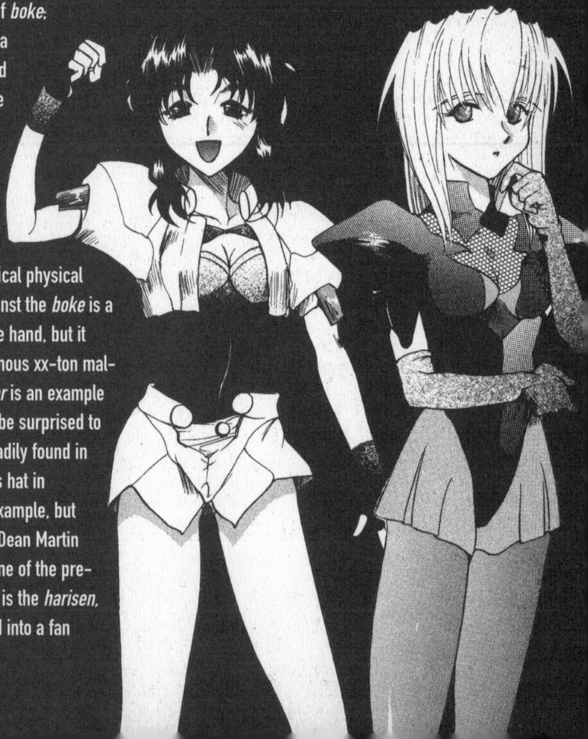

Guide to *Excel Saga* 02's Sound Effects!

FOOTNOTES

Written by translator Dan Kanemitsu

With additions by editor Carl Gustav Horn

1: This whole exchange is making fun at the fact that this was the first time one of Rikdo's series managed to make it past one volume in terms of compilations.

11-1: Note that we are not meant to be sure if he is directing his contempt at himself or at Excel. The easy answer is that it is directed at Excel, but we must remember that Il Palazzo—in this sole respect only perhaps like Walt Whitman—often appears to contain multitudes.

25-4-3: By this, Hyatt means, "well, at least we can go back to doing what we're good at." Or "Oh, it looks like our dear Il Palazzo has come back to his senses."

35-5-2: A reminder that Sumiyoshi not only speaks only in floating captions, he speaks in an accent that says he hails from Okayama, a large city on Japan's "Inland Sea" that stretches between the largest of its four main islands, Honshû, and its smallest, Shikoku. *Excel Saga* itself takes place in Fukuoka, a city on the second-smallest, and southernmost, of the main islands, Kyûshû (that leaves the northernmost, Hokkaidô, a frontier land for the Japanese in the 19th century; entirely uninhabited, except for, you know, all its indigenous inhabitants). The translator suggests a "Northern England" feel to the Okayama sound, so some attempt has been made towards that here. *Excel Saga*'s a good reminder that not everyone in Japan lives in Tokyo or some anonymous suburb—an impression you might sometimes get from manga.

36-4-2: He actually said two *gou*, which is an old Japanese measurement system. A gou is 1/10 of a *shou*, which is the size those large bottles of saké you see in anime and manga come in. One gou is 180 milliliters, so we're talking a little over six ounces of rice per serving.

37-4-1: Iwata means after the Second World War, when in the devastation you could hardly be expected to find many restaurants open for business. Of course, he is himself two generations too young to "get" it, so it's as if he's doing a Grumpy Old Man routine.

51-1-1: These names are supposed to sound horrible, like something no person would ever dare use in real life. *Doskoi* (a shortened *"Dosukoi"*) is the expletive uttered during a Sumo match (hence the wrestling reference) and *Hanako* is an outdated name that you don't hear people use too often. This raises in an interesting issue in Japan with some American parallels, the cultural and social currency of given names. In Japan, some names are regarded as being "too common" and/or "rural," while other names are considered to be "contemporary" and "trend-setting." *Hanako* is one of those names that sound extremely mundane. *Chouchou* (a more immature way of referring to a butterfly, where as the more mature way to refer to them would simply be *chou*) is almost never used as a name. [Consider the different connotations you receive from varying pairs of American names of the past century: Maude and Hazel; Mary and Sally; Kylie and Brittany—*Ed.*]

115-1-3: Matsuya is following standard workplace protocol, where women and men refer to each with a slight difference in hierarchy. Men are supposed to refer to women of equal rank simply by their last name, while women will refer to men of their equal rank with the honorific "-kun"—hence, women are positioned somewhat below the men, even when they are of equal rank.

The chart below is a good diagram of how the social totem pole works in terms of how people refer to each other in Japanese.

Sama / Dono = Lord / Master / Mistress (used to show unusual respect in Japanese, but few contexts exist any more in contemporary English usage, particularly in America, where such equivalents can be used seriously—*Ed.*)

San = Mister / Miss

Kun = (n/a in English)

Just first name with no honorific attached = similar to English use, *but very intimate in context of Japanese culture.*

Chan = as a deliberate use of the diminutive form of someone's name or possibly "my dear ____"

Just last name with no honorific attached = taking a brash tone

Last name + *no yatsu* (an example of detracting reference) = taking an insulting tone

Please note that in terms of how Matsuya interacts with the men of *Excel Saga*, she only follows the protocol in language and does not act at all subservient. This subtle gap in language and behavior adds a particular righteous, stoic, and principled tone to the personality of Matsuya, making her a strong and self-confident woman in Japan, which is still more of a "man's world" in the professional sphere than the United States.

116-5: Matsuya originally used the gender-neutral pronoun *are*, which reinforces the notion that they look upon Kabapu as being a strange character.

122-2: Technical details of the crime: they bought the minimum-fare tickets for the shortest possible trip in order to get inside the transit system, and instead of paying the extra they owed for their much longer trip at the exit station, they took advantage of the fact it was unattended to jump the turnstile.

131-6-2: Watanabe in the original is, more specifically, dealing with this situation by pretending he is on the slopes of the Kitafuji (North Fuji) Training Grounds, used for exercises by both the JGSDF (Japanese Ground Self-Defense Force) and the US Marines.

133-1: The original expression used here was "tanomo~" or *tanomou*, which is an archaic expression used by those visiting someone's home, and seeks to have someone guide or address the needs of the visitor. This expression was used commonly by samurai as they visited a house. A more literal translation would be "I ask upon someone." ("Open the gates!" suggested by my man Toshi Yoshida—*Ed.*)

150-5-2: In the original, the reference was to sômen noodles, which also came up in Vol. 1. The change was made by the editor; sômen are long and straight, and also tend to be packaged much as spaghetti; like spaghetti in America, they are in Japan a cheap but not necessarily healthy staple for those of flimsy means, especially college-age people such as Excel and Hyatt (Excel again made reference to them in the original version of 175-2).

152-5-2: In the original, the air freshener was not a box of baking soda, but "Kimco," a fridge deodorizer manufactured by the Kobayashi Pharmaceuticals Co. of Osaka; Kimco's homepage is http://www.kobayashi.co.jp/seihin/kmk/01.html . But you don't have to journey to Japan to enjoy a fine Kobayashi product; their recently-established subsidiary in Pennsylvania has introduced the "Be Koool" soft gel cooling sheet and the "Cura-Heat" air-activated Therapeutic Heatpack to the US market. Both are currently available at many US stores, including Big Y, Bi-Lo, Fruth, Harris Teeter, H.E.B., HyVee, and Schnucks.

GUIDE TO *EXCEL SAGA* 02's SOUND EFFECTS!

68-1-3: In the original text, Hyatt refuses to take Excel's name because it was spelled out in phonetic *katakana* script (just as most of *Excel Saga*'s sound FX are), as Japanese does when it utilizes imported non-Chinese foreign words. Just as commonly, katakana are used to spell out Japanese terms that are contrived or contract-ed from such foreign words, and part of the joke may be that Japanese such as Hyatt (code name) do not always realize these terms *are* contrived and not the original form of the foreign word. The commonly-used Japanese terms *infure* and *defure* might be two examples, which some Japanese might assume are also the actual English words for "inflation" and "deflation." The fact katakana are used whether an attempt is made to spell out a foreign word in its actual whole, or just shorten it in a way that's easier to pronounce and hence utilize (so *infure* is a Japanese word based on the English word *inflation*, but they are definitely words in two different languages even though they have a common origin and meaning) unfortunately gives no clues. The editor does-n't mean to suggest that such issues don't occur between speakers of many languages, including native speakers of English [Make it your own special pledge today as a manga fan to see that people say "kah-rah-oh-keh," not "carrie-okie."—*Ed.*] But one can easily imagine Hyatt justified her dislike for the name based on how it sounds "so imported." Indeed, many Japanese people, especially the older more conservative types, can't keep up with the influx of foreign words entering into Japanese society, such as "konboi" or "convoy." Therefore we can restructure this sentence to mean Hyatt refused politely because the part about "convoys" just didn't agree with her patterns of language use. Heaven forbid that she couldn't stand it simply because it was such a terrible name.

74-1-2: Notice the italicization of the word *now*—what exactly is meant by such emphasis is just another of the unrevealed mysteries surrounding Il Palazzo.

83-2: This is a common poetic reference in regard to the unique sound of thunderstorms in the spring.

88-5-2: The line game to which he refers is called *Amida kuji*—a form of drawing lots that is done with paper and pencil. You draw parallel lines for each con-testant, and then write out the appropriate results that should be turn up at the end. Next, you draw perpendi-cular lines at random intervals between the original parallel lines. Now each contestant must pick a starting point, and follow the line no matter how many turns it takes. It isn't the most precise way to conduct a ran-dom drawing, but it is popular in Japan.

90: A typical cliched catch-phrase of the sanctity of the medical profession in Japan; in the words of the Geto Boys, "some shit that'll make you throw up."

91-4: Called *yakiniku* in Japan, but using here the term by which this style of cooking is better known in English somehow makes it all the more egregious.

94-3: Excel is simultaneously making the sign of the Cross and also ringing a small metal bowl, which is a Buddhist mourning tradition.

115-1-2: Note that, unlike the US, only people who are intimate with each other will refer to each other by their first names in Japan. Misaki is not happy over the fact Iwata is implying that the two are in a romantic relation-ship with each other. See the following footnote for more information on this issue.

182-183: At one point, the quasi-governmental association given custody over the management of nuclear power plants in Japan objected to the use of the abbreviation of *genshiryoku hatsudensho* to *genpatsu*. They felt that *genpatsu* sounds too similar to *bakuhatsu* ("explosion") and *genbaku* ("atom bomb").

189-3-2: Watanabe's original incredulous query was to confirm that Iwata was going to attempt *yobai*, a wonderful term that dates back to the period in ancient Japanese history where matriarchy and patriarchy were still pushing up against each other. *Yobai* literally means the act of visiting a girl or woman under the darkness of night, in an attempt to make out with her. The editor feels it important to note that the concept predates *Love Hina*, and advise, as you traverse this still-new land of manga, to hate the game and not the player.

190-3-1: At the risk of these notes becoming literally pettifogging, "excessive force in self-defense" is a specific crime under the Japanese penal code; Article 36, Section 2. In U.S. jurisdictions this is more likely to be used as an assertion of fact to justify such a charge as voluntary or involuntary manslaughter (and/or—no, let's face it, this is America—and, a civil tort action such as "wrongful death"). But in Japan they are specific and distinct offenses. The translator on this point has released this statement: "I'm not a lawyer. I just translate one that appears in manga and anime." The editor wishes to aver that he merely *went* to law school. He feels a positive duty, however, to disclose that the letterer actually *is* a lawyer.

191: Elgâla is a character who is in the *Excel Saga* manga but not the anime; I regret that you will have to wait a little while for her first scene (which happens in Vol. 7). Her name is pronounced with a long initial "a," like when you stick out your tongue for a visit to a shabby, sleazy dentist (which happens in Vol. 4). Elgâla (see 173-1 and http://www.elgalahall.co.jp/index2.html) will continue the manga's tradition of naming its characters for Fukuoka's hotels ("Excel," "Hyatt," "Il Palazzo"), convention venues, and civic centers ("Elgala," "Acros" [sic]). The Il Palazzo was designed by Aldo Rossi, winner of the Pritzker Architecture Prize [other recipients including Frank Gehry, I.M. Pei, Rem Koolhaas, and Philip Johnson]. As you can see from Acros's own handy webpage listing, http://www.acros.or.jp/english/interest/syosai/scenic_05.html, the hotel is indeed a fitting base for the eponymous overlord; Dennis Sharp relates that Rossi's design theory has the city as its central theme and stresses the importance of the transformation of Rationalism, while Acros's own site makes note of the fact the building includes "an event hall in the basement." Rates are from 10,000 yen per night for a double.

191.99999: All right, all right. The official English-language website of the Hakata Tokyu Excel Hotel in Fukuoka is http://www.tokyuhotels.co.jp/en/TE/TE_HAKAT/index.shtml. It seems a fitting namesake for *Excel Saga*'s dedicated, career-minded heroine, for the nine different nationwide locations of Tokyu Hotel's special "Excel" chain, whose motto is "Urban refinement and stylish ambience" (there's also one at Tokyo's Narita airport), cater specifically to the female business traveller, with 20 special "Ladies Excel Rooms" available. Check-out time is right now—see all y'all again in Vol. 3 this October.

GUIDE TO *EXCEL SAGA* 02's SOUND EFFECTS!

158-2-1: Excel is reciting a variation on the Japanese saying, "Some gods may disavow (throw away) us, but then there are other gods that adopt us (pick us up.)" In English, this usually is translated to; "When one door closes, another one opens," but we need to include the verb "pick up" or "collect" to reproduce the same variation that was there before. Excel is furthermore chanting a common traditional Japanese expletive associated with festivals and activities involving jubilant exertion.

159-2 Visual puns: Original Japanese saying: "You can't exchange your spine with your stomach;" i.e. Your spine (principles) won't mean much if you have an empty stomach. Also: "[Difficult parting] as it feels like hair from the back of your head is pulling you." English meaning would be, "the anguish of parting with something/someone you do not want to part with."

161-2-2: Originally Nurse Fukuya spoke of a "JIS," or Japan Industrial Standard mark. The process of approval of the JIS mark is different from the UL, or Underwriters' Laboratories mark found in US products, but the cultural meaning is similar.

165-1-1: The original (and traditional) Japanese expression was that Dr. Iwata was willing to become an *oni*, or demon (See *Devilman*). Frankly, this instant promotion to middle-management sounds like a better deal than the Western equivalent of merely selling your soul, which implies you will receive only an entry-level position in hell with little prospects for advancement over the next fiscal eternity. Romans 6:23.

170-5-1: A national holiday in Japan set at the second Monday in October. It was originally inaugurated around the time of 1964 Tokyo Olympics, the first such games to be held in Japan, which greatly increased interest in athletics. *Bodies of Memory: Narratives of War in Postwar Japanese Culture* by Yoshikuni Igarashi (at Vanderbilt) is much-recommended on this subject; it deals in a scholarly (but not at all alienating) way with how memories of the Second World War were gradually faded and transformed (a theme of course of great interest to Mamoru Oshii) through such pop-culture motifs and pursuits as *Gojira*, pro wrestling, and the Olympics.

170-7-1: A Mitsubishi Lancer with a turbo, but not the Evolution. Many people added a turbo to their vanilla Lancers to have it offer more a kick. Note that the Lancer Evolution is a whole different car.

175-2: Of a 16-oz package of sômen noodles— about 448 grams—328 grams will be carbohydrates and only 40 grams protein. There is something about this aspect of the characters' lives that puts the editor in mind of The Dead Milkmen's song "Nutrition." Actually, many aspects of the characters' lives put the editor in mind of many Dead Milkmen songs.

175-5-3: The original Japanese environmental slogan was *Chikyuu ni Yasashiku*, or "Be nice to the Earth." It was used by everybody, including some of the largest polluting corporations, and soon lost whatever meaning it might have had.

180-4-1: Original text referred to *"Osu!"* the expletive most commonly associated to Sumo wrestlers, but it can also be applied to any type of masculine sports as well.

If you enjoy
EXCEL SAGA,
the editor recommends, also from VIZ:

NEON GENESIS EVANGELION

© GAINAX 2001

I'll bet you thought Il Palazzo was going to discover the true meaning of Christmas at the end of Vol. 1, didn't you? But this ain't no Jack Chick tract—HAW HAW! Nobody can resist manga...nobody! If you want to see what Lord Il Palazzo was getting at, check out *Neon Genesis Evangelion*. Don't you ever wonder why people join apocalyptic organizations that claim special divine knowledge, when they all seem to be headed up by such unattractive characters? And Gendo Ikari is *attractive* by the standards of cult leader beardy-weirdies—no wonder NERV has Ritsuko do all the front-office recruiting.

EVEN A MONKEY CAN DRAW MANGA

© 1990 Koji Aihara/
Kentaro Takekuma/
Shogakukan

Even A Monkey Can Draw Manga, which has no doubt gained accidental sales because its nickname in Japanese - is *Saruman* ("Monkey-man"), is Viz's finest satirical manga; if you have good memories of *MAD* magazine, imagine this as a Super-Special about the Japanese comics business. "Professor" Kentaro Takekuma's lectures to the hapless young "I wanna draw manga!" artist Koji Aihara are a must-read for all young people who wanna draw manga, Japanese or American. *Monkey* explains the difference between Viz Comics and VIZ, LLC better than a thousand press releases folded into paper cranes.

DI GI CHARAT

© BROCCOLI 2000

I can't quite figure this one out, but there is something rather *Excel Saga* about it. I don't mean the story or characters—although, like *Excel Saga*, *Di Gi Charat* is a doujinshi that went pro, and its protagonists are attractive young girls who work for minimum wage. It's more the almost Ptolemaic meta-sub-marketing-non-conceptual-conception of *Di Gi Charat* itself—something like an otaku *Adventures of the Big Boy*—which bent its way through strange prisms into America to be sold exclusively through Waldenbooks.

WE INTERRUPT THIS MAGAZINE FOR EXCITING HAPPY NEWS!

EXCEL SAGA IS NOW ON DVD!

with TONS of freakin' EXTRAS!

WHAT'S IT ABOUT YOU ASK?

Wacky show with cute girl heroine

incompetent loser bad guys

good guy afro-wearing bad-a** muthas

super-mysterious overlord types

psycho twisted comic book creator man

and delicious funny singing dog!

★★★★★ *I give it FIVE stars!*
- THE PIG

LOOK!
This is the DVD!

Run not walk to local retailer!
Buy super wacky anime EXCEL SAGA now! DVD!
Every volume contains wacky cool FREE STUFF!

ADV FILMS

www.advfilms.com

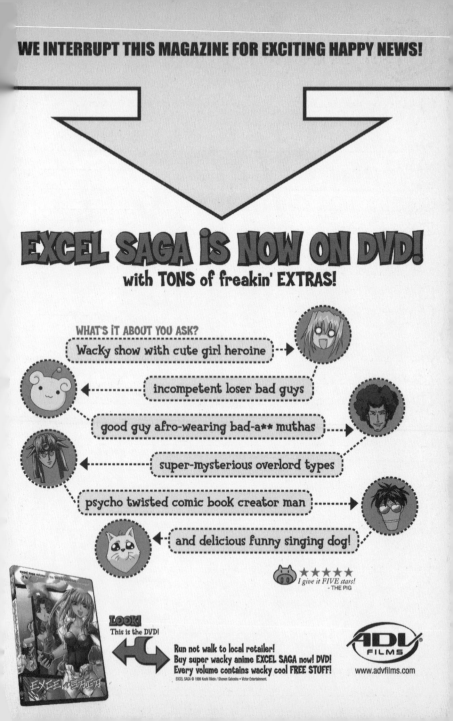

COMPLETE OUR SURVEY AND LET US KNOW WHAT YOU THINK!

☐ Please check here if you DO NOT wish to receive information or future offers from VIZ

Name: _____

Address: _____

City: _____ State: _____ Zip: _____

E-mail: _____

☐ Male ☐ Female Date of Birth (mm/dd/yyyy): ___ / ___ / ___ (Under 13? Parental consent required)

What race/ethnicity do you consider yourself? (please check one)

☐ Asian/Pacific Islander ☐ Black/African American ☐ Hispanic/Latino

☐ Native American/Alaskan Native ☐ White/Caucasian ☐ Other: _____

What VIZ product did you purchase? (check all that apply and indicate title purchased)

☐ DVD/VHS _____

☐ Graphic Novel _____

☐ Magazines _____

☐ Merchandise _____

Reason for purchase: (check all that apply)

☐ Special offer ☐ Favorite title ☐ Gift

☐ Recommendation ☐ Other _____

Where did you make your purchase? (please check one)

☐ Comic store ☐ Bookstore ☐ Mass/Grocery Store

☐ Newsstand ☐ Video/Video Game Store ☐ Other: _____

☐ Online (site: _____)

What other VIZ properties have you purchased/own? _____

How many anime and/or manga titles have you purchased in the last year? How many were VIZ titles? (please check one from each column)

ANIME	MANGA	VIZ
☐ None	☐ None	☐ None
☐ 1-4	☐ 1-4	☐ 1-4
☐ 5-10	☐ 5-10	☐ 5-10
☐ 11+	☐ 11+	☐ 11+

I find the pricing of VIZ products to be: (please check one)

☐ Cheap ☐ Reasonable ☐ Expensive

What genre of manga and anime would you like to see from VIZ? (please check two)

☐ Adventure ☐ Comic Strip ☐ Detective ☐ Fighting

☐ Horror ☐ Romance ☐ Sci-Fi/Fantasy ☐ Sports

What do you think of VIZ's new look?

☐ Love It ☐ It's OK ☐ Hate It ☐ Didn't Notice ☐ No Opinion

THANK YOU! Please send the completed form to:

NJW Research
42 Catharine St.
Poughkeepsie, NY 12601

All information provided will be used for internal purposes only. We promise not to sell or otherwise divulge your information.